WHERE'S WILBER AT?

D0731453

OMEGA BOOKS

The OMEGA BOOKS series from Paragon House is dedicated to classic and contemporary works about human development and the nature of ultimate reality, encompassing the fields of mysticism and spirituality, psychic research and paranormal phenomena, the evolution of consciousness, and the human potential for self-directed growth in body, mind and spirit.

John White, M.A.T., Series Editor of OMEGA BOOKS, is an internationally known author, editor, and educator in the fields of consciousness research and higher human development.

MORE TITLES IN OMEGA BOOKS

WHERE'S WILBER AT?

Ken Wilber's Integral Vision in the New Millennium

By Brad Reynolds

First Edition 2006

Published in the United States by
Paragon House
1925 Oakcrest Avenue, Suite 7
St. Paul, MN 55113

The Omega Books series from Paragon House is dedicated to classic and contemporary works about human development and the nature of ultimate reality, encompassing the fields of mysticism and spirituality, psychic research and paranormal phenomena, the evolution of consciousness, and the human potential for self-directed growth in body, mind and spirit.

Library of Congress Cataloging-in-Publication Data

Reynolds, Brad, 1955-
  Where's Wilber at? : Ken Wilber's integral vision in the new millennium / by Brad Reynolds.-- 1st ed.
    p. cm.
  ISBN 1-55778-846-4 (pbk. : alk. paper) 1. Wilber, Ken. I. Title.
  BF109.W54R495 2006
  191--dc22
                              2005037744

The paper used in this publication meets the minimum requirements of American National Standard for Information Sciences—Permanence of Paper for Printed Library Materials, ANSIZ39.48-1984.

Manufactured in the United States of America

10 9 8 7 6 5 4 3 2 1

For current information about all releases from Paragon House,
visit the web site at http://www.paragonhouse.com

CONTENTS

PART II

WHERE'S WILBER COMING FROM?

PART III

WHERE'S WILBER GOING?

Foreword

If you are truly interested in Ken Wilber's philosophy and work but don't have months to read his many books, articles, and interviews, then you have come to the right place! You hold in your hands the most satisfying and complete book to date on Ken Wilber's integral vision. In it Brad Reynolds leads us step by step with clarity and confidence through the many complex and subtle facets of Wilber's thinking about integral growth, the perennial philosophy, postmodernity, the Wilber-Combs Lattice, post-metaphysical reality and much more. Aided by the clearest graphic illustrations yet seen on these topics, Reynolds offers a superbly readable account of Wilber's astonishing integral Kosmos. His mastery is impressive, and to it he couples a remarkable ability to render difficult ideas into plain English, making this book a genuine pleasure to read.

Here I want to say a few words concerning the person and the vision about which you will be reading. Let's begin by putting Wilber's philosophy into a proper historical perspective.

After the passage of millennia the time has come for our global civilization to seek a deep philosophy that offers hope for uniting a rapidly unraveling world. In truth such times are exceedingly rare, and it is my contention that the remarkable system of thought unfolding in Ken Wilber's writings holds such a promise for our age. Let's step back and take in the long view.

It has been said that all of philosophy is a series of footnotes to Plato. That is to say, Plato posed and set the agendas for all the great questions philosophers would grapple with over the ages:

What is the true nature of reality?
What is beauty?
What is virtue?
What is truth?
What are the limits of knowledge?
What is the best political system?

Historically, Plato stood at the doorway between an archaic world of myth and magic and an emerging world of reason, mathematics, and science. Elements of both of these worlds are seen in his writings, and indeed modern scholars find it difficult understand whether some of his stories should be taken as pure mythology or are meant as metaphors to be deciphered by the rational mind. There is no question, however, that his primary way of thinking was rational, and each of the above questions gave birth to a whole field of philosophy.[1]

The question of the true nature of reality gave birth to the field of metaphysics.

The question of what is beautiful gave birth to the field of esthetics.

The question of what is virtuous gave birth to the study of ethics and morality.

Questions of truth and the limits of knowledge gave birth to the field of epistemology.

The question of what is the best political system gave birth to political philosophy, and later to political science.

A thinker of Plato's monumental influence could only have come at a time when one world, the world of myth and magic, was passing away and another world, the world of rationality and reason, was being born. It has been said that the 19th century German philosopher Friedrich Wilhelm Nietzsche was the next comparable thinker, binding together all strands of philosophy into a single framework and giving each a new form and a new life in the postmodern world.[2] I don't dispute this notion, but for several reasons it is clear that the great body of Nietzsche's work, as unquestionably influential as it is, fails to speak to a readership beyond a relatively small intelligentsia.[3] Moreover, there is a good case to be made for the idea that the advent of postmodernity did not represent a fundamental historical shift in mindset at all, but was simply the fireworks accompanying the final meltdown of the modernist agenda of hyperrationality.[4]

Jean Gebser, a 20th century European social philosopher and one of the many predecessors of modern integral thought, viewed the entire span of time that began with the age of Plato all the way down to the present as being dominated by *mental consciousness*, a phrase that is pretty much self-explanatory. After a pause for the Dark Ages, this form of consciousness shifted into high gear during the Renaissance and the Enlightenment, and modernity has been the dominant theme ever since. Today, however, we are truly living in an age of transition. The world has not seen a period of such fundamental change since Plato. American historian William Irwin

Thompson characterizes our cultural situation as if we are living in different worlds. Walking down the street we pass others who have already moved over into an emerging new era, while many more still reside in the mental age of hyperrationality. At the same time it is perhaps not surprising that others have reacted in large numbers to the frighteningly barren landscapes of hyperrationality and the postmodernity it has spawned by holding back or even regressing into the magic-mythic worldviews of the past. Today, as Gebser predicted, cultures are unraveling and confusion reigns on every side. It is time for a new and encompassing world vision, one that can reunite us in our basic humanity without tossing out the baby of progress with the bathwater of an exhausted civilization.

Gebser considered this era witness to a terrible struggle for the birth of a new integral civilization informed by an emergent integral consciousness. In the following pages you will see how Wilber and his colleagues have mapped out just this evolutionary struggle. You will also come to understand how Wilber's integral vision has developed and expanded Gebser's original notions, incorporating them into a deeper and wider understanding of what it means to be an integral person in an integral culture.

Wilber's thinking represents a monumental and I believe highly fruitful integration of the principle orienting generalizations, truths if you like, of a vast number of fields of knowledge. It is global in scope and honors the most creative and intelligent productions of human experience throughout history. Let me be clear, however, that the product of this labor is not simply a huge mélange of ideas from hither and thither. It is a grand and sophisticated worldview radically different from anything that came before it. This is not to say that Wilber has no predecessors or influences, but there are so many of them that every writer who tries to characterize his work seems to end up with a different list. For my part I am fascinated with his inclusion of ideas originally articulated by the recent American process philosopher Alfred North Whitehead.

To be honest, for most people, 100 proof Whitehead is nearly impossible to read, and even books that try to dumb him down are pretty much unintelligible. Nevertheless, some of his basic notions are not hard to understand. First, let us note that Whitehead was perhaps the last great metaphysical thinker, that is, one who developed a grand theory of the ultimate nature of reality.[5] His predecessors in this regard range from Plato, with is realm of ideals, to the 18th century European philosopher Emmanuel Kant, who shared with Plato the notion that what we see around us is not what is *real*. For Kant it was the mind itself that shapes our experience of the unknown substances that lie hidden behind what we perceive with our senses. Whitehead's essential idea was that at root reality a process. This process presents itself in *occasions* or *drops of experience*.[6] The birth of the universe in the Big Bang was one such occasion. So is this moment as you read these words. So is a pig! (Because a pig is an event – an occasion – and like all species of reality it is a process and not a thing.) Whitehead's universe is a cosmos of events, or occasions, and not of objects or things.

Wilber also views reality in terms of occasions.[7] In his case, however, each such occasion is rich with multiple *perspectives*, thus redefining the manifest world as a realm of *perspectives*, not of things, and not even events or processes as Whitehead conceived them. Here things can get complex fast. But fortunately the book you have in your hands makes these ideas beautifully lucid. Briefly looking ahead, for instance, let us note that each occasion includes inner, or subjective, and outer, or objective, perspectives. Thus we have the beginning of Wilber's four-fold kosmology: every occasion contains both inner and outer aspects. If we include the fact that some occasions are singular (a goose) and some are plural (a flock of geese) then we also have the basis for the four quadrants, a modeling system that Reynolds has described, I believe, very clearly in the following pages. (See, e.g., Figure ** on page **)

Rising vertically upward from this four-fold pattern emerges a series of stages, or levels, that unfold through evolutionary time as well as in the growth of each individual person. For example, every person grows from infancy up through a series of psychological stages to reach whatever level he or she is fortunate enough to achieve during a lifetime. These stages in turn mirror the evolutionary levels humankind on average has passed through in its long ascent from pre-human ancestors. Jean Gebser was one scholar who mapped out the evolutionary history of these stages. He referred to them in terms of *archaic* consciousness, *magical* consciousness, *mythic* consciousness, *mental* consciousness (including its most recent hyperrational phase), on up to the present period of transition into an *integral* consciousness which, as you will soon see, Wilber has unfolded into several evolutionary or developmental levels.

Backing up to get the big picture now, each occasion, each moment of experience, "lights up"[8] in a complex vertical structure with both inner and outer perspectives. This structure is subjectively experienced from the inside (the left two quadrants of the four-fold diagram) while at the same time it is objectively seen from the outside (right two quadrants of the four-fold diagram). The top two quadrants of the four-fold diagram represent each occasion in its first-person or singular aspects, and the right two quadrants represent it in its third-person or plural aspects. To get down to details here takes some explaining, and I leave that to the fine descriptions on the following pages. Here let us simply note that each occasion has an inner subjective dimension and an outer objective one, and that these can be viewed in singular or plural aspects (I am a person with an objective body and an inner subjectivity, while at the same time I am part of a plural community with others and share intersubjective experiences with them).[9] Meanwhile, if we move vertically we discover a series of increasingly complex nested stages or levels. These include the tiered developmental architecture of cognitive skills and moral thinking, as well as corresponding levels of complexity in the nervous system. They also include stages of cultural growth and societal evolution, each overarching and enfolding those below.

As we can see, the picture grows complicated, but you are fortunate to have such as excellent guide as Brad Reynolds, a long-time student of Wilber's, to explain his comprehensive Integral Vision step by step in the subsequent pages. Here, I only hope to communicate the scope and depth of the exquisite worldview that Ken Wilber has crafted over the years. In it we discover the wonder of each occasion, each moment of experience, as an event of unbounded beauty and complexity arising within an evolutionary yet spiritual reality.

—Allan Combs, author of *The Radiance of Being: Understanding the Grand Integral Vision; Living the Integral Life.*

PART I

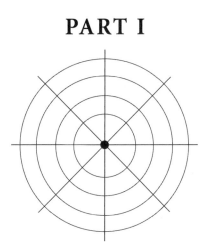

WHERE'S WILBER AT?

The desires of the flesh, the ideas of the mind, and the luminosities of the soul—all are perfect expressions of the radiant Spirit that alone inhabits the universe, sublime gestures of that Great Perfection that alone outshines the world. There is only One Taste in the entire Kosmos, and that taste is divine, whether it appears in the flesh, in the mind, in the soul…. From One Taste all things issue, to One Taste all things return—and in between, which is the story of this moment, there is only the dream, and sometimes the nightmare, from which we would do well to awaken.

—Ken Wilber, *One Taste* (1999)

CHAPTER ONE

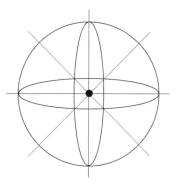

Where Wilber's At: AQAL Reality

It is one thing to merely have God on your side, quite another to have science on your side.

—Ken Wilber, *Sex, Ecology, Spirituality* (1995)

WHERE'S WILBER AT? THAT IS, WHAT IS THE PRESENT PHILOSOPHICAL position of Ken Wilber, the intellectual pundit who many claim to be the world's most intriguing and foremost philosopher? This is not an easy question to answer, for the breadth of Wilber's encyclopedic vision is enormous, covering nearly thirty years of prolific publication and continual modification. In other words, his philosophy keeps evolving. Indeed, the progressive unfoldment of Wilber's "Integral Vision" in complexity and depth allows us to recognize at least *five* consecutive and distinct "phases" or periods in his overall philosophical career. Since this incredible output covers over twenty-some books, with more to come, many people reading from an array of sources have often found him hard to pin down or really understand "where Wilber's at."

Over the years, both critics and students alike have at times complained that these complicated changes in Wilber's theories may indicate he's only a shape-shifter in a philosopher's disguise, or perhaps worse, a lone theoretician

3

cloistered in a mountain hideout totally out of touch with "the real world." In fact, this isn't the case at all, as we'll see when we explore some of the places where Wilber's been and what's he's doing. It's also important to realize that Wilber's always been on the move with his philosophy, since he's constantly integrating more and more, and then writing more and more, therefore, no one person, including this author, could ever express *exactly* where Wilber's at, since only he knows for sure (and that too "shades into Emptiness"). Yet, apparently, even he hasn't completely captured *exactly* where he's at, for he keeps publishing more books and introducing new ideas. In any case, Wilber's all-encompassing integral philosophy has become a clarifying beacon for people throughout the world interested in understanding, and then *applying*, a "more integral" approach to life and existence. As a result, Kenneth Earl Wilber II has earned the right to be called one of the world's most important living philosophers, therefore, it's probably beneficial, perhaps even wise, to check in on where Wilber's at, where he's coming from, and where he's going (the three main sections of this book).

Where Wilber's At: "All-Quadrant, All-Level" AQAL Metatheory

Where Wilber's at, stated quickly and summarily, is what's now known as the "AQAL Approach," or "AQAL Metatheory," or the "AQAL Model" (plus other derivative titles). This odd-sounding acronym "A-Q-A-L" (pronounced *ah-kwul*) stands for "**A**ll-**Q**uadrants, **A**ll-**L**evels," although it really represents the larger embrace of *"all-quadrants, all-levels, all-lines, all-states, all-types, all-worldviews,"* (and even more). The dynamic interplay of all these variables of consciousness and reality is what generates an interwoven, multileveled, pluridimensional, and nested "AQAL Matrix," which is actually an updated version of the traditional "Great Chain of Being." We'll be reviewing in detail why this "all-quadrant, all-level" approach to integral studies has become the primary shorthand phrase for Wilber's "Integral Metatheory," a cognitively reconstructed "Theory of Everything," which, in his words, "attempts to honor and include as much research as possible from the largest number of disciplines in a coherent fashion (which is one definition of an integral or more comprehensive view of the Kosmos)."[1] Most simply stated, this attitude understands that "Everybody is right!" since, as Wilber insists, "No one can be 100% wrong." Consequently, we'll discover that it's possible for every person, every paradigm, every methodology, every worldview, including those of modern science, postmodern philosophy, as well as the traditional religions and authentic mysticism, to have their own valuable yet *partial truths* to contribute to this overall "Big Picture" or "Theory of Everything."

AQAL Metatheory, in this case, reflects the most fundamental elements needed to know where Wilber's at, at a bare minimum (and there's even more):

- **"All-Levels"**—the *basic waves* found in the "spectrum of consciousness," or the AQAL Matrix, based on qualitatively distinct classes of recurrent patterns (within developmental lines) thus measuring degrees of "high" (more complex) and "low" (less complex); synonymous with "wave," "stage" (sequential unfolding) or "structure" (enduring patterns) found in the Great Chain of Being or Great Nest of Spirit (*matter* to *life* to *body* to *mind* to *soul* to *spirit*); thereby, in general, they represent the *premodern* worldview.

- **"All-Quadrants"**—the multiple *perspectives* of holons (or the "whole/parts" of the universe), categorized as having both *interiors* (subjective "I" and intersubjective "We/You" realms) and *exteriors* (objective "It" and interobjective "Its" realms), reaching from subatomic particles to trees to apes to the inner realities of consciousness and spirit; they also involve the "eight zones" or the *inside/outside* of each quadrant's perspective.

- **"The Big Three"**—the "four quadrants" simplified to reflect modernity's "value spheres" or qualitative differentiations of *subjective self/ aesthetics* (languages in the first-person), *interobjective culture/morals* (languages in the second-person), and *objective science/nature* (languages in the third-person); thereby, in a general sense, they represent the *modern* worldview.

- **"All-Lines"**—these are developmental patterns that comprise the evolving components of the self-system, and are defined as being relatively independent streams or capacities that proceed through the unfolding levels of development (including cognitive, morals/ ethics, emotional/affective, interpersonal, needs, self-identity, aesthetics, values, psychosexual, and spiritual).

- **"All-States"**—a clear distinction is being made between the "structures" or basic levels of consciousness, which tend to be *enduring*, and the usually *temporary* "states" of consciousness, which include: *waking* (gross body), *dreaming* (subtle body), and *deep dreamless sleep* (causal body), plus the various *altered* or *nonordinary* states, including peak experiences (of higher levels), meditative, and artificially-induced states; with "life practices" or injunctive methodologies this also involves the sequential unfolding of "States-Stages," usually from the result of intensified training (from gross to subtle to causal to nondual).

According to Wilber, this means that the true and difficult "task of *postmodernity*" is to *integrate* or harmoniously unite the *premodern* wisdom of the Great Chain (or Great Nest) with the invaluable knowledge uncovered by *modernity*, that is, the Big Three differentiations of self, culture, and science. Thus, the integral philosopher defines this important yet elusive goal in *The Marriage of Sense and Soul* (1998): "This integration is actually the single greatest task confronting the postmodern world, what modernity put asunder, postmodernity must heal."[2] This is, in many respects, the most basic underlying goal of Wilber's current AQAL Metatheory and Integral Vision.

At the turn of the century, this means that Wilber claims most *postmodern* philosophy has run aground with dead-end considerations, such as with *deconstructionism* and *pluralistic relativism* (or extreme political correctness). He even points out that many contemporary theories have become badly infected with what he terms *"boomeritis,"* defined as the pervasive narcissism of the "baby-boomer" generation. We'll learn how AQAL Metatheory goes beyond these limitations by offering a "constructive postmodernism," or a "post-postmodern" approach based upon a *universal integralism* that reflects a "unity-in-diversity," because, as Wilber wisely explains, "'Integral' means, if it means anything, the integration of all that is given to humanity."[3] Very importantly, by retaining the truths of both modernity and postmodernity, we'll also learn how the AQAL Approach skillfully and gracefully consummates the long-desired "marriage of science and religion." But most important of all, we'll witness how this integral philosophy, based upon the evolution of consciousness and the methodologies of *authentic spirituality*, also includes Spirit or God itself, yet without resorting to traditional religious conceptions (or their distortions). These are only some of the intriguing topics we'll be discussing throughout this book, while we're constantly reminded that this "Theory of Everything" is fully aware that it's only "a Map," not the actual "Territory," for as our philosopher reveals, "there is only One Taste in the entire Kosmos, and that taste is Divine, whether it appears in the flesh, in the mind, in the soul."[4] And this, when all is said and done, is the deepest place where Wilber's at.

Where Wilber's At: AQAL Phases-4/5

In terms of the span of his career to date, midway through the first decade of the new millennium, "where Wilber's at" is best summarized with what his students now call "Wilber/Phase-5" or "Phase-5" or "Wilber-V,"[5] a cataloging idea that comes from subdividing nearly three decades' worth of Ken Wilber's integral philosophy and psychology. Naturally, since the "fifth phase" is, in many respects, a detailed continuation of Wilber/Phase-4 (begun with *Sex, Ecology, Spirituality* in 1995), I will often use the designator "Phase-4/5" to indicate this current "AQAL" period. Nonetheless, the current Phase-5 writings (many of which are just now being published) do present numerous ideas that continue expanding upon his previous works, such as offering an unprecedented and radically revolutionary *Integral Post-Metaphysics,* or the highly-developed *Integral Operating System,* or an extremely inclusive *Integral Methodological Pluralism,* subjects we'll be reviewing throughout this book.

Indeed, AQAL Metatheory in general, and specifically Wilber/Phase-5, continues to show how well Wilber's integral "theories" are actually applicable in the outer world—or in the "real world"—of social and economic conditions, a feature that's being emphasized with the foundation of the Integral Institute and Integral University. The pragmatic *applications* of integral theories are already having profound effects on the various levels of reality, as they should, for otherwise they're only abstract ideas, and thus can't claim to be very integral at all. Consequently, we'll discover that Wilber's AQAL Metatheory is deeply involved with *Integral Transformative Practices* (ITP), or engaging in actual methodologies that *transform* consciousness and increase valid knowledge acquisition. As already mentioned, with this all-encompassing Integral Vision, even the mysteries of Spirit and the divine nature of the entire universe are thoroughly taken into account and then cognitively modeled in clear and systematic ways (based upon verifiable evidence). Of course, all these topics (and more) are covered in even greater detail in Wilber's much better-written books, a treasure trove of incomparable integral wisdom, which should always, I heartily suggest, become a constant source of study and application, for it's his writing that will naturally best reveal where Wilber's really at.

Wilber/Phase-5: Integral Outreach

Another important shift in the new millennium for the aging fifty-something philosopher is that Ken Wilber has turned to public teaching and outreach like never before. For decades the he had basically shunned public occasions in order to deeply concentrate on his scholastic research and integral writing (and meditative practices), sometimes even giving the erroneous impression that he's a recluse. Since the year 2000, however, Wilber has begun promoting integral education (and countless other activities) in the public forum, including establishing several thriving institutions, specifically Integral Institute and Integral University, his principal conduits for reaching thousands interested in a "more integral" way of life (see chapter 3). By doing so, he's now exercising a wider influence on many walks of life, from business to art, from science to religion, even interfacing with well-known political leaders (such as an ex-president). He's doing this while maintaining a constant dialogue with students and colleagues via multiple outlets and venues, including multimedia events and accessing the information superhighway (or Internet). Indeed, *everyone* is openly invited to join in and participate with this exciting adventure as integral awareness emerges in greater and greater numbers.

This type of public outreach intends to help push forward an "integral revolution," one that's already beginning to emerge from the ruins of postmodernity. This round of activity is attempting to rescue a reductionistic modern flatland caught in a deadly war between science (or modernity) and religion (or premodernity), as well as bringing to a truce the battling factions of the antimodernity forces (or postmodernity). By interfacing more actively with the public (and investors), Wilber wants to bring more integral solutions (that is, "second-tier solutions") to today's current dilemmas by building bridges between a host of competing divisions and philosophical quagmires (a postmodern "Tower of Babel" or aperspectival madness). He's even bringing out an integral critical analysis of "the many faces of terrorism" (the title to his new book), examining how a postconventional perspective might respond to these types of disruptions in the developmental spiral.

The main thrust of Wilber's critical theories is to bring *depth* (or all-levels in the Great Nest) back into a reductionistic scientific materialism known as "Flatland," thus attempting to bring about "the resurrection of the interiors (see part III). Importantly, this philosophy of inclusionary integralism clearly defines and promotes what an *authentic spirituality* (or "real religion") must look like and be in the critical, evidence-driven post-modern world. Such an integral approach to "real religion" openly supports spiritually transformative practices and their accompanying transpersonal disclosures as being fully viable in the modern world of science and critical thinking. This is an extraordinarily exciting venture that, according to Wilber (and many other people), is capable of bringing together and uniting traditional religions with the modern sciences, two of the most powerful forces in today's world with a long history of antagonism based upon multiple confusions.

Morphing Phases & Downloading Pages

One of the first things we notice when studying Wilber's overall oeuvre, as we've already mentioned, is that his integral philosophy has expanded dramatically from his first books. His students, therefore, have found it helpful to use the various "Phases" of his career—Wilber/Phases 1–5 (covering the years 1975–2005)—as a way to better understand the large expanse of his work. This is an organizing technique, first introduced by Wilber himself in *The Eye of Spirit* (1997), as a good way to clarify the staggering breadth of his extensive writings. Importantly, by studying the initial ideas captured in his earlier philosophical phases and published books, it's possible to notice how each succeeding phase transcends-but-includes its preceding phase (a hallmark of evolution itself). Currently, as the AQAL Model continues evolving and morphing into new forms and expressions, Wilber finally conceded what was already obvious to his attentive students, as he explained (in 2003): "The books prior to *Sex, Ecology, Spirituality* are preliminary explorations in integral studies, and, although many of them present what I hope are important pieces of an integral view…the earlier books…[are only] useful in forming the subcomponents of a more integral theory."[6] As we continue to review where Wilber's been coming from during these thirty-some years of his professional career, we'll see he's been very effectively *"phasing"* or expanding his spectrum of consciousness theories into the much more integral embrace of AQAL Metatheory.

Due to a massive amount of published pages, the type of overview attempted here is much easier said than done. Since Wilber's first publication in 1977, up to this current date of 2005, the integral philosopher has published nearly two dozen books and hundreds of articles, all of them composed of fairly difficult and dense material, even though they're eloquently explained and artfully articulated. Significantly, this massive outpouring was accomplished despite a nearly ten-year hiatus from writing and publishing during the mid-eighties while he attended to his second wife's fatal fight with cancer (see chapter 7). Inspired in part from their tragic love story of heartfelt "grace and grit," when Wilber began writing again in earnest during the early-to-mid-1990s, he had soon published *seven* more detailed books between the years 1995-2000; that's over 2,500 pages of printed material!

Recently, during the year 2002 alone, under the influence of another "creative descent" (his words), Wilber wrote out over 2,000 pages of additional material that was pouring through him like a sieve, much of it very complex philosophy indeed (that's at least five books' worth!). Sometimes his endnotes alone comprise a book's worth of material. Also, partly as a way to keep tabs on this prolific output, in the years 1999 and 2000, his principal publisher, Shambhala Publications (headquartered in Boston), released eight bound volumes in *The Collected Works of Ken Wilber* (1999, 2000). This is an impressive set of 800-some-page books containing nearly all of the integral philosopher's previously published work—that in itself is over 5,000 pages of writings, most of which never went out of print since first being published (see chapter 3). With such an extremely prolific output, and its continual publication, and although every page contains incisive scholarship presented with a graceful literary style, it's become nearly impossible to determine exactly "where Wilber's at." As a prerequisite survey of these various phases in Wilber's career, I more thoroughly cover this material in *Embracing Reality: The Integral Vision of Ken Wilber: A Historical Survey and Chapter-By-Chapter Guide of Wilber's Major Works* (2004, Tarcher/Putnam), and therefore suggest its consultation for further details.[7]

By comprehending and following the major "phases" in Ken Wilber's three-decade-long career, it becomes much easier to see how all of his different ideas and theories are actually integrated within a larger whole, thus effectively laying the foundations for the fully developed AQAL Metatheory. In fact, by understanding the important contributions of his earlier books and the advancements of each phase, it's even possible to fully "grok" or truly understand where Wilber's at. This book, therefore, will give a simplified summary of where Wilber's at (part I), where he's coming from (part II), and where he's going (part III), all in an attempt to outline the basic contours of AQAL or the "all-quadrant, all-level" Theory of Everything.

Student's Foil or Critic's Target?

By creating such a generous (some say obsessive) outpouring of philosophical writing that's even difficult for his students and colleagues to absorb, then it's easier to imagine why his flabbergasted "critics" have found it doubly difficult to digest the constant output of Wilber's theoretical writings. Indeed, he's even acknowledged the difficulty presented to his readers, as he recently explained, "In order to really understand my 'system,' a person needs to go through six or seven books, at least, I [therefore] completely understand why most people just don't want to do that."[8] (To see a "best of" list of recommended Wilber books to read first, I'll reserve that task for an endnote.[9])

Often critics have gotten lost in the quagmire of critiquing Wilber's work based on earlier, and now "outdated," books and phases (particularly, it seems, with the evolutionary Phase-2 books). Nevertheless, Wilber has always been attentive to the critical comments of critics and colleagues alike, especially if they show a decent grasp of what he's actually trying to do. Consequently, his response toward many of his critics is "thanks for trying," but they should still do a little more "homework," especially by more comprehensively reading his detailed Phase-4/5 AQAL books (including the endnotes). In other words, in trying to grasp or ascertain "where Wilber's at," one soon realizes that it's really an open-ended, and not a closed, system. Yet, generally, with the right approach and a little diligent study, AQAL Metatheory is fairly easy to comprehend, for it's based on a natural holism that makes rational sense, although admittedly, at its core it will always remain cognitively incomprehensible since all is transcended in Spirit.

Even now, during the opening years of the new millennium, his students are discovering that the more radical—or revolutionary—nature of Phase-5's *Integral Post-Metaphysics* often makes it appear at times he's contradicting some of his more important earlier views; yet this really isn't the case at all. In fact, *this* post-metaphysical integral approach is most certainly where Wilber's at. Amazingly, it appears that this Phase-5 accomplishment of providing a post-Kantian metaphysics may even go beyond (yet include) the incredible strides made by his earlier breakthroughs, such as with the "spectrum of consciousness" (in the 1970s), or with the "pre/trans fallacy" (in the 1980s), or with the "four quadrants" (in the 1990s).

In fact, this post-metaphysical approach is so revolutionary it's even tripping up some of his longtime students, such as with Frank Visser's book *Ken Wilber: Thought as Passion* (2003), a well-documented and critical overview of Ken Wilber's life and philosophical career. Although Visser has an excellent understanding of many important issues presented in his earlier phases, Wilber still maintains that Visser misrepresents his actual views by failing to grasp the significance and radical nature of Integral Post-Metaphysics (and consequently, Wilber/Phase-5). Visser admits that his own theosophical orientation colors his reading of Wilber's integral approach to spirituality, especially since he wants to honor the beloved Perennial Philosophy, another topic Wilber's been critiquing recently (see chapter 5). As a defender of "metaphysics,"[10] Visser finds it hard to agree with Wilber's post-metaphysical approach, therefore, in so many words, he states that Wilber is off-base and is denying his own origins with the "perennial philosophy." Consequently, while offering a sound review of much of Wilber's early work, including some of the corresponding events that took place in the integral philosopher's personal life, Visser's well-researched book still stands as a misreading of where Wilber's at.

In addition, I believe part of the difficulty in interpreting Wilber accurately comes from the fact that there are so many precious gifts of philosophical insight offered in his body of writings that every person walks away with their own valuable understandings and misunderstandings. Plus, by simplifying his complex philosophy for explanatory and introductory purposes, this has sometimes opened the door for unjustified criticism by theorists who haven't taken the time to accurately gauge the true depth of Wilber's original explanation works (which are often buried in extremely detailed endnotes). This shows, in my opinion, that it's not really a weakness of Wilber's presentations, but rather it's reflecting the depth and profundity (and complexity) that comes from studying one of the most passionate philosophical geniuses of our time.

Since Wilber's Integral Vision, as a living philosopher and person, has been evolving in print along with his conceptualizations (in Phases 1-5), even his students and colleagues are finding it difficult to publish a statement about his work, and then have it remain accurate for very long. As only some examples, I'll cite the early version of Allan Combs' *The Radiance of Being* (1995), Brant Cortright's *Psychotherapy and Spirit: Theory and Practice in Transpersonal Psychotherapy* (1997), John Rowan's *The Transpersonal: Psychotherapy and Counseling* (1993, 1998), John Nelson's *Healing The Split: Integrating Spirit into Our Understanding of the Mentally Ill* (1994), or even Roger Walsh's encompassing summary essay "The Worldview of Ken Wilber" (1994, 1996). All of these excellent writings support the Integral Vision, and they offer many important contributions themselves, but they're still not the place to find an accurate representation of Wilber's overall philosophy and integral psychology.

If this shape-shifting or morphing ability makes it difficult for his students, then perhaps it's easier to understand why the misinterpretations and distortions of Wilber's harshest critics are legion. These range from books and essays written by such notable people as Stan Grof, Michael Washburn, Michael Winkelman, Donald Rothberg, Sean Kelly, Jürgen Kramer, Gus DiZerega, Don Frew, and Robert McDermott, to the brilliant but misguided William Irwin Thompson. There's even a new generation trying to make their critical mark, like Ray Harris, Mark Edwards, and Jorge Ferrer, all of whom have important points and considerations, yet each of whom usually couches their work in misconstrued or incomplete comprehensions of where Wilber's at.

Too often these errors arise from a failure to read through the massive volumes of Wilber's numerous books or to recognize their earlier phases. Nonetheless, the critics will say what they will, since critical thinking is a prerequisite for wisdom. Yet, I also believe it's a situation similar to when in 1955 Buddhist scholar T. R. V. Murti observed that "Philosophy never returns to its former placid state after the shock of a great philosopher. It is again a saying of Hegel that the opposition that a philosophy evokes is evidence of its vitality and fruitfulness."[11] This is certainly the case with Ken Wilber and his world-renowned philosophy. However, it also needs to be acknowledged that *every time* Wilber has focused on a critic's concerns or statements, his defense has always been stellar in undermining their distortions and leaving the situation clarified by presenting his actual integral theories (for example, see Wilber's excellent responses to the distorted views presented in *Ken Wilber in Dialogue*).[12]

One of the most consistent scholars faithfully representing Wilber's actual views is philosopher and integral ecologist Michael Zimmerman (from Tulane University), especially in regard to ecology, deep ecology, and now, integral ecology.[13] This is one of the advantages gained by evaluating Wilber's integral ideas as they relate to one's area of expertise, which Zimmerman has done with ecology, instead of attempting an expansive overview and critique of Wilber's entire project, which is what many critics seem wont to do. Zimmerman's excellent work in deep ecology, along with ecologist Sean Hargens (both are in the Department of Integral Ecology at Integral University), shows how effective a genuine integral approach can be when it's adequately applied to ecological systems and the concerns of the natural environment.

Another fine example is the integral work of Allan Combs, especially in his second edition to *The Radiance of Being: Understanding the Grand Integral Vision; Living the Integral Life* (2002), where he adeptly added the AQAL Approach to his integral considerations. Combs has masterfully blended Wilber's integral ideas with his own valuable contributions (and critiques), thus demonstrating a skillful handling of Wilber's shape-shifting, but fully comprehensible, Integral Vision.[14] Nonetheless, although many people grasp only a partial view of Wilber's grand integral vision—or "where Wilber's at"—many have still done commendable jobs of integrating his important ideas and theories into their own work and observations. Thus, in our own ways, we're carrying forward the integral mission as the unfolding brilliance of Wilber's integral philosophy influences and affects us all, even if from a distance.

Dialoguing with Wilber: Integral Conversations

Now with the emergence of Integral Institute, Integral University, Integral Naked, and other public outreach ventures, there are thousands of people and students participating with Wilber personally in a *dialogical approach* to reviewing his AQAL Metatheory and its far-reaching implications (see chapter 3). In fact, the opportunity is now available for anyone to *dialogue,* in a space of mutual understanding and respect, the various details and breadth of integral philosophy, sometimes with Wilber personally, but always with qualified representatives of Integral Institute. Nonetheless, Wilber has always listened hard and intently to his critics' concerns, often incorporating their valid points, or even answering them in future writings. Overall, fortunately, this back-and-forth debate and struggle to clarify ideas has been beneficial to all parties involved. Unfortunately, this has also made it doubly difficult for a reader to know exactly where Wilber's at, however, this is how the Integral Vision stays vital, alive, and effective in the world-at-large—by intersubjective dialoguing and subjective transformative practices verified, confirmed, and checked by the "community of the adequate" or other like-minded people.

Of course, in the sphere of *philosophia* or the "love of wisdom," it's totally appropriate, healthy, natural, and just plain smart to intellectually critique Wilber's writings and so-called theories as you go along (or with any other theories or statements made by anybody). All propositions must be questioned and submitted to critical thinking, the doorway to discovery. That's how we learn in real-life circumstances and maintain our autonomy and freedom. Nonetheless, Wilber's ideas are boundless, and full of stimulating considerations to be enjoyed and pondered, for they reach from science to the arts to philosophy to politics, from psyche to cosmos, from myths to mysticism, from religion to spirit (or God, Brahman, BuddhaNature). Pick and choose what's useful for you. Learn to integrate the plurality of ideas and worldviews streaming off his pages and that are alive and active in the world around us.

Ultimately, as we'll consistently witness, Wilber's main thrust is to encourage everyone to *practice* and *grow,* to reach and evolve, to develop further in order to see for oneself the truths of authentic spirituality and Enlightenment (or God-Realization); in other words, get involved in real *transformative practices—do the yoga!* With an integral philosophy claiming "Everybody is Right!" then there's really no need to believe anything, or anyone, let alone believe everything. Although this Grand AQAL Theory of Everything is undeniably brilliant in its scope and saturated with liberating power, it will always be somewhat difficult to grasp, and definitely impossible to finalize, because it's paradoxically nondual and "Empty" (or inexplicably Divine). Besides, the entire display is only an integral dance anyway just trying to engage you in authentic transpersonal practices and sacred spiritual wisdom.

Empty-Headed Philosopher or Crazy-Wise Mystic?

Since this spiritual or transrational quality of Ken Wilber's writings will seep in sooner or later, then it usually only makes matters worse for both students and critics alike as they try to rationally comprehend where Wilber's at. One of the central reasons is that with Wilber's nondual spirituality he can many times come across as a philosophical "shape-shifter," a theoretical "trickster," or one who is "crazy-wise" and exercising "crazy wisdom";[15] that is, he often makes paradoxical statements, sometimes even negating all he's said before. This makes Ken Wilber even harder to handle, impossible to contain, an enigma in disguise…a slippery devil. This seems to be especially true for the fearful, limited ego-I who seeks (and needs) to know it all, to contain everything within its comfortable grasp, which is exactly the reason why many spiritual teachers will play the role of the trickster, or one who intentionally slips things up for the trembling ego. Ultimately, as you'll find out, Wilber seems to have no boundaries. For example, what other world-renowned philosopher would write a foreword to a book called *Finding God Through Sex* (2002) by David Deida? Wilber begins with the statement: "Finding God through sex? And why not? The only thing that is astonishing in that equation is that it ever should have seemed odd to begin with."[16] I suggest it's only a philosopher with an *extremely* comprehensive worldview who would even begin to make such statements in today's conventional world, that is, one who's deep enough and tolerant enough to talk about sex and God with the requisite freedom and valuable insight, as Wilber does quite proficiently, yet without resorting to irony or narcissistic hedonism.

Interestingly, the noted yoga scholar and philosopher Georg Feuerstein had reason to mention Wilber in his book on *Holy Madness* (1991), such as when he noticed, "The trickster is not *merely* a personification of the unconscious. We may also see in him [or her] a symbol of the intrapsychic impulse toward higher consciousness, or what Ken Wilber calls the 'Atman project.' As such, the trickster is the mythological precursor of the crazy-wisdom guru who also sees it as his or her task to tear off all our cultural blinders and rational pretensions so that we may see reality unmasked."[17] Removing all boundaries and revealing reality by unveiling its various masks, as history has shown, is also the task of the so-called "mad mystics," those "mad" or unconventional (actually postconventional) people, women and men alike, who have continually appeared throughout world history and in every major culture. These folks have been "mad" and "crazy" enough to claim they've actually had *direct* and *personal communion* with God or the absolute Ultimate Reality, a depth of consciousness that's also been called "no-boundary awareness," as Wilber did in his popular second book, *No Boundary* (1979).

If you could know Ken Wilber personally, then you'd realize a strong case can be made that he is indeed a living mystic, albeit a modern (or postmodern integral) one, for he's unlike hardly anyone you'd ever meet in today's world, on many different levels. Yet, don't misunderstand, he's plainly human as well, warts and all, and also subject to illness and disease (such as with his fight with REDD). This can mean many things to many people, but naturally, Wilber is just a man who's been involved with transpersonal spiritual practices and the great wisdom tradition of humankind—an invitation that's open to all of us. Nonetheless, he is *not* to be mistaken with a spiritual master or enlightened adept, for as he's always claimed: "I am a pandit, not a guru" (see chapter 6).

For Wilber, the truth of reality can *never* be stated or codified—*neti, neti!* or "not this, not that"—the famous Upanishadic phrase of Advaita Vedanta and nondual Buddhism (perhaps perfectly embodied by the great second-century Buddhist sage, Nagarjuna). This is also one of Wilber's favorite nondual mottos as well: "Not this, not that" for no map, no model, not even a grand integral vision will ultimately reveal the real "territory" of nondual Spirit, for that's *only realizable,* never accurately stated, published, or quantified. Yet, don't misunderstand the intentions, this is not some cosmic joke created by smoke and mirrors, for it's a profound philosophical position thoroughly grounded in the world's esoteric religious traditions. There have been many enlightened intellectuals, or "pandits," in the long history of religion and mysticism, from nearly every culture and century, and they have all professed similar conclusions. Perhaps, Wilber's not on par with someone like, say Nagarjuna or Plotinus, but he's no doubt floating around their general sphere of reality, since they also claim, and really mean it, bottom-line: It cannot be stated, *only realized!*

Without idealistically deifying him in any way, but rather in clear recognition of his profound philosophical accomplishments, it makes some sense to compare Wilber to a human "bodhisattva," or a sentient being who's committed to the Enlightenment (or God-Realization) of all other sentient beings. This seems especially true since he knows for sure that the "forms" of his teaching (or any other teaching or model) are ultimately "Formless" and

"Empty," i.e., they're never going to be the real territory of consciousness itself. This type of nondual philosophy is so formless and empty that is usually ends up negating *everything* except Divine Spirit (and Spirit-in-action) itself, including, of course, statements like the one I just made, which are also negated. Now you may better understand why it's nearly impossible to exactly pin down or categorize where Wilber's at.

After negating all things possible, then, paradoxically, these enlightened sages often go on to make elaborate statements and philosophical systems (or even edifices) out of their nondual realizations (or Enlightenment), as does Wilber, to the advantage of us all. It's just another part of their divine dance and contribution to humanity as a whole. And besides, language itself isn't really a limitation, for as Wilber clearly maintains, "Words do just fine as *signifiers* for experience, whether mundane or spiritual, if we both, you and I, have had similar experiences in a context of shared background practices. For instance, Zen Masters talk about Emptiness all the time!"[18]

"Not this, not that," but only *what is always already the case*, this indeed is what guides Wilber to ultimately negate anything he might say or write, thus he's always made quite sure that somewhere in every book there's hidden a sentence that paradoxically proclaims a statement similar to the one below:

> All my books are lies. They are simply maps of a territory, shadows of a reality, gray symbols dragging their bellies across the dead page, suffocated signs full of muffled sound and faded glory, signifying absolutely nothing, And it is the nothing, the Mystery, the Emptiness alone that needs to be realized; not known but felt, not thought but breathed, not an object but an atmosphere, not a lesson but a life.... Please use them [my books] only as a reminder to take up dancing itself, to inquire into this Self of yours, this Self that holds this page and this Kosmos all in a single glance. And then express that glory in integral maps, and sing with passion of the sights you have seen, the sounds that the tender Heart has whispered only to you in the late hours of the quiet night, and come join us and tell us what you have heard, in your own trip to Bermuda, in the vibrant Silence that you alone own, and the radiant Heart that we alone, together, can discover.[19]

CHAPTER TWO

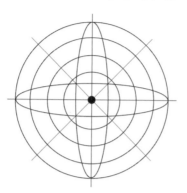

Unitas Multiplex: *An Integral Theory of Everything*

Integral: the word means to integrate, to bring together, to join, to link, to embrace. Not in the sense of uniformity, and not in the sense of ironing out all the wonderful differences, colors, zigs and zags of a rainbow-hued humanity, but in the sense of *unity-in-diversity*, shared commonalities along with our wonderful differences.

—Ken Wilber, *A Theory of Everything* (2000)

An Integral Critical Theory of Everything

BY CONSTRUCTING A "THEORY OF EVERYTHING" OR T.O.E. THAT'S attempting to account for the multiple variables in a pluridimensional yet unified reality, Ken Wilber is offering the world an Integral Vision (with its accompanying AQAL Metatheory) that extends far beyond the reductionistic materialism of modern science or even the metaphysics of ancient spirituality. By doing so, the pandit-scholar has been instrumental in the further innovation of a new language, an integral vocabulary that's capable of communicating across numerous disciplines and methods of inquiry (as we will amply see). Although this new terminology may not initially be familiar, it was designed to be a language of connectivity for it bridges a spectrum of worldviews and the various levels of reality by using a simple and skillful means of discourse and understanding.[1] For example, even the acronym A-Q-A-L with its own set of technical jargon is itself a creative expression of a more integral approach to reality.

As a result, such a comprehensive and inclusionary AQAL Approach can make, as Wilber clearly claims, "legitimate room for art, morals, science, and religion, and doesn't merely attempt to reduce them all to one's favorite slice of the Kosmic pie."[2] Consequently, it also effectively outlines a new type of *critical theory*—an integral critical theory—for in examining and including the full scope of reality, from matter to humans to the spiritual, it makes sure nothing is overlooked or excluded, on any level, in any quadrant. Indeed, this is one of its most valuable contributions, for as the integral philosopher points out in the aptly titled *A Theory of Everything* (2000): "If we succeed in developing a truly holistic or integral view of reality, then we will also develop a new type of *critical theory*—that is, a theory that is critical of the present state of affairs in light of a more encompassing and desirable state, both in the individual and the culture at large. The integral paradigm will inherently be critical of those approaches that are, by comparison, partial, narrow, shallow, less encompassing, less integrative."[3] To be *more integral*, in other words, actually entails embracing more and more of reality.

As only one example of a more inclusive integral language, with the debut of the AQAL Approach (in 1995), Wilber began reintroducing the original spelling of *"Kosmos"* (spelled with a "k") as being a better signifier, indicating that the universe is really a harmonious yet multileveled reality of matter, body, mind, soul, and spirit. Obviously, this view is in direct opposition to the current worldview of science that only sees a physical universe of colliding particles driven only by blind chance, which is generally what the word "cosmos" (spelled with a "c") implies in the modern lexicon. According to Wilber, therefore, it's time to shift from "cosmos to Kosmos" and embrace the full spectrum of reality and consciousness as being our rightful inheritance. Wilber continues to explain these concerns in *A Theory of Everything* (2000): "The Greeks had a beautiful word, *Kosmos*, which means the patterned Whole of existence, including the physical, emotional, mental, and spiritual realms. Ultimate reality was not merely the cosmos, or the physical dimension, but the Kosmos, or the physical and emotional and mental and spiritual dimensions altogether. Not just matter, lifeless and insentient, but the living Totality of matter, body, mind, soul, and spirit. The Kosmos!—now there is a real Theory of Everything!"[4]

By providing a viable Theory of Everything or AQAL Model that embraces both science and spirituality, both the ancient and the modern/postmodern worldviews, Wilber is attracting many contemporary theorists and people who deeply appreciate the vast scope of his integral enterprise (although, naturally, they'll still beg to differ on certain points, as we all should). For instance, human potential pioneer and philosopher Michael Murphy recognized where Wilber's at when he confirmed: "By assembling material from the physical, biological, and human sciences, Wilber helps us see the world as a whole and liberates us from narrow perspectives on the human adventure."[5] Even transpersonal pioneer and psychiatrist Stanislav Grof, sometimes cited as a critic of Wilber's system (yet they share much more in common than not), has also conceded: "Ken Wilber has done more than any other single individual in terms of laying solid philosophical foundations for future reconciliation of science and spirituality. The series of his groundbreaking books has been a *tour de force*, offering an extraordinary synthesis of data drawn from a vast variety of areas and disciplines, Eastern and Western…. Wilber has formulated an extraordinary interdisciplinary framework that provides the necessary philosophical foundations for such an integral understanding of reality."[6]

Integral psychiatrist and author Roger Walsh chimes in as well after examining "The Worldview of Ken Wilber" (in 1996): "Wilber's theoretical system has its limits, but it also has enormous strengths. He has forged a systematic, broad-ranging, multidisciplinary, integrative, visionary yet scholarly worldview based in psychology, grounded in philosophy, spanning sociology and anthropology, and reaching to religion and mysticism."[7] With this type of inclusionary approach, as we'll continue to see, this "Theory of Everything" includes and incorporates the whole Kosmos, from matter to mind to God, from id to ego to Spirit, in all its dimensions and manifestations of interiors and exteriors arising and falling as Spirit-in-action yet grounded in radiant Divine Emptiness. We shall continue to review some of the reasons behind these thoughtful claims, coming from both Wilber's critics and supporters alike.

What's "Integral"?—The Whole Kosmos

Since the word "integral" keeps appearing throughout Ken Wilber's writings, it's probably a good idea to more carefully consider what's being referred to with this ubiquitous term. Simply put, integral (from Latin, *integralis* or "whole") means *comprehensive* or *inclusive*, i.e., to include all of the parts that make up the whole, thus the dictionary defines it as "necessary for completeness," "wholeness," "essential (an *integral* part)," and "composed of parts forming a whole." An integral "map," therefore, is a working model of reality that includes the interior and exterior dimensions of existence, thus it aspires in some way to be a comprehensive cartography covering the "Totality of Reality," no simple task, to say the least.

Nonetheless, as we already learned, and as Wilber constantly reminds us, these types of intellectual integrative approaches or "grand theories" are only "A Map," a facsimile representation, *not* the actual "Territory of Reality" itself; indeed, it's nothing more than some Zen master pointing to the moon, not the moon itself. As we've also seen, Wilber sees the vast encompassing nature of his AQAL Metatheory as being something like a "Theory of Everything," a phrase borrowed from physics in its search for a "Grand Unified Theory" or G.U.T., the long-sought "Theory of Everything" or scientific T.O.E. This mathematical quest of science has been the elusive goal of science since the Einsteinian and quantum revolutions of the twentieth century, where even now scientists are still trying to unite the physical laws of both cosmology (which measures incredibly large astronomical spaces) and quantum physics (which measures extremely small atomic spaces). String theory, for example, is today's most likely candidate for a possible unified scientific T.O.E., but still, that's only the material world.

Beyond the world of physics (which doesn't measure mind, soul, or spirit), Wilber's integral approach is using a mapping scheme or "theory" to *really* unite *everything*, that is, from physical matter to living nature to sensational bodies to mental minds to soulful archetypes to Divine Spirit, etc., all the various levels composing the multifaceted, pluridimensional Kosmos. For Wilber this has evolved into the AQAL or "all-quadrant, all-level" approach, or more generally speaking, he describes this type of *integralism* as the "Integral Approach," the "Integral Model," or the "Integral Agenda" (and other derivatives), all of which appear and reappear throughout his collected works (and in this book). In this case, the title "Integral Vision" has become one of the best catchall phrases signifying "where Wilber's at"—a vision that's been expanding and developing its AQAL Metatheory with each publication for nearly thirty years.

Another descriptive term for this integrative attitude is "universal integralism" for it's designed to be a "world philosophy" used by "*Homo universalis*" to celebrate the rich depth of diversity displayed on this multicultural planet. This genuine universal approach is fully capable of embodying and living what's been called *"Unitas Multiplex"* (Latin, meaning "unity-in-diversity"), which is literally a "multiple unity," therefore, Wilber openly claims "'*Unitas multiplex*' is actually a good motto for my work, and there are signs that it is itself an idea whose time has truly come."[8] This approach allows us to honor the extreme diversity of all the various *relative* "surface features" while simultaneously acknowledging the *universal* "deep features" of our common humanity, for as the integral theorist points out, "The *deep features* are generally similar wherever we find them, while the *surface features* are local, culturally constructed, and relative, usually differing from culture to culture."[9] He continues by explaining, "There are, of course, enormous local variations in content, so that, once again, *'unitas multiplex'* is still the best motto: universal deep features, but culturally relative surface features, are what we find in the growth to goodness."[10] This way it's possible to include all the local surface features without getting lost in the merely relative and constructed variations of endless possibilities, for it's much easier to identify the universal currents or structures deeper than the multifarious surface shapes and forms.

This Integral Vision, therefore, is the *real* "Theory of Everything" for it includes more than physics with its reductionistic T.O.E. that covers only the physical cosmos or the "four forces" of nature: the electromagnetic, gravity, weak/strong nuclear forces. AQAL Metatheory, on the other hand, is not just about uniting the theories of relativity with quantum mechanics, but it intends to include *all* of the spheres of existence, from the *physiosphere* (of matter-energy) to the *biosphere* (of biological/life) to the *noosphere* (of psychological/mind) to the *theosphere* (of soul/spirit), where each higher-order emergent embraces or envelops each lower (or less shallow) level in a *transcend-and-include* manner (see part II). So far, at least, it appears that no one else has offered a more viable inclusionary "theory" than the one being proposed by Ken Wilber, or at least at this time…until, of course, the next one comes along.

However, let's not be mistaken, although he's proposing an all-inclusive AQAL T.O.E., Wilber has never claimed that "his version" of humanity's integral project is the only right one. He's smart enough to know that he's only presenting *his version* of a possible Integral Vision. Thus he becomes perplexed when critics suggest otherwise, for he stated years ago (in 1984): "Some people take my system and make it into a be-all and end-all, as if Emptiness could ever be radically objectified in mental-linguistic forms. And so let me say, for the record, that that is not at all the way I view my own work. Not only do I hold *all* of it in provisional status, the so-called 'highest' state is specifically 'defined' as Formless, Mystery, Unknowing, Divine Ignorance, etc., radically beyond *any* particular objective phenomena, including any mental models, that might parade by in the face of formless Infinity.... If certain individuals insist on misusing my work in this fashion, all I can do is decry it, and repeat again the words from the Preface to *The Atman Project*: the model that follows is of relative use but is 'finally a lie in the face of that Mystery which only alone is'."[11] Nonetheless, if held within its proper context, AQAL Metatheory becomes a brilliant guide to embracing everything from matter to mind to God, and all things and processes in-between creating a Kosmic Mandala of Being/Reality and Knowing/Consciousness (see Chapter 8).

Naturally, there are other versions of integral approaches in today's postmodern world, in which case, Wilber is only inviting anyone to see for themselves by review the evidence and results with an open mind and heart. As we've explained, he's very aware of the limitations of mental modeling systems, including his own, as he recently qualified (in 2000): "The real intent of my writing is not to say, you must think in this way. The real intent is to enrich: here are some of the many important facets of this extraordinary Kosmos; have you thought about including them in your own worldview? My work is an attempt to make room in the Kosmos for all of the dimensions, levels, domains, waves, memes, modes, individuals, cultures, and so on ad infinitum.... My critical writings have never attacked the central beliefs of any discipline, only the claims that the particular discipline has the only truth—and on those grounds I have often been harsh. But every approach, I honestly believe, is essentially true but partial, true but partial, true but partial."[12] "True but partial" means everybody is right at least to some degree, thus this becomes the secret key to being *more integral.*

The Integral Approach: Everybody Is Right (True but Partial)

The Integral Approach or AQAL Metatheory, from Wilber's point of view, begins with the simple premise that "Everybody is Right," although any view is, at best, only *partially* correct. This is the "true but partial" or "correct but partial" approach that Wilber has employed from his earliest writings to his most recent, as he recently explained in *A Theory of Everything* (2000): "In this Theory of Everything, I have one major rule: *Everybody* is right. More specifically, everybody—including me—has some important piece of truth, and all of those pieces need to be honored, cherished, and included in a more gracious, spacious, and compassionate embrace, a genuine T.O.E.... To Freudians I say, Have you looked at Buddhism? To Buddhists I say, Have you studied Freud? To liberals I say, Have you thought about how important some conservative ideas are? To conservatives I say, Can you perhaps include a more liberal perspective? And so on, and so on, and so on.... At no point have I ever said: Freud is wrong. I have only suggested that they are true but partial."[13] Only with this approach could anybody ever be truly right.

Yet, as always, Wilber comes full circle and goes straight to the heart of Spirit by completely understanding that "one abandons a theory of everything in order simply to be Everything."[14] In other words, the maps made by the ego-self, although providing guidance and vital functions of orientation, must sooner or later be totally released in order to realize the real territory of Truth, God, Reality, the essence of all things. There's an important consequence with this type of inclusionary yet "true but partial" approach, because "if everybody is right, then some are more right than others,"[15] and this "value ranking" releases a "holarchy of values" (see chapter 11). In an early autobiographical essay, Wilber further explained what led him to this all-embracing attitude from the very beginning of his integral studies (in 1982): "For my own part, I simply could not imagine that any mind of genius (whether Freud's or Buddha's) could manufacture *only* falsehoods and errors. This was inconceivable to me. Rather, if we must form an early conclusion, the only possible one would be: Freud was correct but partial; Buddha was correct but partial; and so with Perls, Kierkegaard, the existentialists, the behaviorists. And it was on that tentative basis that I proceeded. We are faced not with several errors and one truth, but with several partial truths, and how to fit them together is the supreme puzzle."[16] A supreme picture of many partial puzzle pieces united as a whole produces a genuine Integral Vision, by whatever name, which is most simply where Wilber's at.

Overall, any authentic Integral Theory, by definition, must be willing to accept or integrate *any* new evidence that's being disclosed or revealed by a wide variety of paradigms, worldviews, and methodologies of human inquiry. In reviewing this type of integral approach, cultural historian Jack Crittenden investigates the true meaning of "integral" in his excellent introductory essay called "What Is the Meaning of 'Integral'?" first published as the foreword to *The Eye of Spirit* (1997). Crittenden panoramically reviews the scope of Wilber's world-embracing enterprise:

> Wilber's approach is the opposite of eclecticism. He has provided a coherent and consistent vision that seamlessly weaves together truth-claims from such fields as physics and biology; the ecosciences; chaos theory and the systems sciences; medicine, neurophysiology, biochemistry; art, poetry, and aesthetics in general; developmental psychology and a spectrum of psychotherapeutic endeavors, from Freud to Jung to Piaget; the Great Chain theorists from Plato and Plotinus in the West to Shankara and Nagarjuna in the East; the modernists from Descartes and Locke to Kant; the Idealists from Schelling to Hegel; the postmodernists from Foucault and Derrida to Taylor and Habermas; the major hermeneutic tradition, Dilthey to Heidegger to Gadamer; the social systems theorists from Comte and Marx to Parsons and Luhmann; the contemplative and mystical schools of the great meditative traditions, East and West, in the world's major religious traditions. All of this is just a sampling.... [Thus] if his approach is generally valid, it honors and incorporates more truth than any other system in history.[17]

The *"opposite of eclecticism,"* where being "eclectic" means to "pick and choose" from a variety of sources based on personal preferences, whereas this type of *integralism* includes everything (or all holons) as being vital parts to the whole picture. For Wilber, this involves using the concept of "orienting generalizations," a key idea he first introduced in the opening pages of *Sex, Ecology, Spirituality* (1995) by explaining that there are "certain broad, general themes... about which there is actually very little disagreement" coming from "the various fields of human knowledge."[18] With these truth-claims in mind, Wilber has then *reconstructed* and woven together an integrative model of no small consequence, thus he concludes in *A Brief History of Everything* (1996): "In working with *broad orienting generalizations*, we can suggest a *broad orienting map* of the place of men and women in relation to Universe, Life, and Spirit. The details of this map we can all fill in as we like, but its broad outlines really have an awful lot of supporting evidence, culled from the orienting generalizations, simple but sturdy, from the various branches of human knowledge."[19] This is an orienting map of the Kosmos, Human Life, and Divine Spirit, yet let's always remember, the map is never the territory.

By integrating this vast spectrum of orienting "correct but partial" truths, Wilber's AQAL Metatheory is a *reconstructive* model that is subjected to the *falsifiability principle*, which is the capacity to be proven wrong as well as correct. In this case, it's open to continued modification for, at best, it's only *partially* true. Integralism—as a holistic approach with depth—is the secret key to Wilber's success and his intriguing message. Only a truly *integral approach* will work in today's extremely diverse reality, for as the philosopher points out in *Integral Psychology* (2000): "Obviously much work remains to be done. But a staggering amount of evidence—premodern, modern, and postmodern—points most strongly to an *integral approach* that is [AQAL] all-quadrant, all-level. The sheer amount of this evidence inexorably points to the fact that we stand today on the brink, not of fashioning a fully complete and integral view of consciousness, but of being able to settle, from now on, for nothing less."[20] To settle for anything less than being fully integral is to cheat our innate wholeness and refuse the depth of our compound existence. Wouldn't any true *philosophia*, or the real "love of wisdom," especially one applicable around the globe, by its very nature have to be *integral* or truly comprehensive?

Grand Theories: The Map Is Not the Territory

I have always found it interesting, with all of his written philosophy admired around the world, that some of Ken Wilber's critics have often forgotten, or mistakenly overlooked, one of the most important themes running throughout every one of his "phases" and each one of his books. Wilber clearly articulated this principle on his very first pages, and it's a central message he's always abided by, which is simply the sensible warning: "The map is not the territory." Alfred Korzybski and Gregory Bateson immortalized this important phrase, but as E. F. Schumacher pointed out in *A Guide for the Perplexed* (1977), a faithful, reliable map is simply a necessity because humanity has a great need for such reliable maps.[21] As the aspiring philosopher first pointed out in *The Spectrum of Consciousness* (1977): "Now in itself, there is nothing particularly damaging or misleading about symbolic maps—they are of immense practical value and are quite indispensable to a civilized society.... However, the problem comes as soon as we forget that *the map is not the territory*, as soon as we confuse our symbols of reality with reality itself. Reality, so to speak, lies 'beyond' or 'behind' the shadowy symbols that are, at best, a second-hand facsimile. Not realizing this, humans become lost in a world of arid abstractions, thinking only of symbols about symbols about symbols about nothing, and the reality never gets in at all."[22] Forgetting this simple truth that the map is not the reality it's mapping has never been an accusation that can be accurately aimed at Ken Wilber.

Similar to the Zen fable that warns us not to mistake the finger *pointing at* the moon for the moon itself, it's our responsibility not to confuse the symbolic maps we make and use for reality itself (whatever that *is*). Consequently, Wilber has always gone out of his way to be crystal clear that any Integral Vision, "Grand Theories," "Big Pictures," or T.O.E.s (Theories of Everything), must first *consciously* recognize this simple and straightforward fact: "the map is not the territory," especially really Big (or Spiritual) Maps. However, at the same time, by including all these partial truths and being *more integral* or comprehensive, then Wilber has also acknowledged the immense value that really good maps and intellectual models have as orienting guides and developmental tools. Higher human capacities, he confirmed nearly twenty-five years later in *A Theory of Everything* (2000), are best "exercised and encouraged by engaging these *integral maps,* because such maps open our minds, and thus our hearts, to a more expansive, inclusive, compassionate, and *integral embrace* of the Kosmos and all of its inhabitants. Big pictures and big maps help open the mind, and thus the heart, to an *integral transformation.*"[23] Since Wilber's main interest in having a "Big Map" or "Grand Theory" is to encourage people in achieving the Good, the True, and the Beautiful, he finds it absolutely necessary to include integral applications (or "integral apps") and transformative disciplines (or "integral transformative practices"). In this case, by better knowing the "Big Picture of Reality," including the "idea" of God (or the real Divine), then we only gain for we have a clearer guiding light serving our journey through life and the Kosmos.

Integral Philosophia: *A World Philosophy*

The power of Ken Wilber's writings in these current millennial times has a strong appeal for both professionals and laypeople alike, being especially vibrant for those many modern people wanting to know about *real* philosophy, i.e., authentic *philosophia*—the true "love of wisdom" (ancient Greek, literally, *philos* = loving; *sophia* = wisdom). By opening the treasure chests of wisdom that come from reading his collected works, you will find Wilber is very clear about how to revive a true and authentic *spirituality* in our modern world, yet without having to rely on traditional mythic religions (though, of course, they're included in any theory of *everything*). For some postmodern critics, however, such "grand visions of everything" sometimes seem like nothing more than an endless mental trap, a philosophical edifice of towering egoity, and they certainly can be, if one isn't careful; therefore, the recommendation from this particular integral theorist has always been *to practice*—to *do the yoga!*—*engage* the injunction, not just sit around and theorize, but to learn how to actually drop the bodymind and awaken to the infinity and freedom of God-Realization. Overall, this is just another reason why Wilber's particular version is so stunning and awe-inspiring for many students and critics alike, as we'll continue to see.

In recent twentieth-century scholarship, the term *"integral"* has often been used by theorists and researchers who are attempting to *integrate* the differences between the East and West, that is, they're working toward the possible integration of the modern scientific mind with the ancient mystical worldview. Such important integral scholars and visionaries include the twentieth-century evolutionist from India, Sri Aurobindo Ghose (1872-1950), who, in Wilber's estimation, is "perhaps India's greatest modern philosopher-sage."[24] It was Aurobindo, for instance, who coined the term "integral yoga," which is similar to Wilber's Integral Transformative Practice (ITP). Yet, most important, it was Aurobindo's brilliant synthesis of the monumental discovery of evolution by Western science, combined with India's ancient spiritual tradition of Enlightenment, that has exerted its greatest influence on Wilber's philosophical formative years (although, naturally, he's also quick to critique Aurobindo's liabilities).

Aurobindo's diplomatic student, philosopher, and educator Haridas Chaudhuri (1913–1975) traveled to the United States to encourage this integration, thus he ended up establishing an East-West graduate school in San Francisco, which is now called an "institute of integral studies" (CIIS).

Chaudhuri gave many explanatory definitions for "integral," such as in his book *The Evolution of Integral Consciousness* (1977), where he points out: "An adequate comprehension of reality in its multiform and multi-dimensional fullness can alone lay the foundation for an integrated scheme of human values."[25] This approach was further clarified: "The *integral perspective* is also concerned with encouraging harmony among people by showing that there is room for a multiplicity of perspectives and styles of life within an encompassing human unity."[26] In other words, an acceptance of the great cultural diversity of all humankind is what's possible with a genuine integral philosophy.

Psychiatrist Roger Walsh also encouragingly noted in his essay "The Worldview of Ken Wilber" (1994): "The importance of fostering widespread individual maturation and social evolution is difficult to overestimate. Our willingness and ability to relieve global crises such as pollution, overpopulation, oppression, war, and even to avoid destruction of the planet may depend upon it."[27] By establishing an AQAL Metatheory, which is based upon an evolutionary and developmental dynamic, Wilber is directly encouraging the entire world to grow up (and evolve). Without hesitation, he boldly admits his universal intentions in *A Theory of Everything* (2000): "I sought a world philosophy—or an *integral philosophy*—that would believably weave together the many pluralistic contexts of science, morals, aesthetics, Eastern as well as Western philosophy, and the world's great wisdom traditions. Not on the level of details—that is finitely impossible; but on the level of *orienting generalizations:* a way to suggest that the world really is one, undivided, whole, and related to itself in every way: a holistic philosophy for a holistic Kosmos, a plausible Theory of Everything."[28] A true worldwide or global philosophy, in other words, is what's gained with such an *integral approach*, one that includes the rich and varied spectrum of all the "correct but partial" truths gathered from every era of human history and from all the world's cultures.

To Easterners and Westerners alike, it has become painfully obvious that humanity needs some type of all-encompassing model or philosophical map capable of honoring and including the countless partial truths and perspectives of humanity as a whole. The world's people need effective solutions that can *transcend-yet-include* our premodern ethnocentric heritage while fulfilling the postmodern necessity for a multicultural "multiple unity" of "unity-in-diversity" for humankind. Only by becoming *more integral* will there be a significant reduction in tensions and intolerant hostilities evident in "a world gone slightly mad" (as Wilber once titled it). Indeed, this goal of tolerant world peace, social freedom, individual liberty, including the actualization of every human being's potential, has always been a primary motive for many to seek out a wider, more tolerant, more integral path and vision. Yet, such grand visions or metatheories of everything must always be garnered and applied with wise judgments grounded in a compassionate heart, thus they suggest a willingness to grow beyond current and past limitations and pathologies, at whatever stage of development.

Now, perhaps, we're getting a small hint of the grand scope that's involved with Wilber's comprehensive and coherent worldview or "grand metatheory of everything." Yet, as this philosopher thoroughly understands, such an Integral Model can't be static or existing as some sort of rigid, linear, steady-state universe, for the Kosmos, as science has proven, is a dynamic swirl that forms "order out of chaos" while all set in *evolutionary motion* (the "arrow of time"), in which case, both Aurobindo and Wilber, and not them alone, see the evolution of the universe (and all of us) as being "Spirit-in-action."

Spirit-in-Action: Emergent Evolution to Enlightenment

By including the great modern discovery of evolution, in all the domains of nature: cosmological, biological, and psychological, Ken Wilber's AQAL Metatheory includes a *developmental-logic* or *evolutionary perspective*—or what he simply calls "Spirit-in-action" (similar to Schelling's "God-in-the-Making"). This perspective follows the *emergent evolution* of the entire universe unfolding as the *basic waves* and spheres of existence, which naturally includes the development of all individual sentient beings and all collective systems, from the Big Bang to the present time, chronicled in fine detail by modern science. This is our modern "Universe Story," as cosmologists like Brian Swimme would have it, but in this case it's not just the story of reductionistic materialism suggested by orthodox science, nor is it a "creationist" or even an "intelligent design" explanation, for an integral view of evolution is thoroughly grounded in both modern science and authentic spirituality (see chapter 4).

At its deepest levels, Wilber explains the significance involved with the modern discovery of evolution in *The Marriage of Sense and Soul* (1998): "Suddenly, within the span of a mere century or so, serious minds were entertaining a notion that premodern cultures, for the most part, had never even once considered, namely that—like all other living systems—we human are in the process of *growing toward our own higher potential*, and if that highest potential is God, then we are growing toward our own Godhood."[29] Without resorting to mythic creation stories, this narrative embraces an evolutionary understanding that also accepts the developmental truth of Enlightenment (or God-Realization), the esoteric goal of the world's great religions. Yet, paradoxically, this realization of nondual Spirit also liberates people from the seriousness of the whole evolutionary display and its torturous drama.

As a result, the integral story of the Kosmos has *spiritual* value and meaning sewn into its very fabric, for as Wilber points out in *A Brief History of Everything* (1996): "Because the universe has direction, we ourselves have direction. There is meaning in the movement, intrinsic value in the embrace."[30] To find *meaning* and *value* in the universe by understanding the evolutionary impulse is another one of the great gifts being offered by an integral approach, a proposal offered by other evolutionary philosophers, from Aurobindo to Schelling to Hegel to Teilhard de Chardin to Gebser to Adi Da, among numerous others. In Wilber's case, this integrative approach takes the advantages of the modern mind and unites them with the ancient truths of authentic spirituality, which is what directly leads to AQAL Metatheory's proposed "marriage of science and religion" (see chapter 4).

This evolutionary thesis of Spirit-in-action is indeed the principal scope and import of Wilber's work: It is an inclusionary, intellectual representation of the whole of reality, leading from the quarks of matter to divine Enlightenment. Nevertheless, we're constantly reminded that the Integral Vision or the AQAL Model (by whatever name) is still only a representative map, not the actual territory of consciousness and reality; but, if used properly, it's an extremely beneficial guide for any person (or society) on their transformative journey from *birth* to *childhood* to *adulthood* to *selfhood* to *spiritual Enlightenment*, in which case, you'll discover that Spirit even extends *beyond death* (see last chapter). This grand scope of reality, whether partially right or wrong, seems fairly "integral" by any definition. Although this Metatheory of Everything is certainly worthy of further consideration, let's not take it too seriously (as we'll do throughout this book). But, first, let's turn our attention to where Wilber's at *physically*, that is, where he resides beyond his written integral theories and is embodied in the "real world" of institutes, universities, and the worldwide web of intellectual jewels.

CHAPTER THREE

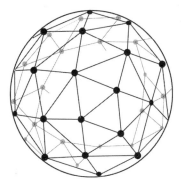

Wilber's Integral Internet of Jewels: Integral Institute & Integral University

> The entire universe is a transparent shimmering of the Divine, of primordial Purity. But the Divine is not someplace else, it is just all of this shimmering. It is self-seen. It has One Taste. It is nowhere else.
>
> —Ken Wilber, *A Brief History of Everything* (1996)

IN MORE PRACTICAL TERMS, WE CAN STILL ASK, "SO WHERE IS WILBER *at*?" Well, *physically*, Ken Wilber's been mostly located in Boulder, Colorado, where he's been living for over twenty years after moving there in 1986 with his late wife, Treya. Although he used to reside in this self-styled mountain home in the outskirts of Boulder, lately the integral philosopher has been spending more and more of his time in Colorado's capital, Denver, living in a rented loft so he can personally promote and establish his newest and most public project: Integral Institute (or I-I for short) and all of its various offshoots.

Inaccurately, Wilber's often bee accused of being a recluse, sheltered in his inner sanctum, yet the truth stands far outside this solipsist claim (usually perpetuated by disgruntled critics). Today, Wilber's been generously available to the growing group of professionals who can adeptly comment on his writings, as well as being available to field questions from gathering students, especially since he's increased his public outreach in the new millennium. In addition, as many writers and visitors have already testified, Wilber is a very sociable and gracious host, for example, since once he grants time for an interview or dinner, he openly avails himself to questions and considerations about his integral positions and philosophy while also being entertaining and quite humorous.[1] Recently, due to the activities of I-I, he has been interacting with a wide variety of interesting personalities and entertaining people (see integral-naked.com), far from the rumored recluse or unsociable character.

There has in fact been an open invitation to visit, or even move, to the Denver-Boulder area, also home to Naropa University, in order to more readily participate in the public integral movement that Wilber and his colleagues are initiating with Integral Institute and its various projects. But if you really want to find out where the philosophy of Ken Wilber is at, then first you need to open and *read* and study his books and articles. Then go surf the Internet because his presence is expanding and ever-growing in the "virtual reality" of the World Wide Web. This interconnected network is linking integral thinkers from around the world, all involved in a plethora of diverse fields, thus allowing anyone to share their individual information, ideas, and inspirations about the integral approach with many others. We'll see that this is similar to the Buddhist notion that pictures "Indra's Net of Jewels," an interconnected web or matrix of lights glistening with its multifarious reflections of every other part in the whole. But first, let's take a brief tour of where Wilber's at, or where you're most likely to find him, and that, of course, begins with the thousands of printed pages amassed in over three decades of publishing, all of which has resulted in Ken Wilber's far-reaching reputation and Integral Vision.

In Print: The Collected Works of Ken Wilber

Where Wilber's at, in terms of his actual presence on this planet and in relation to the world (other than with his body, of course), is most keenly felt and known through his writings, a massive outpouring of over twenty books in twenty-five years. Since the publication of his first book, *The Spectrum of Consciousness* in 1977 (by Quest Books), he has come to be regarded as "the most translated American author of academic books,"[2] for he has been published in over thirty languages and growing. He has written forewords to nearly fifty books, generously articulating an excellent synopsis of what he has just read or reviewed (one of the reasons why his forewords are so widely valued and requested). And to make matters "worse" for the interested reader, he also publishes numerous letters, reviews, answers to critics, and general statements on numerous websites, many of which will never reach a printed book; just search for the countless links and you'll discover for yourself. Yet, it is on the written pages of his published books that the "real" Wilber resides and radiates most fully, alive in his words and integral ideas that are free to everyone who takes the time and interest to read and absorb or "grok" his meanings. Those words, found on thousands and thousands of pages, are the best place to really find out where Wilber's at, unequivocally (by the way, be sure to read the detailed explanatory footnotes to get the Big Picture).

The popularity of his books, although not supported by a major publishing house (Shambhala being mostly a specialized publisher of Eastern mysticism), have nearly all remained in print over the intervening decades (except for some edited editions). Due to this continual demand for his written word and integral ideas, his principal publisher and supporter over the years, Shambhala Publications in Boston (run by his good friend, Sam Bercholz), has released an eight-volume set aptly titled *The Collected Works of Ken Wilber* (1999, 2000, 2006), with more on the way (2006). Being only 50 years old when these volumes came out, this was an unprecedented and distinguished honor since it seems that Wilber is the first psychologist or philosopher in history to have his "Collected Works" published while still alive (although that doesn't mean that much). In the end, the published pages of his eloquently expressed collected writings is where history will turn in order to make its own assessment and best evaluation of Wilber's integral philosophy. Indeed, only *there* will you really find the answers to the complicated question of "where is Wilber at?"

The Collected Works themselves are handsomely bound six-by-nine-inch hardback books in eloquent brown covers, with each ranging from over 400 to 800-some pages. They contain his first books to the most recent ones that are being published in the new millennium. Some have slight grammatical upgrades (with a few revised editions), as well as each having a new and valuable index. In addition, there was the premier publication of two sets of unpublished "papers" that are really short books in themselves (one being the recently written *Integral Psychology* (2000), the other is *Sociocultural Evolution* (1983). They also contain most of his important journal articles, essays, interviews, and even numerous book forewords that he's done for other authors and theorists, themselves sparkling jewels of insight and immaculate writing that recapitulates some of the brightest minds of today.

Importantly, and of significance to any serious student of Wilber's integral philosophy, is that each volume contains a new introduction that offers an insightful and reflective essay written by Wilber in the late 1990s as the *Collected Works* were being prepared for publication (meticulously guided along by lead editor Kendra Crossen Burroughs). This gave the integral theorist the opportunity to look back over his career and weigh in on his original motivations, and then to integrally place each book within the recently proposed "four phases" of his career, thus setting them all within the context of his current AQAL "all-quadrants, all-levels" perspective.

As the years move on into the twenty-first century, other volumes will be added as Wilber's overall oeuvre continues to grow and evolve until, no doubt, the day he stops writing or simply dies. *The Collected Works of Ken Wilber* were originally bound together in eight volumes, but now three new volumes are being released in 2005 and 2006. A list of these valuable resource books, therefore, is a useful guide in getting a grand overview of Wilber's writings or his "Collected Works" (often abbreviated as *CW#*), thus I've listed the original books within the "Wilber/Phase" in which they first appeared (as we'll review in part II):

The Collected Works of Ken Wilber:

WILBER/PHASE-1
_____

CW1 / Volume 1 (1999):
- *The Spectrum of Consciousness* (1977);
- *No Boundary: Eastern and Western Approaches to Personal Growth* (1979); plus selected essays;

WILBER/PHASE-2
_____

CW2 / Volume 2 (1999):
- *The Atman Project: A Transpersonal View of Human Development* (1980);

- *Up from Eden: A Transpersonal View of Human Evolution* (1981); biographical essay "Odyssey: A Personal Inquiry into Humanistic and Transpersonal Psychology";

CW3 / Volume 3 (1999):
- *A Sociable God: Towards a New Understanding of Religion* (1983);
- *Eye to Eye: The Quest for the New Paradigm* (1983);

WILBER/PHASE-3
_____

CW4 / Volume 4 (1999):
- *Transformations of Consciousness: Conventional and Contemplative Perspectives on Development* (1986);
- *Integral Psychology: Consciousness, Spirit, Psychology, Therapy* (1999); including contributions to:
- *The Holographic Paradigm and Other Paradoxes: Exploring the Leading Edge of Science* (1982);
- *Quantum Questions: Mystical Writings of the World's Great Physicists* (1984); various forewords, selected essays on transpersonal psychology, and "Sociocultural Evolution" (1983, unpublished);

CW5 / Volume 5 (2000):
- *Grace and Grit: Spirituality and Healing in the Life and Death of Treya Killam Wilber* (1991);

WILBER/PHASE-4
_____

CW6 / Volume 6 (2000):
- *Sex, Ecology, Spirituality: The Spirit of Evolution* (1995, 2000 revised edition);

CW7 / Volume 7 (2000):
- *A Brief History of Everything* (1996, 2000 revised edition);
- *The Eye of Spirit: An Integral Vision for a World Slightly Mad* (1997); includes the AQAL article "An Integral Theory of Consciousness";

CW8 / Volume 8 (2000):
- *The Marriage of Sense and Soul: Integrating Science and Religion* (1998);

- *One Taste: Daily Reflections on Integral Spirituality* (1999); plus one foreword;

CW9 / Volume 9 (forthcoming):
- *Boomeritis: A Novel That Will Set You Free* (2002); plus extensive endnotes and sidebars;

WILBER/PHASE-5

- *Integral Spirituality: A New Role for Religion in the Modern and Postmodern World* (2006)
- *The Many Faces of Terrorism* (forthcoming)

CW10 / Volume 10 (forthcoming):
- *A Theory of Everything: An Integral Vision for Business, Politics, Science, and Spirituality* (2000); plus other material including long interviews, essays, responses to critics;

CW11 / Volume 11 (forthcoming):
- *Sex, Karma, Creativity* (2006) or Volume 2 of *Kosmos Trilogy*.

Naturally, the *Collected Works* presents a complete overview of Wilber's developing Integral Vision (once they contain his most recent writings), for they are the substance of all his various phases, a vision that offers an unprecedented approach to integrating science and spirituality, the premodern past and postmodern present—it's really the world's first "post-postmodern" attempt at a genuine integral philosophy and methodology. Indeed, many people today see Wilber's maturing integral philosophy as a present-day beacon to what future thinkers will better see and understand about the totality of our existence, so if you want a glimpse for yourself, then open these covers and dig deep into the pages with an open mind and heart. Nonetheless, even though it may be hard for someone to understand all the different places and phases of where Wilber's coming from, or where he's currently at, it's still extremely useful to check in on his collected writing in order to consider and contemplate what this philosophical giant has already said, for that is, most simply, where Wilber's at.

And yet, as we've mentioned, they're only "maps" and "models," not the real territory, but only guiding lights to this particular version of the "Integral Vision." Fortunately, without even paying for the price of a book, there's also another very public place that's been collecting Wilber's integral jewels of written wisdom, and that's the worldwide Internet, the new playground and integral academy for this worldwide interconnected integral vision.

On the Web: Wilber's Integral Internet of Jewels

In today's modern technological and multilayered world of global tele-communications, Wilber's presence on the Internet or World Wide Web is another significant factor that will need to be taken into account in determining "where Wilber's at." In his recent work, especially with Phase-5 and volume 2 of the *Kosmos Trilogy*, or in establishing Integral University, Wilber's been using the interactive Buddhist metaphor of "Indra's Net of Jewels" to metaphorically represent the integral interconnectedness of all things. Thus I think it's a good one to use for his Internet presence as well. As he once defined in an earlier book: "The mystical doctrine of mutual interpenetration—'all in one and one in all'—means that each part is *both* perfectly itself and perfectly one with the whole."[3] Indra, the supreme god in the pantheon of the Vedas, India's most ancient and sacred writings, is said to have an endless glistening net that spreads out across the entire universe (in *every* realm) connecting every other thing (or holon) with every other thing. Each connection is symbolized with a perfectly bright jewel which then reflects every other jewel in the great expanse of existence; in other words, a holographic reality of infinite dimensions.

This interconnected picture was elaborated centuries before by Hua-Yen Buddhism and is intended to show that the true nature of the whole universe is contained in every particle, thus their primary sutra declares: "Every living being and every minute thing is significant because even the tiniest atom contains the whole mystery."[4] Consequently, this is also a very effective image (but only a mystical metaphor) for the Integral Vision because it highlights the interconnected and interactive quality of the AQAL Matrix. Wilber has also co-opted this image and is now using it, for example, in conjunction with the "geodesic dome," which also contains numerous nodes or connections to represent the different "schools" or "portals" or "learning centers" in Integral University. Thus you may "link up" with the rest of the Internet universe and become one of the precious "jewels" in Indra's vast electric web of light. These are all apt images and networking metaphors being used by Wilber's Internet presence and all-embracing Integral Vision to represent the endless forms floating in the Emptiness of Spirit.

We'll continue to see that although Wilber's integral theory has been well established in over twenty-five years of publication, his current work and projects are always at the leading edge, keeping them in a constant state of further evolution and continual modification while he interacts with an army of associates, supporters, and students from around the world. To some degree, therefore, the question of "where's Wilber at?" can be answered only by searching and surfing the Internet, his networked "Internet of Jewels" encircling the global noosphere (or the sphere of mind). This is especially true since this vast interconnected network or worldwide matrix has become the new treasure trove for much of Wilber's more recent ideas, presentations, upcoming projects, and future goals, including current Phase-5 writings (often later published in books). If you take the time to visit, explore, and surf these many exciting and interconnected websites with their networked links of light in this radiant "Integral Internet of Jewels," then you'll see not only where Wilber's at, but where he's going.

Nodes & Portals in Wilber's Internet of Jewels

As a preview (of what we'll discuss in more detail below), these are four of Ken Wilber's primary nodes or websites, to date (2004), in his expanding internet of jewels that are offering the latest integral information (including the emergence of even newer sites):

- **KenWilber.com** (www.kenwilber.com)—a new website launched at the end of 2004 that's the first *official* Ken Wilber website (although others have claimed his name before). It will feature exclusive news and promotion of Wilber's current projects and activities as well as present archival materials, photographs, and other documentation. Immaculately designed with 3-D rotating graphics with a state-of-the-art modular design (built entirely in Flash), it also includes a chronological archive of essays and a personal photo gallery of Wilber throughout the decades, plus interactive book covers (the complete set plus a foreign editions gallery), as well as a list of "Integral Launchpads" to other integral websites. In addition, the site offers some ambitious projects, such as the long-promised *Kindred Visions,* a collection of essays from preeminent theorists evaluating Wilber's work and contributions that was basically too large to publish in book form, but now it will be appearing on this site for the first time in its entirety (see footnote for contributors).⁵ It will also keep you up-to-date in a special "Integral Imprint book series" by Shambhala Publications, as well as with numerous other upcoming specials offered no place else but here.

- **Integral Institute** or **I-I** (www.integralinstitute.org)—the principal site for Wilber's public integral enterprise, one of the best places to find out where Wilber's at. This site leads a person into all the portals and links to Ken Wilber's new millennium projects; it introduces you to Integral Institute and its founding mission: "Integral Institute functions as the world's premier site for integral research and applications; as a generator of consulting services, seminars, and conferences; as a network of the most influential integral theorists from around the world; and as an open organization for disseminating and applying integral methods to complex problems in a wide variety of fields, personal to professional";⁶ it is to the public and also accepts memberships for greater access.

- **Integral Naked** or **IN** (www.integralnaked.org)—a freeform *interactive* site open to members that brings various multimedia events about the Integral Vision from a plethora of world-leading integral pioneers. These include the "IN-Live" events that come to you via streaming audio, MP3, video clips, and other cutting-edge Internet technology, offering an interactive look "behind the scenes with the most provocative thinkers in today's world," thus opening a "multimedia doorway to the world of integral awareness";⁷ each week features new audio dialogues with other leading-edge thinkers and visionaries in politics, ecology, spirituality, business, sexuality, art, modern music, and much more; as promoted: "In-depth, interconnected, and raw, these truly are conversations you will hear nowhere else."⁸

- **"Ken Wilber On Line" Shambhala Publications'** (www.wilber/shambhala.com)—an important web site page maintained on Shambhala's website that officially introduces Ken's books as well as publishes, often for the first time, important essays recently written by Wilber, such as "The War in Iraq" (posted 4/19/03), as well as excerpts from forthcoming books, such as excerpts from volume 2 of the *Kosmos Trilogy*, or sidebars and endnotes to *Boomeritis* (posted in 2002); it also includes numerous "Interviews with Ken Wilber," plus important announcements and an archive of past postings; it also offers newsletter updates and other attractive features.

- **Integral Spiritual Center** (www.integralspiritualcenter.org)—a gathering community of integrally-informed spiritual teachers where "the teachers teach the teachers," and thus mutually co-creating a "trans-path path to tomorrow." The Integral Spiritual Center is dedicated to forging an *integral spirituality* for the modern and postmodern world by honoring the unique contributions of each of the world's religious traditions and using today's many growth techniques for further conscious evolution.

Integral Institute: The Site Where Wilber's Mostly At

INTEGRAL INSTITUTE

In the summer of 1999, admiring philanthropists and enthusiastic businesspeople approached Wilber about establishing a nonprofit organization that he designated "Integral Institute" ("the" is usually dropped) or, for short, "I-I." Incidentally, "I-I" itself is an interesting and appropriate play on words for "I-I" is a phrase of Sri Ramana Maharshi, one of Wilber's most admired sages, representing the awakened divine consciousness of the Witness or the True Self of "I AM," which transcends-yet-includes the individual egoic "I," understandings that are fully embraced with Wilber's Integral Vision.[9] Growing out of some fundamental grants by interested parties, Integral Institute is a type of "think tank" designed to assist, finance, and *interconnect* the growing network of integral theorists, many leaders in their own fields, who were responding to the fully developed Integral Vision proposed by Wilber, especially since 1995 with the emergence of "Phase-4." This specifically includes the AQAL or "all-quadrants, all-levels, all-lines, etc." methodology, plus an integral philosophy of "constructive postmodernism" that boldly "reconstructs deconstructionism," or the failures of postmodernity, while simultaneously integrating the best from the premodern and modern worldviews.

The domain of Integral Institute (see: www.integralinstitute.org), an eloquently designed website, is where Wilber's "official" presence is at on the Internet in conjunction with his fellow associates and members of I-I, who as a group encircle the planet from numerous countries on every continent. Thus it's really the best site to learn about this leading-edge organization, especially with its "Bulletin Board" posting the latest news and updates on its numerous projects and many branches, including Institute of Integral Art to Institute of Integral Medicine to Institute of Integral Psychology, Institute of Integral Politics, Institute of Integral Business, and more. Ultimately, I-I's main interest is in exercising the practical and pragmatic *applications* (or *apps*) of integral theory in the real world, a juncture for moving theory into practice, and thus reaching into most of today's current issues, suggesting more integral solutions. As a vehicle for Wilber's current AQAL Model (especially with its IOS or Integral Operating System, Integral Methodological Pluralism, and Integral Transformative Practice), it's directly dedicated to: "The integration of body, mind, soul, and spirit in self, culture, and nature by honoring and integrating the largest amount of research from the greatest number of disciplines,"[10] as stated by the founder, president, and chairman of the board (Ken Wilber).

By doing so, Integral Institute projects will act as an "information clearinghouse" with a "multidimensional feedback dynamism," a center of "creative synergy" and "cross-domain dialogues" for various fields of integral study. Thus I-I is being likened to the center hub in a wheel with all the spokes radiating outward as the various integral branches and colleges stimulate *interconnected learning across domains,* like an interconnected feedback loop. Consequently, numerous members, associates, and affiliates are diligently working toward completing a slew of integral projects and endeavors (which, as we've mentioned, can be best monitored via Integral Institute's main website). Yet of course, the overall plan continues to move steadily forward, especially with the energetic work of Ken Wilber himself pushing it through to maintain integrity and a clear expression of the AQAL Vision. By doing so, the mission for Integral Institute and its various members is to act as a vehicle for having *integral influence* on the major institutions of politics, business, science, medicine, and higher education in our global society as it naturally solidifies and stabilizes the already emerging Integral Age.

Integral University: The Multiplex

One of the more ambitious projects to emerge from Integral Institute in the early years of the new millennium (due to take off by the end of 2004) is Integral University, also known as "IU" (found at www.integraluniversity.org). This interactive learning portal is also known as the "Multiplex" because IU will be, according to Wilber's plans, the world's first "Integral Learning Community," an event that could have historical implications. Integral University is an online learning community providing the world's first extensive library of integral knowledge and interactive learning environments, often using leading-edge computer technology and graphics.

Integral University will also be affiliated with some prestigious universities and thus will end up offering accredited courses and graduate-level degrees, including certificates of learning, and training seminars. But mostly it's intended to link together, through the Integral Commons, all the various integral centers, integral salons or incubators of integral thinking, and worldwide integral communities that will create an unprecedented global network of integral thinkers energizing "the global brain."

The initial launch of Integral University (aka the Multiplex) itself will begin with a simultaneous linkup of numerous website domains where each domain is a "college" or "school" of integral learning and practice. These sites or colleges are hosted by various associates of I-I, many of whom are

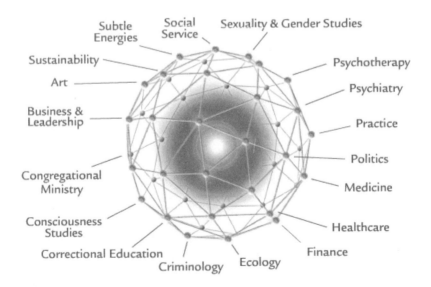

the foremost authorities in their particular profession or field of study. These colleges or domains will include websites for Integral Ecology, Integral Psychology, Integral Art, Integral Sex and Gender, Integral Medicine, Integral Business, Integral Law, Integral Finance, Integral Transformative Practice, and so on. In other words, anywhere from 20 to 50 original websites or nodes will all be launched at the same time, thus creating a matrix of interconnectivity between like-minded integral explorers and visionaries.

Wilber envisions that entry through one of these website colleges or portals in the Multiplex leads out onto the Integral Commons, the core of the interlinked geodesic sphere. The Integral Commons offers learning opportunities, archives (word, audio, visual), discussion areas, starter kits (practical tools for applying integral theory to that field or domain), plus a newsletter connecting members with a wide variety of upcoming integral seminars, accredited courses, workshops, and integral salons, and the like, all of which will be initiated by fellow I-I members gathered from around the world. Each domain will also include recent seminal writings about that particular field being posted by some of the brightest integral visionaries on the planet; nothing less than this. Overall, it's hoped that such a huge interactive, interconnected worldwide "mega-feedback loop" of integral information will be shared and cross-pollinated by all active participants and compatriots—like a shimmering net of Manjushri's inter-networked jewels. This gives the world and global culture an *integral* alternative to the mass of confusion and brutal solutions propagated by most of today's institutional structures.

As we saw, other than using the electric interactive image of Indra's net of jewels, Wilber has also been using the multilayered and interconnected image of the geodesic sphere as an apt image because its numerous "nodes" or "hubs" are interconnected to all the other hubs (or centers of activity) via the main hub of the Integral Commons, thus representing "the Multiplex" of Integral University. Wilber is thus fashioning this integral enterprise as "a *multidimensional matrix of integral learning*...grounded in knowledge and compassion, theory and practice, care and justice, consciousness and culture."[11] Importantly, with the dawning of a worldwide integral community, therefore he tells us it "reaches beyond (and yet includes) any existing cultural types—beyond the culture creatives, beyond traditional, modern, and postmodern habits—to create, by its own learning and self-organizing, a more genuinely integral and embracing culture of consciousness."[12] Incredibly, then, Wilber's Integral Vision is an embrace of all that's come before and might possibly unfold in the future, from premodern to modern to postmodern to "post-postmodern" to integral, all grounded with a critical eye to making adequate judgments and compassionate decisions for individuals and collective institutions and societal systems.

This worldwide project, if successful, will at least affect the programs of major universities and consequently new generations of leaders and thinkers, artists and entrepreneurs, and thus will help promote the global "Rising Culture" (after Toynbee). Inspired, in part, by theologian Paul Tillich's observation that "what we call the 'Renaissance' was participated in by about one thousand people," and the fact that those thousand seem to have been financed by about a dozen patrons, Wilber is attempting to plant the seeds for a nonviolent, compassionate, synergistic "Integral Revolution"[13] that uses both traditional and advanced technological means (see chapter 18). Therefore, all interested people and parties, including financers, the "New Medici," are all invited to join in and actively participate by making their own important contributions to the emerging Integral Age. As Wilber likes to point out, this is how people become part of "a small cultural elite at the leading edge," part of "an integral age at the leading edge,"[14] a leading-edge that is open and available to everyone.

On Multimedia: Speaking of Everything

In this modern, high-tech world of multimedia outlets, there is another growing presence of where Wilber's at, and that is with the integral philosopher recently making numerous appearances in various multimedia packages, from CDs to DVDs to glossy magazines. This is a venue that Wilber has previously shied away from, preferring instead to concentrate on his writings and theoretical ideas (see Chapter 1) However, now with the establishment of the fully-developed AQAL perspective in the late 1990s, and with the founding of Integral Institute at the century's cusp, he's become much more publicly engaged in *teaching* his version of the Integral Vision. Because, as we've mentioned, if he wants to effectively and truly represent his intentions (instead of being misrepresented), then he must play an active role in their dissemination, and he has come up with numerous engaging products.

One of the ways Wilber has been responding to this demand is to release a number of interviews about the AQAL Approach and more fully explaining in person "where he's at," many of which have been released on CDs and spoken word formats (cassettes) as well as being documented on the World Wide Web (as we've already mentioned), including the following:

- ***The Marriage of Sense and Soul*** (four audiocassettes, Random House, 1998)—released in promotion of Wilber's book of the same title. This concise Phase-4 book, read by Denis deBoisblance, shows the power and efficacy of hearing the integral language and how its unique terms are properly enunciated and applied. This method is a very effective tool in spreading the integral message.

- ***Speaking of Everything*** (2-CDs, Enlightenment.com, 2001)—this "first-ever interview released to the public" in Wilber's 30-year career, available on two audio CDs, was released in 2001 by Jordan Gruber, founder and CEO of Enligthenment.Com. Gordon engagingly interviewed Wilber covering a wide range of topics, from intimate discussions of his personal life to humorous and insightful considerations about his integral AQAL theories and the then-budding Integral Institute.

- ***Kosmic Consciousness*** (10 CDs, Sounds True, Inc., 2003)—the tour de force at this time would have to be this 10-CD, 12-hour affair released in the fall of 2003, produced by Tami Simon of Sounds True (see: www.soundstrue.com), a successful audio-education business. *Kosmic Consciousness* is billed as "Ken Wilber's First In-Depth Audio Learning Course," thus it's an amazing presentation and thorough overview of Wilber's AQAL Phase-4/5 approach, yet it also shows his uncanny ability to scan a wide spectrum of topics, a plethora of unprecedented integral information.

- ***The Integral Operating System, Version 1.0*** (one booklet, 2-CDs, 1-DVD, plus a wall reference chart; Sounds True, Inc., 2005) – a beginner's package introducing people on how to *practice* the "integral lifestyle" or "a way of living from day to day that consciously exercises body, mind, and spirit in self, culture, and nature," thus fulfilling its promise to "upgrade the way you think—and live."

The Guru & The Pandit: What Is Enlightenment?

One of the brightest media events that Wilber, as an American spiritual pandit (or intellectual), has been involved with since 2002 is a series of interview-dialogues featured in the cutting-edge magazine *What Is Enlightenment?* (or *WIE*), a glossy, well-produced journal that's bringing an integral perspective to modern spirituality. *WIE* began in 1996 as a publication vehicle for and edited by the American spiritual guru Andrew Cohen, who is bringing his own version of the ancient teachings into American mainstream media. The collaboration between these two sympathetic and enlightened intellectuals is being presented as an ongoing series of interviews titled "The Guru and the Pandit," with Cohen as "the Guru" (his spiritual function), and with Wilber being "the Pandit" (his intellectual function). Many of Wilber's main concerns in their discussions, such as boomeritis, evolutionary enlightenment, or the differences between translation and transformation, have also been supported by engaging articles written by *WIE*'s talented staff. They also use state-of-the-art graphic art production that deftly highlights many of Wilber's integral ideas in stunning full-color and visually powerful ways.

In their dialogues, Wilber and Cohen begin by taking a piercing look at the contemporary spiritual scene, such as asking if people's spiritual practices are really engaging them in serious *transformation,* or the continual growth of "vertical" evolution into and through the higher transpersonal stages of consciousness. Both pioneers suggest that most modern "spiritual people" have become too well-adapted to "horizontal" *translations* by becoming complacent in challenging the limitations of the ego, thus indicating they're not real interested in genuine transcendence or authentic transformation. These two serious spiritual practitioners go on to consider the unorthodox conclusion that *"Enlightenment is evolving,"* a process they call "evolutionary Enlightenment," which comes from today's leading-edge knowledge that suggests "the world of form is itself *changing,* ever-complexifying, forward-moving, and increasingly conscious."[15] Enlightenment and evolution: two faces of the same nondual Divine Spirit.

Obviously, these are topics that go straight to the heart of "where Wilber's at," therefore *What Is Enlightenment?* under the masterful guidance of Andrew Cohen and his accomplished team has beautifully presented may of the core issues involved with Wilber's recent critiques and integral ideas. Surrounded by gorgeous visuals, it even takes a daring look at his criticisms of "boomeritis," which is aimed at the narcissistic tendencies of the boomer generation, as well as other important Phase-5 topics such as absorbing the complex "post-metaphysical" ideas of where Wilber is at during these opening years of the new millennium. Consequently, another good place to find where Wilber is at, is at your neighborhood magazine rack or local bookstore.

AQAL Matrix: Reviews The Matrix *Films*

The nodes in a matrix are infinite and multidimensional, as we've said, like the jewels in Indra's vast Kosmic net (or Nest of Spirit), thus sometimes it's hard to know what's for real, what's an illusion, or what is God, what is samsara, maya, or sin? Therefore any type of guiding map (or "red pill") that promises to help a person sort out what's *really* going on becomes a very valuable tool, perhaps even a sacred gift or blessing because it's serving one's understanding and ultimate liberation (from the lies and deceptions coming from all directions, even inside). Consequently, a map (that's not the territory, remember) that covers every realm of existence, from dirt and dust to chimps and computer chips to deities and divinity, can be quite a useful key to seeing what's already here to be seen (and known).

Therefore, when Ken Wilber went into the marvelous sci-fi world of *The Matrix* motion pictures, the incredible trend-setting films created by brothers Larry and Andy Wachowski, he saw them through integral eyes, and so was invited to participate in the "director's commentary" to *The Matrix* 10-DVD box set. Previously, the directors and visionaries behind the mega-financially successful *Matrix* trilogy, the Wachowski brothers, had been thunderously silent about their hidden meanings in these ground-breaking movies. This was particularly evident since everyone has their own valuable interpretations of these novel and philosophical films, even spawning a mini-industry of books and essays, with many being written by college professors. In response to their refusal to give any interpretations themselves, the Wachowskis asked some well-known philosophers to add their own interpretations about *The Matrix* movies. Therefore, during the summer of 2004, Ken Wilber (who Larry reportedly has said, "Ken Wilber is our Neo")[16] met with Afro-American scholar Cornel West (who played Councilor West in the last two episodes) in Los Angeles, and they responded with over 15 hours of commentary (which has been edited down to 6 hours to cover all three films).

As only a brief preview, Ken points out that the first movie, *The Matrix* (1999), one of the most original movies of the past decade, was fairly straightforward, i.e., everything in the Matrix is bad, while everything out of it is good; everyone inside the Matrix is trapped, while everyone outside is free, and so forth. However, with the next two pictures, *Reloaded* (2003) and *Revolutions* (2003), this theme was not so clear, therefore, Ken suggests that it's not until the last 20 minutes of part 3 that the secret key to the entire trilogy is revealed. This is when a physically blind Neo sees the machines as luminous, golden light, which suggests, according to Ken, that the machines (or the "bad guys") really represent Spirit, yet it's Spirit alienated from itself, and therefore attacking.... As it turns out, Wilber's more integral interpretation uses the hierarchy (or holarchy) of the Great Nest of Spirit to analyze these high-tech science fiction movies.

Ken and Larry also discussed their shared lifelong passion for philosophy, both of whom are extremely well-read, with Larry saying that when he found Ken's work "It was like Schopenhauer discovering the Upanishads."[17] In any case, *The Matrix* trilogy is ripe for interpretations, including integral ones, which is one of the main objectives of the filmmakers and the more enjoyable aspects for audiences. Nonetheless, by placing Ken Wilber inside an immensely popular DVD box set, viewers will find him making even "more integral" interpretations of *The Matrix*, thus Hollywood's just one more place to find where Wilber's at.

CHAPTER FOUR

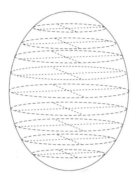

Wilber/Phase-4: The Marriage of Science & Religion: Correlating Exteriors & Interiors

Since the core of premodern religion was the Great Chain of Being (matter, body, mind, soul, spirit), and since the essence of modernity was the differentiation of the value spheres (the Big Three or the four quadrants), then, in order to *integrate* religion and science, we sought to integrate the Great Chain with the four quadrants.... And it is only by acknowledging, honoring, and including all four quadrants that the long sought integration of premodern religion and modern science might finally become a reality.

—Ken Wilber, *The Marriage of Sense and Soul* (1998)

TO PRESENT A TASTE OF THE PROFOUND SIGNIFICANCE OF WHERE WILBER IS AT, I thought it would be a good idea to jump ahead and go to the core of his integral theories and show how he proposes to conduct "the marriage of science and religion" (before reviewing this material in depth throughout the rest of the book). Ken Wilber's AQAL Approach (initiated in 1995 with *Sex, Ecology, Spirituality* and the following Phase-4 books) provides a new way to solidify this needed integration of spirituality and science beyond what he had originally proposed with his spectrum of consciousness model (debuting in the 1970s), a union that was, for author Tony Schwartz, "How Ken Wilber Married Freud and the Buddha."[1] Importantly, this "marriage" is not just a theoretical accomplishment (although it's that too), but it's a "Metatheory" intending to be inclusive of all possible methodologies (an *Integral Methodological Pluralism*), thus it provides the theoretical incentives for legitimate investigative research into, at a minimum, the physical (gross), mental (subtle), and spiritual (causal) realms of existence. According to the AQAL Approach, as we'll see next, this is conducted by both a science, as a *"deep science,"* and religion, as an *"authentic spirituality,"* and done in ways that can be confirmed by a community of the adequately trained. In other words, there is verifiable evidence and empirical tests, based on actual paradigms or injunctive *practices,* that can check the results (or data) and validate the conclusions of these "theories" and "metatheories," as all genuine science (and real religion) already does.

Postmodernity's Task: Integrating Premodernity (Religion) & Modernity (Science)

Since the *modern world* or modernity (arising from the Renaissance/Western Enlightenment and epitomized with science and individual freedoms), can be contrasted with what came before it, the *premodern world* or premodernity (arising from magical tribes to mythic empires and epitomized with their advanced-tip religious systems), then Wilber concludes that the *real task* of postmodernity is to integrate the two; and the sooner, the better. However, he also claims that postmodern philosophy, following in the wake of modernity, has not yet achieved this necessary integration (see part IV). Rather, much of postmodern philosophy has tragically slipped into the pitfalls of deconstructionism, relativism, and nihilism, thus failing to provide real workable solutions to our current global crisis (since any position can be deconstructed or made relative). The integral solution, on the other hand, offers such a hope for uniting the premodern religious traditions and the modern/postmodern world—thus it's really a "post-postmodern" solution—but in any case, it's still the real task of our times and for future generations.

Wilber's ideas for uniting science and spirituality via the AQAL Model were perhaps best summarized in his Phase-4 book titled *The Marriage of*

Sense and Soul: Integrating Science and Religion (published in 1998 by Random House), although he originally tagged the treatise "The Integration of Science and Religion: The Union of Ancient Wisdom and Modern Knowledge."[2] In this book, he outlines how an AQAL or an *"all-quadrant, all-level"* approach could provide a genuine postmodern integration of religion and science by uniting the "core claim of the premodern religions," which he summarizes as the *basic levels* in the Great Chain of Being (of matter to mind to soul to God), with the "central claim of modernity," summarized as the differentiation of the *quadrants* (of individual/collective interiors/exteriors) into the "Big Three" value spheres (of self, culture, and nature; art, morals, and science, etc.). AQAL Metatheory, therefore, generates workable solutions to this centuries-old philosophical dilemma and "the challenge of our times," simply because it integrates *all the levels* of premodernity (i.e., the Great Chain) with *all the quadrants* of modernity (the appropriate separation of self, culture, and nature/science). This means for humanity, as Wilber explains, that "such a synthesis would unite the best of the premodern wisdom with the brightest of modern knowledge, bringing together truth and meaning in a way that has thus far eluded the modern mind."[3] It's an integration that today's world, and certainly the future's, can ill afford to do without.

This post-postmodern AQAL "all-quadrant, all-level" integration could be quantified in the simple formula: "premodern worldview (Great Chain/religion) + modern worldview (Big Three/science) = postmodern integration (AQAL),"[4] which is more fully defined below:

- **Premodernity**—epitomized with traditional religion's "Great Chain of Being" (i.e., *matter* to *body* to *mind* to *soul* to *spirit*), although reinterpreted today as the Great Nest of Being and Knowing (i.e., *all-levels* in the spectrum of consciousness-reality).

- **Modernity**—epitomized as the modern *differentiation* (not dissociation) of the cultural value spheres ("Big Three" of *self, culture, nature,* or *art, morals, science*), which equates with the *all-quadrants* (of "I, We, It, Its"); includes the modern discoveries of "evolution" in all the quadrants (through all the levels).

- **Postmodernity**—the true "task of postmodernity" (or the "all-quadrants, all-levels" integration of science and religion) goes beyond the

importance of *interpretation*[5] uncovered by recent postmodern movements (such as *constructivism* and *contextualism*) by offering an *integral-aperspectival* approach, or when multiple perspectives (aperspectival) shows that "cognition must privilege no single perspective."[6]

Since Wilber maintains that the real task of postmodernity is to *integrate* the important differentiations of modernity (self, culture, science, and
evolution), with the basic levels of existence recognized by premodern spirituality, then he also argues that it still must reject or eliminate their various
fallacies (such as with premodernity's superstitions or modernity's reductionism). As he pointed out in *The Eye of Spirit* (1997): "The integral vision
embodies an attempt to take the best of both worlds, ancient and modern.
But that demands a critical stance willing to reject unflinchingly the worst of
both as well."[7] Thus Wilber insists, as he did in *A Brief History of Everything*
(1996): "Much of postmodern thought is regressive, attempting to heal the
differentiations and dissociations of modernity by regressing prior to the
differentiations of the Big Three.... Nor should we seek our solutions by
regressing to mythic or magic indissociation of the Big Three, where self and
culture and nature were *not yet* differentiated. We must preserve the dignity
[differentiation] of modernity, even while we attempt to overcome the disaster [dissociation] of modernity."[8] It is to this gesture, as we'll see, that the
AQAL Metatheory leans.

The other important gift from modernity that Wilber contends must be
integrated into any overall "Theory of Everything" is the modern discovery
of evolution (or the "arrow of time")—defined not only as the mechanism
of natural selection ("descent by modification"), but as the grand unfolding
of the entire Kosmos in all its dimensions (our "Universe Story"). Growing
out of the differentiations of modernity, scientists have been uncovering the
processes and mechanisms of natural evolution (geological, biological, cosmological), yet without resorting to mythical or metaphysical explanations.
Therefore, Wilber concludes in *Integral Psychology* (2000): "Since evolution
is one of the crucial ingredients—some would say *the* crucial ingredient—of
the modern scientific worldview, and if we truly wish an integral embrace of
premodern, modern, and postmodern, then we need a way to put the theory
of evolution in a context that both honors its truths and curtails it abuses."[9]
The AQAL Approach, as we'll continue to see, is designed to accomplish
both of these formable goals.

Only a higher synthesis, such as with AQAL Metatheory, is capable of embracing both of these important (but partial) truths, thereby providing an effective, pragmatic, and *scientific* integration of spirituality and science. By accomplishing this goal, the AQAL Model offers a sound *critical theory* that engages the *falsifiability* principle (based on verifiable evidence and valid knowledge accumulation), so therefore it's able to better critique the various versions of the premodern, modern, and postmodern worldviews. Let's continue exploring some of the ways Wilber is proposing to consummate this "marriage of science and religion," which if registered and found compatible, could possibly give birth to a better tomorrow and new era of humankind.

The Marriage of "Value-Free" Science & "Value-Laden" Religion

After premiering the AQAL postmodern approach with Wilber/Phase-4 (in the mid-to-late 1990s), by the end of the twentieth-century Ken Wilber had further refined his arguments for meeting "the challenge of our times: integrating science and religion," especially in his book *The Marriage of Sense and Soul* (1998). Here the integral philosopher confronts this "philosophical cold war" by starting with the premise that "*both* science and religion must find the argument acceptable in their own terms. For this marriage to be genuine it must have the free consent of both spouses."[10] This seems to be especially critical since, as Wilber points out, a modern value-free science "might offer us truth, but how to use that truth wisely: on this science is, and always has been, utterly silent…. Truth, not wisdom or value or worth, is the province of science," whereas a premodern value-laden religion "offers what it believes is a genuine *wisdom*…. For literally billions of people around the world, religion provides the basic meaning of their lives," therefore he can only conclude, "It is a strange and grotesque coexistence, with value-free science and value-laden religion, deeply distrustful of each other, aggressively attempting to colonize the same small planet."[11] However, as any psychologist would, he maintains that if certain pathologies and inadequacies of development can be addressed on both sides, then perhaps a healing will take place and set this marriage on firmer ground.

In better comprehending modernity, as he's done in all of his Phase-4 books, Wilber distinguishes between what he calls the "Good News" or the "dignity of modernity" (best described as "*the differentiation of art, morals, and science*")[12] from its "Bad News" or the "disaster of modernity" (best described as the reductionistic "collapse of the Kosmos" into the "Flatland" of only energy-matter). Nevertheless, Wilber also maintains, the positive distinctions and dignities of our modern heritage are certainly worth keeping, since they have "contributed to the rise of modern democracies, feminism, ecology, and the postconventional ideals of liberty, freedom, and equality."[13] The problem with modernity, of course, is its "Bad News," a condition Wilber maintains is more about the *dissociations* or fragmentations of the modern world, than the developmental differentiations of the Big Three (or the clear distinction of self, culture, and nature, or aesthetics, morality, and science).

Using integral psychology, the theorist points to a basic principle of developmental pathology: "If differentiation begins but goes too far, the result is *dissociation* or fragmentation. Differentiation gets out of control, and the various subsystems cannot be easily integrated: they fly apart instead of fitting together."[14] In this case, when the differentiations of art, morals, and science turn into the various modern dissociations, then humanity ends up with a fragmented and alienated world of value-free materialism, one where "depth takes a vacation," and consequently, one where there's an onslaught of repression and painful pathological symptoms. Understanding the differences between the *differentiations* and *dissociations* of the modern world, between its dignities and disasters, according to Wilber is "the key to modernity—and therefore the key to the integration of science and religion."[15] Therapeutically, this means that "the cure for the disaster of modernity is to address the dissociation, not attempt to erase the differentiation."[16] In short, this suggests that some sort of return to the prediffferentiated past will not do, for it's only with progressive evolution that humanity will be able to more fully embrace its positive developments while still healing its past and present pathological maladies.

Historically, the crucial turning point for the modern world came when the explosion of empirical science and technology, coupled with rampant modes of industrial production, generated a *materialism* that began to dominate the other value spheres (especially the interiors). In AQAL terms, this means the *interiors* (Left-Hand quadrants) were collapsed into only *exteriors* (Right-Hand quadrants), thereby gutting values, depth, and consciousness from the modern worldview. This has led to the dominance of a materialistic "Flatland," as tagged by Wilber, which is the monological gaze that sees *only* physical matter in the universe and nothing else, a condition other theorists have identified as the "disqualified universe" (Mumford), the "disenchantment of the world" (Weber), the "dawn of wasteland" (T. S. Eliot), the birth of "one-dimensional man" (Marcuse), or the "desacralization of the world" (Schuon).

One of the best ways to counter this flatland is to therefore deal directly with the modern world's elimination of *depth* and *meaning*. When science and modernity slipped into the reductionistic move of rejecting the interior realities of the Great Chain (i.e., mind/soul/spirit), then it profoundly rejected the core wisdom of the world's spiritual traditions. Most tragically, as Wilber has often pointed out: *"The modern West became the first and only major civilization in the history of humankind to be without the Great Chain of Being."*[17] In this case, he can only conclude that we must "confront the most important and central issue in the relation of science and spirituality, namely, the actual relation of any *interior realities* to *exterior realities.*"[18] Therefore, the pandit goes on to explain how this integration of the premodern Great Nest (all-levels) with modernity's Big Three (all-quadrants) is actually the integration of *interiors* and *exteriors*. This is because the premodern religions emphasized the *interior* modes of knowing (mental/spiritual), whereas modernity places its emphasis mostly on the *exteriors* (empirical/physical), so to integrate the two is to bring both together.

AQAL Metatheory, therefore, brings "a more sophisticated integration" to the table where, as Wilber explains, "science is not *under* but *alongside* [the levels in the Great Nest], and this profoundly reorients the knowledge quest, placing premodernity and modernity hand in hand in the quest for the real, and thus bringing science and religion together in a most intimate embrace."[19] For one, this is accomplished by recognizing the *correlates* or *correspondences* between the *interior* modes of knowing, the principle domain of religion, with the *exterior* forms of the physical world, the main domain of science. This becomes possible because the AQAL Matrix portrays all holons as being intimately intermeshed and interconnected, since all holons have four quadrants, as well as being involved with the numerous levels or stages of development. Since the AQAL Matrix provides a complex but readable gird or mapping system for these multiple variables, then this allows them to also be "teased apart" or "unpacked" with intelligent care and valid investigative methodologies. Let's explore some of the ways this is possible.

Real Science & Broad Empiricism

Ken Wilber has always found it necessary to properly define the words *"science"* and *"religion,"* as being a crucial ingredient in bringing together their reconciliation, especially since they're such loaded terms for most people. In *A Sociable God: A New Understanding of Religion* (1983), Wilber came up with nearly a dozen definitions for religion as it's commonly used in the modern world. Without identifying the various definitions for science and religion, the problem of their compatible integration is only compounded. In *The Marriage of Sense and Soul* (1998), Wilber tackled some of the different definitions for a "value-free science" by first pointing out that it contradicts itself when it tries to deny the interior reality of consciousness since science obviously uses the mind to study, measure, and theorize about the physical realm. In order to highlight the real task of science, the integral philosopher proceeds to unravel two types of *empiricism*, emphasizing its justifiable demand for evidence:

- **Narrow empiricism**—reduces the demand for evidence to mean "sensory experience alone," which produces philosophies and generates actions based on reductionist materialism, or what Wilber critically calls "the myth of the given, the brain-dead flatland stare, the monological gaze, the modern nightmare."[20]

- **Broad empiricism**—simply means "to demand *evidence* for assertions, and not merely to rely on dogma, faith, or nonverifiable conjectures," and also, importantly, that experiential evidence is "actually quite *public* or shared, because each [field or eye of knowing] can be trained or educated with the help of a teacher, and an educated eye is a shared eye."[21]

The integral approach has a deep sympathy for this type of scientific approach to broad empiricism, which also has a long philosophical history in the West. With a demand for actual evidence that can be publicly shared and verified via a community of the adequately trained, then the integral approach asserts that authentic "validity claims" can justifiably be made, not only for the domains of sensory experience, but also for mental and spiritual experience as well. With this dual meaning of empiricism then it's possible to have, in Wilber's words, "a science of sensory experience, a science of mental experience, and a science of spiritual experience—a monological science, a dialogical science, and a translogical science—a science of the eye of the flesh, a science of the eye of mind, and a science of the eye of contemplation—with the traditional concerns of religion joining hands with the assurances of modern science."[22] This type of "resurrection of the interiors" would indeed be a revolutionary breakthrough, and it is, in fact, already under way.

Three Strands of Valid Knowledge: The Scientific Method

From this empirical grounding, the integral philosopher goes on to review the essence of the scientific method, the backbone of modern science, which he labels as the "three strands of all valid knowing," or the "three strands of knowledge accumulation" (an idea he first proposed in Phase-2's *Eye to Eye,* 1983). These strands are, for Wilber, "the essential aspects of scientific inquiry," since they are "the three strands of valid knowledge," briefly listed below:

1) **Instrumental Injunction**—"an *actual practice,* an *exemplar,* a *paradigm,* an *experiment,* an *ordinance,"* in other words, "If you want to know this, do this"; therefore it meets the demand of Thomas Kuhn's observations about paradigms (or *injunctive practices*) that says "genuine scientific knowledge is grounded in paradigms, exemplars, or injunctions,"

2) **Data/Direct Apprehension**—"a *direct experience* or *apprehension of data"* or "knowing this"; therefore it meets the demand of empiricism because it provides *experiential evidence* or "the empiricists' demand that *all genuine knowledge [needs to] be grounded in experience,* in data, in evidence";

3) **Communal Confirmation (or rejection)**—"a *checking of the results...* with others who have *adequately completed* the injunctive and apprehensive strands;"[23] therefore it meets the demand of the falsifiability principle, which is Sir Karl Popper's emphasis on "the importance of falsifiability: genuine knowledge must be open to disproof, or else it is simply dogma in disguise."[24]

For Wilber, this importantly means the integral approach meets all of these requirements provided by a methodological pluralism based on "the importance of the *injunctive strand* in the knowledge quest," since, he claims, these principles (the three strands of valid knowledge) are "operative in *every domain,* sensory to mental to spiritual."[25] In other words, the demand for valid and verifiable evidence is a test that can also be applied to the interiors realms, those domains of psychology and spirituality. Thus, perhaps, all that's needed for a true integration of marriage of science and religion, the theorist suggests, is for both science and religion to "give a little" in their rigid definitions of one another, and expand their own understanding of themselves. By taking these broad, and deeper, approaches to both science and religion, then the AQAL Approach could actually come closer to advancing their true and real meanings.

Real Religion & Authentic Spirituality: The Contemplative Core

Next, in *The Marriage of Sense and Soul* (1998), Wilber critically examines a "value-laden religion" in the modern world, another loaded term with multiple meanings (such as legitimate, authentic, translative, transformative, etc.). Consequently, the integral philosopher strongly concludes that "with the irreversible differentiations of modernity, most of the premodern beliefs and functions of religion are no longer and can no longer be sustained in modern consciousness (except by those who remain at a premodern level in their own development)."[26] In other words, religion needs to grow beyond its mythic traditions and beliefs (often not based on verifiable evidence), and increase their relationship to authentic transformative practices.

As a result, Wilber clearly claims this means that a true and "authentic spirituality," including the possibilities of a "modern science of spirituality," will have to exclude the premodern mythological and mythopoetic themes. As he makes perfectly clear in *The Marriage of Sense and Soul* (1998): "Religious *mythological* proclamations are clearly dogmatic, which means that when they are taken to be literal truths, they are simply asserted without any supporting evidence."[27] This may appear rather harsh to some, but particularly when the *pre/trans fallacy* is factored in it makes extremely good sense for it will further the developmental growth in consciousness (not regressive tendencies). Besides, Wilber insists that his critical demand is only for "religion to accept a more authentic self-image," which shouldn't be much of a problem because the "contemplative core" of all the world's religions, as he points out, is "a series of direct mystical, transcendental, meditative, contemplative or yogic experiences—*not sensory* and *not mental,* but transsensual, transmental, transpersonal transcendental consciousness—data seen not merely with the eye of flesh or with the eye of mind, but with the eye of contemplation."[28] In other words, authentic consciousness transformation is the *real business* of *real religion* or an *authentic spirituality,* that is, transpersonal evolution and moral development to God knows where.

Since an "authentic spirituality," or a "real religion," is found only in the "esoteric" (or inner) contemplative core of premodern religion, then Wilber claims that a real religion (or true spirituality) in the modern and postmodern world will have to rest on *mystical contemplation* (including meditation) and *direct experiential realizations* (from peak to plateau experiences). Otherwise, the integral pandit warns, religion "will serve merely to support a premodern, predifferentiated level of development in its own adherents: not an engine of growth and transformation, but a regressive, antiliberal, reactionary force of lesser engagements."[29] Yet, since mystical experience or transpersonal development is the actual method proposed by the historical founders of the world's major religions, then this too should not be too difficult to overcome (although being a *spiritual practitioner* is usually a difficult path). Indeed, these evolutionary pioneers to spiritual wisdom and compassionate love (i.e., the revered saints and sages of human history) are in fact humanity's global inheritance and birthright, not the proponents of ethnocentric intolerance and mythic superstitions.

In fact, Wilber points out, since a broad science and a real religion would demand evidence based on authentic paradigms (or injunctions), then they both should rigorously stand against any bogus or false claims made by either side. Therefore, the philosopher-pandit wisely summarizes: "If we are to effect a genuine integration of science and religion, it will have to be an integration of real science and real religion, not bogus science and bogus religion. And that means each camp must jettison its narrow and/or dogmatic remnants, and thus accept a more accurate self-concept, a more accurate image of its own estate."[30] In other words, when religion *transcends* (yet includes) its mythic elements and partial truths, then it's on the way to more fully embracing its authentic transpersonal truths validated by proper investigative attitudes and by communities of the qualified, even in the modern/postmodern world, as it's been done *authentically* for millennia.

Deep Science & Real Religion: The Quest for Integration

When all the philosophical considerations presented in *The Marriage of Sense and Soul* (1998) are taken into account, that is, by recognizing the capacities for a real or broad science (based on broad empiricism), and the already proven capacities for a real religion (based on authentic spirituality), then Wilber concludes that "science and religion would fast be approaching a common grounding in experiential data that finds the existence of rocks, mathematics, and Spirit equally demonstrable."[31] In other words, by expanding science and religion just slightly, even based on their own principles for evaluating data and knowledge, then the AQAL Approach has serious ramifications for both. Therefore, Wilber makes an integral call for a genuine "deep science," or a *real science*, not a narrow science of materialism, but one grounded in *broad empiricism*. This integral approach also calls for a "real religion," or a *deep religion* based on *authentic spirituality*, not a narrow religion that denies evidence and resorts to mythic or imaginal explanations (often ethnocentric and intolerant). Rather, real religion will affirm authentic consciousness development based on *transformative* practices and injunctions. In summary, the integral philosopher maintains for there to be such a marriage of science and religion, then they'd each have to meet the following basic requirements:

- **Real Science**—must "expand from *narrow empiricism* (sensory experience only) to *broad empiricism* (direct experience in general)" and therefore be open to evidence from all possible realms and methodologies (including the mental and spiritual);

- **Real Religion/Authentic Spirituality**—must reject its dogmatic limitations and "open its truth claims to *direct verification*—or *rejection*—by experiential evidence... [and therefore] engage the three strands of all valid knowledge and anchor its claims in direct experience."

The AQAL Approach of "all-quadrants, all-levels, all-lines, all-states," based on an *Integral Post-Metaphysics* that doesn't rely on pregiven (a priori) structures or archetypes (see next chapter), therefore points to the possibility of revising and updating the depth and validity of knowledge acquisition being gathered by both science (which is investigating exteriors) and religion (which is developing interiors). Wilber continues to outline some of these contours in defining a "deep science" and "real religion" below:

- **Deep Science**—is based upon a *broad science* (and *broad empiricism*) that "applies the three strands of valid knowing to any and all direct experience, evidence, and data," therefore, a *deep science* is a science of a particular field that "includes not just the *exteriors* of Its but the *interiors* of I and We," thus there's generated "a broad science of each quadrant" that uses "experience in general (sensory, mental, spiritual)."[32]

- **Real Religion/Deep Spirituality**—is based on an *authentic spirituality* that also uses a *broad science* (and *broad empiricism*) that's grounded in the three strands of valid knowledge (i.e., instrumental injunctions, direct apprehensions, communal confirmations) in order to investigate the higher transpersonal levels of the Great Nest of Spirit; Wilber summarizes: "My thesis is simply this: *deep spirituality* involves the direct investigation of the experiential evidence disclosed in the higher stages of consciousness development."[33]

These deeper understandings of science and religion can lead the way to a genuine reconciliation of science and religion simply because the AQAL Model includes all possible methodologies offered by both approaches to human knowledge (from the somatic to the psychological to the intellectual to the contemplative). This is possible since reality can be effectively modeled as one continuous spectrum of existence involving interiors and exteriors, from the prepersonal to personal to transpersonal, from instinct to ego to God, all of which the AQAL Metatheory affirms to be the case (see part III). As we'll see next, this also involves scientifically measuring the "footprints" left by the transpersonal and spiritual domains as they interact with the physical world, although this can obviously be an extremely complex venture since they're usually very subtle and difficult to detect, yet with a good integral map leading the way, it's possible to have a greater chance of success.

Integral Correlates: "Footprints" in the Real World

As far back as Wilber/Phase-2 (in the late 1970s), the integral theorist strongly maintained that these various modes of knowing or "sciences" (i.e., the physical, mental, and contemplative) are deeply related and intimately interactive. As a result, the interaction of the *interiors* (or Left-Hand quadrants) and *exteriors* (or Right-Hand quadrants) actually have *correlates* or *correspondences* or "footprints"[34] that are detectable and measurable by a deep science (or real religion). In 1983, Wilber was already recognizing this vital link between science and religion, as he explained in *Eye to Eye* (1983): "The point is that the higher [transpersonal] realms everywhere leave their *footprints* in the lower. The higher realms form and inform, create and mold, produce and alter, all manner of forms in the lower realms. But those productions cannot be grasped *by* the lower realms nor reduced *to* them."[35] Nearly twenty years later, he mentions the same thing in *Integral Psychology* (2000); "An integral approach allows us to map the *exterior correlates* of *interior states*, without attempting to reduce one to the other."[36] This revolutionary marriage of the physical and metaphysical, of the transcendental and the empirical, of interiors and exteriors, a methodology for "the new and truly higher sciences," has become one of the principal concerns of the AQAL Metatheory, especially with Phase-5's *Integral Post-Metaphysics* (see next chapter).

The AQAL Metatheory, therefore, is designed to support and facilitate the scientific investigation of these higher-level correlates of consciousness making their mark in the exterior dimensions, for as Wilber recently pointed out, "In the manifest world, what we call 'matter' is not the lowest rung in the great spectrum of existence, but the exterior form of every rung in the spectrum."[37] As an example, in *A Theory of Everything* (2000), the integral theorist reviews this topic with a consideration on "the brain of a mystic," where he suggests that by studying meditative states, then a person's *subjective* experiences will have *objective* factual correlates in the brain itself, such as in monitoring brainwave patterns or neurotransmitters. This has important implications, for it means, as he explains, "from bodily feelings to mental ideas to spiritual illuminations (Left-Hand quadrants), there are at least some *physical correlates* (Right-Hand quadrants) for all of the states and stages of consciousness evolution."[38] Yet, even more important, with an AQAL Matrix analysis then the interactions of "all-quadrants, all-levels, etc." must all be included and honored, for consciousness is not merely located in the brain, but it's anchored in, and distributed across, all four quadrants and all of their available levels in the Great Nest of Spirit. Some of these integral ideas about psychophysical correlates are summarized below:

- **Interior/Exterior Correlates**—are monitored or tracked or traced by "simultracking" the *interiors* (Left-Hand quadrants) as they leave their "footprints" (or correspondences) in the *exteriors* (Right-Hand quadrants), which are detectable as "*objective correlates* that are not lower and higher, but outer and inner,"[39] consequently, AQAL Metatheory maintains that deep sciences can investigate and measure these correlates in AQAL terms (i.e., such as using an *Integral Operating System* or *holonic indexing systems*, etc.).

In a truly revolutionary way, AQAL Metatheory, Wilber explains, "finds ample room for the traditional Great Chain of Being and Knowing—from matter to body to mind to soul to spirit—but it plugs those realities into empirical facts in a definite and specifiable fashion."[40] Nonetheless, as he had reminded us years ago in *Eye to Eye* (1983): "Life is synergistic in reference to matter and cannot be reduced to, or fully explained by, matter.... We would also expect spiritual processes to leave their footprints in the biophysical substrate, either directly or via the mind. But in no case could mind or spirit be reduced to brain or explained entirely or merely by brain physiology.... Mind transcends but includes physiology, and the truths of the former cannot be entirely contained in the truths of the latter."[41] Only an AQAL Model, or something similar, could accomplish this task with any type of efficiency and comprehensive understanding. By using the authentic forms of science and religion, i.e., their "deep" forms, then an "all-quadrants, all-levels" AQAL Approach can gather verifiable data from all the realms of human experience (physical, mental, spiritual), yet without reducing any one to the others, and therefore it provides a seamless marriage of science and religion for the modern/postmodern world.

The figure below is a graphic representation of the four quadrants and the natural integration of interiors and exteriors, of the physical and metaphysical, or simply, "the marriage of sense and soul," the integration of science and religion into one seamless totality of reality, or one that can rightly be called the AQAL Matrix (see part III). See Figure 4-1.

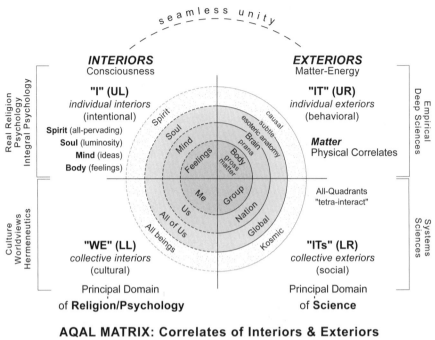

AQAL MATRIX: Correlates of Interiors & Exteriors
(The Marriage of Science & Religion)

Figure 4-1

This integral or holonic model is a monumental change from the traditionalist version because *every level* (including the transpersonal ones) has an "IT-component" (or Right-Hand exterior), that is, a physical correlate that leaves empirical imprints or "footprints" in the "real world" (or in the physical domains). This means interiors aren't just disembodied realities, or the fabled "ghost" in the machine, but they're actually intimately related and intertwined with the exteriors as one continual spectrum of existence. This is a fundamental understanding now being embraced and more clearly articulated with the revolutionary advance of Phase-5's *Integral Post-Metaphysics* (as we'll continue to see in the next chapter), yet it has always been implicit, if not explicit (in passages), throughout every one of Wilber's phases and writings. By relying on this integration of science and religion, of interiors and exteriors, this creates a post-postmodern call for the development of actual spiritual sciences, the next integral idea we'll explore as the marriage of science and religion unfolds its benefits.

Spiritual Sciences: Transcendental Naturalism

On the last page of *Sex, Ecology, Spirituality* (1995), the principal text of the AQAL Model, Wilber tagged this type of sophisticated and integral understanding of science with the Latin title *"Scientia Visionis,"* a vision of science that marries the rational and the transrational (see chapter 17). Yet back in Wilber/Phase-2 with *Eye to Eye* (1983), the integral philosopher already had suggested that by following the "three eyes of knowing" (i.e., physical, mental, spiritual), at a minimum, it's possible to speak legitimately about a "hierarchy of sciences" that's available to human beings in their knowledge quest, which he outlined below:

- **Monological Sciences**—a "science of *sensibilia*" is based upon *empiric-analytic inquiry*, such as physics, chemistry, biology, astronomy, geology, etc.;

- **Dialogical Sciences**—a "science of *intelligibilia*" is based upon a *mental-phenomenological inquiry*, such as with linguistics, mathematics, hermeneutics, logic, etc.;

- **Contemplative Sciences**—a "science of *transcendelia*" is based on *transcendental inquiry*, such as with contemplation, meditation, yoga, integral transformative practices, etc., which can be carefully subdivided into:

    (a) **Mandalic Sciences**—use "mandalic maps" or inadequate mental cartographies that acknowledge that Spirit is ultimately translogical, and therefore paradoxical, not characterizable in mental terms, yet they are still able to "translate the higher realms (downward) into mental maps, cartographies, and so on... [therefore] they are simply pictures of reality, not reality itself,"[42] i.e., "the map is not the territory";

    (b) **Noumenological Sciences** or **"Gnostic Sciences"** or **"Geist Sciences"**—use actual methodologies and injunctions needed to apprehend transpersonal disclosures, including direct and intuitive apprehension of spirit, noumenon, *dharmakaya*, which is disclosed only via *gnosis, satori, wu, prajna,* Enlightenment, God-Realization, etc.; currently involves Wilber/Phase-5 concerns such *Integral Method-ological Pluralism* and *Integral Life Practices.*

As we'll learn later, this integral approach to the spectrum of sciences generates an *Integral Methodological Pluralism* that includes empirical-analytic hypotheses and tests (Upper-Right), hermeneutic-historical investigations and interpretations, conceptual analyses and syntheses (Left-Hand interiors), as well as admitting possible paradoxical or mandalic cartographies of the higher realms. In *The Marriage of Sense and Soul* (1998), Wilber calls this "new roles of science" and knowledge acquisition as being a "transcendental naturalism," or "naturalistic transcendentalism," because they "allow us to thoroughly 'ground' or 'embody' metaphysical or transcendental claims, in effect providing a seamless union of transcendental and empirical, otherworldly and this-worldly. For the higher transpersonal levels are not *above* the natural or empirical or objective, they are *within* the natural and empirical and objective. Not on top of, but alongside of, Spirit does not physically rise above nature (or the Right-Hand world); *Spirit is the interior of nature, the within of the Kosmos. We do not look up, we look within.*"[43] In other words, Wilber boldly claims, this "type of transcendental naturalism, uniting Left and Right, interior and exterior, transcendental and empirical, is just another way to summarize the marriage of the best of premodern wisdom and modern knowledge."[44] As we've seen, it's an accomplishment realized by taking an all-level (great Chain) and all-quadrant (modern) approach.

Importantly, by modeling the fact that *all interior events have exterior correlates*, then this dramatically changes the role of sensory-empirical science itself. This is because, as Wilber explains, "objective empirical science is no longer relegated to the bottom rung of the hierarchy (which the traditional approach gave it).... Rather, empirical science is accessing the *exterior* modes of *all the higher levels as well.*"[45] In addition, by modeling a union of the natural (physical) and spiritual (metaphysical) domains, then this postmodern integration of exteriors and interiors fortuitously "avoids the insuperable difficulties of either position taken alone."[46] In this case, this AQAL union of science and religion is capable of actually generating "spiritual sciences"—a *Scientia Visionis*—whose contours are briefly outlined below:

- **Spiritual Sciences**—combines both "deep sciences" and "real religion," which is how the AQAL Model depicts "the new role of sci-

ence" as being a "deep science," which is when an "empirical science…
accessing the *exterior* modes of *all of the higher levels as well*," therefore
AQAL Metatheory makes its "radical claim: deep spirituality involves
in part *a broad science of the higher levels of human development*"[47]—thus
accomplishing the "marriage of science and religion."

As a result, with a fully developed AQAL Model, then science is seen
as investigating every level in the Great Holarchy of Being and Knowing,
for these spiritual sciences can exist *alongside,* not *below,* the transpersonal
domains, which is the classic error made by a rigid epistemological pluralism and traditional metaphysics. In other words, by making these types
of adjustments, an AQAL Metatheory establishes the foundation for a
genuine science (not a scientific materialism) that's based on a methodological pluralism that can adequately investigate the *subjective interiors* of
consciousness while tracking their *objective correlates* in the exteriors (yet
without reductionism), and while still being open to critical evaluation
and consensual verification.

Yet, perhaps most important, Wilber never loses sight that such "theories" need to have, must have, pragmatic applications (and "practices")
in the real world, to be most effective and truly integrative of the noble
goals of both religion and science. Insightfully, he summarized the goals
of his "overall paradigm," which has now become the fully developed
AQAL Metatheory, in an interview published in *Eye to Eye* (1983): "An
overall paradigm, in my opinion, would have to include all of the modes
of knowing, and all the correlative methodologies…. Further, the overall paradigm, its simple existence, would demand a social evolutionary
stance, a social policy geared to help human beings evolve through the
stage-levels of existence. This would involve both attempts to help vertical
transformation to higher levels and also attempts to clear up the distortions and oppressions that have occurred horizontally on the levels already
in existence…. [Yet] in this paradigm transcendence cannot be forced.
There are only *participants* in emancipation. You can only force slavery;
you can't force a person to be free."[48] This is the type of *real* postmodern
wisdom that provides humanity with the opportunity for a future based
on a deeper understanding of the Kosmos and the sacred wholeness of the
human being, all of which includes the physical, the mental, and the spiritual domains of existence interacting as one harmonious reality.

Holonic Indexing: Simultracking & Cross-Level Analysis

Although the AQAL Model may at times appear complex with all its levels, quadrants, and a multitude of variables, it actually forms a very simple skeleton capable of integrating a wide variety of different perspectives, once the terms are more familiar. Since this AQAL Matrix carefully outlines all the levels, quadrants (interiors and exteriors), lines, streams, states, types, et al., then its principal architect maintains that such a comprehensive approach also provide a careful analysis for the "'simultracking' of levels and quadrants,"[49] which is similar to a "cross-level analysis" and "double-tracking," since they follow the *levels of the subject* (interiors) and the *levels of reality* (exteriors) as the self (or society) evolves through the Great Nest of Spirit. The matrix of "all-quadrants, all-levels, all-lines, all-states" outlined by the AQAL Map, therefore, provides a fairly decent and complex (yet simple) grid that can at least partially track many of these interrelated variables found in the Matrix of Reality.

The AQAL Matrix, as we'll see in part IV, has a great capacity for this type of highly developed "holonic indexing system," especially since it's thoroughly based upon an *Integral Methodological Pluralism* (or actual methodologies) that can adequately investigate these various multidimensional cross-references. By taking an "all-levels, all-quadrants, all-lines, etc." approach to research and the human knowledge quest, this approach makes sure it "touches bases" with all the basic *levels* and *quadrants* in the Great Nest of Spirit, and, most important, to the exclusion or privileging of none. By performing an incredible balancing act of integrating the *qualitative* interior modes of consciousness (Left-Hand quadrants of epistemology) with the empirical *quantitative* exteriors of existence (Right-Hand quadrants of ontology), then the integral model also includes both interior *interpretations* (subjective, intersubjective) and exterior *measurements* (objective) in collecting data. Naturally, these are some of the current investigations being undertaken, promoted, published, and taught by the growing legions of scholars at Integral Institute and Integral University (see chapter 3).

Yet, beyond all the theories and data gathering, in the essay "An Integral Theory of Consciousness" (1997), Wilber also strongly insists on the paramount importance of engaging the *actual transformation of the researcher*, especially when researching the transpersonal domains of consciousness. Actual *transformation* (not just *translation*), of course, can be accessed only through the appropriate *injunctions* (exemplars, practices), whatever the particular mode of inquiry (physical, mental, spiritual, etc.). Wilber therefore outlines "two broad wings" involved with the AQAL Metatheory that involves this "methodology of an integral study of consciousness," as he summarizes below (from the aforementioned essay):

1) "The first is the *simultaneous tracking of the various levels and lines in each of the quadrants*, and then noting their *correlations*, each to all the others, and in no way trying to reduce any to the others.

2) The second is the *interior transformation of the researchers themselves.*… Any Right-Hand path of knowledge can be engaged without a demand for interior *transformation* (or change in level of consciousness: one merely learns a new *translation* (within the same level of consciousness)…. But the Left-Hand paths, at the point that they begin to go postformal, *demand a transformation of consciousness in the researchers themselves.*"[50]

In this case, unless researchers (or people in general) actually *transform consciousness* by engaging the various *modes of inquiry* (bodily, mental, spiritual), then it's not possible to draw accurate conclusions from the knowledge gained from these realms of existence. Otherwise, as everybody has seen all too often, it's easy to become lost in the endless display of kosmic phenomena and the onslaught of multiple perspectives (aperspectival madness). This is especially true, Wilber maintains, with the tendency to make the pre/trans fallacy (i.e., confusing prepersonal and transpersonal), or to commit category errors (i.e., confusing levels or quadrants), especially since the lower levels of awareness (first-tier thinking) often erroneously fuse together or misuse the many dimensions and realms of the Kosmos, thus further distorting their significance. Fortunately, with evolutionary metatheories (like AQAL) that can support a marriage of deep science and authentic spirituality, based on real experiential data, then it should only heighten our capacity to more fully participate in and develop the deepest potentials of ourselves and the Kosmos, a potential that begins anew with every human birth.

AQAL Matrix: All-Quadrants, All-Levels

Later, we will see in more detail that Wilber's AQAL Model is so synergistic and holistic that it pictures the Totality of Reality as vast "morphogenetic developmental space" where all holons (or whole/parts) evolve and unfold in a Kosmic Mandala of Spirit-in-action (see part III). This AQAL Matrix of "all-quadrants, all-levels, all-lines, all-states, etc.," where a "matrix" is a space in which something originates and develops, can cognitively differentiate the many "levels" (of matter, nature, body, mind, soul, and spirit) and the "quadrants" (of interiors/exteriors situated in self, culture, and nature), and the many other variables of consciousness and reality. As we've already discussed, this provides a very powerful *"holonic indexing system"* for "unpacking" or "teasing apart" the endless patterns of these interacting holons as they "tetra-mesh" with each other and their collective interdependent environments. In addition, by integrating science (or the careful measurements of the exterior domains) and authentic spirituality (or the careful disclosures of the interior realms), then the AQAL Matrix also pictures this entire evolutionary reality as being *always already* grounded in nondual Spirit or God.

Although the figure below takes some creative license (since it's never appeared in a Wilber book), and inherently falls far short since it's only a graphic representation of a thoroughly intermeshed pluridimensional reality, it does attempt to schematically show the *basic waves* or *levels* and the *quadrants* in some type of holarchical order of transcend-and-include (sans *all-lines, all-states, all-types*, etc.). Also, the basic levels are named after the predominant *worldview* popularized in Wilber's earlier Phase-2 books (now found in the Lower-Left quadrant), thus it's only a limited spherical map (and certainly not the territory), but it does show some of the multidimensional complexity involved with the AQAL Matrix and its various tracking systems. See Figure 4-2.

Constructive Postmodernism: Integral Metatheory

As we've learned, the AQAL Metatheory of Wilber/Phase-4/5 has made it abundantly clear that by integrating the *all-levels* of the Great Nest of Spirit (matter to mind to God), plus the *all-quadrants* of the modern world (the differentiated domains of self, culture, and nature), then humanity finally has a viable map, or a good start, that includes and honors all the domains

AQAL MATRIX: All-Quadrants, All-Levels
(configured by Brad Reynolds)
Figure 4-2

of the Kosmos, and by doing so, it rescues the Great Nest of premodernity from the Flatland materialism of modernity. Instead of being limited to the deconstruction or nihilism suggested by recent versions of postmodernism, Wilber's integral approach actually provides a "post-postmodern" integration based on the *reconstruction* of evidence, not just theoretical speculations. Consequently, he calls this integral approach a "Constructive

Postmodernism," since it attempts to regain the lost promise of postmodernity, which has still, although trying in various ways, failed to make the necessary integration of the premodern world and the modern one (see part IV). As an alternative, Wilber claims that "the 'bright promise' of a *constructive postmodernity*... involves the integration of the best of *premodernity* (the Great Nest) and *modernity* (the differentiation and evolution of the Big Three), resulting in a more integral 'all-level, all-quadrant' [AQAL] approach."[51] In this case, the advantages gained with this more holistic (and realistic) attempt will involve the "integration of art, morals, and science, at every level of the extraordinary spectrum of consciousness, body to mind to soul to spirit."[52] To say the least, subjects of grave importance.

As we'll see (in later chapters), Wilber's integral psychology claims that this type of AQAL Model is a cognitive expression of *"vision-logic"* or *"network-logic,"* for it adds up the various perspectives into a unified whole, like fitting together the partial pieces in the supreme puzzle (see Chapter 17). This involves the stage or basic wave of self-development termed the integral-centaur (the *integrated bodymind*), which supports the worldview of *"universal integralism"* (or *integral-aperspectivism*), or what's also called "second-tier thinking" (by Spiral Dynamics). Wilber explains the potential significance of this integral development of consciousness in *Integral Psychology* (2000): "Constructive postmodernism takes up the multiple contexts freed by pluralism, and then goes one step further and weaves them together into mutually interrelated networks. This *integral-aperspectivism*—this unity-in-diversity, this *universal integralism*—discloses global interconnections, nests within nests within nests, and vast holarchies of mutually enriching embrace, thus converting pluralistic heapism into integral holism.... It is the emergence of this second-tier thinking upon which any truly *integral model* will depend—and this is the path of constructive postmodernism."[53] By constructively integrating the best of modern science and the best of premodern religion, AQAL Metatheory has accomplished a task that so far has eluded humanity, but now it's within our grasp, or at least it's close.

Whether the integral task Wilber has set out for himself, or rather, what was demanded by his *daemon* (or one's life purpose) will be successful, well, that remains to be seen. In a letter written in the mid-1990s to his dear friend, yet traditionalist antagonist Huston Smith, Wilber philosophically considered some of his noble objectives by sharing these poetic musings (1995): "So it's not that spirituality takes up where science leaves off, but that *they develop up the Great Nest of Spirit* together. The I and We and It domains—investigated by subjective introspection, intersubjective mutual understanding, and objective apprehension—*all develop together* through the entire Great Nest, until every I is seen as Buddha, every We as Sangha, every It as Dharma: the ultimate aesthetics, ultimate ethics, and ultimate science: the Beautiful, the Good, the True, each of which develops from the prepersonal to personal to transpersonal."[54] This is, indeed, the heart of Ken Wilber's Integral Vision.

Nonetheless, even with this updated understanding suggested by AQAL Metatheory, one that even includes spiritual truths and religious values, then it's still important to remember that as a "post-postmodern" integral pandit, Wilber is *definitely not* continuing the premodern values or traditional worldviews suggested by many of the world's great religions. As we'll see next, the particular concerns of Wilber/Phase-5 continues to emphasize that neither the earlier spectrum model (Wilber/Phases 1-3), nor its expanded AQAL version (Wilber/Phase-4), was ever intended to be described as being constructed with a priori (or pregiven) metaphysical structures, as some critics presuppose. As the integral philosopher reaffirmed in one of his first AQAL essays (1997): "The holons in each of those four quadrants were not postulated in any sort of a priori or 'metaphysical' fashion; they were rather suggested by an *a posteriori* data search across several hundred disciplines."[55] As we've just seen, this even includes the realms of soul and spirit, for all levels, all quadrants, and so on, exist as an intermeshed evolutionary AQAL Matrix , a psycho-physical existence of interacting correlates, not a dualistic reality that's separated into a physical world versus a metaphysical reality (see next chapter).

Consequently, and with a beautifully articulated comprehensiveness, Wilber's fully-advanced AQAL Metatheory has even transcended the traditional understanding and need for metaphysics itself, which also means it finds it necessary to critique some of the most benign models of the premodern era, including the "Perennial Philosophy" (although their partial truths will be gratefully included). As a result, the AQAL Model has radical and truly revolutionary implications, such as we just saw with the integral marriage of science and religion, for it also includes a depth of understanding that produces a genuine "post-metaphysics," an idea we'll explore next, one that truly reveals where Wilber's at.

CHAPTER FIVE

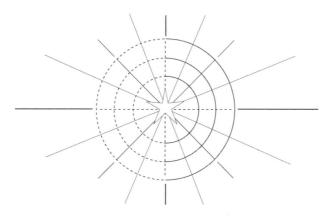

Wilber/Phase-5: Integral Post-Metaphysics: Transcending Spiritual Traditions

> In the smoking ruins left by Kant, the only possible conclusion is that all future metaphysics and *authentic spirituality* must offer *direct experiential* evidence. And that means, in addition to *sensory experience* and its empiricism (scientific and pragmatic) and *mental experience* and its rationalism (pure and practical), there must be added *spiritual experience* and its mysticism (spiritual practice and its experiential data).
>
> —Ken Wilber, *The Marriage of Sense and Soul* (1998)

WE BEGAN IN THE FIRST CHAPTER SUGGESTING THE BEST PLACE TO find "where Wilber's at" is to see him placed within the fourth and fifth phases of his unfolding thirty-some-year-long career, or what we called Wilber/Phase-4/5. This culmination of Ken Wilber's collected works (or Integral Vision) is best represented by his comprehensive AQAL or "all-quadrant, all-level, all-line, all-states, all-types" Metatheory, which we will cover in more depth in the next section (see Part II). Practically speaking, we also reviewed that the integral philosopher is involved with the establishment of Integral Institute and

Integral University (among other ventures), all of which is already influencing everything from education to medicine, business to politics, ecological theory to feminism, avant-garde art and rock music to motion pictures, as well as continuing to have profound effects on modern psychology, philosophy, and spirituality, and other numerous fields (see chapter 3).

Theoretically speaking, Wilber/Phase-5 is just beginning to be released in publication format as the integral philosopher releases yet another magnum opus of over 900 pages in 2006 with volume 2 of *The Kosmos Trilogy*—what he has recently called "the finest work I've ever done."[1] Probably the crowning achievement, and most revolutionary advance, of Phase-5 is the clear articulation of an "Integral Post-Metaphysics," a view that directly addresses the modern and postmodern critiques of traditional metaphysics initiated by the likes of Kant, Heidegger, and Habermas. In short, with Wilber/Phase-5 the world-renowned philosopher is attempting to answer modernity's devastating critique of metaphysics begun by Kant and modern/postmodern philosophy, and, by doing so, he's attempting to rescue depth and Spirit, or authentic spirituality, from the flatland scrapheaps of the modern mind; nothing short of this. Yet, remarkably, although this post-metaphysical Phase-5 appears complex and far outside the traditional "box" of spirituality, it's still fairly simple and straightforward, that is, once you've included and understood the important contributions made by the postmodern mind.

By honoring the many significant but partial truths of *postmodernity*, and while combining them with the partial truths of *modernity* and the *premodern* world, Wilber's integral system has provided a genuine "marriage of science and religion" by keeping the best aspects from all of these inherited gold mines of human knowledge and wisdom, while simultaneously jettisoning their limitations and absolutisms (see previous chapter). In addition, Phase-5 adds a solid theoretical foundation for the further extension of Wilber's *epistemological pluralism,* a paradigm that applies all the various forms of inquiry, from empirical sciences to hermeneutics to system sciences to inner psychology and spiritual inquiries that are grouped together as an " *Integral Methodological Pluralism*" (IMP). This overall integral AQAL Metatheory is also coordinated with what Phase-5 now calls an " *Integral Operating System*" (IOS), which cross-references and double-checks that "all-levels" (in the spectrum of consciousness and Kosmos) and "all-quadrants" (or interiors and exteriors) are all being included so as not to be overlooked, thus being even "more integral" (see chapter 11). At best, we have suggested, this may be the first truly integral system in the history of the world that actually *includes* all the possible modes of knowing or methodologies available to men and women, thus generating an *Integral Methodological Pluralism*; at worst, it's one that's close, at least close enough to warrant some serious study and a genuine inspection on the way to reconstructing an even better integral system.

Deconstructing the Perennial Philosophy: The Neo-Perennial Philosophy

The "Perennial Philosophy" is the idea that certain religious truths are "perennial" or are "reoccurring year after year," and thus it represents "universal" or "timeless truths" about our human condition and the spiritual nature of reality. Although Ken Wilber has used this "universal" concept of the "Perennial Philosophy" (or *philosophia perennis*) as a backbone or support for many of his statements about spirituality in general, and, in particular, about the higher transpersonal levels of consciousness, he does *not* consider himself a "perennialist" or a defender of the Perennial Philosophy. This often comes as a shocking surprise to many of his admirers and students, especially those who are drawn to his earlier writings (particularly the evolutionary presentations of Wilber/Phase-2). Nonetheless, the current Wilber/Phase-4/5 approach is taking a strong critical stance in rejecting many claims made by twentieth-century Perennial Philosophy scholars, such as Huston Smith, Fritjof Schuon, Ananda Coomaraswamy, Rene Guénon, and others.

This "deconstructing of the perennial philosophy" sometimes gives the appearance that Wilber is contradicting some of his statements made in earlier phases and books. Much of this stems from Wilber's insistence on taking an *evolutionary* view of human history, or one that acknowledges the continual progression of humanity's understanding and knowledge, even with its sacred spiritual wisdom and the contours of Enlightenment. Therefore, according to Wilber, it's also critical to include the viable truths uncovered by modernity and postmodernity in making any comparative and comprehensive assessment of the world's great wisdom traditions, or what's known as the Perennial Philosophy. The integral philosopher forcefully summarizes his recent suggestions for an "Integral Post-Metaphysics" in an excerpt for Volume 2 of *The Kosmos Trilogy* (2003): "First and foremost, no system (spiritual or otherwise) that does not come to terms with modern Kantian and postmodern Heideggerian thought can hope to survive with any intellectual respectability (agree with them or disagree with them, they have to be addressed)—and that means all spirituality must be post-metaphysical in some sense."[2] Wilber is directly addressing these important concerns now with Wilber/Phase-5.

Nonetheless, the Perennial Philosophy has always had a strong appeal to spiritually-minded moderns, for even Wilber has usually defined this notion, as he did in *Grace and Grit* (1991), as being "The worldview that has been embraced by the vast majority of the world's greatest spiritual teachers, philosophers, thinkers, and even scientists. It's called 'perennial' or 'universal' because it shows up in virtually all cultures across the globe and across the ages."[3] Nevertheless, the position of Wilber's current AQAL Phase-4/5 stance is clarifying in more stringent terms his relationship with this noble Perennial Philosophy, such as this example from the introduction to *Collected Works, Volume Eight (CW8)* published in 2000:

> When critics identify me with the perennial philosophy, they fail to notice that the only item of the perennial philosophy that I have actually *defended* is the notion of dimensions of being and knowing, and then I only staunchly defend three of them: matter, mind, and spirit (or gross, subtle, and causal). I sometimes expand those dimensions to five (matter, body, mind, soul, and spirit), but I am willing to strongly defend only the former. That is, I claim that every major human culture, at least by the time of *homo sapiens,* recognized these three main dimensions or realms of existence (as evidenced also in waking, dreaming, and sleeping). That is almost the *only* item of the "perennial philosophy" that I have defended.[4]

Consequently, Wilber's position is actually pointing to what he's termed the "Neo-Perennial Philosophy," which he defines by telling us that "at the core of the neoperennial philosophy is the same Radical and Formless Truth glimpsed by the wisdom cultures of the past... but its outward *form,* its clothing cut in the relative and manifest world, has naturally changed and evolved to keep pace with the progressive evolution of the manifest world itself—and that includes, of course, the very idea of evolution."[5] Although often overlooked by critics, this is a position he's maintained since at least 1983 when he first published his groundbreaking essay by the same name, "The Neo-Perennial Philosophy,"[6] which itself appeared in the *American Theosophist* as a counterview to many of the philosophical assumptions made by this prestigious journal on modern spirituality. Indeed, the year 1983 was a turning point for Wilber in many ways, for it's the year he "unofficially" broke ranks with transpersonal psychology, the field with which he was most closely associated. This is when he opted to push his work further into the realm of "integral studies" instead of concentrating on transpersonal or altered states, the principal interest of transpersonal psychology at that time.

With "The Neo-Perennial Philosophy," Wilber claimed that the Perennial Philosophy, as it's usually presented by modern scholars, is still inadequate for our times, therefore he clarified his position: "Now if we use 'Ancient' (with a capital 'A') to represent radical, timeless, and formless Truth, and if we use 'ancient' (small 'a') for the particular past forms and expressions of radical Truth—then we can summarize our major point thus: modern culture needs Ancient Truth, not ancient truth. And our corollary point: the best and most appropriate form of Ancient Truth is now the *neo-perennial philosophy* (and not a blind allegiance to 'what the old folks said'; modern culture is by-and-large incompatible with ancient culture, and their forced fit could never benefit more than a small percentage of nostalgically-oriented)."[7] It's the radical, timeless Truth that Ken Wilber is pointing to, not the revival of past, ancient truths.

This view of an ever-evolving philosophy arises because Wilber, unlike practically any other scholar in the field, has always been pointing to the critical necessity for incorporating the *modern discovery of evolution* (including the evolution of human consciousness) in making any estimation of a "perennial philosophy." Thus, he perceptively explains in the essay, "The Neo-Perennial Philosophy," that "both the *quality* of humanity's spiritual understanding and the *form* of its presentation is deepening and becoming more adequate in modern times, not less."[8] No other philosopher had ever been quite so clear in recognizing the real growth of spiritual expression and teaching throughout human history, although, granted, it has been present among a few in our time (such as with Aurobindo, Hegel, Adi Da, Schelling, Teilhard de Chardin, and Radhakrishnan, to name a few), but nevertheless, the case had never been so persuasively made as it has in Wilber's writings.[9]

As a result, the integral philosopher has been unequivocally abiding by this more critical position, especially with his Phase-4/5 writings, especially since he's only relied on the Perennial Philosophy to *introduce* his integral studies. In particular, he introduces the idea that the "Great Chain of Being" is best seen as a *nested hierarchy* (a "Great Nest of Spirit") that reaches from matter to body to mind to soul to spirit (see chapter 8). However, as we'll continue to see, he's modified it by adding the scientifically proven sub-levels of evolution, including the interior developments of consciousness, which consequently creates an "all-level, all-quadrant" AQAL Matrix or a "morphogenetic developmental space" (see part II). This is highlighted in even greater depth with Wilber/Phase-5, now that he has more fully integrated the critical philosophies of modernity and postmodernity, even providing a highly developed Integral Post-Metaphysics.

Although sympathetic to using the Perennial Philosophy as a vehicle for better understanding the "spectrum of consciousness" as a "Great Nest of Spirit," Wilber has never really claimed total support for all of its tenets, especially the notion of being "perennial" or "ever-repeating year after year" without fail. Most versions of a "perennial philosophy," especially contemporary ones, according to Wilber, are not really "perennial" but stem from certain eras of religious history and consciousness evolution (such as from the magical, mythic, and mythic-rational eras of human history). In this case, Wilber strictly clarifies his critical analysis of the Perennial Philosophy in *CW8* (2000): "Most of the other aspects of the traditional version of the perennial philosophy (as maintained by e.g., Fritjof Schuon, Ananda Coomaraswamy, Henry Corbin, Seyyed Nasr, Huston Smith, Marco Pallis, Rene Guénon, etc.)—aspects such as unchanging archetypes, involution and evolution as fixed and predetermined, the strictly hierarchical (as opposed to holonic/quadratic) nature of reality, etc.—I do not believe are either universal or true."[10] This has, obviously, become his current stance toward the Perennial Philosophy.

Nevertheless, unlike some of today's harsher critics of the Perennial Philosophy, usually relative pluralists or the "green meme" postmodernists who often arrogantly claim there is no such thing as universal truths for humankind, Wilber still supports the general notion of sacred wisdom and the teachings of nondual mysticism (or Enlightenment).[11] Perhaps this is part of what gives rise to what some perceive as Wilber's apparently contradictory stance to the Perennial Philosophy, thus he quickly qualifies his position by saying, "Although I have been a harsh critic of the perennial philosophy, I still believe that, especially in its most sophisticated forms, it is a fountain of unsurpassed wisdom, even if we have to dust it off a bit."[12] Once again, it only *seems like* a paradoxical quandary that's making it difficult to know exactly where Wilber's at, for he's made himself quite clear, especially in his recent Phase-4/5 writings. In other words, in my opinion, it's generally our resistance to hearing what Wilber really means that creates the perceived quandary rather than his actual position.

The positive contributions of a "Perennial Philosophy" include the fact that there are certain universal currents, or "deep structures," in the human mind and psyche that appear as deep patterns throughout most world cultures and in many eras of human history. Consequently, Wilber still maintains this universal sweep in *The Eye of Spirit* (1997), a recent Phase-4 writing: "Known as the 'perennial philosophy'—'perennial' precisely because it shows up across cultures and across the ages with essentially similar features—this worldview has, indeed, formed the core not only of the world's great wisdom traditions, from Christianity to Judaism to Buddhism to Taoism, but also the thinking of some of the greatest philosophers, scientists, and psychologists East and West, North and South. So overwhelmingly widespread is the perennial philosophy…that it is either the single greatest intellectual error ever to appear in humankind's history—an error so colossally widespread as to literally stagger the mind—or it is the single most accurate reflection of reality yet to appear."[13] Consequently, it becomes an important contribution to any genuine integral philosophy.

Even with only a cursory reading of Wilber's collected works, one finds that he often uses the Perennial Philosophy to *introduce* a number of ideas expounded by this cross-cultural, mystical understanding, especially the fact that spiritual (or transpersonal) development reaches a pinnacle with Enlightenment (or God-Realization). But with a closer reading, especially beyond the Phase-2 books, it's revealed that basically it's only been the central idea of the "Great Chain of Being" that Wilber has supported in using the "Perennial Philosophy," as he summarized again in *The Eye of Spirit* (1997): "The central claim of the perennial philosophy is that *men and women can grow and develop (or evolve) all the way up the hierarchy to Spirit itself,* therein to realize a 'supreme identity' with Godhead—the *ens perfectissimum* toward which all growth and evolution yearns."[14] Again, in *Integral Psychology* (2000), he points to the only principle of the Perennial Philosophy he is willing to defend: "The Great Holarchy of Being and Knowing: such is the priceless gift of the ages. This is the core of the perennial philosophy, and, we might say, it is the part of the perennial philosophy that has empirically been found most enduring. The evidence continues overwhelmingly to mount in its favor: human beings have available to them an extraordinary spectrum of consciousness, reaching from prepersonal to personal to transpersonal states…. And the evidence says, in short, that there exists a richly textured rainbow of consciousness, spanning subconscious to self-conscious to super-conscious."[15] Or perhaps most straightforward of all, he tells us in *One Taste* (1999): "So what are the details of this perennial philosophy? Very simple: *the Great Nest of Being, culminating in One Taste*—there, in a nutshell, is the perennial philosophy…. The core of the world's great wisdom traditions is a framework we ought to consult seriously and reverentially in our own attempts to understand the Kosmos. And at its heart is the experience of One Taste—clear, obvious, unmistakable, unshakable."[16] This "One Taste" of Enlightenment (as we'll see in the next chapter) is also the core insight beating at the heart of Wilber's Integral Vision as well.

Beyond these basic principles, Wilber is no longer much of an advocate of the Perennial Philosophy in general; especially since the wealth of its wisdom tends to concentrate mostly on individual consciousness evolution (thus it's mostly about the Upper-Left quadrant reflecting individual interiors). Therefore, having paid his debt to the Perennial Philosophy, so to speak, Wilber is now more directly, and more integrally, including the valid but partial truths of modernity and postmodernity as also having valuable contributions to make toward any genuine integral approach. In this way, the pandit continues to balance all of theses concerns, as he explains in *Integral Psychology* (2000): "At the same time, the fact that the perennial philosophers were the first to spot many of the colors in this extraordinary rainbow [of consciousness and reality] doesn't mean that modernity and postmodernity must come mute to the meeting…. Modernity and postmodernity are not without their geniuses; the perennial philosophy is not without limitations and inadequacies; a more complete spectrum of consciousness will necessarily include and balance all of their insights and discoveries. But the general nature of the waves in the great River of Life: the perennial philosophers were often right on the money."[17] Once more, uniting pre-modernity, modernity, and postmodernity is the goal behind any genuine integral enterprise or "theory of everything."

In introducing his work, therefore, Wilber often presents the *basic waves* in the Great Nest of Spirit, or AQAL Matrix, by looking "first to the perennial philosophy for the general contours of the various levels; and then to significantly supplement that understanding with the many *refinements* (and sometimes *corrections*) offered by modernity and postmodernity."[18] Consequently, the Integral Model calls for cognitively cross-indexing *(holonic indexing systems)*, such as with the Wilber/Combs Matrix, as a way of verifying the legitimacy and authenticity of all possible spiritual engagements. Nonetheless, the integral philosopher can no longer be considered a defender or proponent of the Perennial Philosophy, per se, especially as critiqued by various postmodern critics, nor a traditionalist or revivalists of premodern religious traditions.

Not a Traditionalist, an Evolutionist

Since Ken Wilber is no longer a true defender of the Perennial Philosophy, then let's also clarify that he certainly doesn't consider himself a "traditionalist" either, or one of those scholars who defend the "traditional" religious systems of the world, such as those profound twentieth-century philosophers like Fritjof Schuon, Ananda Coomaraswamy, Seyyed Nasr, Rene Guénon, et al., or even his dear friend, Huston Smith (this is one of their main areas of disagreement). Traditionalists also include the various nineteenth-century Westerners who have supported the traditional notions of an a priori metaphysics based on versions of the esoteric or "inner" (versus the exoteric or "outer") teachings of spirituality, such as with the Theosophists. These mystically-inclined scholars, often trained in numerous religious traditions, usually point to the "esoteric core," or the inner teachings and meanings, hidden at the center of all the world religions, or what Schuon accurately termed "the transcendent unity of religions" (the title to his classic and complex first book published in 1957).

Since these writers, who were usually very serious practitioners, support the real essence (or esotericism) of the traditional world religions (such as Sufism, Buddhism, Hinduism, mystical Christianity, Islam, and so on.), as well as a hierarchy of religious experiences, therefore they're often called "traditionalists." In giving their profound presentations of esoteric religion, they are usually harsh critics of modernity and the modern mind, especially regarding the fallacies of scientific materialism, whereas, according to Wilber, they are mostly criticizing the "bad news" or dissociated rationality of modernity (see part III). Nonetheless, they have done an excellent job of collecting cross-cultural observations about the different insights and transformative practices as well as the common deep structures of the world's wisdom traditions, and so they should be eagerly, though cautiously, consulted (especially by holding in mind Wilber's integral critique). Huston Smith, for one, has presented an excellent summary of many of these cross-cultural parallels spotted and clarified by this insightful group of scholars, especially in his wonderful book *Forgotten Truth: The Common Vision of the World Religions* (1976) about a Great Chain of Being and Knowing (see Chapter 8).

To highlight some of the advances in religious scholarship uncovered by the traditionalists in discovering the universal currents of a Perennial Philosophy, Huston Smith compiled a mandala of the various levels in the Great Nest of Spirit as seen (and named) by the world's major religious traditions, which I was honored to graphically lay out for my kind teacher and friend. See Figure 5-1.

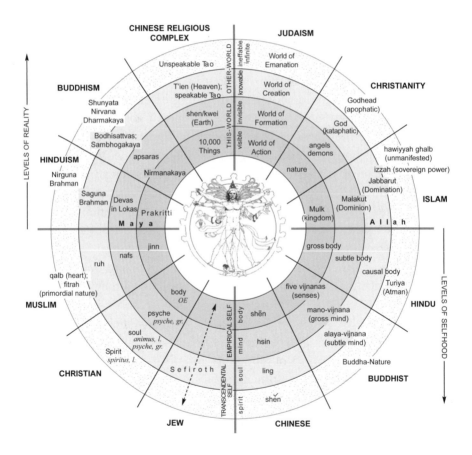

The Perennial Philosophy's Great Nest:
Self and World Envisioned Cross-Culturally
(with permission from Huston Smith, graphic by Brad Reynolds)

Figure 5-1

As excellent and profound as these writers and philosophers are, all making their own valuable contributions to religious studies and cross-cultural spirituality, Wilber has found that he must take a critical (but compassionate) stance against many of their concerns, yet while still building upon their noble research and insights. He's accomplished this principally by including, in a more integral manner, the valuable truths of modernity and postmodernity instead of promoting some type of return to the past or a revival of traditional religious thinking. This specifically means the necessity to fully include modern science's discovery of universal evolution. This is a very subtle and complex issue that can be fully understood only within the context of AQAL Metatheory, specifically with Wilber/Phase-5 and its Integral Post-Metaphysics, therefore it should be explored with care. This confusing and slippery notion, especially with Wilber's rigid stance on the Perennial Philosophy, as we mentioned, has been hard to accept by some of his best students, such as with Frank Visser's *Ken Wilber: Thought as Passion* (2003). Nevertheless, it's imperative to come to terms with this complex view in order to more fully understand where Wilber's at.

Perhaps the best way to recognize that Wilber does not fall into the category of a traditionalist, or even a modified "perennialist" (as Visser claims), is to see that he speaks with a loud voice acknowledging the "good news" or "dignities" of modernity and postmodernity while also condemning their "disasters" (such as with reductionism). By doing so, he seems more willing to transcend the various limitations of the premodern traditional view, such as their reliance on a priori structures, or mythic-archetypal explanations, to describe the human psyche and reality. By taking this approach, Wilber is trying to acknowledge the *partial truths* of the premodern traditions while remaining critical of their exoteric or outer forms (such as blind beliefs, dogmatic assertions, refusal of evidence, and the like). This obviously includes many of their pre-rational aspects as well, such as with magical and mythic consciousness, thus he fires up his rational sword of enlightened insight to bear down on their premodern metaphysical conceptions and distorted assumptions.

This is some of the genesis and reason behind Wilber's new millennium *Integral Post-Metaphysics* project, which includes an AQAL or all-quadrants, all-levels, holonic, multilevel methodology, for it's setting forth a new program of study and deep scientific investigation by bringing an all-embracing approach to reality (grounded in its ultimate nondual realization). As we've

seen, one of Ken Wilber's major accomplishments, or what he's been struggling to do his entire career, is to actually fit the Great Chain of Being or
Great Nest of Spirit into the modern and postmodern world, which he does
by creating a "deep science" and "deep religion" (see previous chapter). His
modeling of the "four quadrants" of the Kosmos, for instance, has integrally
determined that it's not enough to simply speak of the Great Nest in traditional premodern terms (such as simply being matter, body, mind, soul, and
spirit), but rather it needs to more fully expand into an AQAL or "all-quadrants, all-levels" understanding that's fully capable of including, yet critiquing, the *premodern, modern, postmodern,* and *integral* (or "post-postmodern")
currents of wisdom. Only by including all of these concerns in making our
assessments will we really discover where Wilber's at.

Integral Post-Metaphysics: Moving Beyond Premodern Metaphysics

As the twenty-first century dawns, Wilber's strong stance against the Perennial Philosophy has become totally obvious with the concerns of Wilber/
Phase-5, although many of these ideas have been present in his earlier phases
(certainly since the early 1980s). Responding in part to Jürgen Habermas's
call for a "post-metaphysical" understanding as presented in his 1992 book
Post-Metaphysical Thinking (Nachmetaphysisches Denken), Phase-5 is thoroughly establishing an "Integral Post-Metaphysics" (IMP), as Wilber's
recently published writings demonstrate. In short, Wilber's "post-metaphysics" is attempting to answer the modern critique of metaphysical philosophies that was initiated by the empiricists, such as Newton, Locke, Hume,
and finalized most fully with the brilliant critiques of Kant and his devastating attack on traditional metaphysics (as a way of limiting the ability of the
rational mind or pure thought).

Wilber is responding to these demands by clearly demonstrating the
necessity for some type of *epistemological pluralism* (yet recast in a postmodern form), which is an expansion of the "three eyes of knowing" methodology (i.e., including physical, mental, and spiritual modes of inquiry).
According to the integral philosopher, real human knowledge needs to be
accumulated with a multidimensional (or quadratic) spectrum of multiple
perspectives and methods of knowing (including injunctions, data, confirmation) or using a pluralism of methodologies. By providing data, i.e.,

conformational data for each realm of human experience, Wilber is also presenting an answer to Popper's *falsifiability principle* (or the capacity to prove or disprove by testing), which therefore can offer some sort of measurement of observation that can be confirmed by other investigators (i.e., consensual validation, if they engage the required injunctions). This brief review only hints at some of the subtle details being suggested by Wilber's emerging Phase-5 ideas, especially as being proposed in the upcoming volume 2 of *The Kosmos Trilogy* (which has already, in part, been posted on Shambhala's website since late 2002).

In other words, Wilber's philosophical mission is to go post-Kantian, since in order for *spirituality* in the contemporary world to be intellectually respectable and acceptable to both the modern and postmodern currents of world history, then it must address the concerns of our recent and most learned philosophers and brilliant modern thinkers. It is because of these modern and postmodern philosophers that Wilber has begun his tireless task in introducing and insisting on an "Integral Post-Metaphysics." He explains his attempted contribution in a recent writing (2003): "Integral Post-Metaphysics can generate all the essentials of premodern spiritual and metaphysical systems *but without their now discredited ontological baggage.* This, to my mind, is the central contribution of an Integral Post-Metaphysics—it does not itself contain metaphysics, but it can generate metaphysics as one possible AQAL Matrix configuration under the limit conditions of premodern cultures… but without relying on any pregiven archetypal, or independently existing ontological structures, levels, planes, etc."[19]

Specifically, Wilber is suggesting that if we truly embrace the great postmodern truth that our objective world is always *interpreted* by the *subject,* then we must understand that there are *no* ontological planes (or levels) of reality just lying around waiting to be discovered in the higher spiritual or transpersonal realms. Since for Wilber "one of the great and noble aims of postmodernism was to *introduce interpretation as an intrinsic aspect of the Kosmos,*" then his AQAL Metatheory claims that "every holon has a *interior* and *exterior* dimension, and therefore every holon without exception has an *objective* and an *interpretive* component."[20] The "myth of the given," one of the main paradigms of modern science (and the fundamental Enlightenment paradigm), has been sufficiently disproved by postmodernity in such a way that Wilber feels this interpretive consideration must also apply to transpersonal consciousness. Wilber previewed some of these recent ideas in the introduction to *CW8* (2000): "In my view, although features of the various realms of reality are interdependent of any particular observer, and are thus 'objective realities' in a very real sense, they cannot be separated from the interaction that perceiving subjects bring to their disclosure."[21] Rather, it is with *paradigms* or *practices* (injunctions, exemplars) that these various modes of knowing (physical, mental, contemplative) are *enacted* by the subject so that certain worldviews or worldspaces (magical, mythic, rational, vision-logic, etc.) are brought forth, illumined, and disclosed, including the transpersonal domains (psychic, subtle, causal, nondual).

In this case, Wilber seems to be asserting that the traditional means of postulating metaphysical realities is an error that must be addressed by any integral attempt of resurrecting transpersonal and spiritual worldviews in a postmodern world. His current position suggests it's possible with an AQAL or integral approach to unite ancient and modern knowledge with this type of "Integral Post-Metaphysics" and its pragmatic corollary of an "Integral Methodological Pluralism." In this way, as he now explains, "All of those [premodern] spiritual worldviews (from shamanism to Plotinus to Padmasambhava to Aurobindo) can be reanimated and utilized within a broader, non-metaphysical AQAL Matrix, which can generate the same rainbow of existence but without their profound wisdom succumbing to the devastating attacks of modern and postmodern currents."[22] For Wilber, therefore, sitting on a lotus of postmodern research, this contemporary Manjushri swings his sword of insight to reanimate and protect the Rainbow of Existence (or the Great Nest of Being and Knowing) from the critical blows fired by modern critiques and postmodern deconstructions. Yet by doing it this AQAL way, he also makes a compassionate but strong break with the premodern religious models as well. This is in fact a *revolutionary* and thoroughly *radical* gesture ("radical" meaning "root" or "fundamental"), thus it makes it more difficult to understand and "grok" exactly where Wilber's at, but on the other hand it also makes perfect sense within an integral, all-inclusionary worldview, especially one that's ultimately grounded in nondual Spirit.

As a result, with a clear and incisive Integral Post-Metaphysics as a crucial component in his overall AQAL Metatheory, Wilber cannot justifiably endorse any traditional version of the Great Nest of Being as being composed of *pregiven* levels or a priori structures supporting a preexisting ontological reality, including with the inner transpersonal domains. Instead, Wilber proposes an AQAL Matrix with interiors and exteriors and quadrants "all the way down, all the way up," with correlates running throughout the entire spectrum on every level and in every quadrant. This understanding involves evolutionary emergents and novel creative potentials that are unfolding with the already developing "evolutionary grooves" or the "kosmic karma" of past developments. Consequently, Wilber has taken a thoroughly dynamic and much stronger evolutionary position than most of his contemporary post-modern theorists; therefore he summed up his Phase-5 concerns in *Integral Psychology* (2000):

> The higher levels in the Great Nest are *potentials*, not absolute givens. The lower levels—matter, body, mind—have already emerged on a large scale, so they already exist full-fledged in this manifest world. But the higher structures—psychic, subtle, causal—are not yet consciously manifest on a collective scale; they remain, for most people, potentials of the human bodymind, not fully actualized realities. What the Great Nest represents, in my opinion, is most basically a great *morphogenetic field* or *developmental space*— stretching from matter to mind to spirit—in which various potentials unfold into actuality. Although for convenience I will often speak of the higher levels as if they were simply given, they are in many ways still plastic, still open to being formed as more and more people coevolve into them (which is why, as I said, the basic structures are more like Kosmic habits than pregiven molds). As these higher potentials become actualized, they will be given more form and content, and thus increasingly become everyday realities. Until then, they are, in part, great and grand potentials, which nonetheless still exert an undeniable attraction, still are present in many profound ways, still can be directly realized by higher growth and development, and still show a great deal of similarity wherever they appear.[23]

Since Wilber sees that the pregiven ontological structures or levels in the traditional Great Chain of Spirit have become a constant confusion among critics and students alike, he's been moved to take a stronger critical stance toward them. Nonetheless, it's a real compassion that compels him to critically swing his sword of wisdom through the subtle fallacies surrounding such benign yet traditional models of reality, even those as beautiful as a universal *philosophia perennis,* yet still, doing so in a way that scientifically supports authentic spirituality and the unfolding disclosures (or truths) found in the transpersonal domains of existence. Therefore, regardless if critics and students agree, or necessarily understand, the importance of Wilber's current Phase-5 move to checkmate the Perennial Philosophy or not, he's still off in this radical direction of generating an "Integral Post-Metaphysics reconstruction of the spiritual traditions."[24] Although his new Phase-5 writings will clarify the situation further, it's still easy to see why the deeply revolutionary nature of this Integral Post-Metaphysics makes it doubly difficult to understand exactly where Wilber's at.

Nevertheless, in truly understanding "where Wilber's at," we must continue emphasizing that Ken Wilber is *not* presenting an updated version of the traditional premodern spiritual point-of-view, including that of an apparent "metaphysics," or even a continuation of what's often been tagged the "Perennial Philosophy." Instead, it's much more accurate to see this Integral Vision as being a third millennium "update" of the basic "Bliss-Void-Emptiness" *(sunyata)* teachings of Enlightenment, although this time it's a nondual spiritual worldview appearing in a fully contemporary manner. This is because, like all nondual mystics, whether East or West, North or South, Wilber most fundamentally stands by the claim that Ultimate Truth can never be summarized or stated, *only directly realized*—and so, he insists, please be our guest. Or, as one modern Siddha of the Great Tradition put it: "The truth is revealed, not published."[25]

Even in the face of this absolute truth, the discussion of all relative phenomena and their symbolic "Theories of Everything" will continue to go on, be spoken about, and written down, as it thankfully should, since they provide useful maps for those of us who will benefit from their revealed teaching and wisdom. But with Wilber, let there be no mistake, his integral perspective maintains our maps and models must now include the recently discovered knowledge of the postmodern mind as well as all the branches of modern science, *in addition* to the premodern wisdom of traditional spirituality and religion. Now, it's hard to disagree with that, isn't it? Thus, I'll venture to suggest next, it's probably only some type of "post-postmodern" bodhisattva who could pull off that type of integral embrace, a consideration to which we'll now turn.

CHAPTER SIX

Manjushri with a ThinkPad:
"Spirit Exists"

When I am not an object, I am God. When I seek an object, I cease
to be God, and that catastrophe can never be corrected by more
searching for more objects. Rather, I can only rest as the Witness,
which is already free of objects, free of time, and free of searching.
When I am not an object, I am Spirit. When I rest as the free and
formless Witness, I am with God right now, in this timeless and
endless moment. I taste infinity and am drenched with fullness, precisely because I no longer seek, but simply rest as what I AM.

—Ken Wilber, *The Eye of Spirit* (1997)

SINCE KEN WILBER'S INTEGRAL VISION AND THE ESOTERIC TRADITION
of Buddhism recognize Enlightenment or God-Realization as the purpose
of human existence, then it can be useful, instructive, and somewhat entertaining to view some of the similarities between them. In addition, since
Wilber's principal spiritual practice has generally been Buddhist for over
three decades (he began with Zen), then it's somewhat appropriate to view

him within that lineage, as I have done here in this chapter. Nevertheless, while it may be instructive to use Buddhist models and analogies to more colorfully paint in the full spectrum and enlightened scope of Wilber's integral picture, it's still a limited venture. This limitation stems from the fact that, as we just saw, this Integral Vision is a "post-postmodern" *reconstruction* based on an AQAL or "all-quadrants, all-levels" approach to everything, not very Buddhist-sounding at all. In a certain sense then, it's really not accurate to readapt traditional models or premodern pictures of reality as though they can be equated with Wilber's integral scheme, especially with his *Integral Post-Metaphysics*, which is definitely not very Buddhist. Nonetheless, the similarities and intersections with Buddhism, and mysticism in general, seem too important to pass up.

Instead, out of historical necessity during the dawn of the third millennium, the Integral Vision of Ken Wilber intends to embrace the full scope of human history with all of its developmental stages and discoveries, including the *premodern* (or traditional) and *modern* and *postmodern* worldviews (see chapter 4). Consequently, he's had to critically claim that no matter how "spiritual" or somewhat useful the traditional views are, even the Buddhist's, they still have some serious inadequacies that in our times must be adequately addressed (see previous chapter). An Integral Approach, therefore, is out to unite and integrate *the best* from the premodern traditional past with *the best* of the modern/postmodern present, thus marrying their precious truths yet while simultaneously and carefully ejecting their limitations and absolutisms. With these disclaimers aside, let's explore some of Wilber's enlightened visions about the ultimate nature of our unnamable reality, which does indeed lie at the heart of his work.

Divine Ground & Goal: "Spirit Exists"

Perhaps the simplest statement of where Wilber's ultimately at is best summarized with the succinct phrase: "Spirit exists." This means, in other words, that "God exists" or "God is real." The simplicity of this phrase can be garnered from much of Wilber's writings, yet this particular version was drawn from an unpublished manuscript (1987): "The essence of my work is: God, or the absolute Spirit, exists—and can be proven—and there is a ladder [Great Nest of Spirit] that reaches to that summit, a ladder that you can be shown how to climb, a ladder that leads from time to eternity, and from death to immortality. And all philosophy and psychology swings into a remarkable synthesis around that ladder [the Kosmic Mandala]."[1] As a result, whatever else Ken Wilber's integral theories may offer, they most fundamentally are *spiritual* in nature simply because they're about Spirit (Emptiness), the Great Nest of Spirit (consciousness-reality), and Spirit-in-action (evolution). Nonetheless, Wilber has always been acutely aware that the best any cognitive theory (or *theoria*) can do is *point to* the higher transpersonal or spiritual dimensions, or best yet, to encourage injunctive practices (or *praxis*) so a person can see for oneself (or *gnosis*). Only authentic methods of inquiry and the requisite unfolding stages of development will disclose, and then make enduring, the transpersonal truths of Spirit. Put another way, as we've already pointed out, this makes Wilber not only an integral theorist and a profound philosopher, but a flaming mystic as well.

Although born a Westerner in the state of Oklahoma, located in the middle of the United States, Wilber's adult life philosophy has always been more closely aligned with Eastern mysticism, and that's only partly because he's been a practicing Buddhist for over three decades now. As he once explained in one of his more personal books, the autobiographical *Grace and Grit* (1991): "I would not especially call myself a Buddhist; I have too many affinities with Vedanta Hinduism and Christian mysticism, among many others. But one has to choose a particular path if one is to actually *practice,* and my path has been Buddhist."[2] A serious practitioner who also universally embraces (and transcends) all paths of wisdom is the gateway to an Integral Vision.

Beyond Buddhism, as we saw earlier, Wilber shares a loose but deep affinity with the esoteric (or "inner") teachings of what's been called the "Perennial Philosophy" (originally named by the likes of Steuco, Leibniz, and Aldous Huxley). Alan Watts, for one, defined the Perennial Philosophy as "a single philosophical consensus of universal extent [that] has been held by men and women who report the same insights and teach the same essential doctrine whether living today or six thousand years ago, whether from New Mexico in the Far West or from Japan in the Far East."[3] Embracing this type of appreciation for all cultures and forms of spirituality, whatever one's path, is exactly the comprehensive scope of investigation needed and expected in today's global times. This is especially true since people now have access to this worldwide "Great Tradition"[4] or the "Great Wisdom Tradition" of humankind, which is, as a living human being, our inherited birthright to all the world's cultures and religions. The Perennial Philosophy, in this case, doesn't belong to any one religion, for it's a reoccurring philosophy common to many religious systems. The Perennial Philosophy, however (as we saw in the previous chapter), is *not* where Wilber's at.

With the current phase of Wilber's integral work (Phases-4/5), particularly with its *Integral Post-Metaphysics*, he has found it necessary to critique the notion of a "perennial" philosophy, especially as it has been presented by traditionalist scholars. For instance, as he recently pointed out in a Phase-5 writing (2003): "We can account for *existing* stable structures (from bacteria to ecosystems to levels of consciousness) without resorting to pregiven archetypes, structures, or independently existing ontological levels—that is, we can begin to replace metaphysical speculation with reconstructive inquiry."[5] Nonetheless, the Perennial Philosophy is a universal fountain of wisdom that Wilber defends as a valuable teaching tool, since it reaffirms from a variety of respected sources the validity of the simple statement: "Spirit exists." However, according to Wilber, since this wisdom gives the appearance of being "perennial" and universal, then it's also important not to only associate it with the traditional metaphysical views upheld by the premodern world, which brings with it certain inherent limitations (see previous chapter).

Of course, "Spirit exists" or "God is real" is a statement that's vigorously denied by the philosophical trends of modern science and the postmodern mind, yet still, the integral approach can embrace both positions (see Chapter 4). Nevertheless, since science and the Western modern mind basically believe "God is dead" (echoing the claim of Nietzsche), or it's just your *interpretation* (postmodernism), then, for Wilber, it's probably best *not* to interpret God in conventional Western terms, such as being a Creator God, or one who is "above" and separated from His Creation. Consequently, Wilber's views about God, the Ultimate Reality, or the Absolute are closer to those maintained by mysticism in general, and specifically by Eastern philosophies, particularly Buddhism and Advaita Vedanta (the nondual sect of Hinduism). These philosophies, for one, speak of an ineffable reality that's *transcendent* (or exceeding all limits) while also being totally *immanent* (or all-pervading), another paradoxical claim that's perpetuated by the world's mystics, whether East or West (North or South).

Wilber too has long recognized this paradoxical nature of nondualism throughout his writings (in every phase), thus he often pictures "nondual

Spirit" (by whatever name) as being the "Ground" (or *immanent* aspect) and the "Goal" (or *transcendent* aspect) of the evolutionary "Great Chain of Being." The fact that nondual Spirit is both an *immanence* (Goddess, Ground, Source, the "wood of the ladder") and a *transcendence* (God, Goal, Summit, the "highest rung on the ladder"), brings him to often repeat this metaphorical formula: "Spirit is the summit of being, the highest rung on the ladder of evolution. But it is also true that Spirit is *the wood out of which the entire ladder and all its rungs are made*. Spirit is the suchness, the isness, the essence of each and every thing that exists."[6] In this case, since "Spirit is both the Goal and the Ground of the entire sequence,"[7] then Wilber simply qualifies this seemingly contradictory position as "the most *notorious paradox* in the perennial philosophy."[8] But still, he also claims that any genuine "metatheory" would have to include *this fact* as well; thus he pointed out years ago in *Eye to Eye* (1983): "If spirit is completely *transcendent*, it is also *completely* immanent. I am firmly convinced that if a new and comprehensive paradigm is ever to emerge, that paradox will be its heart"[9]—with Wilber's Integral Vision, this task has been accomplished without compromise.

Only God: Goddess & Godhead

Since the transcendent Absolute Reality is actually One ("not two"), then all names or images (or gender types) are inadequate, since the Divine is immanently part and parcel of all that exists and will ever exist (as Ground) while being totally transcendent of any phenomenal manifestation (as Goal). Mystics therefore don't see Ultimate Reality as being a Great Object, or a Great Parent figure, but rather as being the "suchness" and "isness" of the entire created universe; the warp and woof of all possibilities in all possible universes; the "Truth" behind all partial truths and illusory falsehoods. In this case, "God" or "Spirit" is also the True Self of every individual, since we exist within the radiant embrace of this Ultimate radiant Oneness.

This sacred message has also been at the heart of Wilber's theories from the very beginning, as he eloquently explained in *Up from Eden* (1981): "The essence of the perennial philosophy can be put simply: it is true that there is some sort of Infinite, some type of Godhead, but it cannot properly be conceived as a colossal Being, a great Daddy, or a big Creator set apart from its creations, from things and events and human beings themselves. Rather, it is best conceived (metaphorically) as the ground or suchness or condition of all things and events. It is not a Big Thing set apart from finite things, but rather the reality or suchness or ground of all things…. The Absolute is not Other, but, so to speak, is sewn through the fabric of all that is."[10] Part and parcel of all that is, we too, are That.

For Wilber and the Perennial Philosophy (and the wisdom traditions in general) then, this Absolute Reality doesn't involve only a personal "God" (or Final-God), which is sometimes called "God the Father," as it's named in the West (although it *does* involve That, too). Real God is the transcendent-immanent truth of all reality that cannot be defined, named, or quantified, which is why, for example, Christian theology uses the term "Godhead," or what the great medieval theologian Meister Eckhart (1260–1327) defined as "God beyond God."[11] Fortunately, Wilber's scholarship has become one of the modern world's clearest champions in distinguishing these types of subtle distinctions, such as he did decades ago when he clarified "there is a radical difference between the mental father figure and the Transcendent God or Godhead."[12] In this case, Wilber distinguishes between "the Paternal Image of cultural authority" (whether the basic Father Image or Great Mother) and what's actually being pointed to as *real God*, or "God beyond God." These are truths that are clearly recognized and differentiated throughout the "theories" of Ken Wilber's Integral Vision.

By following the unfolding stages/structures in the spectrum of consciousness evolution *(psychic, subtle, causal, nondual),* Wilber is able to identify a "hierarchy of religious experiences," or the various degrees of mysticism *(nature, deity, formless, nondual)* with an unprecedented precision. Early on, Wilber had become explicitly clear about the progressive unfoldment of divine realization, as he is here in *The Atman Project* (1980): "And so: at the center of the self was shown to be Archetype [of *nature mysticism*]; and as the center of Archetype was shown to be final-God [of *deity mysticism*]; and as the center of final-God was shown to be Formlessness [of *formless mysticism*]—so the center of Formlessness is shown to be not other than the entire world of Form [or *nondual mysticism*]."[13] We'll review further explanations as we proceed, or if you thoroughly read any of Wilber's books (no matter which phase), it is a persistent realization embodied in his "theoretical" works, which themselves are based on following the actual evidence contained in the reports of mystics (as well as his own experiences).

As a result, any true integral embrace of the Totality of Reality would naturally include the feminine face of the Divine as well, or the "Goddess," as being a valid and valuable aspect of reality and human interpretation. For example, in *Up from Eden* (1981), Wilber distinguishes between two commonly perceived notions of the feminine "face" of Spirit, such as with the "Great Mother," which is associated with prepersonal awareness where she is "a simple biological nourisher and fertility token, magically blown up to cosmic proportions," thus often demanding blood sacrifices, and the "Great Goddess," which is the transpersonal or higher-order understanding defined as the "subtle Oneness of actual Transcendence, representative of true Divinity."[14] These are subtle distinctions and clarifications that other scholars of religious studies have generally overlooked, especially since they're usually schooled in traditional patriarchal prejudices. Either that or they haven't acquired the adequate development (via authentic spiritual practices) to more fully appreciate these transpersonal realities (indeed, this is one of the grave limitations of the modern scholastic mind). In this case it's crucial to *include* these multiple types of transpersonal (and sacred) understandings in any genuine integral theory, as you'll find ample evidence in his collected works, since this too is the heart of where Wilber's at.

Two Modes of Truth: Dualistic & Nondual

Since Ken Wilber's first book, *The Spectrum of Consciousness* (1977), he has pointed toward "Two Modes of Knowing": (1) Dualistic/symbolic mode of knowing—"variously termed symbolic, or map, or inferential, or *dualistic knowledge*"; this is the province of philosophy, science, exoteric religion, and the human mind (ego-self); (2) Nondual mode of knowing—"called intimate, or direct, or *nondual knowledge*"; this is the province of mysticism (or self-transcendence), esoteric religion, Enlightenment, and God (Absolute Spirit). Importantly, Wilber continues, "These two modes of knowing are universal, that is to say, they have been recognized in one form or another at various times and places throughout humankind's history, from Taoism to William James, from Vedanta to Alfred North Whitehead, from Zen to Christian theology."[15] Whatever else can be said, Ken Wilber's Integral Vision, although in a post-postmodern form, is most closely aligned with the "tradition" of nondual mysticism, which, as the mystics claim, is only known through the "ultimate state of consciousness" or nondual Enlightenment (whether temporary or permanent).

The Nondual Traditions naturally rely on the "nondual mode of knowing" to reveal the "real territory," whereas the dualistic modes of knowing reveal "the map" and the symbolic representations of reality. With many similar views scattered throughout the great wisdom traditions, this view is similar to the Buddhist's "two truths doctrine," which differentiates between "Absolute Truth" (nondualism), known only via the nondual mode of knowing (or Enlightenment), and the "relative truths," which are uncovered with the symbolic and dualistic modes of knowing. With this awareness, the AQAL Metatheory is only attempting to integrate or weave together the "correct but partial" (or relative) truths into a more efficient model or map of the Kosmos. Thus it's not saddled with disclosing the Ultimate Truth itself, which can only be pointed to, at best, with any modeling system (or even "mandalic maps"). This way it's much easier to hold the maps more lightly, thus seeing them more freely as God's Play in the evolution of self and Kosmos, and not to be mistaken for truth itself.

Nondual Mystery: Sunyata Emptiness

The paradoxes of nondual Spirit have often prompted mystics the world over to speak about absolute reality as being simply the "Mystery," for it cannot be named, captured, contained, quantified, or measured. In truth, the mystics say, "It" is not an Object among other objects, or even One among Many, for it is "One without a second."[16] This is why Wilber relies on the "Nondual Traditions" of mysticism, because they universally promote the absolute highest and deepest (or ultimate) level of consciousness, which he calls *nondual mysticism*. Thus he points out on the first page to the last chapter of *The Eye of Spirit* (1997): "The realization of the Nondual traditions is uncompromising: there is only Spirit, there is only God, there is only Emptiness in all its radiant wonder. All the good and all the evil, the very best and the very worst, the upright and the degenerate—each and all are radically perfect manifestations of Spirit precisely as they are. There is nothing but God, nothing but the Goddess, nothing but Spirit in all directions, and not a grain of sand, nor a speck of dust, is more or less Spirit than any other.... And this simple recognition of an *already present* Spirit is the task, as it were, of the great Nondual traditions."[17] In other words, the world/Kosmos (and us) is part of God/dess, but the Godhead totally transcends the sum total of all the possible universes, and we (the world/Kosmos) are That.

To help explain the slippery paradox of nondualism, Wilber often turns to one of his all-time favorite enlightened spiritual masters, if not his most beloved, the illustrious twentieth-century sage from modern India, Sri Ramana Maharshi (1879–1950), who is undoubtedly one of the most realized souls to ever walk this Earth. Thus the integral philosopher was deeply honored to write the foreword to the compilation book, *Talks with Ramana Maharshi* (2000), where Wilber even claimed it's the one book he would want if stranded on a desert island. Wilber borrows a phrase from Beloved Ramana, which also echoes the influential eighth-century Vedanta master Shankara (788–820), who's also pointing to the heart of the Upanishads (composed circa, 800–400 B.C.E.), to create a concise formula that sums up the nondual message of Enlightenment:

> The world is illusory;
> God alone is real;
> God is the world.

Wilber's nondual stance effectively uses this enlightened expression as a way to point to the paradoxical realization of Nondual Mysticism by more precisely explaining this Enlightened consciousness (if you hear it correctly):

- **The world is illusory**—"means you are not any object at all—nothing that can be seen is ultimately real. You are *neti, neti,* not this, not that….

- **God alone is real**—the Self (unqualifiable Brahman-Atman [or God]) alone is real—the pure Witness, the timeless Unborn, the formless Seer, the radical I-I, radiant Emptiness—is what is real and all that is real. It is your condition, your nature, your essence, your present and your future, your desire and your destiny, and yet it is always ever-present as pure Presence, the alone that is Alone.

- **God is the world**—Emptiness and Form are not-two. *After* you realize that the manifest world is illusory, and *after* you realize that God alone is real, *then* can you see that the absolute and the relative are not-two or nondual… The entire world of Form exists nowhere but in your own present Formless Awareness."[18]

This too is the "central core" of Buddhism, to which Wilber also mines for examples of nondual philosophy, such as from the famous and beautiful *Heart Sutra*, one of the most revered and shortest scriptures (or *sutras*) in the Buddhist canon. Its name means "heartpiece of the *Prajna-paramita-sutra*," the principal teachings of Mahayana Buddhism, for this sutra, we are told, "formulates in a particularly clear and concise way the teaching of *sunyata* (Emptiness), the immediate experience of which is sought by Zen [and Buddhist] practitioners."[19] In less than a page, the *Heart Sutra* summarily chants: "Form is Emptiness, Emptiness is Form." The integral pandit points to this paradoxical position once again in *One Taste* (1999): "The entire world of Form is arising in your own Formless awareness right now. In other words, Emptiness and Form are not-two. They are both One Taste in this moment."[20] Indeed, he's been a master of clarifying this slippery nondual realization for some time, as he shows in this wonderful passage alluding to the *Heart Sutra* from *The Atman Project* (1980):

> "Form is not other than Void, Void is not other than Form," says the most famous Buddhist Sutra (called the 'Heart Sutra'). At that point, the extraordinary and the ordinary, the supernatural and mundane, are precisely one and the same.... This is the radically perfect integration of all prior levels—gross, subtle, and causal, which, now of themselves so, continue to arise moment to moment in an iridescent play of mutual interpenetration.... whereupon Consciousness as Such is released in Perfect Transcendence, which is not a transcendence from the world but a final transcendence as the World. Consciousness henceforth *operates,* not on the world, but only as the entire World Process, integrating and interpenetrating all levels, realms, and planes, high or low, sacred or profane."[21]

Again, the integral pandit brings our attention to this important equation in *Integral Psychology* (2000): "Consciousness is always 'transcend and include' and having completely *transcended* the world of Form, consciousness awakens to a radical *embrace* of all form: 'That which is Form is not other than Emptiness, that which is Emptiness is not other than Form,' says the *Heart Sutra,* in what is perhaps the most famous formula for this eternal, sacred equation. For pure Spirit (Emptiness) and the entire manifest world (Form) have become one eternal embrace."[22] Emptiness, in this case, is *real*

God for it is "empty" of human definitions or classifications. This too applies to Wilber's "Theory of Everything," for it is deeply reflected and repeated in every one of his books, and thus is the foundation of each "phase" of his career (Wilber/Phases 1–5). This is also the message or realization that's confirmed by the esoteric or inner teachings of the world's major religions, and also, by your own psychic development and consciousness evolution.

Consequently, Wilber often follows the example of Advaita Vedanta (from Hinduism) and Mahayana Buddhism, as well as the deeper esoteric teachings from Christianity, Islam, and Judaism, by agreeing that Divine Reality is actually "Formless," "Void," or "Emptiness" (*sunyata* in Buddhism). Because the Ultimate is absolutely Free, Infinite, and Eternal, then Mahayana Buddhists, especially Nagarjuna (ca. 2nd/3rd century), insists that the best way to convey the Absolute is *"neti, neti"* (meaning "not this, not that"), for it's truly "empty" of all human conceptions. Yet, paradoxically, it's also an Absolute Fullness, thus it's sometimes referred to as being "Radiant Emptiness," or "Bliss-Void-Emptiness," or "One Taste," or the "Superconscious All," or the "Divine Domain," or the "Clear Light of Bliss," all terms periodically used by Wilber to name the unnamable. However, this is not the void of nihilism, or a blank nothingness, as Wilber adeptly reminds us throughout his writings, exemplified by this passage in *Up from Eden* (1981): "According to Buddhism—actually, to the perennial philosophy in general—the ultimate nature of reality is *sunyata*, which is usually translated as 'voidness,' 'emptiness,' or 'nothingness.' But sunyata does *not* mean blankness or vacant absence. The void does not mean featureless, but seamless—'the seamless coat of the universe,' as Whitehead would have it…. This holds, obviously, for men and women as well. The ultimate psychology is a psychology of ultimate Wholeness, or the superconscious All."[23] Most simply stated (and it cannot be fully stated), the Absolute just *is*—"Spirit exists."

These wisdom traditions of humankind, as always, are only *pointing to* the same Divine Truth and Reality, yet they still use words as "signifiers" to indicate the various "referents" that are being referred to and indicated by with the gift of language. According to Wilber, these technical topics of language can be accounted for with an authentic mysticism, thus he humorously but seriously points out that "Zen masters talk about Enlightenment all the time!" This involves Wilber's "integral semiotics" (which incorporates the "linguistic turn" of postmodernism begun by Ferdinand de Saussure), and the paradoxical nature of language, which have recently been discussed in detail.[24] Nonetheless, whatever words are used, it is absolutely crucial to include "Emptiness" (or the divine reality of *sunyata*) in any so-called integral theory, which is exactly what this American Buddhist has done with his metatheory of "everything."

Enlightenment: One Taste ("I AM" Always Already)

Although the Absolute Truth is only truly known through the nondual mode of knowing, then this still means it can indeed be known and *realized!* This is the complete transcendence of all dualistic and symbolic knowledge, including, most importantly, the "Primal Dualism" between subject (self) and object (reality). Importantly, this divine disclosure usually relies on specific practices or exercises (such as meditation and self-inquiry) in order to reveal this transpersonal truth and reality. With a nondual but factual understanding of the Divine (or God), then the mystics of the Perennial Philosophy (and Wilber) unanimously claim that the *purpose of human life* is to personally and directly *discover* or *realize* the real truth of the Absolute Reality for oneself.

The great discovery of one's true nature as being Divine or God is traditionally known as Enlightenment, God-Realization, Buddhahood, liberation, *gnosis, moksha, bodhi, wu, satori, prajna, sahaj samadhi,* and so forth; it is the conscious recognition of our ultimate Wholeness and Divinity, the rediscovery of our "own true nature," as Zen says. According to the world's mystics, this occurs with "ego death," or when the subject or separate-self sense is totally transcended or "dies," and thus all separation dissolves in realizing the One that is "always already the case." Then one realizes "what every individual *is,* before he/she is anything else," as Wilber once noted, "Every conscious being, precisely as he or she is, is a perfect embodiment and expression of the Ultimate."[25] In our essence, we are all already liberated and completely free, full of pure love, absolute Happiness, infinite and eternal, etc.—totally indescribable, in other words, but certainly a good thing (or what Plato might call the Good, the True, and the Beautiful).

Once again, the integral philosopher succinctly emphasizes this point in the opening pages of *Up from Eden* (1981): "According to the perennial philosophy, this 'discovery of Wholeness,' the removal of the optical delusion of separateness, is not merely a belief—it is not a dogma one accepts on mere faith. For if the Ultimate is indeed a real integral Wholeness, if it is equally part and parcel of all that is, then it is also completely present in men and women. And, unlike rocks, plants, or animals, human beings—because they are *conscious*—can potentially discover this Wholeness. They can, as it were, awaken to the Ultimate. Not believe in it, but discover it."[26] The importance of *consciously* realizing this truth (through disciplined spiritual *practices*) cannot be overestimated, for it is the heart of mysticism itself. This is the condition Wilber points to when the "eye of contemplation," or the "Eye of Spirit," is fully opened and awake in the natural human condition, such as with *sahaj samadhi,* which means "innate," "spontaneous," or more literally (in Sanskrit) "together born," thus it's sometimes referred to as the enlightened condition of "open eyes" (or whole-body Enlightenment). This understanding is paradoxically "beyond" the causal Emptiness or the Void where the last stand of the Witness has been transcended so there is Only God, and God Only, since reality is *always already* a nondual or indivisible Oneness.

Naturally, Wilber has provided excellent descriptions of this enlightened awareness, such as in this brief passage from *The Atman Project* (1980): "Passing through *nirvikalpa samadhi* [causal Formlessness], Consciousness totally awakens as its Original Condition and Suchness *(tathata),* which is, at the same time, the condition and suchness of all that is, gross, subtle, or causal. That which witnesses, and that which is witnessed, are only one and the same. The entire World Process then arises, moment to moment, as one's own Being, outside of which, and prior to which, nothing exists. That Being is totally beyond and prior to anything that arises, and yet no part of that Being is other than what arises."[27] In other words, the form of the world/Kosmos arises as the Formlessness of one's own True Being or nondual divine nature.

This "rediscovery" of our true condition is why mystics the world over have reaffirmed what the wise sages of ancient India declared millennia ago: *"Tat tvam asi,"* which means "Thou Art That," or "You are God." Our innate divinity, therefore, can be summarized with the declaration "I AM," since the essence of your *ever-present consciousness* is God or the Divine Condition itself. This statement is scattered throughout world history, but one famous Western example is when Yahweh (of the Old Testament) declared "I AM" at the burning bush when Moses asked what is God's name. Wilber points to this same realization in *The Eye of Spirit* (1997): "Both God and I are one in the ever-present Witness, which is the nature of intrinsic Spirit itself, which is exactly what I am in the state of my I AMNESS. When I am not an object, I am God. (And every I in the entire Kosmos can say that truth-fully.)"[28] It's up to each and every soul to *know* this truth beyond the limitations and self-centered activities of the ego-I (or self). Yet, such absolute awakening ultimately entails the difficult practice of transformative consciousness evolution (involving self-development and self-transcendence) and, importantly, divine grace.

As is to be expected, Wilber has always been very clear in explaining that this "ultimate state of consciousness" is really not a "state," per se, but it is ever-present awareness, thus he clarified in *The Atman Project* (1980): "This is not itself a state apart from other states; it is not an altered state; it is not a special state—it is rather the suchness of all states."[29] In this case, "Always Already" is another phrase the integral philosopher uses to indicate this ever-present divine condition of consciousness, thus he artfully articulated this point in his popular second book *No Boundary* (1979): "Since unity consciousness [nondual awareness] is of the timeless moment, it is entirely present now. And obviously, there is no way to reach now. There is no way to *arrive* at that which already is."[30] In fact, Wilber usually closes his mentally engaging books detailing complex philosophy with another mystical consideration pointing to our "always already" divine consciousness and condition.[31] Consequently, he reaffirms the teachings of the enlightened mystics who teach that this awakening is more like a "re-discovery," or a "re-membering," a re-cognition of what is *always already* the case, i.e., that you *are* God, than an acquisition gained by mental acuity. As we'll continue to see, Wilber displays impeccable scholarship presented with immaculate prose supporting these enlightened expressions, especially since his own understanding is founded in personal practice and direct experiences, not just theoretical estimations.

Ken's Kensho: *Wilber/Phase-1 to Wilber/Phase-2*

From the very beginning of Ken Wilber's career (in the 1970s), his theoretical ideas have been embodied in and arise from his own personal spiritual practices, which have included numerous disciplines, such as meditation, psychotherapy, and somatic bodywork (including healthy eating and exercise).[32] After years of *"engaging the injunction"* (originally practicing Zen and zazen under well-known Zen masters), and after meditating for over an hour or more every day (with a day-long every week), the aspiring student finally began to discover what the mystical teachings had been talking about in their spiritual literature and sacred texts. These included, for Wilber, experiences of cosmic consciousness (or *nature mysticism*), and "a tour of the subtle realms" or the subtle lights, sounds, and archetypal forms (or *deity mysticism*).[33] Then, in the late 1970s, these experiences were gracefully released with the transcendence of all experiences (or *formless mysticism*), which is when the young man found out: "The real awakening is the dissolution of the Witness itself, and not a change of state in that which is witnessed."[34] In Zen Buddhism, this "non-experience" of "ego-death" is known as *satori* or *kensho* (Japanese, literally, for "directly seeing one's true nature"), which is a temporary experience of Enlightenment (or God-Realization), the indescribable heart of *nondual mysticism*.

At a Zen meditation retreat taking place on Pawnee sacred ground in the late seventies, when Wilber was around thirty years old, his Zen master Katagiri Roshi instructed him by saying: "The Witness is the last stand of the ego." Soon thereafter Wilber realized, as recounted in an autobiographical essay (1982): "There was no subject anywhere in the universe; there was no object anywhere in the universe; there was only the universe. Everything was arising moment to moment, and it was arising in me and as me; yet there was no me.... This radically open, undefended, and perfectly *nondual state* was both incredibly and profoundly ordinary, so extraordinarily ordinary that it did not even register. There was nobody there to comprehend it, until I fell *out* of it. (I guess about three hours later)."[35] The sense of being a separate self (or Ken) had "died," or was totally transcended (although this was only a temporary "taste" of enlightenment and not permanent enlightenment itself).

Such an indelible and sacred revelation of his own divinity, and the divine nature of the universe, let alone the culmination of all Wilber had been studying in the great wisdom traditions, would only further serve to inform and clarify his theoretical orientations and integral studies. As one consequence, he tells us soon thereafter (1982): "I became profoundly suspicious of any transpersonalist who spoke of the highest states as 'experiential realities,' even as I had tended to do in *The Spectrum of Consciousness*."[36] Importantly, Ken's *kensho* (or "small *satori*") confirmed the correctness of the huge intellectual changes that were underway in his major philosophical shift from Wilber/Phase-1 (or the Romantic "recaptured-goodness" model) to Wilber/Phase-2 (or the evolutionary "growth-to-goodness" model). In support of this move, the young philosopher found that his brief *satori* helped resolve the vast intellectual quagmire he was soon embroiled in after his first "spectrum of consciousness" writings had been published to high acclaim. In the end, this American Buddhist has incorporated these divine understandings into his integral "Theory of Every-thing" by fully realizing that it is really "No-thing."

A Western Vedanta American Buddhist

In a manner similar to Nagarjuna, the second-century Buddhist master of negation—*neti, neti* ("not this, not that")—Wilber too never defines or categorizes the "ultimate state of consciousness" or the realization of Enlightenment. Rather he only confirms its *always already* inherent nature and that ultimately it cannot be stated or gained, but *only realized* in the *present moment* (for that's all there really *is*). When this realization (or Enlightenment) finally dawns on any sentient being, whether temporarily *(satori),* or when it becomes more permanently stabilized through adequate development *(sahaj samadhi),* then we find that the nondual paradox of Divine Spirit is indeed our ever-present condition and awareness.

This bald American Buddhist philosopher, like the Buddhist *Heart Sutra,* chants over and over: "Emptiness is form, form is Emptiness," therefore, he is moved to conclude: "[This is] the standard message of all Nondual schools: *transcend* absolutely every single thing in the Kosmos, *embrace* absolutely every single thing in the Kosmos—with choiceless compassion or love."[37] By updating the nondual wisdom in a form that's applicable for the modern West, Wilber is helping to reignite a movement (especially in transpersonal psychology and its tributaries) that fully acknowledges and includes the psychological significance of this nondual realization (Enlightenment). With such pure and clear communications, a reader will often find that Wilber becomes like a close friend or wise teacher, in the truest sense, for he gives us a larger vision of reality that inspires us to grow and develop and evolve, in an integral fashion, to our own higher and highest potentials.

Since the work of Ken Wilber is appropriately aligned with the lineage of the nondual traditions, then in his recent Phase-4 books he introduces the term "Western Vedanta"[38] to account for the fact that there has always been a stream of nondual currents running through Western philosophers. In an enlightening clarification of Western history, Wilber identifies some of these philosophers who have emphasized the ever-present awareness of consciousness itself, although historically they are usually suppressed and persecuted by traditional religious systems, especially the Christian Church (a group of "frustrated Ascenders"). For example, the pandit points to the Neoplatonic tradition (extending from the masterful Plotinus) in the West (which has had profound influence in Arabia) as being a representative of this "Nondual revolution," as he mentions in *One Taste* (1999): "In the West, the great Neoplatonic tradition would carry [the Nondual revolution] bravely forward, but it was everywhere resisted by the Church, which had officially pledged allegiance to the Ascending path, for my kingdom is not of this world, and render unto Caesar…. But for those with eyes to see and soul to hear, the Neoplatonic current blazed a trail of Nonduality across the first and second millennia. When it was realized that the Great Nest actually unfolded or *developed* in time, the Neoplatonic tradition directly fueled the great Idealist vision of Fichte, Schelling, and Hegel."[39] Indeed, these are some of the deep currents running through Wilber's Integral Vision as well.

For Wilber, these Western thinkers still have great intellectual potency and valuable gifts to offer all of humanity, whether Eastern or Western. In fact, since "it takes one to know one," then he further explains in *The Eye of Spirit* (1997): "Rare is the philosopher who uses the mind to transcend the mind. Jnana yoga is quite common in the East, but it only occasionally makes its appearance in the West, although when it does, it is sometimes quite profound (if sporadic). In *Sex, Ecology, Spirituality* I identified this as 'Western Vedanta,' and pointed out a few of its practitioners… from Augustine to Descartes, Spinoza, Berkeley, Kant, Fichte, Schelling, Hegel, Husserl, Heidegger, and Sartre, to mention a few…. Spirit, as basic Wakefulness, is not something that needs to be proven, but something that even the existence of doubt *always presupposes* as its own ground. And thus, Spirit (or consciousness or pure Ego or transcendental Self or basic openness) is not something hard to find but rather is impossible to avoid."[40] For our purposes, it's another useful way to understand where Wilber's at: He's a Western Vedanta American Buddhist.

These philosophers have concluded that our very consciousness, our "basic wakefulness" in the ever-present *now* is indeed the essence of the nondual reality, thus there's "nothing to be attained!" Once again our attention is brought back to what's *always already* the case, i.e., our innate

Divine Condition. Wilber focuses on these Western philosophers, similarity with Eastern mysticism (1995): "God is the ground, not just of all being, but of our own immediate and primordial awareness—this is the call of Augustine. How similar to the Eastern traditions!"[41] In other words, as this twenty-first-century integral philosopher continues explaining, "These traditions are not saying that you have BuddhaNature but don't know it; you know it but won't admit it."[42] What kind of person, I wonder, could clearly explain such outrageous claims, and then skillfully prove them with brilliant philosophical arguments, expositions that could even nudge a person toward their own spiritual practice, possibly even igniting further evolution to Divine Enlightenment itself? I suggest that, perhaps, it's some type of modern-day or post-postmodern *bodhisattva*, an intellectual wizard of enlightening wisdom.

Manjushri with a ThinkPad

In this same light, I have found it useful to envision Ken Wilber and his complex integral studies as being the devoted work of some type of postmodern "Bodhisattva," because he basically serves the Enlightenment of other sentient beings. This is the common definition of a *bodhi-sattva* (in Sanskrit, literally, *bodhi* = Enlightenment; *sattva* = being),[43] a title used in Buddhism to describe any being, human or archetypal (or otherwise), who shows signs of advanced spiritual realization by sincerely exercising efforts to awaken nondual Enlightenment (or God-Realization) in others. Personally, after working under Wilber's tutelage for over a decade, I have seen the commanding power and adeptness to which he pursues this aim, although his human foibles are evident, too, as in all people, including enlightened ones. Nonetheless, Wilber is dedicated to the awakening of others, but in the manner of a *pandit* (or scholar), not a *guru* (see below). To read and "grok" his writings is the only proof needed to verify this personal observation; therefore, in my opinion, it's appropriate to suggest that Ken Wilber gracefully leans toward embodying bodhisattva-like characteristics. Nonetheless, let me be clear, I am not saying, nor has he ever claimed, that Wilber is a fully enlightened being, for those terms are too paradoxical to define (although I will explain further in an endnote).[44]

To emphasize this observation, there is a famous bodhisattva known throughout Asia, and especially loved in Tibet, named Manjushri (Sanskrit, literally, "One Who Is Noble and Gentle"), known as the bodhisattva of enlightened wisdom (or *prajna*). Manjushri is associated with Mahayana and Vajrayana Buddhism, and specifically with the Madhyamika (or "Middle Way") and its teaching of Bliss-Void Emptiness (*sunyata*), a path that is one of Wilber's closest affiliations (as we've already seen). In iconography, Manjushri is usually depicted with two lotus blossoms at the level of his head displaying his twin attributes of a sword (representing penetrating wisdom), and in his other hand there's a book (representing the *Prajnaparamita Sutras* or the great "Scriptures of Transcendental Realization"). These images symbolize the clear light of wisdom that dispels the darkness of ignorance or that which prevents en-light-enment. Manjushri is thus the symbol for the experience of Enlightenment that's manifested in intellectual enterprises and expositions (or written teachings). I contend it's possible to see Wilber in this light, yet without elevating him to the status of a deity, per se, but as being a human representative of this enlightened awareness who displays an incredible mastery of language and ideas.

At its basic core, the nondual worldview of Buddhism is the one that's most closely aligned with Wilber's integral philosophy of nondualism. He clarified this in a mid-1990s interview about his own spiritual practices (1998): "I am a longtime practicing Buddhist, and many of the key ideas in my approach are Buddhist or Buddhist inspired. First and foremost, Nagarjuna and Madhyamika; pure Emptiness and primordial Purity is the 'central philosophy' of my approach as well. Also Yogachara, Hua Yen, a great deal of Dzogchen and Mahamudra, and yes, the fundamentals of Abhidharma…. Again, I'm trying to take the best from each of these traditions and bring them together in what I hope is a fruitful fashion."[45] Combined with the knowledge of the West (in its many forms, including Western Vedanta), these are indeed some of the essential ingredients in Wilber's integral stew. Therefore, in my mind (and in the opinions of others), this integral philosopher is justifiably associated with Manjushri-like qualities, especially since he falls within the parameters of this enlightened nondual tradition.

Although Wilber has *never* personally claimed to be the incarnation of a Buddhist anything (let alone a deity), my point is that his Integral Vision, ultimately, has the same overriding theme demonstrated by a bodhisattva like Manjushri, i.e., *all* is negated as *neti, neti* or transcended in the Divine Love-Bliss (*sunyata)* of One Taste. In this case, since "Spirit is not other than the Kosmos, and the Kosmos is not other than Spirit," then both Manjushri and Wilber argue that while models and "maps" (or dharmas and teachings) are useful tools for guidance and assistance, they're ultimately unreal (and dualistic) for nondual reality (the real "territory") is known only through *direct experience* via the transcendence of all mental dilemmas created by the egoic separate self.

The American Buddhist scholar Robert Thurman (another possible modern-day Manjushri) verifies this notion when he explains that bodhisattvas, such as Manjushri, are disciples of the Buddha who act as "Enlightenment Heroes," for their aim, he tells us, "is to help people develop the transcendent wisdom that is the sole cause of the ultimate freedom from suffering that is Enlightenment."[46] Additionally, the Buddhists also tell us Manjushri is called "Lord of the Word" *(vagisvara),* for when language is consciously and adeptly applied, it becomes another valuable tool for liberation. The words and phrases of language, if properly used, can cut away the tangles of ignorance and misknowledge, which, as Professor Thurman clarifies, "traps humans and gods in the automatic habit patterns of cyclic living."[47] For me, this is also an apt image for *The Collected Works of Ken Wilber:* piercing sword of critical insight in one hand; a book of enlightened word in the other. This certainly isn't true of everything he says (that's not my point), but this archetype certainly runs through the deeper currents of this pandit's philosophy as well with words that are executed with an eloquent flair and articulate grace unsurpassed in our times.

In the ancient East, the spiritual hero Manjushri is often depicted as wielding with his right arm the flame-tipped "sword" of transcendent wisdom *(prajna),* as we've indicated. This represents the liberating truth of enlightening wisdom because it "cuts through" all delusions and ignorance (including human models and maps). This makes it a powerful symbol of razor-sharp intelligence and penetrating critical wisdom that's been mastered by the intellectual insight and heartfelt compassion of nondual Enlightenment. This "sword of wisdom" tears through the partial or relative truths that cloud the mind and egoity in order to reveal the pristine purity of Ultimate Reality. Combined with the thundering shout of the awakened heart, and exercised with compassionate "skillful means" (or *upaya*), this wise bodhisattva uses the intellect to break through the confused philosophies and distorted worldviews of his (or her) historical time and place.

In the modern West, instead of waving a sword high above his head, Wilber writes away on yellow legal pads and types at lightning speed on his IBM

ThinkPad (high-tech notebook computer), to get his integral ideas across, written down, and printed out. Instead of "cutting though" the shrouds of ignorance with a sharp saber, he glides over his feather-light-touch keyboard, creating a vast series of words and integral ideas, which, if properly understood, have the power to dispel darkness and shine a light on our own innate awareness—or at least, he guides you to be *more integral*. Similar to the geniuslike Manjushri, Wilber (with an IQ of 160) engages in a skillful job of balancing the compassion of enlightened love with the need for piercingly brilliant wisdom, for like any true bodhisattva, the heart (with compassion) is as awake and as real as the mind (with wisdom). Yet, of course, this particular postmodern version plugs into the Internet and uploads ideas and essays, even providing multimedia extravagances (such as with Integral-Naked.org). Nonetheless, it is authentic spiritual practices (such as meditation) that truly reveal the contemplative core of where Wilber's at.

Wilber as a Champion of Meditation

Another reason it can be appropriate to see Wilber as a modern-day embodiment of Manjushri, sitting cross-legged in the full-lotus posture (he's a long-time meditator), wielding in one hand his IBM ThinkPad (or his "sword") and in his other an "Internet of Jewels," is that he's also one of today's most articulate defenders and loudest champions of meditation and contemplative practices in general. Wilber's intellectual integral philosophy always circles back to persistently suggesting that we need open all of "the eyes of knowing," from body to mind to spirit, by actively engaging *Integral Transformative Practices* (including traditional paths), to gracefully open the "Eye of Spirit" to see your own Original Face as the Face of God, present here and now.

By clearly eliminating the *pre/trans fallacy*, or the confusion between *pre*-rational and *trans*-rational truths, then integral psychology adeptly argues for the methodologies of progressive inner development, countering narcissistic regressions to *prepersonal* oceanic awareness or magical-mythical cults. Nor does he *elevate* prepersonal stages to transpersonal status, or does he *reduce* transpersonal domains to the prepersonal id, or as he once critically put it, "And so they [orthodox psychology] trace samadhi back to infantile breast-union; they reduce transpersonal unity to prepersonal fusion in the pleroma; God is reduced to a teething nipple and all congratulate themselves on explaining the Mystery."[48] For integral psychology, therefore, as Wilber explains, "Meditation is not primarily a way to dig back into, or uncover, prerational impulses, but rather a way to carry development or evolution forward into transrational and superconscious states."[49] By using evidence gained from a wide variety of *conventional* (or psychological) and *contemplative* (or mystical) sources, Wilber has deftly explained how meditation is a tool for positive growth into the *transpersonal* realms and authentic spiritual maturity. Yet, only meditation (or spiritual contemplation) itself will reaffirm this truth via appropriate knowledge acquisition and subsequent community confirmation.

In conjunction with the transpersonal movement in general, which sprung from the concerns of humanistic psychology in the fifties and sixties, Wilber is helping rescue the spiritual or transpersonal levels of consciousness from the "Flatland" collapse of the modern world's materialism (see chapter 14). This approach counters the failures of reductionism and elevationism by placing meditation back into a revered place of academic respectability, obviously benefiting the entire global culture. Moreover, in very pristine terms, the integral psychologist has clearly emphasized the necessity to include the reality of nondual Enlightenment, "the ultimate state of consciousness," in any package of transpersonal experiences studied by an advanced psychology. In a manner similar, then, to a bodhisattva, Wilber's Integral Vision promotes a psychology of liberation, one that can guide integral studies, transpersonal psychology, and psychology in general, in their noble quest for optimal human health and mental functioning.

Wilber as Pandit, Not Guru

In this postmodern age of the new millennium, Ken Wilber's intellectual defense of meditation and Enlightenment is another reason why he's best described as a "pandit" (in Sanskrit, literally, "scholar"), which is the root of the English word "pundit," or learned teacher and intellectual authority. In India a pandit is seen as a *sacred scholar* who is a "defender of the dharma, an intellectual samurai,"[50] which is a vastly different role than that of a guru. The sacred role of "guru" (Sanskrit, literally, "heavy one") is more akin to a spiritual "therapist," or one who has a direct and personal relationship with a student (or devotee) that intimately serves their karmic purification and awakening to Enlightenment. In other words, a guru gets "heavy" on the limitations of the contracted ego-I (or separate self). Therefore, from his earliest writings to his most recent, Wilber has always placed himself within the parameters of a "teacher-student" relationship, not a "guru-devotee" one.[51]

Most important, an effective Guru will initiate or baptize a person with a spiritual transmission that stimulates psycho-physical changes in the body-mind-soul structures of the dedicated aspirant. Indeed, this widely misunderstood technique has been the most revered and sacred process in the entire Great Tradition of humankind. Every great shaman, yogi, saint, sage, or siddha has had some type of direct contact or a personal relationship with another living spiritually advanced person or teacher. Examples include some of the world's greatest and most famous spiritual masters, such as Jesus of Nazareth (whose master/guru was John the Baptist), Socrates (who's master/guru was Diotima), Plato (whose master/guru was Socrates), Plotinus (whose master/guru was Ammonius Saccas), Marpa (whose master/guru was Milarepa), or Chuang-Tzu (whose master/guru was Lao-Tzu), among many others. This is the case even if a particular student's realization and historical import exceed his teacher's. As a sacred pandit or intellectual defender of Enlightenment, then Wilber's Integral "Theory of Everything" would naturally embrace this spiritual and sacred aspect of reality, which it heartily does.

This *living relationship* between student and teacher, between master and disciple, between Guru and devotee, is the vital psycho-physical link generated from an actual *transmission* or spiritual power that connects everyone to the religious history of this planet. This indeed is the "spiritual fire" that baptizes the nervous system of an individual with grace and love, opening the heart and higher chakras or structures of our existence. Naturally, Wilber also acknowledges this phenomenon of spiritual transmission (from adept to disciple), which is confirmed by his own personal experiences, as he once explained in his private journals published as *One Taste* (1999): "In my experience, when a person is fairly enlightened, they can transmit—actually *transmit*—that enlightened awareness through a touch, a look, a gesture, or even through the written word. It's not as weird as it sounds. We are all 'transmitting' our present state to each other all the time…. Just so with the higher states. In the presence of a *psychic-level yogi* [or shaman], you tend to feel power. In the presence of a *subtle-level saint*, you tend to feel great peace. In the presence of a *causal-level sage*, you tend to feel massive equanimity. In the presence of a *nondual siddha*—these are often very ordinary people—you simply find yourself smiling a lot."[52] Consequently, these higher functions of teaching and initiation are the unique role of the Guru, whereas the pandit is predominantly using the mental intellect and their study of sacred literature to support and perhaps sometimes criticize these important techniques of transpersonal development.

Wilber, of course, openly acknowledges and totally supports the necessity for both forms of guidance and communion (i.e., pandit and guru), especially since both methods are vital and important tools used by the nondual Enlightenment traditions. This American pandit once explained his role in becoming an intellectual proponent of the Ultimate Truth (1995): "It has been my good fortune to find that when the intellect is polished until it becomes radiant and shining, it is a staunch defender of a Truth and Beauty that reaches quite far beyond its own capacities, and in that reach it serves its master more than faithfully."[53] These words are the resounding echo of Manjushri's wisdom, even if today he's appearing in a postmodern form, for they still carry great capacity to reveal the truth of enlightened awareness as well as dispel some of the darkness and despair drowning the world that's floating around us.

Today there are probably several "post-postmodern" Manjushris, or spiritual pandits from the West (look for them); (in fact, not surprisingly, many of these "advanced-tip" individuals have been good friends of Wilber's throughout the years). Although this group of wonderful scholars has been or is living in our contemporary times, its roots are still founded upon and grounded in this "great tradition" of Enlightenment or Ultimate Consciousness, yet without being necessarily restricted to the metaphysical philosophies of premodern religions, but to the timelessness of the Infinite or Ultimate Reality. Since this "tradition" or "Perennial Philosophy," if you will, has historically evolved in its expression over the millennia, then its transcendent goal and immanent ground is always already "perennial" only in the sense nondual Spirit transcends *any human* tradition, model, teaching, conceptualization, or utterance, including, of course, the massive metatheory of where Wilber's at.

PART II

WHERE'S WILBER COMING FROM?

Spirit is not merely or even especially the summit of the scale of evolution, or some sort of Divine omega point (although that is part of the story). Spirit is preeminently the empty Ground, or groundless Emptiness, fully present at each and every stage of evolution, as the openness in which the particular stage unfolds, as well as the substance of that which is unfolded. Spirit *transcends* and *includes* the world: *transcends,* in the sense that it is prior to the world, prior to the Big Bang, prior to any manifestation; *includes,* in the sense that the world is not other to Spirit, form is not other to Emptiness. Manifestation is not "apart from" Spirit but an activity of Spirit: the evolving Kosmos is Spirit-in-action.

—Ken Wilber, *Sex, Ecology, Spirituality* (1995)

CHAPTER SEVEN

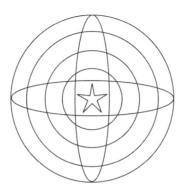

AQAL Metatheory: A Kosmos of Holons

According to the nearly universal view [of a Great Nest of Spirit], reality is a rich tapestry of interwoven levels, *reaching from matter to body to mind to soul to spirit.* Each senior level "envelopes" or "enfolds" its junior dimensions—a series of nests within nests within nests of Being—so that every thing and event in the world is interwoven with every other, and all are ultimately enveloped and enfolded by Spirit, by God, by Goddess, by Tao, by Brahman, by the Absolute itself.

—Ken Wilber, *A Theory of Everything* (2000)

Grace and Grit: The Death of Treya & the Transformation of Ken

THE ARTICULATED COMPLETION OF THE FULL-SPECTRUM MODEL DURING the early-to-mid 1980s, which covers Wilber/Phases 1–3 (1977–1989), culminating with *Transformations of Consciousness* (1986), also marked a personal transformational cauldron for Ken Wilber. After falling madly in love, or "love at first touch," with Treya Killam in the summer of 1983, it was only ten days after their marriage in the autumn of 1983 that his new wife

119

was diagnosed with terminal cancer. Treya (whose name *Estrella* is Spanish for "star") lived such a noble life and practiced such a conscious death that she exemplified her other name of "Dakini Wind" (meaning "the wind of enlightenment") given to her by the couple's mutual Tibetan Buddhist guru, Kalu Rinpoche, thus Ken lovingly calls her "the most enlightened person I've ever known."[1] A star of the Heart.

The heartbreaking and beautiful story of their losing but inspiring battle against cancer, and the further discovery of their own depths and capacity to love, is captured with sublime eloquence in the aptly titled *Grace and Grit: Spirituality and Healing in the Life of Treya Killam Wilber* (published in 1991 by Shambhala Publications). Completed two years after her passing in January 1989, the book was named after Treya's last written diary entry: "It takes grace, *yes*—and grit,"[2] their love story is told as a dialogue for it wonderfully includes entries from her own personal journals (used with her insistence and blessing). *Grace and Grit* has inspired many people the world over in their own fight against cancer and other illnesses, thus it's become Wilber's most popular book, stimulating the most moving letters from his readers, many of whom have their own story to tell.[3]

As a positive consequence of this time of "grace and grit" with Treya, and empowered with her incredible love, the spectrum psychologist and maturing man was transformed into a full-fledged integral philosopher and wiser soul. After a nearly ten-year hiatus from writing and publishing in order to devotedly serve his ailing wife (1984–1994), Wilber would emerge with a new phase of his career in 1995 (Wilber/Phase-4). It was Treya, therefore, who helped Ken Wilber birth a new and expanded integral approach that's still based upon the same integrative principles as before (the evolutionary "growth-to-goodness" model of Wilber/Phases-2–3), but this time it's presented as an even more embracing vision: an AQAL Approach to integral studies and research.

Ken Wilber's Integral Vision: The Kosmos Trilogy

During the early years of the 1990s, after Treya had died in early 1989, Ken Wilber unintentionally found his hiatus from writing and publishing had so annealed his ideas with the fire of love and sacrifice that he was now passionately invigorated to continue expounding on his spiritual Integral Vision. Treya's profound love and life had transformed Wilber in ways he would later affirm were partly responsible for the emergence of Wilber/Phase-4, or the most-developed period of his philosophy yet to emerge. One of the first things it did, after completing *Grace and Grit*, was push him into an intensive three-year reading and research retreat between 1991 and 1994 at his comfortable self-styled home in the mountains of Boulder, Colorado. This three-year seclusion was somewhat like a traditional Tibetan meditation retreat involving extended periods of meditation training and focused attention, since, like a secluded monk, Wilber too hardly saw anyone for the entire period, including close friends.

One of the fruits coming out of this intense intellectual study, following another bitter theoretical struggle that resulted from running a data search across the various developmental and evolutionary fields, was the conception of the "the four quadrants," an observation that would lead directly to the A-Q-A-L (pronounced *aw-quil*)—"all-quadrants, all-levels"—Metatheory.[4] This idea that theoretically recognizes and accounts for both the interiors *and* exteriors of reality (intentional, behavioral, cultural, social) basically dawned on Wilber after he realized the different hierarchies from numerous fields of study, from stellar physics to molecular biology, from anthropology to linguistics, from developmental psychology to ethical orientations, from cultural hermeneutics to contemplative endeavors, gathered from Eastern, Western, premodern, modern, and postmodern sources, were confusing the fact of whether they were using individual *or* collective hierarchies, or a mixture of both (see chapter 9). When these *"quadrants"* were separately distinguished and defined, and then combined with the developmental *"levels"* from the spectrum of consciousness (outlined in his previous studies), then the AQAL Metatheory was born as a viable and inclusive integral map embracing more of the various "correct but partial" truths and possible methodologies than any model before it.

Once Wilber figured this out, the manuscript to *Sex, Ecology, Spirituality*, originally titled *The Spirit of Evolution: Cosmos, Bios, Psyche, Theos*, began to "write itself" in only a few months during 1994. The AQAL Approach of Wilber/Phase-4, therefore, officially began in 1995 with the publication of *Sex, Ecology, Spirituality: The Spirit of Evolution* (by Shambhala Publications, with a revised second edition[5] in 2000), also known as *SES*, for short. This nearly three-pound tome of over 500 pages of text, and over 200 pages of endnotes was so encompassing, it literally included "two books" (or sections), where each one could be justifiably published as a separate book (then perhaps they would've been a little easier to digest). What *SES* did do, without a doubt, other than become the "best-selling academic book" for that year, was to establish Wilber's AQAL Approach to integral studies… and, of course, in doing so it began another "Wilber revolution," which ended up creating another huge wave of reaction, mostly positive, certainly negative, but totally undeniable.

The overriding theme highlighted in this treatise on "The Spirit of Evolution," which builds upon the accomplishments of his earlier evolutionary theories, was that Wilber continued to unabashedly maintain that the entire evolutionary journey of the Kosmos, or the multileveled and pluridimensional universe (not just a material "cosmos"), is ultimately being driven by, or pushed and pulled by, a divine *telos* (Greek, for "end, completion"), the movement of *Eros* (Greek, for "love"); what Whitehead referred to as "the gentle persuasion toward love." Following in the footsteps of other notable evolutionary philosophers, Wilber effectively argued that evolution is actually best seen as "Spirit-in-action" (the original title to "book one"), because this "secret impulse of evolution" is in fact "the single and all-pervading principle of manifestation."[6] The brilliant pages of *SES* (and the following books) outlined and explained in detail these integral ideas, along with countless others, and once again they were done with a graceful literary style and depth of research that's never quite been seen before, at least in the eyes of many observers and critics alike.

Not without significance, *Sex, Ecology, Spirituality* (1995) is only considered to be volume 1 in a projected three-volume set, titled either *"Kosmos, or The Kosmos Trilogy,"*[7] a foretold series outlined by Wilber during his three-year intensive research retreat (1991–1994). Each volume will be at least as large as *SES*, and they're expected to be published every ten years (ca. 2005, 2015).[8] Originally, volume 2 was to be titled *Sex, God, Gender: The Ecology of Men and Women*, for it would present a detailed application of AQAL Metatheory to the fields of anthropology, sociology, gender issues, politics, and so forth. Volume 3 (now the upcoming volume 2) was originally titled *The Spirit of Post/Modernity*, for it concentrates mostly on an integral but critical review of the modern and postmodern worldviews. Together, with Wilber's other books published to supplement this task, these three towering tomes will be what officially outlines the expanse and depth of Ken Wilber's Integral Vision, or most fully "where Wilber's at."

Now, however, their order has been reversed, so that 2006 will present the actual *Kosmos Trilogy,* volume 2 (as *Collected Works, Volume 11*), which will probably be called *Kosmic Karma and Creativity* or *Sex, Karma, Creativity,* another incredible testament of advanced integral thinking. This Wilber/Phase-5 book will "officially" introduce many of the principal Phase-5 themes, including Integral Post-Metaphysics, Integral Methodological Pluralism (IMP), Integral Operating System (IOS), an integral calculus, and numerous other advances in AQAL thinking while still continuing Wilber's strong critique of relative pluralism and postmodern nihilism (the green meme) and their integration with a *universal integralism* (second-tier solutions). In addition, following these same themes in more detail, Wilber will release two more books, *Integral Spirituality: A Startling New Role for Religion in the Modern and Postmodern World* (Shambhala Publications), and also *The Many Faces of Terrorism* (Shambhala Publications).

After *Sex, Ecology, Spirituality* (1995), there was a successive series of books published every year into the new millennium (see Appendix), which all together set Wilber/Phase-4 in motion. Within those five or six years these integral ideas blossomed into the fully developed AQAL Metatheory with its "all-quadrant, all-level, all-line, all-state, all-type" matrix of reality. Nevertheless, it's still important to note again that this approach is actually based upon a hermeneutical *reconstruction* (or interpretation) of the Kosmos, one that amply includes the verifiable evidence of science (as a deep science) as being *alongside* (not underneath) the transpersonal or spiritual realities (see chapter 4). This integral view, therefore, models the entire universe, from the Big Bang to the present to the future, from birth to death to beyond, from matter to body to mind to soul to spirit, as all being manifested as the grand evolutionary display of "Spirit-in-action," the glorious *uni-versum* or "one-turning all together," a Divine Dance of incomparable complexity and beauty. In the infinite heart of Wilber's love for Treya, the seeds of an AQAL "multi-paradigmatic" Metatheory were planted, to be further cultivated and harvested over the next ten years by expanding into the new century with numerous books, articles, and voluminous website postings, all written to support the next phases of his Integral Vision, which are what, in the end, best shows where Wilber's at.

Wilber/Phase-4 Books & "Sutras": Further Evolution of AQAL

In the wake of *Sex, Ecology, Spirituality: The Spirit of Evolution* (1995), the AQAL Approach of Wilber/Phase-4 was further refined and expanded with a series of succeeding books published each year between 1995 and 2000. Even that exact term "A-Q-A-L" (pronounced *al-kwul*) was just beginning to emerge in the later years of these writings, so with each book the integral philosopher further outlined and refined the AQAL trend to integral studies. During these intensely creative years, Wilber unleashed a bundle of seriously detailed works (including dense, complicated endnotes offering profound philosophical considerations and semantic clarifications), which all emphasized the necessity for a "more integral" or "AQAL Approach" that must include, in his words, "all quadrants, levels, lines, types, and states in self, culture, and nature." Let's briefly review the series of these principal Wilber/Phase-4 books or the "sutras" of Wilber's Integral Vision and their role in the further evolution of AQAL:

- The year following the publication of *SES*, Wilber released a shorter and more user-friendly version with the popular ***A Brief History of Everything*** (published in 1996 by Shambhala Publications as a paperback only). Since it's written as an interview conversation, it's much easier to read while still covering the same basic themes as *SES* (and, as usual, introduces a few more novel ideas as well). Wilber again covers in detail the implications and story of the dynamic and evolving "Great Nest of Spirit," for part I is "Spirit-In-Action" and part II is "The Further Reaches of Spirit-In-Action" (basically covering book one of *SES*). Part III is "Flatland," where Wilber again aggressively addresses and attacks the crippling materialism of the modern world, or "the collapse of the Kosmos," while he continues to convincingly call for an integral approach that can bring depth and meaning back to respectability within the context of the modern/postmodern world (instead of perpetuating the irony and cynicism that pervades in today's dominant culture). At the same time, Wilber brilliantly, yet with compassionate care and integral wisdom, shows how the integral approach can simultaneously "unpack" the Good, the True, and the Beautiful (the "Big Three"), the unfolding truths of Spirit-in-action.

- The year 1997 saw the publication of ***The Eye of Spirit: An Integral Vision for a World Gone Slightly Mad*** (by Shambhala Publications) which is basically a contemporary update and analysis of Wilber's previous books and theories (Phases 1–3) with the "four quadrant" AQAL Model first presented in *SES* (1995). This is also where Wilber introduced the "phase" concept as a way to review his earlier works through the lens of his current AQAL Metatheory; therefore, some of these essays/chapters incorporate newly written forewords to the recent reprint editions of his various Phase-2 and Phase-3 books. Overall, it is an excellent recapitulation of the AQAL Approach to Wilber's spectrum psychology and integral theories.

- The year 1998 saw the publication of ***The Marriage of Sense and Soul: Integrating Science and Religion*** (by Random House), a relatively short book (200-some pages), since it was intended for the general public and leaders in religion and science, therefore, he had it published by a larger publisher, Random House. Specifically it claimed that the integral "task of postmodernity" is to "marry" all the levels of the premodern "Great Chain" with the "four quadrants" (or "Big Three") of self, culture, and nature, the important differentiations of modernity and postmodernity. In a stunning display by a master philosopher, Wilber reviews the history and important truths of *premodernity* (the "Great Chain"), *modernity* (including its "Dignity and Disaster") while also giving a masterful critique and acknowledgment of *postmodernity*, from deconstructionism to the "linguistic turn" (or the work of Saussure and the "transition from modernity to postmodernity"). Wilber concludes by suggesting that only something like the AQAL Approach can bring about a post-postmodern "resurrection of the interior" from modern Flatland. He does so by calling for a "real religion" (or *authentic spirituality*) and a "deep science" (based on a *broad empiricism*), which again highlights the importance of using clear definitions to propose a genuine integration of science (modern knowledge) with religion (ancient wisdom) that will be acceptable to both parties.

- The year 1999 saw the publication of ***One Taste: Daily Reflections on Integral Spirituality*** (by Shambhala Publications), a personal account of Wilber's daily life written during the year 1997; therefore, it's a more reader-friendly way to reflect on a variety of integral issues while more easily explaining the all-embracing attitude of a fully AQAL "all-quadrant, all-level" Approach to consciousness studies and the mapping of reality. It also gives the reader some intimate insights into Wilber's own personal "tastes" and meditative experiences, from meetings with rock stars to his favorite movies, from avant-garde art to meditative experiences of *One Taste,* a Buddhist term which means, he explains, "There is only One Taste in the entire Kosmos, and that taste is Divine, whether it appears in the flesh, in the mind, in the soul."[9] Importantly, as the revised subtitle suggests (the original was "The Journals of Ken Wilber"), it continued introducing the outlines for authentic *Integral Transformative Practices* (ITP), a lifestyle that exercises all levels of consciousness in self, culture, and nature.

- The year 1999 also saw the debut publication of one of Wilber's most important books, called **Integral Psychology: Consciousness, Spirit, Psychology, Therapy** (by Shambhala Publications), which first appeared in *CW4* and was later released in 2000 as a paperback. *Integral Psychology,* in my opinion, is Wilber's most summary overview work to date for it upgrades the plethora of terms and ideas found in his earlier phases (Phases 1–3) into a thoroughly AQAL Approach (Phase-4/5). Instead of just offering a "spectrum psychology," which was already a huge expansion over traditional psychology (including all the basic *levels* and developmental *lines* of consciousness), Wilber made it abundantly clear that a fully developed *integral psychology* would have to look something like the "AQAL Model," that is, it would need to include all *levels, lines, states, types, worldviews,* et al., of consciousness as they appear in self, culture, and nature (or in all *quadrants*). Perhaps one of the most outstanding features of this detailed but relatively concise presentation (around 200 pages) is the "correlative charts" placed in the back of the book that cross-reference the hundreds of models from contemporary researchers and the mystical traditions, all compiled by Wilber himself; therefore, they amply demonstrate the integrative effectiveness of using a truly full-spectrum, all-quadrant approach to human psychology (Knowing) and reality (Being).

- The year 2000, the first year of the new millennium, also brought publication of *A Theory of Everything: An Integral Vision for Business, Politics, Science, and Spirituality* (by Shambhala Publications), a finely poised and succinct book (at less than 150 pages) introducing the basic parameters of AQAL Metatheory, thus the author concedes it's "probably the best introduction to my work on the whole."[10] The first chapters introduce integral psychology's critique of *"boomeritis,"* a postmodern dis-ease of the "Baby Boomers" and the "green meme" of relative pluralism, thus, it's a companion volume to Wilber's first novel *Boomeritis* (published in 2002). As an antidote, the AQAL Approach offers "an integral vision for business, politics, science, spirituality" by proposing a real "Theory of Everything" (or T.O.E.), a "metatheory" that embraces everything from matter to mind to God, including the valuable contributions from each of the premodern, modern, and postmodern eras.

By any measure, this prolific output is an amazing feat—the culmination of twenty books and hundreds of articles written in around twenty-five years (even less when the ten-year hiatus is factored in)! These are the "sutras" of Ken Wilber's Integral Vision, now compiled in a growing *Collected Works* already containing over 5,000 pages, with thousands more ready to be added! Since this incredible outpouring is backed with enlightened wisdom and compassion, this has led many to agree that this man must be something like a post-postmodern apparition of the bodhisattva Manjushri, especially since this intellectual pandit is influencing thousands of people worldwide by touching their minds, hearts, and souls. From writing his first books by hand in spiral-bound notebooks to pounding away on crude typewriters, to executing keyboard commands on digital ThinkPads, to uploading essays onto the World Wide Web, Wilber has proven time and time again there's a creative descent of eloquent language and integral reasoning awake to the One Taste of God running straight into the heart of nearly everything he writes. In this case, these "sutras" of the Integral Vision—the clearest indication of "where Wilber's at"—began by seeing a shimmering similarity to some of the most complex Buddhist models of reality available, as we'll review next, yet importantly, they're also offering something more by adding modern scientific knowledge and postmodern insights to this all-encompassing matrix of reality.

AQAL Matrix: A Post-Postmodern Dharmadhatu

As I mentioned at the beginning of this book, it's nearly impossible to explain exactly "where Wilber's at" since it's so complex and multilayered, and, in the end, only he really knows for sure where he's at, although naturally he does his best to communicate and dialogue his many ideas about "everything." With that limitation in mind, however, it's still quite instructive, in my opinion, to picture Wilber's grand "Theory of Everything," especially the AQAL Matrix, as being somewhat similar to the notion of the "Dharmadhatu," or a "Bodhimandala," philosophical models of the "totality of reality" used by the Hua-Yen and Yogachara schools of Buddhism (thus being extremely influential on all subsequent Buddhist history and philosophy). Already in his first monumental book, *The Spectrum of Consciousness* (1977), Wilber acknowledged these ancient wisdom models of enlightenment and reality as significantly reflecting his spectrum approach (some of which I will outline in an endnote).[11] In this case, today's current AQAL or "all-quadrant, all-level" Matrix itself is somewhat like a post-postmodern update of the Dharmadhatu.

Although Wilber's Integral Vision has been expressed in a different language, sociocultural milieu, and context, I still believe it's fairly easy to see that his integral model reflects a tone similar to the more complex and subtle Buddhist models of reality developed by some of the East's most brilliant sages and pandits, such as with the influential brothers Asanga and Vasubandhu (fl. fourth–fifth century CE), or Tsong Khapa (1357–1419), or the aforementioned Aurobindo (1872–1950) (however, we don't have the space to explore these suggestions in detail). Simply put, however, they both recognize that all phenomena, or the totality of reality, all arises from within and is embodied as, the pure Emptiness of nondual Divine Spirit, the Clear Light that can never be quantified, modeled or published, but *only realized!* This alone, we may note once again, aligns this postmodern Manjushri (see chapter 6) with the real depths of Buddhism or authentic spirituality and mysticism itself: *Go practice to see for yourself—do the yoga!*

As an indication of this similarity, in *The Spectrum of Consciousness* (1977), Wilber began by pointing to a "Matrix" as being a good organizing principle and metaphor for reality as a whole, since it's defined as the space in which things originate, take form, and develop. In his first published pages, the young philosopher explained this important correlation with Buddhist philosophy when he recognized, "The word 'matrix' suggests the universal field-like nature of reality, and thus is reminiscent of the Dharmadhatu or Universal Field."[12] The *Dharmadhatu* literally means "Realm of Dharma" (in Sanskrit, *dharma* = truth; *dhatu* = realm), therefore it's often translated as the "Sphere of Reality,"[13] or the "Truth-Realm."[14] These early Wilber/Phase-1 books also referred to it as the "Matrix of Reality," the "Universal Field," or the "Universal System,"[15] simply because it pictures the vast universe of all relative forms (i.e., the universe or Kosmos) as arising in absolute divine formlessness or Emptiness *(sunyata)*. Today, however, as we've already seen, Wilber's Integral Vision presents these deeply spiritual models of reality with a new language based on modern and postmodern terms since it incorporates the vast reams of knowledge that are available from all premodern, modern, and postmodern philosophies and research. Therefore, Wilber does not necessarily *equate* his integral model with these premodern Buddhist ones, although there's a noticeable similarity, especially in the end result (i.e., all dualistic models are always transcended in nondual Spirit).

Specifically, the *Dharmadhatu* is an idea or philosophical principle (arising from the enlightened mind) designed to portray that there's an ineffable true nature *(sunyata)* that pervades and encompasses all possible phenomena, thus it's seen as both immanent and transcendent beyond description (thus "Empty"). Consequently, this Dharmadhatu is the foundational "ground" or "suchness" *(tathata)* of all possible models and philosophies created by the human mind. This approach brilliantly (and paradoxically) depicts the "Totality of Reality," or "Universal Field," as being a vast "realm of mutual interpenetration" where everything arises *within* and *as* the "field" of Divine Emptiness, the indescribable and indivisible Clear Light of Reality or real God itself. This is also a notion that rings true with Wilber's Integral Vision, although this version integrates the essence of the premodern mystical wisdom with the wealth of modern and postmodern evidence, thus it depicts and reconstructs a vast AQAL Matrix as being an evolutionary morphogenetic field of arising and falling forms (or holons) which are *always already* Spirit-in-action.

Far from being a rigid, linear model of reality that some of Wilber's critics have accused him of, this AQAL Matrix is a dynamic coevolving (actually, tetra-evolving) matrix where the basic structures or "the levels of consciousness are largely plastic" best seen as, he tells us, "a field of potentials and not a predetermined set of levels through which humanity must rigidly march on the way to its own realization."[16] Nonetheless, as he acknowledged in the first chapters of his first book, even these types of grand esoteric systems, such as the Buddhist's Dharmadhatu, are just another intellectual "approach to the Void."[17] At best, they can only point to the ultimate truth of Reality itself, which is ineffable, but certainly *realizable*. Naturally, this holds true for any AQAL Metatheory as well, even one that's a bona fide marriage of East and West, of real science and authentic religion, of rationality and mysticism (the transrational)—a *scientia visionis* –for our millennium and troubled times.

AQAL Matrix: A "Morphogenetic Developmental Space"

Since Wilber's work is a post-postmodern AQAL Approach, instead of being an Eastern Dharmadhatu model, or even a modern scientific theory, or a post-modern New Age paradigm, then we're presented with an interactive AQAL Matrix of "all-quadrants, all-levels, etc." In his current Phase-4/5 writings, Wilber has redefined and described this Dharmadhatu as being more like a "morphogenetic developmental space," which is, he explains, "a *developmental space* in which human potentials can unfold."[18] He continues in *Integral Psychology* (2000): "What is worth keeping in mind is that, taken together, the basic levels in virtually every major system, ancient and modern, Eastern and Western, simply describe a vast *morphogenetic field*, or *developmental space*, and one that is *migratory* [evolutionary]—it grades holarchically, transcending and including, nests within nests indefinitely, inviting *a development that is envelopment*."[19] In other words, it is a universal field of reality itself arising as an endless array of forms (in this case, *holons*), which creates an evolutionary AQAL Matrix (or universe) within which all the integral theories and methodologies apply and exist—a Grand Theory of Everything.

"*Morphogenesis*" (*morphic*, literally, meaning "pattern-related") is the coming into being of form, and it is, as Wilber explained in an essay on the subject in 1984, "perhaps the most persistent problem in developmental biology," because the creation of forms "cannot be predicted or even accounted for in terms of its constituent material parts."[20] "Morphogenetic fields" is an explanatory idea from biology (pioneered by Waddington in the early twentieth century), yet it was Rupert Sheldrake (in the late twentieth century), who further developed this idea and backed it with scientific evidence, one of his great contributions to the field. Sheldrake defined *"formative causation"* as the causal influence of one form on another and the means by which this causation occurs he calls *"morphic resonance,"* which is generated by "morphogenetic fields," or the habitual patterns of energy, simplified as *"morphic fields."* [21] These morphogenetic fields include the past patterns of behavioral, social, cultural, and mental fields (the four quadrants), which all play a causal role in morphogenesis, thus they're acting as "blueprints" in the creation of all forms. In other words, the "morphogenetic developmental space" is the entire "matrix of reality" in which *all forms,* gross to biological to mental to subtle, all arise, thrive, and pass away.

Wilber has incorporated these well-thought ideas (backed with evidence), and even suggests one of the measurable mechanisms by which this might occur (1984): "It is therefore possible—I would say probable—that *morphogenetic fields* are not completely formal [or abstract] but rather possess some sort of *very subtle energy,* and it is the influence of these subtler energies on the denser ones that constitutes the formative capacity of morphogenetic fields." [22] The integral philosopher has been exploring these complicated and controversial ideas further with his Phase-5 writings, even outlining a spectrum of "subtle energies," such as with the essay titled "Toward a Comprehensive Theory of Subtle Energies," where he identifies that the "complexification of gross form is accompanied by subtler energies," [23] as only one example.

In any case, AQAL Metatheory reflects a deep understanding of these modern scientific models (of morphogenetic fields), while also combining them with the premodern concept of the Great Chain of Being (yet, importantly, *without* a priori or metaphysical structures). He explains more clearly in *Integral Psychology* (2000): "What I have done is to take the results of that research, along with dozens of other modern theorists, and attempted to integrate it with the best of the perennial philosophers, to arrive at a master template of a *full-spectrum developmental space,* reaching from matter to body to mind to soul to spirit. As we have seen, these are the basic waves of being and knowing through which the various developmental streams will flow, all of which are balanced and (ideally) integrated by the self in its remarkable journey from subconscious to self-conscious to superconscious." [24] In other words, the Great Nest of Spirit as an AQAL Matrix models *all-levels and all-quadrants* as "fields within fields within fields, nests within nests within nests," all being interdependent and influencing one another, while being *always already* grounded in nondual Divine Spirit.

This is, of course, set within the context of Phase-5's *Integral Post-Meta-physics* (see chapter 5), which he clarified again in *Integral Psychology* (2000): "What the Great Nest represents, in my opinion, is most basically a *great morphogenetic field* or *developmental space*—a stretching from matter to mind to spirit—in which various potentials unfold into actuality. Although for convenience I will often speak of the higher levels as if they were simply given, they are in many ways still plastic, still open to being formed as more and more people coevolve into them (which is why, as I said, the basic struc-tures are more like Kosmic habits than pregiven molds)."[25] Whatever the degree of sophistication one is looking for, there's a good chance Ken Wil-ber's integral theories have reviewed them somewhere in fine detail (be sure to check the copious endnotes), complicated ideas that I can only skim over here. But, importantly, this allows him, in concert with numerous other sci-entists, to unequivocally announce: "From Rupert Sheldrake and his 'nested hierarchy of morphogenetic fields' [to numerous others]—the Great Chain is back."[26] And in Wilber's case, the Great Chain is "back" and present in the new millennium as the AQAL Matrix or the "all-quadrants, all-levels morphogenetic developmental space" of Reality, a post-postmodern form of the enlightened Dharmadhatu (by whatever name).

AQAL Matrix: Multivariable Model (IOS Basic)

We have seen from the first chapter that Wilber's AQAL Model and Matrix is described as incorporating a series of variables that gives it its acronym of "A-Q-A-L," meaning, at a minimum, "all-quadrants, all-levels," but more completely is "all-quadrants, all-levels, all-lines, all-states, all-types, etc." Some critics have complained that Wilber's early books focused mostly on the *basic structures* or "levels" or "stages" of human development—the entire spectrum of consciousness (from *archaic* to *magic* to *mythic* to *rational* to *integral* to *psychic* to *soul* to *spirit*)—yet, he was always embracing much, much more. Consequently, by criticizing (and misinterpreting) Wilber's structural "stage model," many critics have too often overlooked the sig-nificance of this model having always been incredibly *multidimensional* and *multivariable* in nature, not rigid and only progressively linear, but one that involves the interdependent and intermeshing of both ontological exteriors and epistemological interiors (see next chapter).

The AQAL Model, therefore, most basically includes—now called "IOS

Basic"—anywhere from *three to six major variables,* or clearly defined independent scales, which Wilber claims must always be accounted for in any genuine integral model. Recently, the multimedia package titled *The Integral Operating System, Version 1.0* (2005, Sounds True, Inc.), has been released outlining these ideas in detail and how their understanding and *practice* can "upgrade the way you think – and live." These include the "five elements" needed to operate or run the AQAL Integral Operating System (or IOS), the components of IOS Basic listed below:

1) **Levels** of consciousness (or the *planes* of reality);

2) **States** of consciousness (or waking, dreaming, deep sleep, altered, meditative);

3) **Types** of consciousness (or horizontal typologies of translation);

4) **Developmental Lines** of consciousness (or the cognitive, affective, spiritual, etc., lines of development) or the "multiple intelligences" of selfhood;

5) **Quadrants** (the individual-interiors, individual-exteriors, of collective-interiors, collective-exteriors, holons), as we've seen, summarized as the "Big Three" (of self, culture, nature, or art, morals, science, or I, We, It).

These are the general guidelines of AQAL Metatheory; consequently, Wilber maintains this is simply one of the easiest ways to include all the various factors of existence that interact as the Matrix of Reality. For beginners it may seem complex, or perhaps just another nasty theory to memorize, but for Wilber it's one of the most accurate approaches to a genuine *integralism,* an inclusion of *everything,* as he recently conceded in a Phase-5 writing (2003):

> Seem complicated? In a sense it is. But in another sense, the extraordinary complexity of humans and their relation to the universe can be simplified enormously by touching bases with the *quadrants* (the fact that every event can be looked at as an I, we, or it);

developmental lines (or multiple intelligences), all of which move through *developmental levels* (*from* body to mind to spirit); with *states* and *types* at each of those levels. That Integral Model—"all quadrants, all levels, all lines, all states, all types"—is the simplest model that can handle all of the truly essential items. We sometimes shorten all of that to simply "all quadrants, all levels"—or AQAL—where the quadrants are, for example, self, culture, and nature, and the levels are body, mind, and spirit, so we say that the Integral Approach involves *the cultivation of body, mind, and spirit in self, culture, and nature.*[27]

Today, with the AQAL Approach emerging in the twenty-first century, Wilber and his Integral Institute are creatively picturing this "vast developmental space" with a degree of sophistication that is unparalleled in depth. Now, instead of relying too much on traditional Eastern models or mystical terms, the integral pandit prefers instead to designate the matrix of reality, or the Great Chain of Being, with other *more integral* names (yet, to some, perhaps ones just as exotic), but, in any case, they're now being cast in a decidedly more "post-postmodern" and integral language. Therefore, especially in Wilber's current writings, you'll read such phrases as the aforementioned "morphogenetic developmental space," or "AQAL Matrix," "AQAL Lattice," "Great Holarchy of Spirit," "Holarchy of Being and Knowing," "Great Nest of Spirit," "Mandalic Map of Consciousness," or "Kosmic Mandala," and numerous other variations. We'll continue to briefly review (especially compared to Wilber's detailed discussions) some of these integral ideas below, starting with the holistic idea of how it all fits together.

Holism & Holarchy: How Holons Fit Together

Since Ken Wilber has been *reconstructing* his integral model based upon available (and verifiable) evidence, not just by picking and choosing from his personal preferences (known as eclecticism), then such an approach holds together as a unified system because it's reflecting the inherent holism of the universe itself. As Jan Smuts, the statesman-scientist who originated the term "holism," pointed out in his early-twentieth-century book *Holism and Evolution* (1926): "Wholeness is the most characteristic expression of the nature of the universe in its forward movement in time. It marks the line of evolutionary progress…. Holism is the term here coined (from *holos* = whole) to designate this fundamental factor operative towards the making or creation of wholes in the universe."[28] Wilber's integral model reflects this same understanding, especially after the "spectrum of consciousness" theories shifted into the evolutionary dynamics of Phase-2 (in the late 1970s). The integral philosopher affirmed in *The Atman Project* (1980): "Everywhere we look in nature, said the philosopher Jan Smuts, we see nothing but *wholes*. And not just simple wholes, but hierarchical ones: each whole is part of a larger whole which is itself part of a larger whole. Fields within fields within fields, stretching through the cosmos, interlacing each and every thing with each and every other…. This overall cosmic process, as it unfolds in time, is nothing other than *evolution*. And the drive to ever-higher unities Smuts called *holism*."[29] In other words, it is evolution itself that creates the holism of the Kosmos (driven by divine *telos*).

True holism, therefore, always involves evolution or the development of higher-order wholes where each emergent "level" *transcends-yet-includes* (or envelops) the lower levels, but they do so by adding "something more" (the new emergent). For example, molecules "transcend-but-include" atoms, cells "transcend-but-include" molecules, apes "transcend-but-include" cells, and so on. This evolutionary holism is still Wilber's overriding thesis, as he first explained in his third book, *The Atman Project* (1980):

> As a general approximation, then, we may conclude that the psyche—like the cosmos at large—is many-layered ("pluridimensional"), composed of successively higher-order wholes and unities and integrations. The holistic evolution of nature—which produces everywhere higher and higher wholes—shows up in the human psyche as *development* or *growth*. The same force that produced man from amoebas produces adults from infants. That is, a person's growth, from infancy to adulthood, is simply a miniature version of cosmic evolution… the unfolding of ever higher-order unities and integrations. And this is one of the major reasons that the psyche is, indeed, stratified [as a spectrum of consciousness].[30]

Yet, such an integrative scheme has not been universally accepted, especially in today's modern world of scientific materialism and postmodern deconstructionism. With modern and postmodern visions that claim everything is equal since "all things are relative,"[31] or that all things are reducible to matter, then terms and ideas like "hierarchy," "development," "transcendental," "universal" have been out of favor in today's intellectual world. Nonetheless, with an evolutionary holism, Wilber is taking a strong stance in critically defending the evolving nature of the Great Nest of Spirit, since it's the most viable way to accurately portray the vast display of the universe (with exteriors) and consciousness (with interiors), even constructed with the aid of a broad science and empiricism (see Chapter 4). In fact, this is a motivating factor behind debuting the AQAL Approach in the mid-1990s, for the integral theorist needed to directly address this "problem with hierarchy" in contemporary culture.

In response, with the AQAL Approach, Wilber began emphasizing a new set of terms, such as "holons" and "holarchy," which are also rooted in the ancient Greek word *holos*, literally, meaning "whole, organism, universe."[32] These terms were originally proposed by science-philosopher Arthur Koestler (1905–1983), who was building upon Smuts's use of *holism* as a way to emphasize the necessity for using a *hierarchical* approach to explain the structure of the universe. In support of this, the economist and philosopher, E. F. Schumacher (1930–1977) clearly agreed when he pointed out, "The ability to see the Great Truth of the hierarchic structure of the world, which makes it possible to distinguish between *higher and lower Levels of Being*, is one of the indispensable conditions of understanding. Without it, it is not possible to find out every thing's proper and legitimate place. Everything, everywhere, can be understood only when its *Level of Being* is fully taken into account."[33] A good map, in other words, when used properly, is an invaluable tool for better knowing the deep complexities of reality, and none more so than using a holistic hierarchy that discerns the various dimensions and levels of existence.

By the 1960s, Koestler had coined the term "holon" to indicate a "subwhole," which is an autonomous *part* that's also set within larger *wholes*, thus a holon is defined as a "whole/part." This is why Koestler described them as being "Janus-faced" (or "two-faced"), since all things in nature are simultaneously: (1) a *whole*, or "a stable, integrated structure," and (2) a *part*, which is always "a dependent part" that's set within more and more wholes (nests within nests within nests, etc.). As Koestler put it, the universe is "not parts, not wholes, but holons,"[34] which is exactly the same for Wilber who explained in *Sex, Ecology, Spirituality* (1995): "Reality as a whole is not composed of things or processes; it is not composed of atoms or quarks; it is not composed of wholes nor does it have any parts. Rather, it is composed of *whole/parts*, or holons."[35] Importantly, the *wholeness* of a holon gives it a degree of autonomy (or *agency*), while its *partness* puts it in relationship (or *communion*) with other wholes, in other words, as the integral evolutionist simply puts it: "All holons are *agency-in-communion*" (see next chapter).

In addition, Koestler was also keenly aware of the sticky problem of using a hierarchical vision in today's modern egalitarian world, mostly because there's a justifiable need to distinguish "pathological hierarchies" of social domination, including its authoritative "military and ecclesiastic associations" (Koestler's words), from the "natural hierarchies" that reflect the natural order of all things (or of all holons). Although the term *hierarchy* originally meant "sacred order," it's too often been a word for social oppression, therefore Wilber too has been very clear about distinguishing "normal or *natural hierarchies*," or even *"actualization hierarchies,"* from the "pathological or *dominator hierarchies*."[36] This too has often been overlooked by postmodern critics who are too quick to criticize hierarchical structural organizations.

To counter this dilemma, Koestler cleverly suggested using more holistic derivatives, which Wilber has also incorporated, such as "holarchy" and "holarchic" and "holonic" as being a better way to indicate that a true "hierarchy consists of autonomous, self-governing holons endowed with varying degrees of flexibility and freedom."[37] By definition then, Wilber also concludes in *The Eye of Spirit* (1997): "A [natural] *hierarchy* is simply a ranking of orders of events *according to their holistic capacity*. In any development sequence, what is whole at one stage becomes merely a part of a larger whole at the next stage."[38] Consequently, Wilber agrees with Koestler, who argued in *The Ghost in the Machine* (1967): "A hierarchy of holons should rightly be called a *holarchy*."[39] This has important implications, as Wilber points out in *Sex, Ecology, Spirituality* (1995): "With the understanding that *the only way you get a holism is via a holarchy*, we are not in a position to realign facts and values in a gentler embrace, with science working with us, not against us, in constructing a truly holistic, not heapistic, worldview."[40]

As a result, with the current AQAL Metatheory, Wilber also distinguishes between the *vertical* integration of a *holarchy* (or "the *holism between levels*") and the *horizontal* adaptation of *heterarchy* (or the "holism *within* any level").[41] He therefore explains his intended usage, "When I use the term 'holarchy,' I will especially mean the balance of *normal hierarchy* and *normal heterarchy* (as the context will make clear). 'Holarchy' undercuts both extreme hierarchy and extreme heterarchy, and allows the discussion to move forward with, I believe, the best of both worlds kept firmly in mind."[42] In both cases there are the *normal* versions of hierarchy and heterarchy, and also their pathological versions, which must always be clearly differentiated, as the AQAL Model does so well. Wilber perfectly summarizes these observations about this natural *holonic* order of the Kosmos in a passage from *A Theory of Everything* (2000):

> What *all* of those entities are, before they are anything else, are *holons*—they are all whole/parts. The Kosmos is made of holons at various levels of organization (physical holons, emotional holons, mental holons, spiritual holons). This insight relieves us from saying that, for example, the entire Kosmos is made of nothing but quarks, which is horribly reductionistic. Rather, each higher level of holons has emergent qualities that cannot be derived from, nor totally reduced to, its junior levels—and this gives us the Kosmos, not merely the cosmos.[43]

Any genuine integral theory, therefore, will have to see all mutually interpenetrating processes and things as *holons,* or as interlaced whole/parts nested within one another as a *holarchy,* or a "nested hierarchy" of the Kosmos. Wilber explains, "Further, let us simply note that the Great Chain of Being was in fact a Great Holarchy of Being—with each link being an intrinsic whole that was simultaneously a part of a larger whole—and the entire series nested in Spirit."[44] These are just some of the new AQAL terms laying the foundation for Wilber's current integral theories that have transformed the traditional "Great Chain of Being" into a post-postmodern "Great Holarchy of Spirit," an interactive matrix modeling the indescribable spectrum of consciousness and Kosmos as One Taste of Divine Spirit.

Holons, Not Heaps or Aggregates

The idea of holons can sometimes appear more difficult to grasp than it really is; for instance, not *everything* is a holon, since holons are only whole entities with depth, that is, as wholes they are composed (or compounded) of smaller whole/parts (holons), yet they're always an autonomous part of larger wholes (with agency). For example, bodies are composed of cells that are composed of cells that are composed of molecules that are composed of atoms, and so on, not the other way around (or vice versa). In addition, there is a difference between an *individual holon* and a *social holon*, where each has an interior dimension but in a different way, and then there are *heaps* or *aggregates,* which are not holons but only a collection of holons. Wilber began defining these characteristics in *Sex, Ecology, Spirituality* (1995), but his subsequent AQAL writings have clarified these basic definitions:

- **Individual Holon**—a *whole* that is also a *part* (with four quadrants) of larger wholes, therefore, they possess "actual wholeness (identifiable pattern, *agency,* regime, etc.),"[45] such as with quarks, electrons, atoms, cells, organisms, etc., which also include *interiors,* such as prehension, propensity, irritability, sensation, tropism, perception, impulse, image, etc.

- **Heaps**—are holons that are accidentally thrown together, e.g., a pile of sand; heaps do not have agency and interiors.

- **Aggregates**—like heaps, are associated holons that are the gathering of units into in mass, for example, rocks; aggregates do not have agency and interiors.

- **Social Holon**—is more than a mere heap (or collection of holons) because "individual [holons] are united by patterns of *relational exchange,* but it is less than an individual holon in terms of tightness of its regime: social holons do not possess a locus of self-awareness at any stage of their development, whereas higher-level individual holons have interiors that become increasingly conscious, so that at the level of human compound individuals, self-awareness is possible in individuals, but not in societies."[46]

Transfinite Turtles: All the Way Up, All the Way Down

In his immensely popular yet difficult book on physics and black holes called *A Brief History of Time* (1988), the renowned British physicist Stephen

Hawking began by telling a story of a well-known scientist (some say it was Bertrand Russell) who gave a lecture on astronomy that ended with a little old lady saying it was all rubbish because the universe was supported on the back of a giant tortoise. When the lecturer smirkingly asked, "What is the tortoise standing on?" she unhesitatingly replied, "It's turtles all the way down."[47] In another difficult book, but one outlining an integral vision that integrates all the elements of existence, called *A Brief History of Everything* (1996), Ken Wilber also resorted to a tale of turtles to explain the fact that the universe is composed of "holons" or "wholes that are simultaneously parts of other wholes," and that they go on endlessly "all the way down." In other words, the "rings" or "spheres" or "levels" of the Great Nest of Being are actually holons composed of endlessly more holons (whole/parts), and so why not call these holons "turtles"?[48] Again (and metaphorically), "It's turtles all the way down," which is another way of saying *"the system is sliding"* (or *transfinite*).

Yet, of course, in an expansive Kosmos of great depth and mighty span, Wilber also tells us it's not only "turtles all the way down… but it's also turtles all the way up," thus he's invoking the famous saying attributed to the ancient Greek philosopher Heraclitus (540–475 B.C.E.): "The Way Up Is the Way Down."[49] This is a good metaphor for the AQAL Matrix, because, as Wilber explains, "The *system is sliding*. The Kosmos is the unending All, and the All is composed of holons [turtles]—all the way up, all the way down." [50] In other words, this means Wilber's trying to emphasize the fact that since the Kosmos (or all holons) are actually arising from, and are pervaded by, the infinite and eternal Spirit (or God), then it's really *without* any foundation at all, for it's simply arising in "pure groundless Emptiness, or radically *nondual* Spirit."[51] In other words, all things really do shade into God.

Another way to say this is holons are "transfinite," or as Wilber defines in *SES* (1995): "Every holon is actually a holon within other holons *transfinitely*—that is, every holon is *simultaneously* both a *subholon* (a part of some other holon) and a *superholon* (itself containing holons)."[52] Therefore, since "the Kosmos is composed of holons, all the way up, all the way down," then the integral philosopher recognizes that "'transfinite' (turtles all the way up) means that the sum total of all the whole/parts in the universe is *not itself a Whole,* because the moment it comes to be (as a 'whole'), that totality is merely a *part* of the very next moment's whole, which in turn is merely a part of the next… and so ad infinitum."[53] In other words, all emergent holons are *transfinite* since they're always *part of* a greater whole, including this moment, which then leads into the next, and so on, forever, yet, nonetheless, all holons (or all things) are *always already* released (or absolutely free) in "One Taste," or the radiant formlessness and indivisible unity of God. Wilber thus summarizes these intentions of *SES,* and the entire Phase-4 AQAL Approach in *A Theory of Everything* (2000):

> According to *SES,* reality is fundamentally composed—not of particles, quarks, pointless dimensions, strings, or membranes—but of *holons.* A holon is a whole that is simultaneously a part of other wholes. For example, a whole quark is part of a whole proton; a whole proton is part of a whole atom; a whole atom is part of a whole molecule; a whole molecule is part of a whole cell, which is a part of a whole organism, which is part of the whole Kosmos, which is part of the whole Kosmos of the next moment, and so ad infinitum (what *SES* calls *"turtles all the way up, all the way down"*). What *all* of those entities are, before they are anything else, are holons—they are all whole/parts. The Kosmos is made of holons at various levels of organization (physical holons, emotional holons, mental holons, spiritual holons). This insight relieves us from saying that, for example, the entire Kosmos is made of nothing but quarks, which is horribly reductionistic. Rather, each higher level of holons has emergent qualities that cannot be derived from, not totally reduced to, its junior levels—and this gives us the Kosmos, not merely the cosmos.[54]

This understanding has profound implications, such as, for one, this is in complete agreement with postmodernity's truth claim: "Everything is a context within a context forever," which is why Wilber concludes: "That consciousness is endlessly holonic is the final message of postmodernism."[55] The integral pandit continues to explain in *Sex, Ecology, Spirituality* (1995): "There is a system, but *the system is sliding*, it is unendingly, dizzyingly holarchic.... Turtles all the way up, turtles all the way down…transfinite turtles."[56] By embracing this paradox, Wilber does not, like many scientists and philosophers, declare a final "end point" or "Omega point" for everything ultimately "shades" into nondual Emptiness (or the Divine). Only a model of great depth, actually infinite depth, can include these type of paradoxical conclusions (a mandalic science), which are proven only by actual *transformative practices* (such as meditation), which disclose the transpersonal structures of the Kosmos, including the One Taste of the Divine Domain (or Enlightenment).

Anti-Flatland: A Kosmos *with Depth & Meaning*

By recognizing and reviving the traditional Great Chain of Being into an integral Great Holarchy of Spirit, Wilber is countering the *reductionistic* tendency of "scientific materialism" (or *scientism*) that's generated by the modern mind. Simultaneously he's offering a cure for the relative pluralism and narcissistic nihilism of postmodernity. One of the principal "disasters" or "bad news" of modernity, claims Wilber, is that it promotes "the collapse of the Kosmos," which not only reduces everything in the universe to nothing but material particles, but it also scrubs clean all interiors by claiming they're nothing more than "epiphenomena" or a secondary influence arising from only matter. Wilber calls this "Flatland," for the social critic bemoans the dreadfulness of the situation in *The Marriage of Sense and Soul* (2000): "The interior dimensions of the Kosmos were simply gutted and laid out to dry in the blazing sun of the monological gaze."[57] This reductionistic materialism of modernity is its disaster, and is in a large part responsible for the reactionism expressed by fundamentalists (or traditionalists) and postmodernists, who have not yet proposed a workable and realistic solution (see chapter 14).

Wilber drives his point home by noting it's only the modern West that holds the dubious distinction of becoming "the first major civilization in the history of humanity to deny almost entirely the existence of the Great Nest of Being."[58] For many present-day thinkers and theorists (from postmodernists to new paradigm theorists, et al.), this is an unacceptable intellectual quagmire, which is why the integral view proposes a holarchical or holonic view of evolutionary development (grounded in Spirit) as the means to overcome these reductionistic limitations while maintaining modern critical and scientific thinking. Therefore, by acknowledging *interior realities*, the integral approach is adding *depth* and *meaning* back into today's worldview and philosophical theories. Thus "the resurrection of the interior" is one of the principal challenges of any integral theory, yet an accomplishment the AQAL Model achieves very effectively.

Since the AQAL Approach of Wilber Phase-4/5 builds upon the earlier theories of the spectrum of consciousness, but is now described as a holarchy of holons, Wilber introduced the various *spheres* of the Kosmos as being the realms or structures (basic waves) in the "Great Nest of Spirit" (see next chapter). Thus, he recaps the real meaning of "Kosmos" in *A Brief History of Everything* (1996): "The original meaning of Kosmos was the patterned nature or process of all domains of existence, from matter to math to theos, and not merely the physical universe, which is usually what 'cosmos' and 'universe' mean today. So I would like to reintroduce this term *Kosmos*. The Kosmos contains the *cosmos* (or the physiosphere), the *bios* (or biosphere), *nous* (the noosphere), and *theos* (the theosphere or divine domain)—none of them being foundational (even spirit shades into Emptiness). So we can say in short: The Kosmos is composed of holons, all the way up, all the way down."[59] For Wilber, of course, the pluridimensional and multileveled *Kosmos* is the "Realm of Totality," the "Matrix of Reality," a "morphogenetic developmental space," a postmodern "Dharmadhatu," or an evolving inter-meshed "Kosmic Mandala," a spectrum of reality that paradoxically exists as "One Taste" for there's really nothing *but* the nondual condition of Real God.

The reduction of the natural holarchy of the "Kosmos" into a material-istic Flatland that's defended by modern scientism and capitalistic consum-erism has often been recognized by many profound thinkers as being one of modernity's greatest maladies. The AQAL Model, therefore, with its *all-quadrants, all-levels* and interacting *interiors* and *exteriors* (in self, culture, and nature) is specifically designed to be an antidote to this error of the modern mind, for it adds *depth* and *interiors* back into the Kosmos as a whole. This approach will further enrich our understanding of a genuine "kosmology" as being the real "order of the universe," thus the integral philosopher again acknowledges: "I think what we want to do is *kosmology*, not cosmology."[60] This allows the static "Great Chain" to morph into the dynamic holarchy or morphogenetic matrix of nested holonic quadrants alive with developing levels, lines, states, types, of consciousness, a Whole of holistic holons that's always already grounded in Divine Emptiness. Only this type of multivari-able model that incorporates and integrates all these important discoveries, yet *partial truths*, of the premodern, modern, postmodern, and transpersonal (or spiritual) worldviews will be adequate to meet today's intense challenge of authentic integration, to finally consummate the passion-filled "marriage of science and religion." Such a "Kosmic Mandala" of divine existence is naturally saturated with depth *and* meaning, exteriors *and* interiors, all arising in and as Spirit-in-action, the unfolding dance of evolution itself, which we'll turn to next.

CHAPTER EIGHT

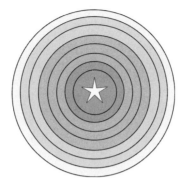

AQAL Matrix: A Kosmic Mandala of Spirit-in-Action

Spirit unfolds in a great *spectrum of consciousness-reality,* from the Big Bang to matter to sensation to perception to impulse to image to symbol to concept to reason to psychic to subtle to causal occasions, on the way to its own shocking self-recognition, Spirit's own self-realization and self-resurrection.

—Ken Wilber, *The Eye of Spirit* (1997)

A Great Chain of Being into a Great Nest of Spirit

IN THE MID-TO-LATE 1970S, BY USING THE METAPHOR OF A "SPECTRUM" to reflect a unified whole composed of different bandwidths with each having its own distinct and recognizable characteristics, Ken Wilber brought an idea similar to the traditional "Great Chain of Being" straight back into modern psychology. This accomplishment brought accolades such as he's "the long-sought Einstein of consciousness research," and prompted the elder scholar of world religions, Huston Smith, to tell the young philosopher, "If all you had done in your life was to move the Great Chain of Being into psychology virtually single-handedly, that alone would be one of the intellectual achievements of our century."[1] Although Wilber began with the conception of a "spectrum of consciousness" (Phase-1), it soon grew into an evolutionary "Great Chain of Being" (Phases-2/3), thus becoming the "Great Nest of Spirit" with successive levels of reality reaching from *matter* to *nature* to *body* to *mind* to *soul* to *spirit,* and then twenty years later it blossomed into the AQAL Matrix of "all-quadrants, all-levels, all-lines, all-types, all-states" (Phases-4/5).

Philosopher Arthur Lovejoy, in his classic study *The Great Chain of Being* (1936), had already demonstrated that some type of hierarchical Great Chain model "has, in one form or another, been the dominant official philosophy of the larger part of civilized humankind through most of its history."[2] In generalized Western terms (with Wilber's subdivisions in parentheses), the "Great Chain of Being" is commonly described as the "basic levels" of Matter (pleroma), Body (uroboros, archaic, magic), Mind (mythic, rational, centaur), Soul (psychic, subtle), and Spirit (causal, nondual). As an important advancement, Wilber's integral theories emphasize that each senior level *transcends-yet-includes* the junior dimensions in an integral embrace.

In these simple Western terms, the accompanying figure represents the nested quality and mandalic embrace of the "Great Chain" or "Great Nest of Spirit," where Wilber often points out that each level has its corresponding fields of study or "modes of knowing" (methodologies). See Figure 8-1.

By building upon this holistic idea, Wilber went on to enormously expand this "Great Chain" into a "Great Nest of Spirit" (or "Great Holarchy of Being"), especially since it's not really a strictly linear progression with separate "links," like the crude chain metaphor suggests, but rather this morphogenetic developmental space is more like a *mandala* of nested spheres. In fact, the traditional Christian metaphor of the Great Chain of Being with its hierarchy of seraphim to angels to demons, and so on, was not what Wilber had in mind at all. As a matter of course, he continues to sketch out this simple idea as being foundational to understanding his theories, as he explained again in the Phase-4 book *The Marriage of Sense and Soul* (1998): "The Great Chain of Being—that is perhaps a bit of a misnomer, because the actual view was more like the Great Nest of Being, with each senior dimension nesting or enfolding its junior dimensions—a situation often described as '*transcend and include.*' Spirit transcends but includes

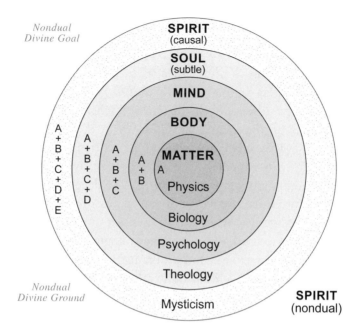

The Great Nest of Spirit:
A Holistic Mandala of Transcend-and-Include
Figure 8-1

soul, which transcends but includes mind, which transcends but includes the vital body, which transcends but includes matter."[3] And this Great Nest is now the AQAL Matrix.

By readapting the "Great Chain of Being" into an AQAL Matrix, Wilber's integral philosophy presents a holistic holarchy of creative evolutionary development, yet it does so without resorting to an outdated metaphysics or to archetypal mythic images upheld by the premodern worldview, whether religious ones or not. AQAL Metatheory retains these significant truths for they are the "dignities" and "good news" of premodernity, modernity. and postmodernity, yet does so in a way that produces an *Integral Post-Metaphysics* that can decidedly answer and rectify Kant's devastating critiques (as we saw in chapter 6). As we've also seen, the approach of this "Theory of Everything" is crucially based upon investigative methodologies, not just intellectual speculation, but is grounded in actual methods and paradigms reaching from science to the spiritual quest (see chapter 14).

AQAL Matrix: Great Nest of Being (Reality) & Knowing (Selfhood)

In his acclaimed book *Forgotten Truth: The Common Vision of the World's Religions* (1976), Huston Smith, respected religious studies scholar and author of the immensely popular *The World's Religions* (1958, 1991), made perhaps the definitive defense of the hierarchical scheme of nature (or reality), or what represents the traditional "Great Chain of Being" (which is the "forgotten truth"). This small and wonderfully written book was released during Wilber's formative intellectual years, thus it was instrumental in supporting his developing philosophy by reaffirming a deep reliance on a hierarchical scheme to outline the whole of reality. Importantly, especially for Wilber, Smith's defense was set within the context of the modern world, a world of modernity, which had become increasingly antihierarchical in its attitudes, especially in its extreme forms of reductionistic scientific materialism, a philosophical malady Smith simply calls *scientism*.

Forgotten Truth (highly recommended to all) exquisitely summarizes the traditional or premodern "Great Chain of Being" as being composed of Body (the "terrestrial realm"), Mind (the "intermediate realm"), Soul (the "celestial realm"), and Spirit ("the infinite"). Traditionally, Smith noted, each level was seen to have corresponding "Levels of Selfhood" and "Planes of Reality,"[4] thus they emphasize two important philosophical ideas traditionally known as "Being" or "Existence" (also called *ontology*), and "Knowing" or "Consciousness" (also called *epistemology*), summarized as follows:

- **Being** (or *ontology*)—reflects the "planes of reality" or the "levels" and "realms" of existence, therefore, technically, ontology is usually referred to as being "out there," thus it's commonly seen as the *exterior* world or the universe-at-large (the Kosmos/cosmos);

- **Knowing** (or *epistemology*)—reflects the "levels of selfhood" or the "levels of consciousness," which is our own human psychology that's found "in here," therefore, technically, epistemology studies what and how humans gain knowledge, thus it involves the inner psyche or the *interior* development of the mind.

To summarize these various levels, the accompanying figure shows an expanded view of Professor Smith's arrangement of correlating the "planes of reality" (or Being and *ontology*) with the "levels of selfhood" (or Knowing and *epistemology*), now called the AQAL Matrix. See Figure 8-2.

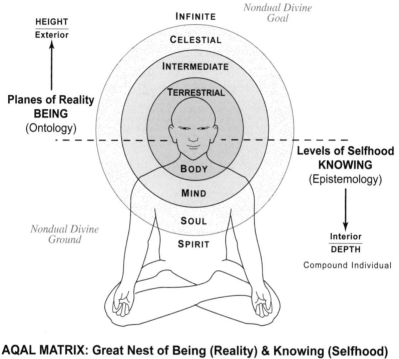

AQAL MATRIX: Great Nest of Being (Reality) & Knowing (Selfhood)
(after Huston Smith)
Figure 8-2

In *Forgotten Truth,* Smith further pointed out that these "planes of reality" (or the external world) are often envisioned with metaphors of *"height,"* while the internal "planes of the self" (or the internal worlds) are seen as having *"depth,"* both metaphors that Wilber's integral approach uses interchangeably. For humans, made of physical body and subtle soul, yet grounded in causal Spirit, there is a correlation between them, for as Professor Smith eloquently explains, "One of the reasons a hierarchical view of reality is indispensable is that Spirit, the human spirit included, is nonspatial and thereby belongs perforce to an order of existence distinct in kind from nature.... That which man seeks externally in the highest heavens he seeks internally in the depths of his soul.... We journey far to reach our origin."[5] Inspired in part by his teacher and dear friend, Huston Smith, Wilber has developed an integral model that agrees that this journey directly involves the spectrum of consciousness and Kosmos evolving together, where *both* are seen as an integral unity, a matrix of interiors and exteriors, embodied as four quadrants in the Great Holarchy of Spirit, an AQAL Matrix that is the totality of reality, from matter to mind to God.

In this case, according to Wilber, the AQAL "all-quadrant, all-level" Matrix is best seen as a "Great Nest of Being and Knowing," and it was even back when he called it a "spectrum of consciousness," because all the *interiors* (or the levels of selfhood) and *exteriors* (or the planes of reality) are intimately intertwined and intermeshed. Recently he specifically clarified this position in *Integral Psychology* (2000): "In my view, the basic structures in the Great Nest are *simultaneously* levels of both Knowing and Being, epistemology and ontology…. However, on occasion it is useful to distinguish them, because *a given level of self can experience a different level or plane of reality.*"[6] He continues to make his definitions clear (2000): "For 'Levels of Reality' (or *'planes of reality'*) I also use *'realms of reality'* (e.g., gross realm, subtle realm, causal realm, etc.) or *'spheres of reality'* (e.g., biosphere, noosphere, theosphere, etc.). For 'Levels of Selfhood' I often use *'levels of consciousness'* or *'levels of subjectivity.'* But I usually refer to them *both* as *basic levels, basic structures,* or Basic Waves, since they are *correlative* (i.e., there are as many levels of selfhood as there are levels of reality)."[7] Obviously, any integral approach needs to fully include and correlate both variables of consciousness and existence, self and kosmos, subject and object, as being one indivisible reality, while also being distinguishable and open to observation, measurement, and mapping (or cross-indexing).

The "AQAL Matrix" continues to depict the "basic structures" or "basic waves" of the Great Nest of Spirit as involving *both* the "levels of selfhood" (or *epistemology*) and the "planes of reality" (or *ontology*), which is why, as Wilber acknowledges, "a given level of self, generally, can interact with different levels of reality, to various degrees, so that we need to keep there two (structures and realms) as independent variables."[8] As he's pointed out since *Eye to Eye* (1983), the self (or consciousness) can turn its attention, via the various modes of knowing (i.e., the *epistemological* "eyes" of flesh, mind, contemplation) to any of the *ontological* levels (i.e., the objects of sensibilia, intelligibilia, transcendelia). Since Wilber began his work oriented toward transpersonal psychology (and psychology in general), even premiering his integral theories by suggesting a *psychologia perennis* (or "perennial psychology"), his presentations have usually favored the psychological structures of the self-system (or the levels of selfhood). This is mostly because the modern world has tended to focus more on epistemology since the levels of ontology have been tragically reduced down by modernity and scientism as being *only* physical matter, instead of reflecting the full depth of existence.

On the other hand, extreme postmodernists (such as deconstructionists) depict the separate self or subject as constructing all possible views of reality, thus they dispense with modernity's "myth of the given" by separating the objective world from the observing self (which, ironically, is the stated role of science). Yet, this creates a divisive dualism in contemporary thought, a deconstructive nihilism that only an integral approach can solve and unify in theory and practice. To overcome these limitations, AQAL Metatheory, especially with its *Integral Post-Metaphysics* (where the levels are not depicted as a priori structures), portrays a *psycho-physical existence* of evolutionary development situated in the basic waves of Kosmos-consciousness, not as a dualistic division between the physical ("this-world") and the metaphysical ("the other world"). The AQAL Matrix depicts a divine dance of Spirit-in-action that's unfolding the spheres of the Kosmic Mandala, from physical matter to biological nature to mental mind to subtle soul and spirit, which we'll review next.

AQAL Matrix: Spheres of the Kosmos (Transcend-and-Include)

To view this AQAL Matrix, or Great Nest of Spirit, in more detail, it's time to examine the various basic levels of reality and selfhood, by first reviewing the principal *spheres* of existence. Wilber pointed out in *Sex, Ecology, Spirituality* (1995) that the "pyramid of development" universally recognized by science generally consists of two (or three) great spheres of evolution: the realm of Matter (physics, etc.) and the realm of Nature (biology, etc.), and with only partial recognition of the sphere of Mind (psychology). The integral philosopher continues to cite some contemporary examples, such as from systems scientist Eric Jantsch, author of *The Self-Organizing Universe* (1980), who refers to these great domains as the *cosmic, biosocial,* and *sociocultural* domains (by correlating "micro" and "macro" dimensions),[9] or systems philosopher Ervin Laszlo, author of *Evolution: The Grand Synthesis* (1987), who calls these realms *matter* (material), *life* (biological), and *society* (historical),[10] or integral philosopher Michael Murphy, author of *The Future of the Body* (1993), who summarizes them as the *inorganic, biological,* and *psychological* realms.[11] In each case, they identify each succeeding sphere of existence as adding "something more," a *novel emergent,* and in a "*transcend-yet-include*" manner.

With the full-spectrum AQAL Model, of course, Wilber added the missing transpersonal realms, thus subdividing these holarchical "spheres" of the Kosmos into the Physiosphere (or the sphere of the *physical* and *matter*), the Biosphere (or the sphere of *biology* and *life*), the Noosphere (or the sphere of *mind* and *psyche*), and the Theosphere (or the sphere of *soul* and *spirit*), all culminating (as Goal) and arising within (as Ground) in the Divine Domain. As he summarized in *Sex, Ecology, Spirituality* (1995): "The Kosmos contains the cosmos (or *physiosphere*), the bios (or *biosphere*), nous (or *noosphere*), and theos (the *theosphere* or divine domain)—none of them being foundational (even spirit shades into Emptiness)."[12]

Let's briefly review these "Spheres of the Kosmos," as they've been identified since the Wilber/Phase-4 AQAL Approach, more closely below:

- **Physiosphere** (*physis,* Gr. "nature")—the sphere of "cosmos" or the domain of physical matter-energy, from subatomic particles to stars, planets, and galaxies, etc.; studied by the physical sciences, such as physics, astronomy, cosmology, chemistry, etc.:

  a) **Subatomic/Atomic Matter-Energy**—quarks and subatomic particles (energy) that comprise atoms; atoms then lay the foundation for molecules;

  b) **Molecular Matter**—the range of the elements in the periodic table comprised from the combination of subatomic particles and atoms;

  c) **Chemical Matter**—or the chemical construction and combination of elemental systems and polymers, etc., all comprised of molecular configurations.

- **Biosphere** (*bios,* Gr. "life")—the sphere of the natural world, the domain of biology and the diversity of life, living biological systems including *prana* or "life-energy/bio-energy" and Gaia (Earth) life-systems; studied by the life sciences:

a) **Simple Life-Forms**—viruses; bacteria; cells without a nucleus (prokaryotes), etc.;

b) **Complex Life-Forms**—cells with a nucleus (eukaryotes), multicellular life-forms, etc.;

c) **Flora** and **Fauna**—plants and animals whose interconnected Web-of-Life can be subdivided almost ad infinitum since the diversity is so great, including past life-forms, such as dinosaurs, etc.;

d) **Higher Life-forms**—complex-brained mammals, from dolphins to dogs to horses to apes, etc.;

• **Noosphere** (*nous*, Gr. "mind, intellect")—culminating with the human "triune brain," i.e., (1) the reptilian brain stem, (2) paleo-mammalian limbic system, and (3) neomammalian neocortex, together generating the sphere of "nous" or "mind," including the bilateral (two-hemisphere) brain, the domain of the personal mind or self-reflexive consciousness and intelligence, mostly highly evident in human beings (as far as we know); studied by the human sciences and psychology:

a) **Early Mind**—the higher intelligence of higher mammals and early mental structures of hominids (protohumans), peaking with early *Homo sapiens* and Neandertals;

b) **Late Mind**—begins with transition to *Homo sapiens sapiens* (anatomically modern human beings), including the spectrum of worldviews or worldspaces (memes) generated from the emerging structures of consciousness (deep structures) displaying a wide variety of sociocultural forms (surface structures); involves human development from birth to maturity (centaur) to Enlightenment and is the inalienable right of every person on planet Earth;

• **Theosphere** (*theos*, Gr. "divine")—the sphere of "theos" or "the spiritual" realms indicates the transpersonal or superconsciousness structures of soul and spirit (reviewed in chapter 6 as the "spectrum of mysticism"), which are basically subdivided into:

a)   **Higher Realms**—the "subtle sphere," both low and high: the "low-subtle" is the *psychic* dimension, including "paranormal events... the lowest of the transcendental realms"; the "high-subtle" is when the self "extends within and beyond to various subphases of extraordinarily higher-order transcendence, differentiation, and integration"; [13]

b)   **Ultimate Realms**—the "causal," low and high: the "low-causal" includes *archetypal form, illumination, intuition,* and beginning *gnosis,* until the realization of "God as an archetypal summit of one's own Consciousness"; the "high-causal" is "total and utter transcendence and release into Formless Consciousness, Boundless Radiance," traditionally known as *enlightenment* (or *sahaja samadhi*) in which "ultimate unity consciousness... completes that absolute gestalt toward which all manifestation moves.";

•   **Divine Domain**—the "non-sphere," the paradoxical Ground and Goal or inexplicable nondual Divine Spirit to which everything "shades" and ultimately dissolves into Infinity (beyond space) and Eternity (beyond time), thus ultimately translating into the Original Source and Condition of Absolute Consciousness and Transcendent God-Light, therefore, totally indescribable, *only realizable.*

The accompanying figure pictures this "Holarchy of Spheres" as a Kosmic Mandala based on Wilber expanding "The Great Chain of Being" into "The Great Nest of Spirit," now an AQAL Matrix of "basic waves" or "basic structures" of matter, body, mind, soul, spirit, including subdivisions, appearing in self, culture, and nature (with the "star" representing the all-pervading Divine Domain). See Figure 8-3.

The spheres of the Kosmos, as Wilber has maintained since the important transition to a "growth-to-goodness" model (Phase-2), shows that evolution is a *"transcend-yet-include"* process of developmental unfolding where "at each point in evolution, what is the *whole* of one level becomes merely a *part* of the higher-order whole of the next level."[14] Or as Hegel would have it, "development is envelopment."[15] Wilber calls this transcendence "the form of development," which means it's "the secret impulse of evolution,"[16]

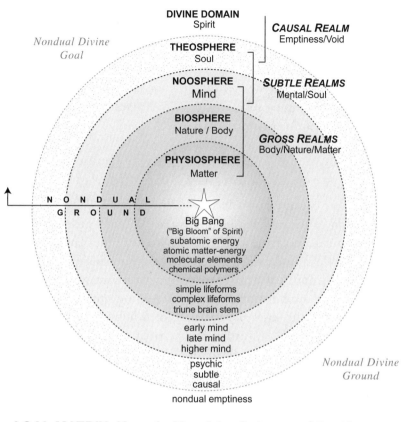

AQAL MATRIX: Kosmic Mandala: Spheres of the Kosmos

Figure 8-3

thus he summarizes in *A Brief History of Everything* (1996): "Evolution is a process of transcend and include, transcend and include. And this begins to open onto the very heart of Spirit-in-action, the very secret of the evolutionary impulse."[17] The emergence of higher-order holons means they are compounded of the previous levels, yet they add "something more," which is the novel emergent, from matter to biology to the mind to the soul and spirit.

Since each sphere is Spirit in essence, and since each senior sphere transcends-yet-includes the junior ones, then Wilber beautifully expressed this idea in *The Eye of Spirit* (1997): "Spirit manifests as the entire world in a series of increasingly holistic and holarchic spheres, stretching from *matter* to *body* to *mind* to *soul* to *spirit* itself. But all of these different dimensions are actually just forms of spirit, in various degrees of self-realization and self-actualization. Thus, there is really spirit-as-matter, spirit-as-prana, spirit-as-mind, spirit-as-soul, and spirit-as-spirit."[18] Huston Smith expressed the same idea in *Forgotten Truth* (1976): "Spirit is Infinite, but a person is finite because s/he is not Spirit only. One's specifically human overlay— body, mind, and soul—veils the Spirit within oneself."[19] One Kosmos with intermeshing and developing spheres of existence, always already grounded in God—this is the AQAL Matrix.

Kosmic Patterns: 20-Tenets (of Spirit-in-Action)

When Ken Wilber began Phase-4 in the 1990s, he codified the basic patterns of evolution or the evolving holons as the 20-Tenets of Evolution or "the patterns that connect," the "patterns of existence," the "laws of form," or "propensities of manifestation"[20] in the Kosmos. He explained his intentions in *Sex, Ecology, Spirituality* (1995): "Starting with the notion of holons, and proceeding by a combination of a priori reasoning and *a posteriori* evidence, we can attempt to discern what all known holons seem to have in common."[21] Consequently, he further clarifies that "the twenty tenets are simply some of the tendencies of evolutionary patterns wherever we find them [in any sphere]; they are 'Kosmic patterns.'"[22] As important as the 20-Tenets are, Wilber also concedes "the twenty tenets—by which I mean dynamic systems theory in general—are the *most fundamental* tenets of *all* of development, and therefore the *least* interesting, least significant, least telling tenets." In other words, he continues, "There is nothing in the twenty tenets that will tell us how to resolve an Oedipus complex, or why pride can be wounded, or what honor means, or whether life is worth living."[23] Nonetheless, they outline the dynamics of development, including the evolution of consciousness, and so will be a crucial part of any integral theory.

Although the actual number of "twenty" is malleable (for "there is nothing special about twenty,"[24] and again, "there is nothing sacrosanct about the number 'twenty'"),[25] Wilber maintains these are the active patterns of evolution as they appear in the *physiosphere, biosphere, noosphere,* and even the *theosphere* (although he has not tried to be exhaustive in compiling the list). In *Sex, Ecology, Spirituality* (1995) and *A Brief History of Everything* (1996),[26] the "20-Tenets" of evolution are carefully defined, which I have briefly condensed below:

1) *Reality as a whole is not composed of things or processes, but of* holons (*wholes* that are *part* of other *wholes*). Composed, that is, of wholes that are simultaneously parts of other wholes, with no upward or downward limit.... Thus, holons within holons within holons means that the world is without foundation in either wholes or parts...but pure groundless Emptiness [*sunyata*], or radically *nondual* Spirit.

2) *Holons display four fundamental capacities,* or the four "forces" that are in constant tension that can be pictured as a cross, with two *horizontal* "opposites" *(agency and communion)* and two *vertical* "opposites" *(self-transcendence and self-dissolution):*

   a) **self-preservation** (or *agency*)—All holons display some capacity to preserve their individuality, to preserve their own particular wholeness or autonomy;

   b) **self-adaptation** (or *communion*)—A holon functions not only as a self-preserving *whole* but also as a *part* of a larger whole, and in its capacity as a *part* it must adapt or accommodate itself to other holons;

   c) **self-transcendence** or self-transformation (or *eros*)—Self-transcendence is simply a system's capacity to reach beyond the given and introduce some measure of novelty.... through the introduction of new and creative twists in the evolutionary stream;

   d) **self-dissolution** (or *thanatos*)—Holons that are built up (through vertical self-transformation) can also break down. Not surprisingly, when holons "dissolve" or "come unglued," they tend to do so along the same vertical sequence in which they were built up (only, of course, in the reverse direction);

3) *Holons emerge.* Owing to the self-transcendent capacity of holons, new holons emerge.... *emergent holons* are in some sense *novel;* they possess properties and qualities that cannot be strictly and totally deduced from their components; and therefore they, and their descriptions, cannot be reduced without remainder to their component parts.

4) *Holons emerge holarchically.* That is, *hierarchically.* That is, as a series of increasing whole/parts. Organisms contain cells, but not vice

versa; cells contain molecules, but not vice versa; molecules contain atoms, but not vice versa. And it is that *not vice versa*, at *each* stage, that constitutes unavoidable asymmetry and hierarchy (holarchy).

5) *Each emergent holon transcends but includes its predecessor(s).* Hegel: "To supersede is at once to preserve and to negate," but not in detail, but in fundamental feature. Another way to express this is: *All of the lower is in the higher, but not all of the higher is in the lower.*

6) *The lower sets the possibilities of the higher; the higher sets the probabilities of the lower....* This is what is meant by saying that a lower sets the possibilities, or the larger framework, within which the higher will have to operate, but to which it is not confined.

7) *The number of levels that a holarchy comprises determines whether it is "shallow" or "deep" [depth]; and the number of holons on any given level we shall call its "span."* The greater the *vertical* dimension of a holon (the more levels it contains), then the *greater* the *depth* of that holon; and the more holons on that level, the *wider* its *span.*

8) *Each successive level of evolution produces greater depth* and *less span.* The greater the depth of a holon, the more precarious is its existence, since its existence depends also on the existence of a whole series of other holons internal to it.... Thus, greater depth always means less span, in relation to a holon's predecessor(s).... Evolution is *not* bigger and better, but smaller and better (greater depth, less span).

9] Addition 1: *The greater the depth of a holon, the greater its degree of consciousness.* The spectrum of evolution is a spectrum of consciousness. And one can perhaps begin to see that a spiritual dimension is built into the very fabric, the very *depth,* of the Kosmos.... *Translation* shuffles parts; *Transformation* produces wholes.... The point, then, is that evolution is first and foremost a series of transformations ("self-realization through self-transcendence").

9) [10] *Destroy any holon, and you will destroy all of the holons above it and none of the holons below it....* In other words, destroy any type of holon, and that also destroys all the *higher* holons in the sequence, because those higher wholes depend upon the lower as constituent parts....

- The *less depth* a holon has, the *more fundamental* it is to the Kosmos, because it is a *component* of so many other holons....

- At the same time, the *less depth* a holon has, the *less significant* it is to the Kosmos, because it embraces (as its own components) so little of the Kosmos....

- On the other hand, the *greater the depth,* or the greater the particular wholeness of a holon, then the *less fundamental* it is, because fewer other holons depend on it for their own existence....

- But by the same token, the less fundamental, the more significant: the *more significant* that holon is for the universe, because more of the universe is reflected or embraced in that particular wholeness (more of the Kosmos is internal to it, as part of its own being).

10) [11] *Holarchies coevolve.* Holons do not evolve alone, because there are no alone holons (there are only fields within fields within fields). This principle is often referred to as *coevolution,* which simply means that the "unit" of evolution is not an isolated holon (individual molecule or plant to animal) but a holon plus its inseparable environment.

11) [12] *The micro is in relational exchange with the macro at all levels of its depth.* This tenet is extremely important, particularly when it comes to holons of greater depth and the types of ecosystems (in the broad sense) that they must co-reate and upon which their existence depends... a network of relationships with other holons at the *same level of structural organization* ["same-level relational exchange"].

12) [13] *Evolution has directionality* [the "arrow of time"]. This is the famous arrow of evolutionary time first recognized in the biosphere, but now understood, in the sciences of complexity, to be present in all three of the great domains of evolution. This *directionality* is usually stated as being one of increasing differentiation, variety, complexity, and organization.... Here are some others. Aside from regressions, dissolutions, arrest, etc., evolution tends in the direction of:

a) **[14]** *Increasing complexity*—The central and universal feature of nature: the emergence of ever-increasing complexity;

b) **[15]** *Increasing differentiation/integration*—*Differentiation* produces partness, or a new "manyness"; *Integration* produces wholeness, or a new "oneness."... In sum, evolution requires both differentiation and integration operating together... The dialectics of depth;

c) **[16]** *Increasing organization/structuration*—Laszlo: "Evolution moves from the simpler to the more complex type of system, and from the lower to the higher levels of organization."... This is, for example, behind the standard distinction, in evolutionary biology, between clades and grades... *Grade*, of course, is another term for depth;

d) **[17]** *Increasing relative autonomy* [agency-in-communion]—This simply refers to a holon's capacity for self-preservation in the midst of environmental fluctuations.... *As a whole*, a holon possesses a degree of autonomy, expressed in its identifying and enduring pattern, its self-preservation.... *As a part*, every holon—the autonomy of every holon—is subjected to larger forces and systems of which it is merely a component.... In other words, all agency is *agency-in-communion...;*

e) **[18]** *Increasing Telos*—The regime, canon, code, or deep structure of a holon acts as a magnet, an attractor, a miniature omega point, for the *actualization* of that holon in space and time. That is, the end point of the system tends to "pull" the holon's actualization (or development) in that direction,.... Telos—the miniature omega-point pull of the end state of a holon's regime—is, of course, rampant not only in physical systems but in the biosphere and noosphere as well... perhaps telos, perhaps Eros, moves the entire Kosmos, and God may indeed be an all-embracing chaotic Attractor, acting, as Whitehead said, throughout the world by gentle persuasion toward love;

[19] Addition 2: *Every holon issues an IOU to the Kosmos*—where *IOU* means "Incomplete Or Uncertain," and which specifically means, the more complete or encompassing a holon, the less consistent or certain, and vice versa.... And no holon *ever* delivers, or *can* deliver, on that promise;

[20] Addition 3: *All IOUs are redeemed in Emptiness*—Emptiness *[sunyata]* is neither a Whole nor a Part nor a Whole/Part. Emptiness is the reality of which all wholes and all parts are simply manifestations.... And there is the *message of the mystics,* ever so simply put: Emptiness and Emptiness alone redeems all IOUs.

Once more, especially with Additions 2/3, we can see how radically Buddhist Wilber's integral model is by referring again to "Emptiness" or *sunyata,* and putting him in deep accord with the world's mystical traditions, thus reflecting the deepest stream of where Wilber's at (see chapter 6). Nonetheless, these integral revelations of the 20-Tenets of evolution showing the most fundamental "patterns that connect" the Kosmos from matter to mind to God, are now being updated with post-postmodern or integral consciousness and modeling systems that incorporate science and spirituality together in harmony.

Agency & Communion: Rights & Responsibilities

The implications of seeing the Kosmos (or the totality of reality) as an embrace of *holons* or unfolding whole/parts comprising a nested *holarchy* will, no doubt, have reverberating effects for generations to come. The integral approach will unlock keys for insightful individuals, women and men alike, that will have untold influences on various fields of study that can only be hinted at today. The reason for this is because the idea of holons with four so-called quadrants in all levels of existence (or AQAL) reflects the natural order of the universe (a *kosmos*), all set within an evolutionary dynamic displaying universal features that are reflected in a wide variety of surface features. Wilber has begun, as we just saw, with the 20-Tenets to carefully "unpack" some of their characteristics and significance—and everyone is invited to add their contributions.

One of the more interesting aspects of seeing a Kosmos of holons that becomes immediately applicable is understanding that holons have *agency* (or autonomy as a *whole*) as well as being in *communion* (or relationship as a *part*), therefore he simply defines: "All holons are always *agency-in-communion* (or *coherence-in-correspondence,* or *being-in-the-world*)."[27] He extrapolated these

ideas in *A Theory of Everything* (2000): "Agency means *rights*, and communion means *responsibilities*, and thus *agency-in-communion* means that each
self (at whatever level) is always a series of *rights-in-responsibilities* or *freedom-
with-duties*."[28] Therefore, as a human holon we have rights, as an autonomous whole, *and* responsibilities as part of a whole, which Wilber summed
up below:

- **Rights** (via *agency*)—"As a *whole*, a holon has *rights* which express its
  relative autonomy. These rights are simply a *description* of the conditions that are necessary to sustain its wholeness. If the rights aren't
  met, the wholeness dissolves into subholons.... *Rights* express the *conditions* for the *intrinsic value* of a holon to exist, the conditions necessary to sustain its wholeness, sustain it *agency*, sustain its depth."

- **Responsibilities** (via *communion*)—"Each holon is also a part of
  some other whole(s), and as a *part*, it has *responsibilities* to the maintenance of that whole. Responsibilities are simply a *description* of
  the conditions that any holon must meet in order to be a part of the
  whole.... *Responsibilities* express the *conditions* for the *extrinsic value*
  of a holon to exist, the conditions necessary to sustain its partness,
  sustain its *communion*, sustain its span."[29]

This obviously has profound implications for the human and social
holon, and for a genuine integral politics (see part III). Wilber clarifies
his point in *A Theory of Everything* (2000): "One of the first items on the
agenda of a truly integral politics is to reconnect *rights* and *responsibilities*
at a postconventional level (orange or higher), without regressing to merely
blue [mythic meme] rights-and-responsibilities."[30] As a result, this becomes
a rich territory for further exploration (and application), from politicians
to activists, from local to national to international systems of governance,
and so on. It certainly indicates the type of integrative power that's emerging with a greater understanding of the holonic AQAL Approach provided
by Wilber's emerging Integral Vision that's critically applicable in the "real
world" (see chapter 14).

AQAL Matrix: Spirit-in-Action (Emergent Evolution)

Ken Wilber has clearly maintained, especially since Phase-2 of his work in
the late 1970s, that "Development is evolution; evolution is transcendence...

and transcendence has as its final goal Atman, or ultimate Unity Consciousness in only God."[31] With AQAL Phase-4 emerging during the late 1990s and 2000s, the integral philosopher began regularly using the term "Spirit-in-action," a phrase similar to the Idealists' one of "God-in-the-making" (after Schelling and Hegel). Both convey the same idea by describing this evolutionary movement as being inherently *spiritual* in nature, as Wilber did in *The Marriage of Sense and Soul* (1998): "Evolution is simply Spirit-in-action, God-in-the-making, and that making is destined to carry all of us straight to the Divine."[32] He confirmed again in *A Brief History of Everything* (1996): "Evolution is best thought of as Spirit-in-action, God-in-the-making, where Spirit unfolds itself at every stage of development, thus manifesting more of itself, and realizing more of itself, at every unfolding.... an infinite process that is completely present at every finite stage, but becomes much more available to itself with every evolutionary opening."[33]

Since evolution is the emergence of higher-order holons (which are the basic waves of the Great Nest of Spirit), then they're known as "novel emergents" because they add "something more" than what came before. Evolution, in other words, is *more than* the sum of its parts. These observable "creative leaps" in evolution have consequently led many philosophers and scientists, from Hegel to Whitehead to Bergson to Teilhard de Chardin to Thomas Berry, and countless others, to define "emergent evolution" as the *creative emergence* of higher-order wholes, the unfolding of the novel developments of the Kosmos. This developmental process is well documented by the modern evolutionary sciences (especially in the spheres of matter and biology), therefore, evolution as a general idea is really beyond doubt to any reasonable thinking person (without resorting to mythic explanations of existence).

With a transpersonal or spiritual understanding, then this process convincingly demonstrates evolution has a direction, or a *Telos* (ancient Greek, literally, "end or completion"), an idea used by Wilber since the shift to Phase-2 in the late seventies (and the "growth-to-goodness" model). Telos, claims Wilber, is a concept necessary to explain evolution (especially when including the *involution* of Spirit into matter), and is also useful to counter the reductionist arguments of natural selection and scientific materialism. As he explained in an essay from 1982: "It is an intellectual catastrophe that the concept of *telos* has been scrubbed from modern psychology; philosophers from Aristotle to Hegel have found the universe impossible to comprehend without telos. If the universe is truly interpenetrating and interdependent in all aspects, then not only does the past shape the present, the future also shapes the present, just as an electric current will not leave one terminal until the distant terminal is grounded."[34] Naturally, this developmental process of Spirit-in-action includes *human beings*; therefore the integral philosopher provides a wonderful summary statement of this grand material, biological, psychological, and spiritual process of evolution in *A Brief History of Everything* (1996):

> We—and all beings as such—are drenched in this meaning, afloat in a current of care and profound value, ultimate significance, intrinsic awareness. We are part and parcel of this immense intelligence, this Spirit-in-action, this God-in-the-making. We don't have to think of God as some mythic figure outside of the display, running the show. Nor must we picture it as some merely immanent Goddess, lost in the forms of her own production. Evolution is both God and Goddess, transcendence and immanence. It is immanent in the process itself, woven into the very fabric of the Kosmos; but it everywhere transcends its own productions, and brings forth anew in every moment.[35]

This is one of the outstanding beauties and gifts of Wilber's Integral Vision, for it does express an "idealist" evolutionary vision of life and the Kosmos, yet it does so without the crippling metaphysics or a priori assumptions that, for instance, contributed to the collapsing of Hegel's great evolutionary vision. Rather, this type of *reconstructive* model is based upon evidence gathered from the numerous methodological injunctions, from science to meditation, that all demand verifiable proof (or a set of paradigms and exemplars) to explain and model phenomena. This means, as Wilber has masterfully pointed out, that a real integral vision must include "a yoga" (or *integral transformative practices*), i.e., a verifiable methodology to validate its theoretical claims (which was one of the great failures of the Idealists' enterprise). Verifiable practices of transformation are what AQAL Metatheory readily incorporates and promotes.

Seeing all things, all beings, all processes, all holons, all possibilities in the universe, including interiors and exteriors, as a shimmering manifestation of Spirit-in-action, or more poetically, as the dance of God (transcendence) and Goddess (immanence), gives us an interactive AQAL Matrix of *depth* and *direction* that provides *meaning* and *value* to the universe beyond personal preferences and misguided ideologies. It provides a "holarchy of value" based on the transcendence-and-inclusion of all forms (holons) within and radiating as the formless embrace of Divine Spirit. Thus, Wilber persistently reminds us: "Spirit transcends all, so it includes all.... Transcends all, includes all, as the groundless Ground or Emptiness of all manifestation."[36] The AQAL Matrix, therefore, is a grand Kosmic Mandala of Spirit-in-action, a "morphogenetic developmental space" of pluridimensional glory unfolding from dirt to divinity as the basic waves, streams, states, et al. of consciousness as embodied in self, culture, and nature, the essential nature of the AQAL Approach.

AQAL Matrix: Basic Waves of the Kosmos (All-Level)

Since there are different applications for the word "structure" in today's world, then Wilber's work has often been caught in these different interpretations by various critics, especially since from his earlier phases he identified the levels in the spectrum of consciousness as being "basic structures." This situation has also been compounded by the misinterpretations of numerous critics in regard to Wilber's relationship to *structuralism*, a movement of the twentieth century that analyzed the relatively stable elements in a system, such as with the structures of linguistics or the behavioral sciences. For Wilber, a structure "indicates that each stage has a holistic pattern that blends all of its elements into a structured whole," and a Level "means that these patterns tend to unfold in a relational sequence, with each senior wave transcending but including its juniors," and a Wave "indicates that these levels nonetheless are fluid and flowing affairs; these developmental stages appear to be concentric spheres of increasing embrace, inclusion, and holistic capacity."[37]

With the advent of the AQAL Metatheory, the integral philosopher has been more actively using fluid metaphors and analogies with liquids to better describe and designate these dynamic and interpenetrating aspects of the AQAL Matrix. For example, "structures" have become *"waves"* and developmental lines have become *"streams"* in the current AQAL Matrix (see chapter 10). Nevertheless, such fluid and dynamic metaphors are only adding emphasis to his original intentions that have always pictured the spectrum as not only being "structural," but also having recognizable patterns that are flexible, dynamic, and malleable.

The AQAL Matrix now groups the "Basic Waves" or structures (and stages) in groups of *"functional aggregates"* or *"functional groupings,"* which Wilber identifies as the *sensori-physical* (composed of matter, sensation, perception, exocept), *phantasmic-emotional* (composed of impulse, image, symbol), *rep-mind* (composed of symbol, endocept, concept), *rule/role mind,* and so on (see below). Integral psychology correlates these basic waves of consciousness (in the Overall Life Cycle) with the "Fulcrums" or "milestones" of human self-development, a definition he first presented in Phase-3 included below (fulcrums are further reviewed in chapter 10); these are the *ten to sixteen* **Basic Waves** (in bold) in the AQAL Matrix briefly listed below (without any definition being definitive):

1) **Matter-pleroma**—the structure of physical matter (matter-energy) as the Physiosphere of subatomic, atomic, molecular, polymer holons, etc.; alternate names: pleroma, uroboros, archaic heritage.

2) **Sensation** [sensori-physical]—the structure exhibiting immediate reactions to external stimulation in the environment, such as with any living holon in the Biosphere (or the Earth).

   (F-0) **Fulcrum-0: Perinatal** (conception to birth) or prenatal to neonatal (loosely similar to Grof's Basic Perinatal Matrices);

3) **Perception** [sensori-physical]—the structure exhibiting initial mental awareness of objects, qualities, etc., by means of the senses (sense organs).

   (F-1) **Fulcrum-1: Physical Self** (birth to 5–9 months); worldview: archaic and early archaic-magical; also correlated with Piaget's *sensorimotor* structure (0–2 years); includes "hatching" (after Mahler's research) or differentiation of the physical self from the physical environment; alternate names: sensori-physical self, uroboric.

4) **Impulse/Emotion** [phantasmic-emotional]—the structure (of the early Noosphere) exhibiting incitement to action arising from some external stimulation or mental process, which includes the instincts and *exocepts* (a mental construct or inner representation that is subsequently embodied in movement or action);[38] (*phantasmic*

refers to the ability of consciousness to have a perception of something that has no physical reality; a figment of the mind).

5) **Images** [phantasmic-emotional]—the structure exhibiting the imitation or representation, such as a visual impressions or mental processes, including areas of abstracted images, a generalized "idea," and protoemotions.

> **(F-2)** **Fulcrum-2: Emotional Self** (9 months to 2 years); worldview: archaic-magical, magical, early magic-mythic; also correlated with *preoperational* (preop) thought (2–7 years), or the differentiation of the emotional self from the emotional environment including adherences or magic proper; in *mid-late preop* language begins to emerge; alternate names: phantasmic-emotional, bodyego, body self, typhonic.

6) **Symbols** [rep-mind]—the structure (of the Noosphere) exhibiting the ability to create something that stands for or represents something else, especially an object used to represent something abstract (protolanguage) or even unconscious desires.

7) **Concepts** [rep-mind]—the structure exhibiting generalized ideas or thoughts (mental processes) about a class of objects or an abstracted notion (*late preop* cognition), often using symbols (language) including *endocepts* (or a "felt meaning," i.e., the hazy zone between bodily feelings and mental concepts).

> **(F-3)** **Fulcrum-3: Conceptual Self** (2 to 7 years); worldview: magic-mythic, late magic-mythic; also correlated with *late preop* and *early concrete operational* (conop) thought, or the differentiation of conceptual mind from the emotional body and other conceptual selves (including the "terrible twos"); alternate names: rep-mind.

8) **Rule/Role Mind**—the structure exhibiting the ability to take the *role* of other, and perform *rule* operations (*conop* cognition), which can be subdivided into early and late periods.

> **(F-4)** **Fulcrum-4: Rule/Role Self** (7 to 11 years); worldview: mythic, mythic-rational; also correlated with *late conop* and *early formal operational* (formop) thought (persona), or the differentiation from the previous egocentric mode into

sociocentric capacities (taking the role of other, beginning perspectives, mutuality); alternate names: rule/role mind, role mind, social self.

9) **Formal-Reflexive Mind**—the structure exhibiting the ability to "think about thinking," thus clearly self-reflexive and introspective (*formop* cognition), which can be subdivided into early and late periods.

(**F-5**) **Fulcrum-5: Formal-Reflexive Self** (11 to 21 years); worldview: mental-rational; also correlated with *formal operational* thought, including rational and self-reflexive thinking or "thinking about thought itself"; highly developed separate self-sense using reason or "a space of possibilities" to differentiate from sociocentric modes to worldcentric capacities (global perspectives, perspectival, universal pluralism or perspectivism); alternate names: mature ego, mental-ego, worldcentric self.

10) **Vision-Logic Mind**—the structure exhibiting the ability to integrate the formal and verbal mind with the emotional body (*centaur*) and establish higher *networks* of multiperspectival relationships (*vision-logic* and *network-logic*), which can be further subdivided into early, middle, and late periods.

(**F-6**) **Fulcrum-6: Integral-Centaur (existential) self** (21 years onward); cognitive line: vision-logic, network-logic; also correlated with *post-operational* thought, known as *vision-logic* and *network-logic*, or the integration of a differentiated body and mind, bodymind and nature; alternate names: integral-centaur; worldview: existential, integral, aperspectival, holistic-integralism; beginning of inner, transpersonal consciousness evolution and the transcendence of the ego; alternate names: aperspectival, second-tier.

11) **Psychic**—alternate names: Over Soul, World Soul, Eco-Noetic Self (sometimes termed "Low Subtle"); worldview includes the visions and intuitive insights of nature mysticism, an interconnected oneness with the energies of the physio-biospheres, or Mother Nature, thus having referents in the gross-material realm (as well as intuiting the divine ground).

(F-7)   **Fulcrum-7: Psychic Self**, known as the "Path of the Shaman/ Yogi" (sometimes subdivided into early and late periods).

12) **Subtle**—alternate names: Soul, authentic self; worldview involves the real archetypes, the realm of deity mysticism, involving subtle forms, lights, sounds, deities, archetypal structures, etc. with the "High Subtle" culminating with knowledge of the One God or Great Goddess, the Ground and Goal of Creation that the mystics point us to.

(F-8)   **Fulcrum-8: Subtle Self**, known as the "Path of the Saint" (sometimes subdivided into early and late periods).

13) **Causal**—alternate names: Witness, Absolute Self; worldview involves formless mysticism, or the complete transcendence of all forms in the radiant Emptiness of the Divine Domain, including the complete transcendence of any sense of being a separate self, other than being "the Witness" or True Self (Atman).

(F-9)   **Fulcrum-9: True Self**, known as the "Path of the Sage" (sometimes subdivided into the "low causal" and "high causal").

14) **Nondual**—alternate names: Divine Domain, One Taste, Transcendent-Immanent; worldview is the enlightened realization of nondual mysticism, a complete oneness with the nondual Ground and Goal of the Divine Domain and Kosmic Mandala, ever-present and awake in consciousness in body and beyond in the Absolute.

(F-10)   **Fulcrum-10: Nondual** beyond and embracing the self/Self, known as the "Way of the Siddha/Sage" (sometimes subdivided into early, middle, and late periods).

These basic waves in the AQAL Matrix, or the intermeshed levels in the Great Holarchy of Being (reality) and Knowing (self), can be cross-referenced throughout all four quadrants (or as interiors and exteriors "all the way up, all the way down") unfolding in self, culture, and nature. In the back pages of *Integral Psychology* (2000), Wilber presented a series of detailed correlative charts compiled from hundreds of researches, ancient and modern (a compilation first started in *The Atman Project*), which cross-reference the *sixteen basic waves* comprising the AQAL Matrix, summarized in the following figure. See Figure 8-4.

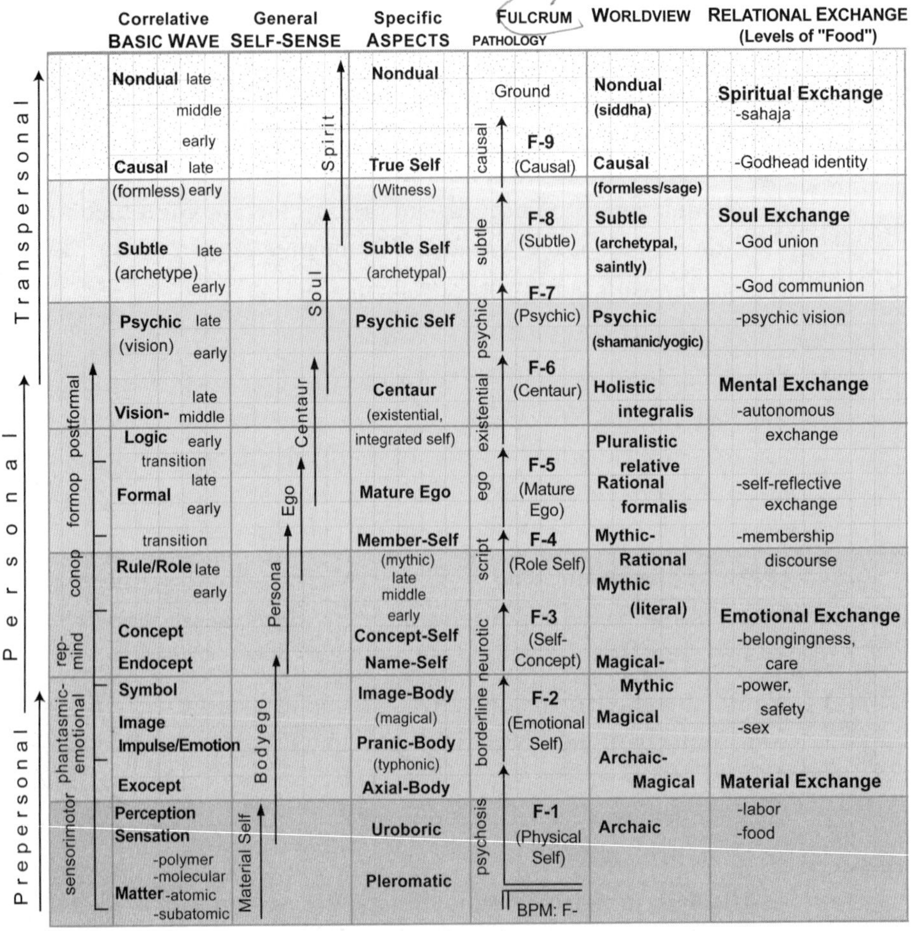

Correlative BASIC WAVE	General SELF-SENSE	Specific ASPECTS	FULCRUM PATHOLOGY	WORLDVIEW	RELATIONAL EXCHANGE (Levels of "Food")
Nondual late		Nondual	Ground	Nondual (siddha)	Spiritual Exchange
middle					-sahaja
early	Spirit		F-9		
Causal late		True Self	(Causal)	Causal	-Godhead identity
(formless) early		(Witness)		(formless/sage)	
			F-8	Subtle	Soul Exchange
Subtle late		Subtle Self	(Subtle)	(archetypal,	-God union
(archetype)	Soul	(archetypal) subtle	saintly)		
early			F-7		-God communion
Psychic late		Psychic Self	(Psychic)	Psychic	-psychic vision
(vision) early				(shamanic/yogic)	
			F-6		
late	Centaur	Centaur	(Centaur)	Holistic	Mental Exchange
Vision- middle		(existential,	existential	integralis	-autonomous
Logic early		integrated self)			exchange
transition			F-5	Pluralistic relative	
Formal late	Ego	Mature Ego	(Mature Ego)	Rational formalis	-self-reflective exchange
early	ego				
transition		Member-Self	F-4	Mythic- Rational	-membership discourse
Rule/Role late	Persona	(mythic) late	(Role Self)	Mythic	
early		middle		(literal)	
Concept		early Concept-Self	F-3		Emotional Exchange
			(Self-	Magical-	-belongingness,
Endocept		Name-Self	Concept)		care
Symbol		Image-Body	F-2	Mythic	-power,
Image	Bodyego	(magical)	(Emotional	Magical	safety
Impulse/Emotion		Pranic-Body	Self)		-sex
		(typhonic)		Archaic-	
Exocept		Axial-Body		Magical	Material Exchange
Perception			F-1		-labor
Sensation	Material Self	Uroboric	(Physical	Archaic	-food
-polymer			Self)		
-molecular		Pleromatic			
Matter -atomic					
-subatomic			BPM: F-		

AQAL MATRIX: Basic Waves and Correlations

(from *Integral Psychology*, 2000)

Figure 8-4

The Kosmic Mandala (of Spirit-in-Action)

The basic waves of the AQAL Matrix are essentially various levels of energy fields or kosmic patterns in a vast morphogenetic developmental space, from matter to body to mind to soul to spirit. It exists as nests within nests within nests, fields within fields within fields, all cocreating, generating, and perpetuating the Great Nest of Spirit pictured as the embracing and inclusive spheres of existence, a Kosmic Mandala or holarchy of transcend-

and-include. As a consequence, we've already mentioned how the "ladder" analogy is not suited to best describe this multi-layered or graded structure of the universe (although it has its advantages), and how the idea of a dominant or suppressive hierarchy is inadequate to convey the pluridimensional and interactive nature of our Divine Kosmos. Rather, as Wilber points out on several occasions, the metaphor of encompassing "Chinese boxes" (the toy of stacking boxes within one another), creating a Great Mandala of concentric circles enveloping one another, is a much better descriptive image to work with (although it too falls far short of conveying the complexity of reality).

In *Sex, Ecology, Spirituality* (1995), Wilber uses an eloquent description from an encyclopedia of philosophy to emphasize his point: "The general scheme of levels is not to be envisioned as akin to a succession of geological strata or to a series of rungs in a ladder. Such images fail to do justice to the complex interrelations that exist in the real world. These interrelations are much more like the one found in a nest of Chinese boxes or in a set of concentric spheres, for according to emergent evolutionists, a given level can contain other levels within it [i.e., holons]."[39] Even if this universal mandala is seen as containing two, three, or four dimensions (or more), it still doesn't capture the vast multi-dimensional, intertwined nature of the Kosmos, let alone the fact that Spirit is not only the paper on which the diagram is written, but it's also the nondual and empty ground of the whole display. Circles, spirals, waves, streams, mandalas, rivers, and the like, are some of the newer images and terms being used by the current AQAL Model (of Wilber/Phase-4/5) to better depict a thoroughly dynamic, developmental, holistic AQAL Matrix of "Spirit-in-action."

The "Kosmic Mandala," therefore, is another reference to the totality of conditional reality, the Kosmos of Being and Knowing, which we saw is also like the premodern Dharmadhatu or the postmodern "morphogenetic developmental space" of the AQAL Matrix. The Sanskrit word *"mandala"* (literally, "circle") is commonly used by the esoteric spiritual traditions to describe and picture the holarchic levels of existence. Although Wilber infrequently uses the term "Kosmic Mandala," I believe it is an excellent, if not the best, way to envision the pluridimensional and hierarchical nature of the Kosmos as the Great Nest of Spirit. He did point out in *The Eye of Spirit* (1997): "A more integral philosophy… attempts to include and coordinate the many faces of the Good (the 'We'), and the True (the 'It'), and the Beautiful (the 'I'), as all of them evolve across the entire spectrum, from their sensory forms (seen with the eye of flesh) to their mental forms (seen with the eye of mind) to their spiritual forms (seen with the eye of contemplation) a pluridimensional Kosmic Mandala of unending embrace."[40] Therefore, I have chosen to use this image liberally as an alternate name for the AQAL Matrix.

The accompanying figure graphically represents the "Basic Waves" in the Kosmic Mandala (which we've just reviewed above), showing a slightly expanded version of Wilber's original "spectrum of consciousness" model which is now more accurately seen as the AQAL Matrix (for it also includes "all-quadrants" as well as "all-levels"), with the evolutionary "arrow of time" indicating Spirit-in-action. See Figure 8-5.

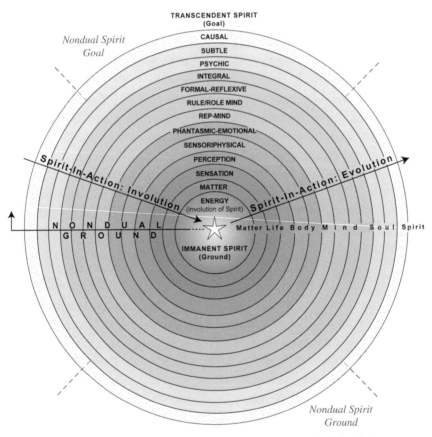

AQAL MATRIX: Basic Waves in the Kosmic Mandala

Figure 8-5

On a more esoteric (or spiritual) level, another wonderful Buddhist analogy that's mentioned in Wilber's first book, and which still rings true for the advanced AQAL Matrix, is that every point or jewel (or holon) in the Kosmos is actually a "Bodhimandala" or "Sphere of Enlightenment" (Sanskrit, *bodhi* = Enlightenment; *mandala* = "circle" or "sphere"). This marvelous radiant image refers to the whole Kosmos being pervaded by and grounded in nondual Emptiness (*sunyata*) since enlightening wisdom (*bodhi*) reveals that Spirit or God is *always already* available to consciousness at *any time*, in *any place*, for *any conscious* being that becomes aware of this absolute truth of reality. This paradoxical truth, as Wilber explained in his initial considerations, involves the *nondual* mode of knowing since there's "a suspension of space, time, form, and dualism, and in this condition an utter mental Silence prevails. *This is remaining with what is.*" Consequently, he follows the way of the Zen Master Huang Po (d. 850), who refers to this as "sitting in a Bodhimandala, that is, sitting in a place where Enlightenment can erupt at any instant."[41] Such wonderful and ecstatic explanations that transcend rational thought aren't necessarily the modern or postmodern way to approach these truths, but they do seem to more fully "color in" the rainbow of existence, the spectrum of reality and consciousness, the holarchy of Being and Knowing. Wilber's AQAL Matrix, of course, lends itself to both views, to our great advantage.

As we'll continue to see (in the next chapter), the Kosmic Mandala includes more than just the *all-levels*, or the basic waves, of the Great Nest of Spirit, for it also includes the *all-quadrants* (and thus is AQAL). To summarize, let's listen to the integral philosopher muse over the profundity of this kosmic integral vision:

> It seems that we are part and parcel of a single and all-encompassing evolutionary current that is itself Spirit-in-action, the mode and manner of Spirit's creation. The same currents that run through our human blood run through swirling galaxies and colossal solar systems, crash through the great oceans and course through the cosmos, move the mightiest of mountains as well as our own moral aspirations—one and the same current moves throughout the All, and drives the entire Kosmos in its every lasting gesture, an extraordinary *morphogenetic field* that exerts a pull and pressure

which refuses to surrender until you remember who and what you are, and that you were carried to this realization by that single current of an all-pervading Love, and here "there came fulfillment in a flash of light, and vigor failed the lofty fantasy, but now my will and my desires were moved like a wheel revolving evenly, by the Love that moves the sun and other stars" [from Dante].[42]

CHAPTER NINE

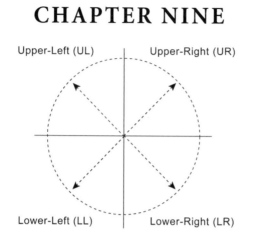

Upper-Left (UL) | Upper-Right (UR)

Lower-Left (LL) | Lower-Right (LR)

AQAL Matrix: Four-Quadrant Holons

My position is that every holon has these four aspects or four dimensions (or "four quadrants") of its existence, and thus it can (and
must) be studied in its *intentional* [Lower-Left], *behavioral* [Upper-
Right], *cultural* [Lower-Left], and *social* settings [Lower-Right]. No
holon simply exists *in* one of the four quadrants; each holon *has*
four quadrants.

—Ken Wilber, *Sex, Ecology, Spirituality* (1995)

AQAL Matrix: Four Quadrants (All-Quadrant)

WHEN KEN WILBER'S INTEGRAL STUDIES MORPHED INTO "A-Q-A-L"
or the "all-quadrants, all-levels, all-lines, all states, etc." approach, he basically expanded his integral vision to more inclusively embrace *all four quadrants* or the "quarters" and "corners" of the Kosmos and their accompanying
perspectives. As we've already seen, the four quadrants are the (1) singular
individual holon (with *agency* and *rights*), situated within (2) plural *collective social holons* (with *communion* and *responsibilities*), each with different
levels of (3) *interiors* (or insides) and (3) *exteriors* (or outsides). The integral
philosopher first made this startling, yet simple, formulation after nearly

175

three years of dedicated research begun in the early 1990s that resulted in the AQAL Approach and *The Kosmos Trilogy* (see Chapter 7). Since these so-called "quadrants" first became obvious after Wilber compiled a data search across various developmental and evolutionary fields, he always emphasizes that his conclusions are based on "*a posteriori* conclusions, not a priori assumptions."[1] As a result, they've become a fundamental thesis of the AQAL Metatheory with its *Integral Post-Metaphysics* in the new millennium, or basically where Wilber's at.

In a stunning breakthrough that would have profound implications in integral theory, Wilber went on to model these four major "corners" or "aspects" of a holon by calling them the "Four Quadrants," or even better, "The Four Faces of Spirit." Since these quadrants or domains of the Kosmos are very real and observable (being the insides and outside of every holon), he goes on to explain "these truths are the golden treasure of a collective humanity, hard won through blood and sweat and tears and turmoil in the face of falsity, error, deception, and deceit. Humanity has slowly and increasingly *learned*, over a million-year history, to separate truth from appearance, goodness from corruption, beauty from degradation, and sincerity from deception. Ultimately, these four truths are simply the four faces of Spirit as it shines in the manifest world. The validity claims are the ways that we connect to Spirit itself, ways that we attune ourselves to the Kosmos."[2] This, obviously, has profound implications.

The "four quadrants" first appeared when Wilber compiled hundreds of hierarchical models and developmental schemes taken from contemporary, scientific, and ancient sources, from stellar physics to molecular biology, from anthropology to linguistics, from developmental psychology to ethical orientations, from cultural hermeneutics to contemplative endeavors, from Eastern and Western disciplines, including premodern, modern, and post-modern sources.[3] When he laid his stack of yellow legal pads out across the floor to gain a wider perspective, he saw these different sources only agreed on using a hierarchical approach; they certainly didn't agree on much else, for there was no consensus on how to bring them all together into a cohesive whole. From the integral perspective, Wilber soon noticed that most of them hadn't distinguished between the hierarchies of *individuals* and *collective systems*, nor had they properly differentiated between the *interior* and *exterior* domains either.[4] A few years later he explained what happened, "I noticed that these various developmental sequences all fell into one of four major classes—the four quadrants—and further, that within those four quadrants there was substantial agreement as to the various stages or levels in each."[5] Philosophically, the integrative concept of the "four quadrants" could theoretically add the interiors or depth back into a modern world that had nearly eliminated the inner world, or at least constantly overlooked it, preferring instead to claim that the only real things are empirical exteriors (scientific materialism).

As we saw with the 20-Tenets of evolution (see previous chapter), the four quadrants are the interior and exteriors of every holon with *agency-in-communion* (or autonomy-in-collectives). Again, Wilber emphasizes his position in *Sex, Ecology, Spirituality* (1995): "No holon whatsoever simply exists in one or another quadrant; all holons *possess* these four quadrants, and each quadrant is intimately correlated with, dependent upon, but not reducible to, the others."[6] This is precisely why the "four-quadrant" (or "all-quadrant") aspect plays such an important role in the acronym A-Q-A-L ("all-quadrant, all-level") and its accompanying metatheory.

Of course, since it's only for matters of convenience and as language referents that the "Left" and "Right" designators were chosen as arbitrary assignments (it's only a map, after all), then Wilber's schematic diagrams usually show the *interior* aspects of a holon as being on the left side (Left-Hand quadrants) with the *exterior* aspects of a holon being on the right side (Right-Hand quadrants). Consequently, the *individual* holon is usually shown on the top half (Upper), while the collective socio-cultural-environmental systems of a holon are the bottom half (Lower); therefore, they're translated and abbreviated as the Upper-Left (UL) quadrant or the *individual interior*, the Upper-Right (UR) quadrant or the *individual exterior*, the Lower-Left (LL) or the *collective interior*, and the Lower-Right (LR) or *collective exteriors*.

The figure below represents "the four quadrants in the compound human holon," as often presented in Wilber's Phase-4 books (although, as he would say, "it is very schematic and leaves out more than it includes"), in addition to showing the evolutionary milestones up to the present-day, i.e., up to vision-logic (Upper-Left quadrant), including the *worldviews* and "value memes" of Spiral Dynamics (Upper-Left and Lower-Left quadrants), with the *sociocultural-economic* eras (Lower-Right), all evolving through the "basic waves" of the AQAL Matrix. See Figure 9-1.

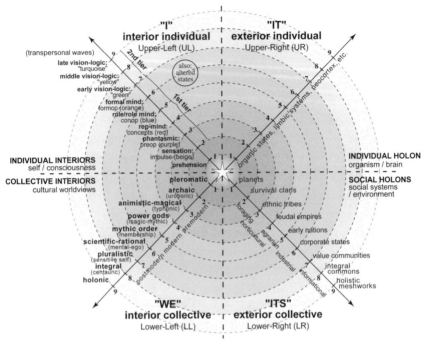

AQAL MATRIX: Four Quadrants of the Compound Human Holon
Figure 9-1

A more detailed but brief review of the four quadrants continues below:

- **Individual Interiors** or **Upper-Left (UL) quadrant**—*Subjective* "I" (intentional), the *interiors* of *individual* holons (in humans called "I") generating *first-person* perspectives (expressed in first-person language of I/you/she/he); studied by disciplines such as psychology, religion, and mysticism, thus originally covered by Wilber's "spectrum of consciousness" psychology (the basic structures of interior individual development). Upper-Left quadrant is the *within*, inner, inside, subjective, interpretive capacity and experience of *individual* holons (particularly in human beings), ranging from *prehension* (Whitehead's term for the contact or "feeling" of an object by a subject) to *irritability* (experienced by nonliving forms) and *protosensation* (experienced by simply living forms) to *perception* and *impulse* (found in lower life forms) to *symbols, concepts, cognitive-operational thinking* (appearing in higher life forms), then extending into the *transpersonal* domains of awareness (most evident in advanced-tip human beings).

• **Collective Interiors** or **Lower-Left (LL) quadrant**—*Intersubjective* "We" (cultural), the *interiors* of *collective* social holons generating *second-person* perspectives (expressed in second-person language of we/us); involving culture and social "worldviews" mostly evident in the stages of collective historical evolution. Lower-Left quadrant is the *within*, inner, inside, intersubjective, interpretive capacity and "worldspace" of *collective* holons or societies, ranging from *pleroma* to *archaic* to *magical* to *mythic* to *integral* to *transpersonal* communities; these worldviews generally correlate with Spiral Dynamics "value memes" (beige, purple, red, blue, orange, green yellow, turquoise, etc.).

• **Individual Exteriors** or **Upper-Right (UR) quadrant**—*Objective* "It" (behavioral), the *exteriors* of *individual* holons generating *third-person* perspectives (expressed in third-person language of it/its); studied by empirical science (and its collective counterpart of systems sciences) involving exterior nature, such as measuring the *without*, outside, empirical, objective or physical correlates of individual holons. Upper-Right quadrant ranges from the agency (or autonomy) of a *subatomic particle* to a *molecule* to a *star* to a *eukaryote cell* (cells with nucleus) to the *triune brain* (human beings) to *physical-chemical correlates* in the brain-mind (indicated in the AQAL diagrams by the "structural functions" SF1, SF2, etc.).

• **Collective Exteriors** or **Lower-Right (LR) quadrant**—*Interobjective* "Its" (*social systems*), the *exteriors* of *collective* holons or *exterior forms* of social holons generating *third-person* perspectives (expressed in third-person language of it/its); involving social and natural systems. Lower-Right quadrant is measured and studied by system sciences and social sciences, ranging from *galaxies* to *solar systems* to *planetary eco-systems* (Gaia) to *human groups* to *tribes* to *nation-states* to *united planetary organizations* (where human holons have more depth); Lower-Right exteriors are also correlated with *techno-economic* stages of development, evolving from the historical eras of *horticulture* to *agrarian* to *industrial* to *information* modalities of *relational exchange.*

The figure below simplifies some of the major characteristics of the four quadrants (the "Left-Hand" *interiors* and "Right-Hand" *exteriors* of *individual* and *collective* holons), as well as portraying the directionality of evolution (Spirit-in-action) throughout all the levels or basic waves (signified with the arrows), thus it crudely portrays the pluridimensional AQAL "all-quadrant, all-level" Matrix. See: Figure 9-2.

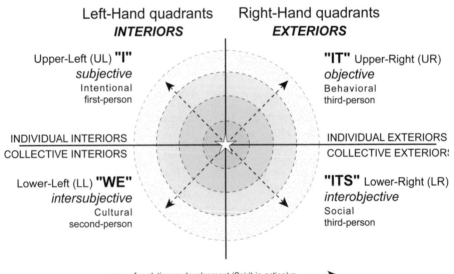

AQAL MATRIX: Four Quadrants of a Holon
Figure 9-2

Attuned to the Kosmos: Four Truths (Validity Claims)

Another one of the advantages gained from the four-quadrant approach, is that it recognizes that each quadrant has its own set of *truths* or "validity claims," what Wilber defines as "different types of knowledge with different types of evidence and validation procedures."[7] For Wilber, therefore, "Truth, in the broadest sense, means being *attuned* with the real.... And that implies that we can also be out of touch with the real. We can be lost, or obscured, or mistaken, or wrong in our assessments."[8] If we could better understand the spectrum of validity claims, then it could have a profound effect on all of us and the world-at-large, for as the integral pandit reminds us, "The validity claims are the ways that we connect to Spirit itself, ways that we attune ourselves to the Kosmos. The validity claims force us to confront reality; they curb our egoic fantasies and self-centered ways; the demand evidence from the rest of the Kosmos; they force us outside of ourselves! They are the check and balances of the Kosmic Constitution."[9]

The validity claims of the four quadrants are disclosed with various methodologies that test the veracity of their claims *(Integral Methodological Pluralism)*, which can at least be investigated with the "three eyes of knowing," i.e., the eye of flesh, the eye of mind, and the eye of spirit. Wilber has clarified his position again in "An Integral Theory of Consciousness" (1997): "Each quadrant has a different architecture and thus a *different type of validity claim* through which the three strands [of knowledge acquisition: paradigm, apprehension, confirmation] operate: *propositional truth* (Upper-Right), *subjective truthfulness* (Upper-Left), *cultural meaning* (Lower-Left), and *functional fit* (Lower-Right)."[10] These validity claims or the various truths of the four quadrants are briefly summarized below:

- **Propositional Truths (objectivity)—"It"** (Upper-Right)—correspondence, representation (representational truth), propositional truth; an *objective state of affairs* (the brain, planets, organisms, ecosystems, etc.), therefore they are *seen* (by the senses and their extensions); they all have *simple location* and can be objectively measured (by science); empirical mapping;

- **Truthfulness (subjectivity)—"I"** (Upper-Left)—sincerity, integrity, trustworthiness; a *subjective truthfulness* (to oneself and others), therefore they are *interpreted* (by oneself and others); Wilber: "Therapy is to help people *interpret* themselves more *truthfully*";[11] doesn't have simple location therefore it's blocked by deceit and deception; context-bound; truthful (or false) interpretations;

- **Cultural Truths (intersubjectivity)—"We"** (Lower-Left)—mutual understanding, cultural fit, rightness, justness (justice); a *common context* involving *cultural backgrounds*; Wilber: "the *subjective* world is *situated* in an *intersubjective* space, a cultural space… the *subjective* space is inseparable from the *intersubjective* space";[12] the intersubjective networks that allow the subjective space to develop in the first place;

- **Functional Fit (interobjectivity)—"Its"** (Lower-Right)—*systems theory* (web-of-life), structural-functionalism, environmental-social systems mesh, collective systems (minus *subtle reductionism*); objective exterior systems; social integration.

The figure below graphically summarizes these "four truths" and their validity claims of individual interiors and exteriors situated in collective interiors and exteriors (the four quadrants). See Figure 9-3.

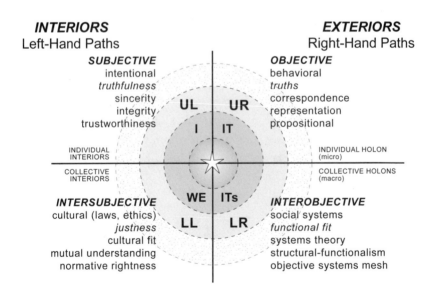

Four Truths: Four-Quadrant Validity Claims
Figure 9-3

Not only are these four large camps of human knowledge—the *intentional, behavioral, cultural,* and *social* domains—persistent and real as the nonreducible aspects of any holon, but they're all intimately intertwined and interdependent (or tetra-meshed), like a morphogenetic developmental matrix. The AQAL Matrix, therefore, is designed to model the fact that "apparently each quadrant causes, and is caused by the others, in a *circular* and nonreducible fashion, which is precisely why all four types of truth (validity claims) are necessary to access the various dimensions of any holon."[13] In whatever terms, the four quadrants of a holon and their validity claims, are active in and operating on all the levels comprising the Great Nest of Spirit, therefore, they're an indispensable component of any genuine integral theory.

As a result, Wilber has made the four-quadrant analysis of holons the backbone of his integral approach (coupled, of course, with all the levels in the spectrum and the other variables of consciousness). From this perspective, the AQAL Model of "all-quadrants, all-levels, et al." is one of the best methodologies for becoming *more integral* (or comprehensive), since it provides the guidelines for making sure all the essential elements of the Kosmos are included when we're assessing truth and implementing our research. Indeed, the universality of these basic elements shows up in all human languages (as "I, We, and It"), therefore, as we'll see next, they correlate precisely with the "Big Three," or the important differentiations of modernity.

The "Big Three" of Modernity

Beginning with the dawn of Wilber/Phase-4, another useful and simplified way Wilber represents the four quadrants is to align them with the principal differentiations or "value spheres" of modernity (following Max Weber and other researchers). As we've already seen, Wilber simply titles them the "Big Three" by combining the two exterior Right-Hand quadrants (exteriors) into the one domain of empirical objectivity (i.e., "It/Its" into "It"). This allows the four quadrants to be aligned with modernity's differentiation of *Self* or "I," *Culture* or "We," and *Nature* or "It/Its," also seen as *Art, Morals,* and *Science,* respectively. More philosophically, Wilber also recognized that the Big Three can correspond with Plato's the Good, the True, and the Beautiful, or with Kant's immensely influential trilogy, or with Habermas's three validity claims, among numerous other correspondences, but perhaps most esoterically with the Three Jewels of Buddhism (*Buddha, Dharma,* and

Sangha).[14] The basic characteristics and definition of AQAL's "Big Three" are summarized below:

(I) I—individual interiors (Upper-Left quadrant)—*subjective* interpretation: *Self* (self-system), *Art* (aesthetics), the *Beautiful* ("beauty in the I of the beholder"), the *Buddha* (the enlightened "I" or mind);

(II) We—collective interiors (Lower-left quadrant)—*intersubjective* interpretation: *Culture* (worldviews), *Morals* (mutual understandings and justness), the *Good* (ground of collective morality), the *Sangha* (spiritual community);

(III) It/Its—objective exteriors (Right-Hand quadrants)—*objective/interobjective* interpretation: *Nature* (objective world/Kosmos), *Science* (objective truth and knowledge/studies), the *True* (nature's deep science), and the *Dharma* (enlightened science or teaching of truth).

Again, Wilber points out the AQAL Matrix of "all quadrants, all levels" really aren't that difficult to understand, since all these elements are natural universals based on differentiating-and-including the basic realities of existence. Indeed, these aspects of a holon are universally recognized by every major culture in the world since everyone recognizes the pronouns of "I, We, and It." As a result, the elements of *all-quadrants* (or the Big Three), plus the full-spectrum of *all-levels*, as well as with the additional variables of *all-lines, states, types, worldviews,* et al., have all become the indispensable tools for understanding exactly "where Wilber's at" in the new millennium, thus, we'll look a little deeper into the languages of the Big Three.

The Big Three Languages: "I, We, It" Perspectives

Since the Big Three (or four quadrants) reflect the natural universals of the Kosmos, Wilber emphasizes that they're already innately expressed in all human languages, that is, as the *first-person, second-person,* and *third-person* perspectives of a holon. Indeed, one of the more complicated, albeit confusing, aspects of Wilber/Phase-5 is his detailed analysis of the perspectives, or the "primordial perspectives" of any holon. This generates at least *eight major perspectives* that Wilber claims "are the fewest that we need in order to get a fairly well-rounded view of any occasion."[15] Although Phase-4 had seen the four quadrants providing a holon's perspective, now with Phase-5, the integral philosopher is finding it necessary to add perspectives upon perspectives, even creating a revolutionary "integral calculus."[16] This is because the four perspectives of each quadrant can be looked at, or studied from, a holon's *within* (its insides), as well as from its *without* (its outsides), therefore all of these perspectives should be taken into account with any comprehensive integral model.

In the four-quadrant scheme, Wilber begins by identifying the major "language" of each quadrant, i.e., with the *expressive-aesthetic* sphere described in "I" language, with the *moral-ethical* sphere described in "We" language, and with the objective-science sphere described in "It" language. In addition, Wilber also distinguishes between the *surfaces* of exteriors that are *seen* or measured, such as with the senses or their extensions (for they have *simple location*), whereas the *depth* of interiors can only be *interpreted* (with truthfulness and dialogue). He clarifies in *Sex, Ecology, Spirituality* (1995): "Whereas the Right-Half can be *seen*, the Left-Half must be *interpreted*. The reason for this is that *surfaces can be seen*—there they are, anybody can look at them—but depth cannot be directly perceived—*depth must be interpreted*. The Right-Hand path always asks, 'What does it *do?*' The Left-Hand path asks, 'What does it *mean?*'"[17] Let's briefly review the "Big Three Languages" of "I, We, and It" in more detail below:

- **"I" Language/Perspectives** (Upper-Left quadrant)—*first-person subjectivity* ("the person who is speaking") or *I, me, mine* (in the singular)—Wilber: "I-language *is* your presence, your consciousness, your subjective awareness. Everything on the Upper-Left is basically described in I-language, in the language of interior subjectivity. The subjective component of any holon is the I-component"; "Beauty is in the 'I' of the beholder. This subjective domain represents the self and self-expression, aesthetic judgment, and artistic expression in the most general sense. It also represents the irreducible subjective contents of immediate consciousness (and intentionality), all of which can properly be described in first-person accounts, in 'I' language."[18]

- **"WE" Language/Perspectives** (Lower-Left)—*second-person/plural intersubjectivity* ("the person who is spoken to"), including pronouns like *you, yours,* and *we/us* (although technically first-person plural), which are *dialogical*—Wilber: "Ethics is described in 'We' language. It is part of the intersubjective domain, the domain of collective interaction and social awareness, the domain of justness, goodness, reciprocity, and mutual understanding, all of which are described in 'we' language"; "The We-language, is the Lower-Left, the cultural or intersubjective dimension. The Upper-Left is how 'I' see the world; the Lower-Left is how 'we' see it. It is the collective worldview that we of a particular time and place and culture inhabit. These worldviews evolve, of course, and so we find archaic, magic, mythic, rational."[19]

- **"IT" Language/Perspectives** (Right-Hand quadrants)—*third-person objectivity* (Right-Hand quadrants) – *third-person objectivity* ("the person or thing being spoken about), such as *he, him, she, her, they, them, it,* and *its*—Wilber: "Truth, in the sense of objective truth, is described in 'it' language. This is the domain of objective realities, realities that can be seen in an empirical and monological fashion, from atoms to brains, from cells to ecosystems, from rocks to solar systems, all of which are described in 'it' language"; "It-language is objective, neutral, value-free surfaces. This is the standard language of the empirical, analytic, and systems sciences, from physics to biology to ecology to cybernetics to positivistic sociology to behaviorism to systems theory. In other words, it is monological. It is a monologue with surfaces, with 'its.' It-language describes objective exteriors and their interrelations, observable surfaces and patterns that can be seen with the senses or their instrumental extensions—whether those empirical surfaces are 'inside' you, like your brain or lungs, or 'outside' you, like ecosystems."[20]

The accompanying figure graphically subdivides the "four quadrants" into the "Big Three" reflecting modernity's major "value sphere" differentiations of self, culture, and nature (art, morals, and science) and the languages of "I," "We," and "It." See Figure 9-4.

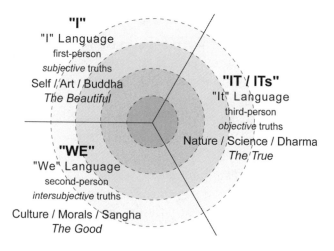

"I"
"I" Language
first-person
subjective truths
Self / Art / Buddha
The Beautiful

"IT / ITs"
"It" Language
third-person
objective truths
Nature / Science / Dharma
The True

"WE"
"We" Language
second-person
intersubjective truths
Culture / Morals / Sangha
The Good

AQAL MATRIX: The "Big Three" of Modernity
Figure 9-4

With the advent of Wilber/Phase-5, this basic understanding of languages and the perspectives of a holon have expanded the AQAL Models into a "quadratic" analysis of a holon's "four major dimensions of being-in-the world," or what Wilber defines as the "four most basic dimensions of being-in-the world, dimensions that are so fundamental they have become embedded in natural languages as variations on first-, second-, and third-person pronouns (which can be summarized as 'I,' 'We,' 'It,' and 'Its')."[21] These are supported and enacted by a set of time-honored methods of inquiry or practices (referred to as *Integral Methodological Pluralism*) that can bring forth, enact, disclose, and illumine these basic dimensions of being-in-the-world (see chapter 14). In these advanced AQAL writings, the integral-pandit outlines his case by building upon the work of Alfred North Whitehead, whose philosophy of "process and reality" is particularly good with handling the *subjective* and *intersubjective* domains (Left-Hand interiors), while Rupert Sheldrake's work with "morphogenetic fields" is especially good with the *objective* and *interobjective* quadrants (Right-Hand exteriors). Yet, these are the complicated extensions of Phase-5, whereas we still want to review some of the implications of the AQAL Approach in relation to consciousness studies in particular, and integral studies in general.

1-2-3 of Consciousness Studies (All-Perspective)

By acknowledging and applying the four-quadrant scheme, and its corollary of the Big Three (self, culture, nature), then AQAL Metatheory maintains this is a major step toward solving the reductionism of modernity and scientific materialism (see chapter 4). Beginning in the late 1990s, Wilber also quantified the AQAL Approach by calling it "The 1-2-3 of Consciousness Studies" (as he did in chapter 14 of *Integral Psychology*). Apparently, this was an idea first proposed in a talk by the transpersonal/integral psychologist and author Frances Vaughan as a way to make sure all four quadrants are being reviewed, since she was noticing that people tend to prefer "their favorite quadrant, pushing one approach to the exclusion of others."[22] Wilber agrees and explains, "I have stressed the need for an approach to consciousness that *differentiates-and-integrates all four quadrants* (or simply the Big Three of I, We, and It); or first-person, second-person, and third-person accounts: the 1-2-3 of consciousness studies."[23] This includes the subjective, intersubjective, and objective points-of-view (of being-in-the-world).

The "1-2-3 approach" of *integral studies* is mostly intended to make sure all the perspectives of the four quadrants, or the Big Three, are always included in any comprehensive analysis or research project. By doing so, it also provides a well-developed *integral critical theory* (see chapter 1). Wilber further reviews what this means in *Integral Psychology* (2000): "The time is certainly ripe for the beginning of an all-quadrant approach, or simply an approach that equally honors *first-person* phenomenal accounts, *second-person* intersubjective structures, and *third-person* scientific/objective systems: the 1-2-3 of consciousness studies."[24] This critical approach is also in its infancy, so that a fully integral view acknowledging all the quadrants still awaits more primary discoveries in various fields. For example, an AQAL analysis can be run on cognitive science and brain physiology (in the Upper-Right), or on the modes and forces of production (in the Lower-Right), or on the pluralistic cultural worldviews and their contextual backgrounds (in the Lower-Left), or on developmental integral psychology (in the Upper-Left). As the integral theorist puts it once again in *A Theory of Everything* (2000): "An 'all-quadrant, all-level' [AQAL] approach—or a 1-2-3 approach—makes ample room for I, We, and It research."[25] Their cross-analyses will therefore afford a more integral view.

The benefits are just beginning to manifest in a wide variety of integral applications and research agendas (see chapter 14). For now, we'll let Wilber summarize with an excellent quote from the last chapter to *Integral Psychology* (2000):

> For any integral studies, this means that we must take great care to insure that the important differentiations of modernity are in fact integrated, that the Big Three do not fly apart; that subtle reductionism does not creep into the picture, yielding a flatland holism; and that any approach to consciousness is indeed a 1-2-3 approach, including and equally honoring first-person, second-person, and third-person accounts of consciousness: *first-person* or phenomenal accounts of the stream of consciousness as it directly experienced by a person (Upper-Left); *second-person* communication of those facts, set in particular linguistic structures, worldviews, and background contexts (Lower-Left); and third-person scientific descriptions of the corresponding mechanisms, systems, and material networks, from brain structures to social systems (Right-Hand).
>
> That "all-quadrant" approach is the first step to a truly integral model. The second step adds an "all-level" approach, which investigates the *stages of development* of first-, second-, and third-person consciousness. In other words, it investigates the waves and streams, the levels and lines, in all of the quadrants. The result is an "all-level, all-quadrant" [AQAL] approach to *integral studies*, across the spectrum of disciplines—science, history, religion, anthropology, philosophy, psychology, education, politics, business.[26]

AQAL Tetra-Meshing (All-Quadrant, All-Level)

As we've already learned, an important characteristic of Wilber's integral approach is that the AQAL Matrix pictures all of these interiors and exteriors as being inextricably interwoven and interactive. As we saw, this approach offers the capacity for a "holonic indexing system" and "cross-level analysis" by "simultracking" the various levels and quadrants of the AQAL Matrix (see chapter 4). Therefore, to be even more accurate, this evolutionary AQAL Approach of Spirit-in-action emphasizes that all the quadrants, levels, lines, states, types, worldviews, and so on, continuously "tetra-interact" and "tetra-mesh," therefore, all holons "tetra-evolve" in a "four-quadrant, all-level mesh" (a "morphogenetic developmental space" or AQAL Matrix). Thus Wilber clarifies in *Integral Psychology* (2000): "It is not enough to say that organism and environment coevolve; it is not enough to say that culture and consciousness coevolve. All four of those *'tetra-evolve'* together…. In other words, all four quadrants—organism, environment, consciousness, and culture—cause and are caused by the others: they *'tetra-evolve'.*"[27] Once again we see, the AQAL Matrix is a holarchical Kosmos of holons tetra-evolving and interacting, while *always already* grounded in the Love (or Eros) of Spirit-in-action.

Consequently, Wilber/Phase-4/5 has introduced the AQAL terms "tetra-interaction" and "tetra-evolution" to describe the fact that the Left-Hand *interior* quadrants are always interacting with and has *correlates* in the Right-Hand *exterior* quadrants. With this understanding, AQAL Metatheory can index the the four quadrants as they interact with all the levels of existence to create and mold humans and their Kosmos: "Short of nondual realization, what can be said, in a relative fashion, is that all four quadrants *'tetra-inter-act'*—they are mutually arising and mutually determining. It is not just that the individual mind and consciousness (UL) interacts with the individual body-brain-organism (UR), but that they both equally and mutually interact with the collective cultural mind (LL) and collective social body (LR)."[28] This is exactly why the integral psychologist also highly recommends with an AQAL psychology that "a truly integral therapy is not only individual, but cultural, social, spiritual and political."[29] These observations once again bring forward the AQAL feedback loop (of all-quadrant, all-level).

One of the great advantages of the AQAL Approach, obviously, is that all of these processes and tetra-interactions of holons (in all-quadrants, on all-levels) can be measured and plotted with a comprehensive meta-paradigm, such as using the "holonic indexing" made possible by carefully "unpacking" of the AQAL Matrix of reality with deep sciences (see chapter 4). This lays the foundation for the countless applications of AQAL Metatheory, or "AQAL Apps" (see chapter 14). But first (in the next chapter), we'll turn our attention to Wilber's integral psychology and how it models the self (or self-system) which is intimately involved in the AQAL evolution of consciousness, that is, with you and me (and all of us), subjects that are clearly of concern with where Wilber's at.

CHAPTER TEN

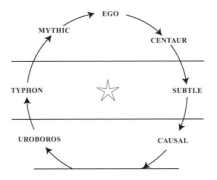

AQAL Matrix: Integral Psychology: Evolution of the Self-System

For an integral psychology, this means that we should attempt to honor the entire spectrum of consciousness, matter to body to mind to soul to spirit—by whatever names, in whatever guises, and in however many levels modern research can confirm… but all such cartographies are simply different approaches to the many waves in the great River of Life, matter to mind to spirit, which is the most precious legacy of the ancient wisdom.

—Ken Wilber, 2000, *Integral Psychology*

Integral Psychology: Human Consciousness Project

THE AQAL APPROACH OF WILBER/PHASE-4 CONTINUED TO FLESH out a fully developed integral psychology, which is the advanced form of Ken Wilber's original spectrum psychology (from Wilber/Phases 1–3). Integral psychology, Wilber asserts, brings together the various therapeutic treatments for the range of psychopathologies (usually thwarted development) into one flexible and comprehensive system of human health and well functioning, thereby integrating the core insights and practices of the

191

major schools of modern psychotherapy. At the same time, he's also aligned integral psychology with the various levels and stages of mysticism, even providing positive encouragement for active transpersonal practice, thereby integrating the core insights and practices of the world's major wisdom traditions. By initiating this "marriage of Freud and the Buddha," by uniting interiors and exteriors, Wilber has helped integrate science and religion in ways never quite seen before (see chapter 4).

All of this was brilliantly summarized in his landmark Phase-4 book, *Integral Psychology: Consciousness, Spirit, Psychology, Therapy* (2000), an abridged version of his long-planned textbook on psychology (originally titled *System, Self, and Structure*). In this AQAL textbook, Wilber further outlines the dynamic and multiple variables that are involved in "the archeology of the self" or the "spiral of development," also known as the evolution of human consciousness. Indeed, in my opinion, there's no one better source than this concise, power-packed volume of around 200 pages in order to get the broadest overview of the AQAL project and its integral psychology, or where Wilber's at. In addition, the back pages of the book presents numerous "correlative charts" compiled by Wilber himself that cross-reference the basic waves of the AQAL Matrix as they've been documented by hundreds of researchers, ancient and modern; they alone are worth the price of the book.

To support a genuine integral psychology, Wilber has also presented the intriguing idea of establishing a type of "Human Consciousness Project" (modeled after the Human Genome Project of biological medicine), but now seen from the AQAL perspective; these are goals already under way with Integral Institute and Integral University. The integral psychologist envisions this complex project, in *A Theory of Everything* (2000), as being "a cross-cultural mapping of all the states, structures, memes, types, levels, stages, and waves of human consciousness. This overall map then becomes the psychological component of a possible Theory of Everything, where it will be supplemented with findings from the physical, biological, cultural, and spiritual dimensions."[1] As we've been exploring, these types of holonic and quadratic indexing systems are exactly the types of comprehensive approaches suggested by an AQAL Theory of Everything (and deep sciences in general). A genuine integral psychology will be one of the contributing fields promoting improved human health by initiating research and study of the human *psyche* by a genuine, all-embracing *psychologia* (Greek, literally, *psyche* = mind/soul; *logia* = study).

Self-System: Overall Life Cycle (of the Proximate-Self)

With Wilber/Phase-3, Wilber defined "the self," or the "self-system," (now called the "overall self," as that which "navigates" and "juggles" the multiple variables of consciousness, including the basic waves (or structures) and developmental streams (or lines), while its self-identity evolves from matter (pleroma) to body (magical) to mind (mythical, rational, vision-logic) to soul (psychic, subtle) to causal spirit (while *always already* grounded in nondual Spirit). In his pinnacle Phase-3 book, *Transformations of Consciousness* (1986), Wilber explained, "Negotiating these structural developments is the *self* (or *self-system*), which is the locus of identification, volition, defense, organization, and 'metabolism' ('digesting' of experience at each level of structural growth and development)."[2] Decades later, the integral pandit gives a similar definition in the Phase-4 book *Integral Psychology* (2000):

> The overall self is an amalgam of all these "selves"… and all of them are important for understanding the development or evolution of consciousness…. What each of us calls an "I" (the proximate self) is both a *constant function* and a *developmental stream.* That is, the self has several *functional invariants* that constitute its central activity—it is the locus of identity, will, metabolism, navigation, defenses, and integration, to name the more important. And this self (with its functions) also undergoes *its own development* through the basic waves in the Great Nest: material self to bodily self to mental self to soul self to selfless Self. Especially significant is the fact that, as the locus of integration, the self is responsible *for balancing and integrating all of the levels, lines, and sates in the individual.* In short, the self as navigator is a juggling act of all of the elements that it will encounter on its extraordinary journey from subconscious to self-conscious to superconscious.[3]

The self (or self-system) is sometimes called the "ego-I," because it's the "separate-self sense" (from Phase-2: "persona + shadow = ego"),[4] yet for a detailed integral psychology this is an oversimplified equation, for the self is actually an amalgam of "selves" developing through the spectrum of consciousness. With integral psychology, therefore, Wilber now defines the self-system, or "Overall Self," as being an interplay of the:

- **proximate self** —the "bounded I" or *observing self,*
- **distal self**—the "me" or *observed self,*
- **Witness**—the "I-I" or *selfless Self.*

Consequently, due to all these different strands and variables of development, Wilber has always maintained that overall development can appear uneven or even chaotic at times. Therefore, he's now making stronger statements about not confusing his developmental model as being strictly linear: "*Overall development*—the sum total of all these different lines—shows no linear or sequential development whatsoever."[5] In this case, Wilber claims the evolution of consciousness is basically the development of the *proximate self* (or the sense of "I"), which is generally equated with what Western psychology has documented as "ego development."

The integral psychologist summarizes these views in *Integral Psychology* (2000): "Proximate-self development is, in my view, at the very heart of the evolution of consciousness. *For it is the proximate self that is the navigator through the basic waves in the Great Nest of Being.* The basic structures or basic waves themselves are devoid of a sense of self.... The basic structures are simply the waves of being and knowing that are available to the self as it develops towards its highest potential."[6] It is this progressive development (or evolutionary growth) that indicates, for integral psychology, that "the proximate self is the navigator of the waves (and streams) in the great River of Life. It is the central source of identity, and that identity expands and deepens as the self navigates from egocentric to sociocentric to worldcentric to theocentric waves (or precon to con to postcon to post-postcon levels of overall development)—an identity that ranges from matter to id to ego to God."[7]

When the Phase-2 book, *The Atman Project: A Transpersonal View of Human Development* (1980) was first published, as we've mentioned, Wilber focused mostly on defining the basic structures of consciousness as the unfolding psychological stages which are involved in individual development (or ontogeny). They reach from infancy to adulthood to self-actualization (the integral-centaur) to nondual Enlightenment. This is when the integral psychologist first premiered the "growth-to-goodness" or evolutionary model of Wilber/Phase-2, and he continued to use the "spectrum of consciousness" model to move the Great Chain of Being straight back into modern psychology (see chapter 7). In *The Atman Project*'s short succinct chapters, based on volumes of meticulous research, Wilber outlined the developmental journey of the human being's "Overall Life Cycle" or "Complete Life Cycle," by documenting how the self unfolds from the "primitive roots of awareness" to the "typhonic self" to the "membership self" to the "mental-egoic realms" to the "centauric realms" to the "subtle realms," and finally, to the "causal and ultimate realms" of awakened God-Realization (or Enlightenment). This developmental process is now referred to by Wilber "the archeology of the self" of "the archeology of Spirit."[8]

The AQAL Model of integral psychology still follows these basic stages in the human life cycle as the self develops in a *transcend-and-include* manner following the "form of development": identification, differentiation/transcendence, and integration, which is, as the integral psychologist once pointed out, "the form of development, the form of transformation—this is constant, as far as I can tell, from the womb to God."[9] The basic subdivisions are the tripartite domains of the *prepersonal* (pre-egoic, pre-rational) to the *personal* (egoic, rational) to the *transpersonal* (trans-egoic, trans-rational) stages of awareness (thus clarifying the *pre/trans fallacy*). This journey of self discovery is what Wilber originally termed the "inward and outward arcs" of development, for it's after stable egoic development there is the "*turn inward*," for then the self is "a soul on the brink of the transpersonal."[10] Then with appropriate practices (or injunctions) and further developmental growth, the transpersonal stages of mysticism (nature/psychic/subtle/causal/nondual) will unfold in consciousness, up to and including Enlightenment (which has "its own post-Enlightenment dynamic").[11] Now, of course, with the AQAL Approach, the self is modeled as also being situated in all four quadrants (intentional, behavioral, cultural, and social) while being simultaneously tetra-meshing with the full-spectrum of consciousness (id to ego to God).[12]

The figure below summarily pictures the evolutionary development of the "proximate self" (or self-system) as it evolves through the basic waves (or structures), with their main subdivisions (or stages) in the Great Nest of Spirit, from the *prepersonal* to the *personal* to the *transpersonal* domains of consciousness (situated mostly in the Upper-Left quadrant of individual interiors). See Figure 10-1.

This is the evolutionary journey of the self through the basic waves or "*fulcrums*" of self-development, from pleromatic infancy to adult selfhood to the "One Taste" of nondual Enlightenment. Integral psychology also defines the sense of self-identity, or what the "I" thinks and feels itself to be, as being a case of "*decreasing egocentrism*,"[13] basically because the self moves from a more narrow or contracted sense of identity to the wider,

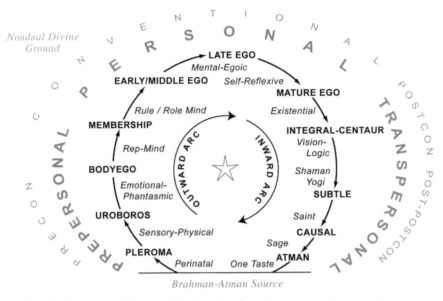

Self-System: Overall Life Cycle (Spectrum of Consciousness)
(based on *The Atman Project*, 1980)
Figure 10-1

more embracing stages of conscious awareness (comparable to "the spiral of compassion"). This unfolding of the self's "structural potentials" develops from the lower levels of prepersonal consciousness (which are *egocentric*), to the various stages of personal awareness (which are *ethno-sociocentric* to *worldcentric*), then to the transpersonal stages (which are *theocentric* or *kosmocentric*) because they exhibit a universal and spiritual sense of identity. That is, until the self finally dissolves (or is fully transcended) when it fully identifies with its ever-present Source and Divine Condition (the "Supreme Identity"). In this case, the play of the universe, the dance of the Kosmos, continues but it is now lived freely and happily. For these reasons altogether, Wilber simply states that the self-system is "where the action is."

Wilber/Phase-3: Transformations of Consciousness

In the cumulative book of Wilber/Phase-3, *Transformations of Consciousness: Conventional and Contemplative Perspectives on Development* (1986), Wilber outlined in detail the various components that are involved with a "spectrum psychology," including a "spectrum of psychopathologies" (generally defined as thwarted development) and their corresponding "treatment modalities." As Wilber clearly summarizes: "The fact that evolution always produces greater transcendence and greater differentiation means that a factor of *possible* pathology is built into every evolutionary step... As always, we want to tease apart the pathological manifestations of any stage from its authentic achievements, and celebrate the latter even as we try to redress the former."[14] A full-spectrum model offered inclusive approach to human psychology in order to include the full-spectrum of human psychology (from birth to Enlightenment), which the *New York Times* recognized as being "the most important and sophisticated synthesis of psychologies East and West to emerge yet."[15]

By expertly accessing the theories and evidence of modern psychology, Wilber shows how the various psychopathologies are often operative on different levels of the spectrum, therefore, each treatment modality can be suited to better address that particular stage of development with a corresponding therapeutic approach. Examples from each level include following: *psychoses* requiring *physiological intervention* (fulcrum-1); *narcissistic-borderline disorders* requiring *structure-building techniques* (fulcrum-2); *psychoneuroses* requiring *uncovering techniques* (fulcrum-3); *script pathology* requiring *cognitive-script analysis* (fulcrum-4); *existential pathology* requiring *existential therapy* (fulcrum-6); *psychic pathology*, such as the "dark night of the soul" requiring "the path of yogis" (fulcrum-7); *subtle pathology*, such as "integration-identification failure" requiring "the path of saints" (fulcrum-8); *causal pathology*, such as "failure to differentiate" requiring "the path of sages" (fulcrum-9).

Phase-3 also concludes that it is *the self* that *translates* (as horizontal integration) and *transforms* (as vertical change) by evolving through a sequence of "*fulcrums*," or the "milestones of development" (see chapter 10). A more integral psychology, therefore, not only claims that the *levels* (or basic waves) of consciousness are important, but so are the various developmental *lines* (or streams), and the other variables of consciousness (*states, types, worldviews,* etc.), thus they must all be differentiated and accounted for in any overall "self-system" of human development, a task not yet accomplished by Wilber's predecessors or peers.

The accompanying figure is a graphic used by Wilber to show the corresponding levels and fulcrums involved in spectrum psychology along with their characteristic psychopathologies and treatment modalities. See Figure 10-2.

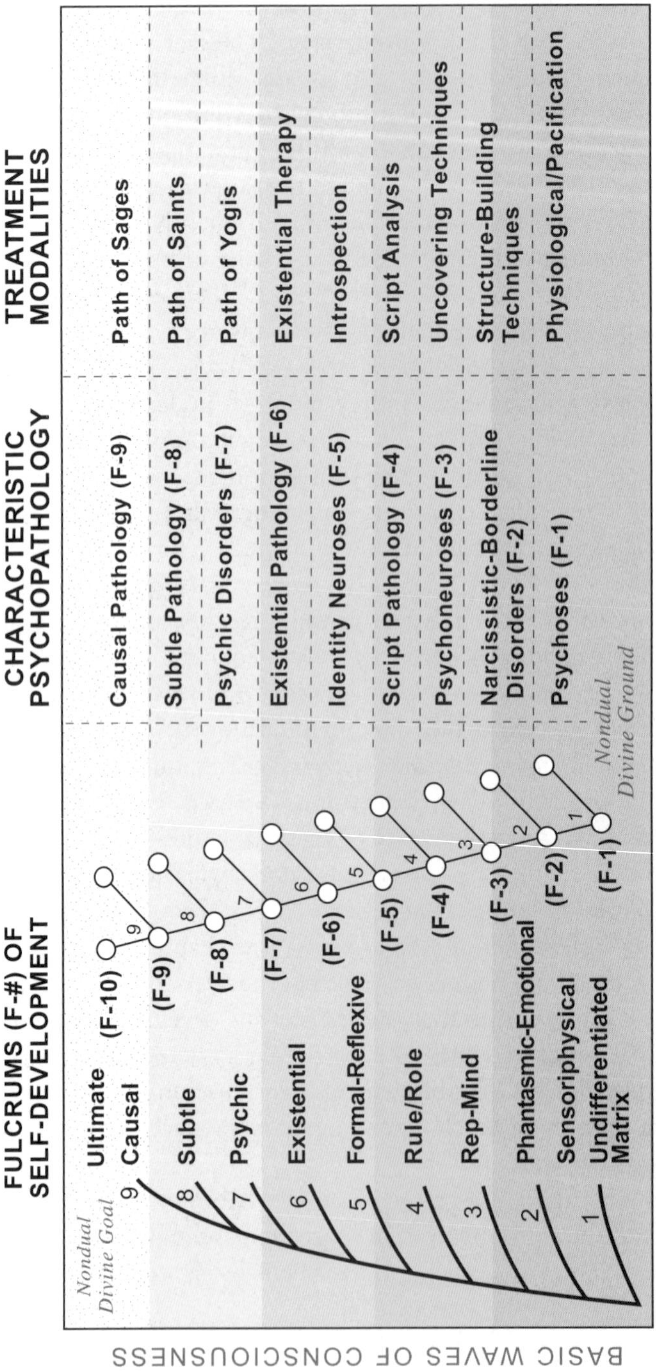

FULCRUMS (F-#) OF SELF-DEVELOPMENT	CHARACTERISTIC PSYCHOPATHOLOGY	TREATMENT MODALITIES
Nondual Divine Goal		
Ultimate (F-10)	Causal Pathology (F-9)	Path of Sages
9 Causal (F-9)	Subtle Pathology (F-8)	Path of Saints
8 Subtle (F-8)	Psychic Disorders (F-7)	Path of Yogis
7 Psychic (F-7)	Existential Pathology (F-6)	Existential Therapy
6 Existential (F-6)	Identity Neuroses (F-5)	Introspection
5 Formal-Reflexive (F-5)	Script Pathology (F-4)	Script Analysis
4 Rule/Role (F-4)	Psychoneuroses (F-3)	Uncovering Techniques
3 Rep-Mind (F-3)	Narcissistic-Borderline Disorders (F-2)	Structure-Building Techniques
2 Phantasmic-Emotional (F-2)	Psychoses (F-1)	Physiological/Pacification
1 Sensoriphysical (F-1)		
Undifferentiated Matrix	*Nondual Divine Ground*	

BASIC WAVES OF CONSCIOUSNESS

INTEGRAL PSYCHOLOGY: A Spectrum of Basic Structures/Waves, Fulcrums, Psychopathologies, and Treatment Modalities

(based on *Transformations of Consciousness*, 1986)

Figure 10-2

When the self identifies with a particular structural level of unfolding development, then this is defined as the self's "center of gravity" or "home base" (until further vertical transformation). In other words, self-identity usually hovers at the level of development to which it is most adequate, known as "adequate competency," although it does have at least temporary (but limited) access to other basic waves in the spectrum of consciousness (called "fluid access"). Therefore, integral psychology maintains there is no set pattern of how exactly development must transpire; nevertheless, Wilber still strongly maintains: "You cannot skip actual stages, but you can accelerate your growth through them by using various types of integral transformative practices."[16] This structural order of holarchical development is demonstrated in overall development (of the compound human holon), must obviously be accounted for in any competent integral model and integral psychology, a task Wilber has covered extensively.

In collecting together into an insightful integral synthesis much of the world's research and wisdom on the human psyche, Wilber has integrated information coming from the very best of the premodern, modern, and postmodern sources to arrive at a genuine integral psychology. He recently recapped this enterprise in *Integral Psychology* (2000): "What I have done is to take the results of that research, along with dozens of other modern theorists, and attempted to integrate it with the best of the perennial philosophers, to arrive at a master template of a *full-spectrum developmental space*, reaching from *matter* to *body* to *mind* to *soul* to *spirit*.... These are the basic waves of Being and Knowing through which the various developmental streams will flow, all of which are balanced and (ideally) integrated by the self in its remarkable journey form subconscious to self-conscious to superconscious. But, of course, this tortuous journey is not without its perils."[17] By embracing the entire evolutionary journey of the self in the great River of Life, this fully-developed AQAL model and integral psychology has obviously gone far beyond the important and valid concerns of traditional psychology (for it includes them as well), or even the advances of Wilber's earlier integrated spectrum psychology, all in its valiant attempt to embrace the entire scope of human development and existence.

Self-System: Three Major Self-Streams (All-Stream)

One of the major clarifications brought forward by the AQAL Approach to integral psychology is that it highlights the "three major self lines," or the "major streams of the self," or what Wilber calls the *frontal-egoic* (ego), the *deeper-psychic* (soul), and the *Witness* (causal Self). These three major self-streams also correlate with the three great domains of the *gross* (matter, body), the *subtle* (mind, soul), and the *causal* (formless spirit) realms, which are universally recognized by the great wisdom traditions. Wilber had already presented the gist of these ideas back in Phase-2 (late 1970s), particularly with the last chapter titled "Involution" in *The Atman Project* (1980), but now with the emergence of Phase-4 and AQAL Metatheory, he's further clarified these distinctive aspects of the self (or self-system), as he did in *Integral Psychology* (2000):

- **Frontal Line / Ego / Egoic Self**—the major line of the separate-self sense or "ego-I," subdivided into the *proximate self* (or "I") and the *distal self* (or "me"), therefore the frontal line of the self is what *evolves* through the developmental transformations or fulcrums involved with the evolution of consciousness; therefore, the frontal line, Wilber explains, "includes all of the self-stages that *orient consciousness to the* **gross realm** (the material self, the bodyself, the persona, the ego, and the centaur—all of which can be generically called 'the ego')."

- **Deeper-Psychic / Soul / Authentic Self** [after Andrew Cohen]— the aspect of self that transcends the frontal personality and ego; the soul is said to transmigrate after death and possibly be reborn, so Wilber defines the "deeper-psychic soul" as that which "includes all the self-streams that *adapt consciousness to the many facets of the* subtle sphere. The soul is the self that depends on the subtle line of cognition (which includes… imagination, reverie, daydreams, creative visions, hypnogogic states, etheric states, visionary revelations, hypnotic states, transcendental illuminations, and numerous types of *savikalpa samadhi* [ecstasy with form]), and thus the soul is the self-stream that orients and integrates consciousness in the subtle domain."

- **Witness / Self** (Atman) / **Absolute Self** [Cohen]—the True Nature of the Self (Atman) that is ultimately transcendent and formless, therefore, it is "the Witness" (as consciousness itself) of all possible forms; Wilber: "The self that depends upon the *causal line of cognition* (the capacity for *attention, detached witnessing, equanimity* in the face of gross and subtle fluctuations, etc.), and thus it is the self that orients and integrates consciousness in the causal domain." In addition, he continues to clarify (in an endnote) that "the pure transcendental Self or Witness does not itself develop, since it is sheer formlessness; however, access to this Self does develop,"[18] that is, via the frontal-ego and deeper-psychic (soul) lines.

The figure below pictures the three major streams of the self as they develop through the various structures and basic waves of the AQAL Matrix (modified slightly by the author).[19] See Figure 10-3.

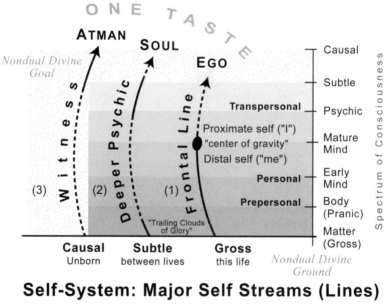

Self-System: Major Self Streams (Lines)

(1) FRONTAL / EGO, (2) DEEPER PSYCHIC / SOUL, (3) WITNESS / ATMAN

Figure 10-3

Although the frontal, psychic, and Witness streams of the self are correlated, respectively, with the realms of the gross, subtle, and causal domains, they also interact independently, as Wilber has also pointed out, "the realms of *gross, subtle,* and *causal* can develop, to some degree, *independently* of each other; and thus the *frontal*, the *soul*, and the *Self* can develop, to some degree, *alongside* each other."[20] For one, this accounts for the evidence of a "soul" presence, or a deeper-psychic self, which can sometimes be observable during the birth process (via psychic remembrance), such as documented with Grof's "perinatal matrices" (or BPMs). This is a notion Wilber compares more to the deeper soul as "trailing clouds of glory" (after Wordsworth) occurring after it incarnates during human birth. Along with everyone's access to the natural states of consciousness, these streams also account for the "fluid access" and "peak experiences" to the higher structures of consciousness. On occasion, the self has access to higher states than its current level of adaptation warrants (its center of gravity), such as, for example, when children have *temporary* transpersonal experiences or when adults have "peak experiences" (see below). However, in these cases, the higher *stages* of development have not yet been stabilized or made permanent and enduring; in other words, temporary *states* must be transformed into permanent *traits* via the further evolution of consciousness.

Moral Development: The Spiral of Compassion

By relying on the detailed research of developmental psychologists, such as Lawrence Kohlberg, Jane Loevinger, Carol Gilligan, and Robert Kegan (and countless others), Wilber has also pointed out that the evolving self's moral development follows the *same stagelike progression* as the unfolding *prepersonal, personal,* and *transpersonal* domains of consciousness. He calls this arc of "moral development" the "Spiral of Compassion," since it is the general trend of self-identity to expand from *egocentric* or preconventional (precon) to *ethnocentric* or conventional (con) to *worldcentric* or postconventional (postcon) to *kosmocentric* or post-postconventional (post-postcon) stages of morality. Integral psychology defines this "spiral of development" again as being one of *"narrowing of egocentrism,"* because it subsequently promotes a greater care, concern, and tolerance for others, as documented extensively by modern psychology. Wilber summarizes this research in *A Theory of Everything* (2000): "The spiral of development is a spiral of compassion expanding from *me*, to *us*, to *all of us*: there standing open to an integral embrace.... The point for now is that each unfolding wave of consciousness brings at least the possibility for a greater expanse of care, compassion, justice, and mercy, on the way to an integral embrace."[21] Integral psychology uses the following terms interchangeably when defining and identifying these basic stages of moral developmental growth briefly summarized below:

- **Preconventional** (precon) / **egocentric** / **"ME"** / (body-oriented)
  The infant born into the world has not yet been acculturated into the society's ethics and norms; therefore it's called the "preconventional" stage of moral development. Since infant awareness is largely body-bound and self-absorbed (bodyself), its view is "egocentric," which Wilber simplifies by saying attention is focused on "me."

- **Conventional** (con) / **ethnocentric** or **sociocentric** / **"US"** / (mind-oriented)
  As the young child develops and grows he/she learns the rules and conventions of its native culture from its parents and caregivers to the larger society; therefore it's called the "conventional" stage of moral development. This stage of self-development, Wilber explains, "centers on the child's particular group, tribe, clan, or nation, and it therefore tends to exclude care for those not of one's group,"[22] therefore its view is "ethnocentric" with attention focused on "us."

- **Postconventional** (postcon) / **worldcentric** / **"ALL OF US"** / (soul-oriented)
  As adulthood matures individual identity can, but not necessarily, expand beyond the bounds of a particular society by discovering a deeper morality and stage of moral development, therefore this view is called the "post-conventional" stage of moral development. In this stage the capacity "to include a care and concern for all peoples, regardless of race, color, sex, or creed" develops into a view that's called "worldcentric" with attention focused on "all of us."

- **Post-postconventional** (post-postcon) / **Kosmocentric** / **"ALL"** / (spirit-oriented)
  Wilber's integral psychology moves beyond the typical stages of development (conventional) perceived by a science blinded to the higher transpersonal stages, therefore it includes what's called the "post-postconventional" or "transpersonal" stages of moral development. Since this view of universal care and concern embraces all

reality, interiors and exteriors, including all beings and all things, Wilber sometimes refers to this view as being "Kosmocentric" with attention focused on "All."

These three simplified stages (there are more substages) of moral development are often graphically depicted in Wilber's work within the context of the four quadrants pictured below. See Figure 10-4.

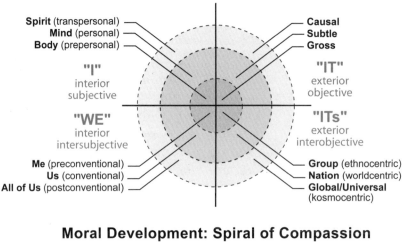

Moral Development: Spiral of Compassion
(in Four Quadrants)
Figure 10-4

Self-System: Developmental Lines & Streams (All-Line)

The unfolding of these "higher, deeper, wider potentials" in the evolution of human consciousness, according to integral psychology, is the meaning and drive of a human life, as well as being vital for culture and society. This is exactly what AQAL metatheory addresses by including the "all-quadrants, all-levels" of consciousness (Knowing) and reality (Being), and so forth. With an eloquent and precise writing style that brought him international attention, Wilber's earlier spectrum books from Phases 1–3 (1977–1994) cataloged and outlined in detail the *basic levels* or *structures* (the *basic waves* and *stages*) in this evolutionary journey of the self through the spectrum of consciousness. Then when he moved his groundbreaking theories from *spectrum psychology* to the more fully developed *integral psychology* with its AQAL Approach (mid-1990s onward), he then applied the four-quadrant scheme to the same basic developmental sequence since it continues to be supported by the available evidence (which has grown considerably since the mid-1970s). This growth of psychological research during the 1980s is what prompted Wilber (in Phase-3) to more fully include the self's various *developmental lines* (or *streams*) along with the various stages and waves in consciousness evolution. As we've seen, these advancements have led to the expanded moniker of "all-quadrants, all-levels, all-lines" to more fully represent the AQAL Matrix (not just the oversimplified "all-quadrant, all-level" abbreviation), especially in relation to charting the evolution of the self-system.

With the current AQAL Model, most of these lines or streams of development are mostly evident in the Upper-left quadrant (the interiors of individuals). However, the main point is that the evolving self is not just a monolithic development of linear progression, as Wilber is at pains to report, but instead, as he summarizes, "The self is all over the place!" Yet, for psychology this also means, "Precisely because the self is 'all over the place,' so is pathology and its treatment."[23] Since the developmental lines evolve *"relatively independently,"* then Wilber is forced to conclude, as he did in *One Taste* (1999): "Even though we can say, based on massive evidence (clinical, phenomenological, and contemplative), that many of these developmental streams proceed through the waves in a stagelike fashion, nonetheless *overall* self development does *not* proceed in a specific, stagelike manner, simply because the self is an amalgam of the various lines, and the possible number of permutations and combinations of those is virtually infinite. Overall individual growth, in other words, follows no set sequence whatsoever."[24] Nonetheless, the integral psychologist also concedes that the general consensus so far is "that no matter how different the developmental lines might be, not only do most of them unfold holarchically, *they do so through the same set of general waves*, which include: a physical/sensorimotor/preconventional stage, a concrete actions/ conventional rules stage, and a more abstract, formal, postconventional stage."[25] Consequently, although the developmental streams of the self often give the impression of uneven development, overall development itself is generally a progressive affair of increasing compassion and wisdom (to Enlightenment).

By accounting for these developmental *streams* or *lines* (as well as the basic development *levels* or *waves*), Wilber's integral psychology acknowledges the observable fact that people develop unevenly and at different rates, although they're still following the same basic universal patterns of consciousness evolution (i.e., from precon to con to postcon to post-post-con). This view is aligned with recent modern research that's identified dozens of developmental streams (also called "multiple intelligences"), where some are more important than others, but nonetheless, all of these variables together contribute to the qualities and substance of the self (or self-system).

Some of the more important Developmental Lines/Streams, which follow the spiral of development, are listed below:

- **Cognitive** line—development of cognition (or awareness of what is); evolving from (in Piaget's terms) from sensorimotor to preoperational (preop) to concrete-operational (conop) to formal-operational (formop) to vision-logic (in Wilber's terms), although his line is often confused as being the only line that develops since it represents intelligence and a sense of self;
- **Moral** line—development of morals and perspectives (or the awareness of what should be); evolving from preconventional to conventional to postconventional to post-postconventional;
- **Emotional** or **Affective** line—the spectrum of emotions and feelings;
- **Interpersonal** line—how a person socially relates to others in social and intersubjective occasions;
- **Needs** line—such as Maslow's need hierarchy: safety, belongingness, self-esteem, etc.;
- **Self-Identity** line—development of identity (or "who am I?"), such as with Loevinger's ego-development;
- **Aesthetic** line—the line of self-expression, beauty, art, and felt-meaning;
- **Psychosexual** line—in its broadest sense it means the entire spectrum of Eros or love (reaching from gross to subtle to causal);
- **Spiritual** line—where "spirit" is viewed not just as Source and Ground, and not just as the highest stage or Goal , but as its own line of unfolding;
- **Values** line—development of values (or what a person considers most important); a line studied by Clare Graves and made popular by Spiral Dynamics.[26]

These developmental lines or streams are graphically pictured in the figure below as appearing in the Upper-Left quadrant or the domain of individual interiors (the "ego-I" or self), yet they're always tetra-meshing (or interacting) with the entire AQAL Matrix. See: Figure 10-5.

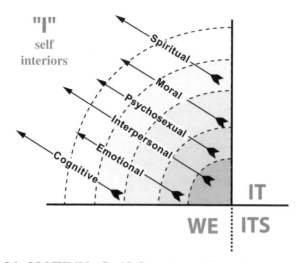

AQAL MATRIX: Self-System: Developmental Streams
(Upper-Left quadrant)
Figure 10-5

As mentioned, these developmental streams have also been called "multiple intelligences," an idea made popular by Howard Gardner with such works as *Frames of Mind: The Theory of Multiple Intelligences* (1983, 1993), which integral psychology see as comparable to the various developmental streams. Gardner pointed out that human beings are a combination of a variety of intelligences, such as cognitive intelligence, emotional intelligence, musical intelligence, kinesthetic intelligence, and so on. Most people, therefore, exercise different *degrees of competence* in each of the various lines, so that they excel in some, do poorly in others, and so forth. An integral approach therefore wants to include all these factors as a way to better find where a person succeeds and where one fails. This will serve to highlight where and how a person may improve, grow, and evolve (overcoming various pathologies and dysfunctions) in order to more properly offer to the world (and themselves) their deepest gifts and talents.

Out of all the possible different developmental streams evolving through the self, Wilber has identified certain "self-related lines or streams" as being more important, since they are, he tells us, "developmental lines that are especially and intimately associated with the self, its needs, its identity, and its development… [in] its extraordinary journey through the great waves."[27] He more fully explains in *Integral Psychology* (2000): "Each time the self's center of gravity orbits around a new level of consciousness, it has a new and different outlook on life. Precisely because each basic level in the Great Nest has a different architecture, the self at each level *sees a different world:* it faces new fears, has different goals, suffers new problems. It has a new set of needs, a new class of morals, a new sense of self."[28] The evolution of consciousness is always a dynamic process of growth, and so must be undertaken with deep resolve, relational support, and discipline.

The figure below lists some of these more important "self-related streams" as they move through the "basic waves," as documented by various modern researchers. See Figure 10-6 (next page).

Integral Psychograph (AQAL)

Since the AQAL Approach includes *all-lines* (or *all-streams*), as well as *all-levels* (or *all-waves*), and *all-quadrants* (the Big Three), then integral psychology proposes the use of an "integral psychograph" to index and plot the various streams and lines in their stages of developmental unfolding through the basic waves of the AQAL Matrix. This allow a composite "picture" or "snapshot," so to speak, of a person's current degree of self-development, since overall, as we've noted and Wilber explains, "a person can be highly evolved in some lines, medium in others, and low in still others."[29] The point is that it's possible to track (simultracks) or index and map the different developmental streams as they flow through the various waves in the Great Nest of Spirit, as a *holonic indexing system* of self-development.

Although these self-related streams can be plotted on a vertical axis (as straight lines), Wilber has also recently suggested that using concentric circles provides a better image, for as he points out, "since the Great Nest is actually a holarchy, we can more accurately represent the *integral psychograph* as [a holarchic mandala]."[30] The nested circles, therefore, represent the basic waves while the developmental streams are the lines radiating throughout them, and thus are extremely useful in self-understanding and therapeutic work. Importantly, Wilber also notes, "both horizontal [heterarchy] and vertical [holarchy]

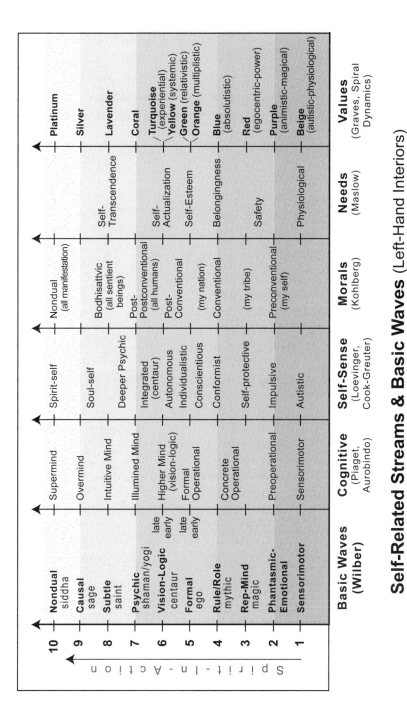

Self-Related Streams & Basic Waves (Left-Hand Interiors)

(from *Integral Psychology*, 2000)

Figure 10-6

analysis would be part of the integral psychograph... [since it] can also include any horizontal typology the particular therapist finds useful."[31] In other words, the AQAL psychograph gives a larger composite "snapshot" of overall development, thus indicating areas for increased focus and improvement.

The figure below pictorially reproduces this holonic indexing idea behind the Integral Psychograph of *basic waves* and *developmental streams* as it's been recently represented in Wilber's Phase-4 books. See Figure 10-7.

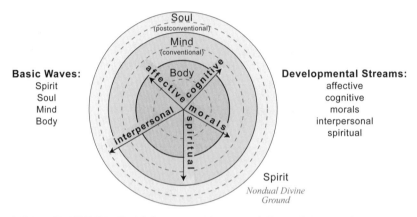

AQAL MATRIX: Self-System: Integral Psychograph
(Basic Waves & Developmental Streams)
Figure 10-7

As a result, by acknowledging and integrating the different developmental streams (or lines), uncovered and documented best by Western psychology, plus by adding the different waves (or levels) of the Great Chain of Being, best recognized by Eastern wisdom, then Wilber realizes that "by recognizing that fact—levels and lines—we can integrate Eastern wisdom with Western knowledge."[32] Although these details may seem complicated (and at times, they are), it actually simplifies an enormous amount of data, which gives the AQAL Approach an upper hand in presenting a truly integral psychology, especially when all the other variables of consciousness must also taken into account, which this approach does, as we'll see next.

Types of Consciousness (All-Type)

Another critical variable in any genuine integral psychology includes what Wilber identifies as the "horizontal typologies" or the "types of consciousness." He defines them in detail in *Integral Psychology* (2000): "For the most part, these [typologies] are not vertical levels, stages, or waves of development, but rather different *types* of orientations *possible at each of the various levels.*"[33] Some examples of these types of horizontal personality systems include the Enneagram, the Myers-Briggs personality system, the Jungian psychological types, astrological traits, and so forth. They tend to give legitimacy to a certain level of awareness by recognizing the unique patterns of each individual self, therefore, they're invaluable in better understanding the activities of the self (and the self-contraction).

Integral psychology acknowledges that these "horizontal types" are *translative* in nature, not the vertically transformative, therefore they're very useful for understanding the tendencies or traits of the self and of others, since they help identify "types of personalities" or "subpersonalities." Nonetheless, according to Wilber, these "horizontal translations" are limited in encouraging further "vertical transformation" into the higher levels of awareness. The important point is, as Wilber explains, "You can be any of those types at virtually any stage of development,"[34] therefore, these types of horizontal characteristics and capacities are fully included in AQAL Metatheory, and its accompanying integral psychology, in order to give a broader and truer picture of the evolving self.

States of Consciousness (All-State)

Since integral psychology outlines a complete cartography of the human psyche by differentiating the various *structures/waves* of consciousness, defined as the various sheaths or levels or *"stable patterns"*[35] of consciousness evolution, from the developmental *lines/streams* and multiple intelligences, then it must also clearly distinguish the various *states* of consciousness, since they're the temporary and ever-changing patterns of daily human awareness. In basic agreement with the wisdom traditions (such as with Vedanta), Wilber begins by acknowledging the states of consciousness known as the *waking* (gross ego), the *dreaming* (subtle soul), and the *deep sleep* (causal spirit) states, which is what every person cycles through every day, as well as including various altered states. Wilber further explains in *Integral Psychology* (2000): "The importance of these three (or four) natural states is that every human being, at no matter what stage or structure or level of development, has available the general spectrum of consciousness—ego to soul to spirit—at least as temporary states, for the simple reason that all humans wake, dream, and sleep."[36] This is obviously a fundamental reality that any true psychology must incorporate and address, which is why, for example, the importance of dreams (and dream interpretation) is widely acknowledged by modern psychology.

Whether arising naturally or at times being artificially induced (medicines, drugs, fasting, prayer, vision quests, etc.), but always effecting consciousness (and self-development) and the awareness of the self, these "States of Consciousness" include at least two or three general types listed below:

1) **Natural states**—are universally recognized by all cultures and in all major world religions:
   - **Waking**—associated with the *Gross* or physical realm (gross-ego, frontal-line stream);
   - **Dreaming**—associated with the *Subtle* or mental and soul realms (subtle soul, deeper-psychic stream);
   - **Deep Sleep**—associated with the *Causal* or formless consciousness (causal spirit, Witness);
   In addition, a full-spectrum integral psychology also acknowledges these transpersonal states (recognized in Advaita Vedanta):
   - **Turiya**—the "fourth state" is the "Witness" of all the states for as consciousness itself it transcends and includes the three states of waking, dreaming, and deep sleep;
   - **Turiyatita**—"beyond the fourth," which is equivalent to, as Wilber says, "One Taste, or the *ever-present awareness* or *constant consciousness* or *basic wakefulness* or *choiceless awareness* that transcends and includes all possible states and is therefore confined to none."[37]

2) **Altered states**—*nonordinary* or non-normal states of consciousness that are always *temporary*, including "peak experiences" ("peek experiences"), which range from drug-activated states to near-death experiences to meditative states. Nonetheless, Wilber emphasizes that "The way in which those [altered] states or realms are experienced

and interpreted depends to some degree on the stage of development of the person having the peak experience."[38]

3) **Meditative states**—those states of consciousness that access the higher and transpersonal realms but in a deliberate and prolonged fashion (such as with "plateau experiences"); therefore, they are an example of when "temporary states must become permanent traits," thus meditative states of transpersonal awareness ultimately transform into the enduring contours of an enlightened mind.

As a further refinement, in Wilber/Phase-4/5 (also by following those same traditional conceptions), Wilber has emphasized that there is always a "Body" that is "the energetic support of the various states and levels of mind,"[39] including:

- **Gross Body**—the "body" of the *waking state* (which supports the material mind);
- **Subtle Body**—the "body" of the *dreaming state* (which supports the emotional, mental, and higher mental levels):
- **Causal Body**—the "body" of *deep sleep* (which supports the spiritual mind).

The fact that all minds or states of consciousness need a "body" to support consciousness has profound implications, since, for example, their observations can be included with *simultracking* (or cross-referencing) the tetra-meshing activity of the AQAL Matrix, now being supported by an *Integral Post-Metaphysics* and the advanced phases of where Wilber's at.

Temporary States into Permanent Traits

Integral psychology acknowledges, as we just saw, that there are differences between the *structures* of consciousness, which evolve in a stagelike manner, and the *states* of consciousness, which are accessible to everyone at any stage of development, particularly since each person (of any age) experiences the three "natural states" of *gross, subtle,* and *causal,* every day when they *wake, dream,* and *sleep,* let alone the various altered and meditative states. As we've mentioned, this involves a certain amount of "fluid access"[40] to the different states of consciousness, which, as Wilber points out, occurs "because the self at every stage of its development has *fluid access* to the great natural states of consciousness (psychic, subtle, causal, and nondual), it can have temporary peak experiences of any or all of those transpersonal realms, thus momentarily leaping forward into greater realities."[41] Consequently, he refers to these aptly named "peak experience," a phrase coined by Abraham Maslow and thoroughly documented by transpersonal psychology, as also being a "peek experience," since they're a fleeting glance or a "peek" at the higher transpersonal states (and structures) of consciousness available to men and women. However, since they're only *temporary* and passing, a person will usually fall back or "come down" to their current level of structural adaptation (or their "center of gravity" and "locus of identification"), where they'll usually *interpret* their higher-order experiences from that level or stage of adaptation.

Since it's possible to have an "influx" of the higher (psychic, subtle, or causal) "poured into" the lower (magical, mythical, or rational) structures of consciousness, then after having a "peek experience" into the higher transpersonal waves, people will often *interpret* that higher experience from their lower level of adaptation. This creates an entire spectrum of possible epiphanies and interpretations, for as Wilber already pointed out in *A Sociable God* (1983): "Notice that even with our simple scheme we have suggested nine substantially different varieties of authentic peak experience: *psychic, subtle,* or *causal* influx poured into *magical, mythical,* or *rational* structures."[42] These "*temporary infusions*" are called a "transpersonal infusion" (when lower adaptation is infused from the higher transpersonal states) and a "downward translation" (translating the higher transpersonal structures through lower adaptations). With AQAL cross-referencing and a holonic indexing system of "simultracking," such as with the Wilber/Combs Matrix (see below), then integral psychology fully accounts for all these possibilities and shows why there's still the need for further research and studies (see chapter 4).

As only one example, when a person in the mythic-membership stage of cognition reinterprets his/her transpersonal experience from that stage or worldspace tends to distort the original experience, for, as Wilber notes, "If an authentic peak experience occurs to a mythic-religious true believer, it often has the awkward effect of energizing his or her mythic immortality symbols."[43] Nonetheless, transpersonal therapists contend these peak (or peek) experiences are often very valuable for further growth since they give a tangible demonstration of the higher potential within human consciousness, therefore, they can positively encourage further consciousness evolution and more serious, responsible behavior.

In this case, in order to stabilize these *"temporary states into permanent traits"* of enduring structural adaptation, the AQAL Approach (and integral psychology) recommends various disciplines or techniques for self-development initiated through enacting paradigms or injunctions of daily transformative practice (to gain adequate competency and mastery). These types of *Integral Transformative Practices* (ITP) encourage developmental growth, for example, from the prepersonal self who's developing language capacities, to the emerging mental-ego who's learning self-reflexive education, to the higher self-cultivating shamanic (psychic), yogic (subtle), or meditative (causal) practices, and so forth. This vert*ical transformation* of consciousness is what Wilber calls changing "states into traits," i.e., transforming "passing states into enduring traits of permanent realization." Back in 1983, when Wilber was shifting from transpersonal psychology (but including it as well) to a more integral psychology, he had already urgently suggested psychological research should move as quickly as possible "from the paradigm of peak experiences to the paradigm of structural adaptation."[44]

These insights prompt the integral psychologist to conclude in *The Eye of Spirit* (1997): "Growth will consist in a gradual conversion of these alternating and temporary states into enduring structures and traits. The mechanism of that conversion is the central story of the growth and development of consciousness in humans and evolution at large."[45] To first differentiate temporary *states* from the enduring *stages* (or structures), as well as to understand the significance of their *pre/trans* or *pre/post* sequence (and fallacies), are indispensable tools in clarifying today's confusion over having temporary "peak experiences" of higher realms of consciousness from the "plateau experiences" of enduring adaptation. Wilber clarified his concerns back in Phase-2's *A Sociable God* (1983): "In my opinion, authentic religious experiences must be differentiated from mere emotional frenzy, from magical trances, and from mythic mass-enthusiasms, all of which result in a temporary suspension of reason via regression to *pre*-rational adaptations, a slide that is altogether different from *trans*-rational epiphany."[46] This is precisely why development and the evolution of consciousness should be encouraged (but not forced) by establishing social support systems and appropriate lifestyles that are required to live from these higher levels of conscious awareness as an enduring structural adaptation. AQAL Metatheory (with its IOS and holonic analysis) will be invaluable in making sure all the four quadrants: intentional, behavioral, cultural, and social are covered, as well as including all the levels (and the other elements of the self-system) in modeling this sacred Kosmic Mandala of Spirit-in-action. But, as always, it's up to each of us to access and open all the "eyes of knowing" available to us, from the eyes of the flesh to the eye of the mind to the eye of Spirit.

A Spectrum of Mysticism: Seeing with the Eye of Spirit

This brings us to one of Wilber's most intriguing and meticulously researched, yet often most misunderstood and controversial positions, and that is the notion that mysticism, or spiritual (transpersonal) experiences, can be critically graded into different levels of attainment and realization. The condemnation of this type of approach is especially intense in these times of *relative pluralism*, a postmodern attitude that sees all things as relative or of equal importance. Indeed, it's quite understandable that people today generally do not like to have their spiritual or transpersonal experiences questioned since they're such personal and exalted experiences lifting us beyond the confines of the ordinary ego (or self). In grading the higher realms of consciousness, Wilber is recognizing a nested hierarchy (or natural *holarchy*) of structural organization based on contemplative practices, not demoting anyone's experience or level of mystical attainment. Besides, integral psychology embraces them all as a natural unfolding to whole-body Enlightenment (or God-Realization). Since most religions themselves acknowledge there's a progressive unfoldment of consciousness, and since, as Wilber explains, "there exists a hierarchy of not only psychosocial development but also of authentic religious development,"[47] then it's possible to outline a genuine "reconstruction of the contemplative path."[48]

In "teasing apart" the characteristics in the "hierarchy of religious experiences," Wilber came to his conclusions by carefully studying and cataloging the testimonies and writings of history's greatest mystics the world over (the "Perennial Philosophy"), as well as comparing them to his own contemplative practices (such as meditation). Unlike many of his generation, Wilber's been personally exercising the "eye of Spirit" under the careful guidance of various adepts or masters of certain wisdom traditions (in his case, mostly

Buddhist and Zen, but involving others).[49] All of them require certain strict injunctions or disciplined practices to elicit and disclose transpersonal data and knowledge. Thus Wilber's personal meditative experiences, coupled with his extensive reading from the world's sacred texts and literature, have allowed him to reaffirm very clear yet broad categorizations regarding the degree of mystical experiences.

Going beyond "a variety of religious experiences" (after William James's classic study), Wilber has expanded upon that approach by outlining a hierarchy of spiritual experiences plotted along the "spectrum of consciousness" and summarily called the *psychic, subtle, causal,* and *nondual* transpersonal structures (see chapter 8). These ideas were concisely summarized in Phase-2's *A Sociable God* (1983): "The point is that not only is there a variety of religious experience, there is a *hierarchy of religious experience,* with each successive stage—*psychic, subtle, causal*—being higher (by developmental, structural, and integrative standards) than its predecessor, and each correlative practice—*yogic, saintly,* and *sagely*—being likewise more ultimately revelatory."[50] As another useful guide, this matrix or grid correlates each structure with an archetypal "Path" or methodology that's used to disclose the knowledge or wisdom inherent in each one of these basic waves of consciousness, including the paths of the yogis/shamans (psychic), the saints (subtle), the sages (causal), and the siddha/sages (nondual), which was a system first suggested by Sri Ad Da Samraj in the 1970s.[51]

With Wilber/Phase-4/5 this "overall hierarchy of structural organization"[52] is pictured as holons tetra-evolving through the basic waves with four quadrants set within the larger context of the AQAL or "all-quadrants, all-levels" Matrix. These stages of mystical attainment, the highest (deepest) levels of consciousness, and their corresponding "paths" or principle methodologies, are briefly outlined below:

- **Nature Mysticism**—the Path of Shamans/Yogis—**Psychic** (low subtle) level including paranormal capacities (precognition, clairvoyance, psychokinesis, etc.), as well as yogic *siddhis* (or "powers"), and shamanic energies, since they still have referents situated in the gross realm (of the body and nature);

- **Deity Mysticism**—the Path of Saints—**Subtle** (high subtle) level or the "overmind," "overself," or "soul" including patterns of light (shabd), sound (nada), and crystalline etheric structures, such as the *real archetypes* or structures read by mathematics,[53] these can be the subtle structural patterns in the crystallization of Spirit into matter (or *involution*); includes various astral realms or soulful deities and other subtle beings (spirit guides, angelic beings, ishtadevas, etc.);

- **Formless Mysticism**—the Path of Sages—**Causal** Emptiness or Void (the Witness), the indefinable, yet where the "early/low phase" can be seen as the "First Cause" (causal) or the "Final God" for all holons and all created things (in whatever form, gross or subtle) arising out of this Uncreated Emptiness (*sunyata*) thus all forms are *witnessed* (as "the Witness") in free consciousness as consciousness itself; "late/high phase" is the "total and utter transcendence and release into Formless Consciousness, Boundless Radiance";[54]

- **Nondual Mysticism**—the Path of Siddhas/Sages—**Nondual** Divine Spirit is totally indescribable, *only realizable*, thus it is both Transcendent and Immanent, both Summit or Goal (or the highest "rung on the ladder") and Source or Ground (the "wood of the entire ladder") of all creation (the Kosmos); the indivisible Oneness of Emptiness that releases all forms (gross, subtle, causal) into the radiant Formless Divine, where, as Wilber mystically muses, "the center of Formlessness is shown to be not other than the entire world of Form."[55]

An effective way to show this cross-referencing is with the figure below taken from the detailed correlative charts found in the back of *Integral Psychology* (2000), which were compiled by Wilber himself from hundreds of researchers and spiritual systems. See Figure 10-8.

These important benefits gained from better "unpacking" or "teasing apart" the various dimensions and depths of reality can even affect the evolution of consciousness, both individually and collectively. For example, in learning the subtle distinctions between the personal God (high subtle) and transcendent Godhead (causal), or between the Great Mother (magic-mythic) and the Great Goddess (subtle/nondual), or between the Witness (Atman) and nondual mysticism (Brahman-Atman), a person can begin to more fully realize the depth of our consciousness and the reality of existence.[56] As another example, by appreciating the important differentiation between

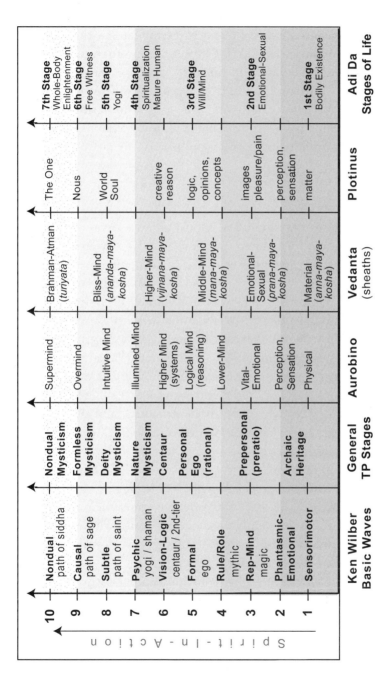

Basic Waves Correlated with the Great Wisdom Traditions

(from *Integral Psychology*, 2000)

Figure 10-8

the "average-mode" awareness of the popular masses (magic, mythic, rational), as well as the sacred wisdom bestowed in us by the "advanced-tip" individuals who are humanity's spiritual pioneers (exemplified by the shamans, yogi, saints, sages, siddhas, et al.), then we can better embrace the entire expanse of our global inheritance. In this case, we'll find the spectrum of mysticism, and the entire spectrum of consciousness, or the AQAL Matrix, is an extremely valuable tool for becoming *more integral,* for it simply asks us to embrace all of reality while transcending it all in mystical liberation, the enlightened pinnacle of human life and happiness.

Wilber-Combs Lattice: States & Structures

One recent example of this multidimensional approach is seen with the "Wilber-Combs Lattice," a holonic indexing or cross-referencing system used to track the various *structures* of enduring adaptation (i.e., magical, mythical, rational, psychic, subtle, causal, and nondual) with the fluid temporary *states* available to the self (i.e., waking, dreaming, deep sleep, altered, meditative, etc). Through a mutual collaboration between Ken Wilber and integral professor Allan Combs, they have expanded upon the grid originally created by the Phase-2's spectrum of consciousness model and its "hierarchy of religious experience" (as we just saw above). The Wilber-Combs Lattice is capable of running a *cross-level analysis* on the various states of consciousness and their relationships with the various structures, and then reviews their interactions and interpretations, such as, for example, by monitoring the various forms of *downward translation* engendered by *transpersonal infusion.* Professor Combs explains this principle nicely in his follow-up edition to *The Radiance of Being: Understanding the Grand Integral Vision; Living the Integral Life* (2002): "The idea that people interpret their experiences of states of consciousness differently, according to their own developmental level, opens the door to a better understanding of why spiritual or religious encounters seem so different for different people."[57] As we saw, since a person usually *interprets* their higher consciousness experiences in terms of the level they presently reside, then it's important to keep track of these differences.

The Wilber-Combs Lattice (which is in harmony with the great wisdom traditions on this account) also accounts for the relationship of structures, states, and realms. It presents a "nesting" or "matrix" where the general or *broad states* (i.e., waking, dreaming, altered, etc.) contain the different *structures* (i.e., magical to rational to causal, etc.), which contains the various *states of mind* (i.e., Combs' term for the emotional/mental states, such as laughter, anger, hurt, surprise, etc.). Wilber further explains, "At the same time, the relationship among these various states and structures is definitely holonic and intermeshing. They are not simply plunked down on top of each other like so many bricks, but are interwoven in mutually influential ways."[58] This produces the basic outline of the Wilber-Combs Lattice summarized below:

- **General States** or *Broad States* of consciousness—the *natural states of* waking (gross-ego), dreaming (subtle soul), and deep sleep (causal spirit), plus *altered* and *meditative* states of consciousness;

- **Structures** of consciousness—the "spectrum of consciousness" (in four quadrants), from archaic to magical to mythic to mental-egoic to centaur, etc. (Lower-Left quadrant), from rep-mind to rule/role to formal to vision-logic, etc. (Upper-Left quadrant), and they exist within the broad states of consciousness;

- **States of Mind** or *Phenomenal States*—such as joy, doubt, determination, sadness, anger, laughter, etc., with many hybrids, and existing within the structures of consciousness.

Obviously, the importance of having a clear understanding of the variety and depth of human experiences, and the methodologies available to disclose the spectrum of awareness and knowledge, is indispensable for developing a tolerant and integrated global unity. This is especially true for any type of "Human Consciousness Project" that needs to explore and embrace the "farthest reaches of human nature." This approach serves our own personal self-development in each individual case, while simultaneously serving the collective evolution of humankind. Nonetheless, the AQAL view being articulated by this particular post-postmodern bodhisattva (Wilber) strongly maintains that it's only with pragmatic (and compassionate) applications of these theories in the "real world" of social and cultural life will the human consciousness project be truly successful. This very directly involves turning theories into practices, a subject we'll turn to next.

CHAPTER ELEVEN

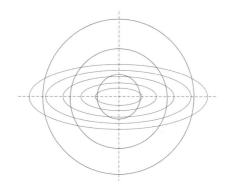

AQAL Apps: Integral Theory into Integral Practice

What is required, in my opinion, is not simply a new integral theory or a new T.O.E., important as that is, but also a new *integral practice*…. We don't just need a map; we need ways to change the mapmaker. Thus, although most of my books attempt to offer a genuinely integral vision, they almost always end with a call for some sort of integral practice—a practice that exercises body, mind, soul, and spirit in self, culture, and nature (all-level, all-quadrant).

—Ken Wilber, *A Theory of Everything* (2000)

Wilber/Phase-5: AQAL Metatheory

IT COULD BE ARGUED THAT WILBER/PHASE-5 IS NOT REALLY A CLEARLY distinguishable phase in Ken Wilber's career, for even he had difficulty conceding that a real shift had taken place, especially since, for him, it's just the further reaches of exploring Phase-4's AQAL Matrix with all its multivariable forms and integral metatheory (floating in the Formless). Nevertheless, as we've seen, there are certain characteristics appearing in Wilber's recent writings that help define a shift into another phase of his integral studies, such as with Integral Post-Metaphysics (see chapter 5). Now let's go on to review some other important Phase-5 emergents, including Integral Methodological Pluralism (IMP) and the Integral Operating System (IOS), all new formulations that have made it useful, especially for his students, to recognize the emergence of Wilber/Phase-5 in first half decade of the new millennium. This will become abundantly evident with the daunting publication of volume 2 of *The Kosmos Trilogy* (over 900 pages), and the other upcoming volumes to be published in the second half-decade of the twenty-first century.

Another highlight of Wilber/Phase-5, which *Integral Post-Metaphysics* deals with directly, is that by seeing the entire AQAL Matrix (the spectrum of consciousness in self, culture, and nature) as an interwoven tapestry of interiors and exteriors, then we can more clearly see that "matter" or the gross physical realm is the *outer* or *external* forms of the AQAL Matrix or Great Nest of Spirit (see chapter 4). As Wilber recently and very clearly stated: "In the manifest world, what we call 'matter' is not the lowest rung in the great spectrum of existence, but the exterior form of every rung in the great spectrum."[1] By applying these revolutionary gains, the integral philosopher has alleviated the theoretical the dualism between "this-world" versus the "other-world," the dualism of traditional metaphysics and the physical world, thereby demonstrating there's no real separation between the physical and spiritual (or the "metaphysical"), for existence is a *psychophysical* or AQAL "all-quadrant, all-level" reality.

By modeling an AQAL Kosmos that has corresponding *correlates* of insides *(interiors)* and outsides *(exteriors)* reaching from the material to the mental to the spiritual, from the *gross* (physical) to the *subtle* (mental) to the *causal* (spiritual) realms, and we saw they generate a *deep science* and *real religion* that can contribute to our knowledge quest (see chapter 4). Yet, of course, as we've also discussed, with the AQAL Matrix, this understanding comes with the spiritual realization that all forms, the entire evolutionary Kosmic Mandala itself, is *always already* "shading into Emptiness," thus it's in deep harmony with authentic spirituality. This way, according to the Integral Vision, we can better appreciate all the possibilities existing in the Kosmic Mandala of Spirit-in-action, and therefore make wiser ethical decisions for appropriate action in our lives and the real world.

These types of revolutionary conceptions imply a more modern way, in fact, a thoroughly "post-postmodern" and *integral* way, to model and investigate spirituality (and Spirit-in-action) as it appears in the real world. Yet, these are not just theoretical constructs but *reconstructions*, since they come from accessing and integrating the various methodologies available to men and women in their knowledge quest. In continuation of his earlier works (especially with *epistemological pluralism*), these forms of data acquisitions or "modes of knowing" come from the *"eye of flesh"* (the physical world), the *"eye of mind"* (the mental world), and the *"eye of Spirit"* (the archetypal, contemplative realities). Ultimately, an integral vision of reality would have to involve and include *all* worldviews, *all* methodologies, *all* paradigms, thus providing a "Metatheory" or "Meta-paradigm," or what Wilber/Phase-5 terms an *Integral Methodological Pluralism*, as a constructive way to open and include *all* the eyes of knowing. This constructive postmodern philosophy, as we'll see, even provides an appropriate "environmental ethics" (based on an integral *value holarchy*), showing the *rights* and *responsibilities* of each and every individual human holon in their quest to be "more integral" (let alone more enlightened, for this approach includes that as well).

As one practical example of application, as we've already learned, each person can use or apply the AQAL Matrix as an integral "scanning device" in order to make sure all quadrants, all levels, all lines, all states, all types, etc., of consciousness are being included, honored, and developed (and even, ultimately, transcended) in our understanding of ourselves and existence. The AQAL Approach, therefore, offers an integral map of knowledge that's awakened to both intellectual wisdom and heartfelt compassion, grounded in the "marriage of science and religion," based on a compatible integration of the premodern (mythic/religious) and modern/postmodern (scientific/critical) worlds. This principle project of Wilber/Phase-5, embodied in the business of Integral Institute and Integral University (and other integral ventures), is certainly a good place to find where Wilber's at.

In the previous chapters we briefly sketched in the some of the basic elements and variables involved with Ken Wilber's Integral Vision and how it's evolved from his groundbreaking spectrum of consciousness model into the fully developed AQAL Approach with its dynamic and evolving AQAL Matrix of all-quadrants, all-levels, all-lines. Now we'll briefly review a few of the pragmatic applications of these integral theories in the "real world," including the harsh realities of *realpolitik* (or real politics), business, education, ecology, and countless other critical endeavors. As we'll see, the AQAL Integral Vision opens up new vistas for an even larger, more expanded embrace of reality.

Correcting the Use of "Paradigm"

When Ken Wilber first began his investigations into psychology, philosophy, world religions (and the Perennial Philosophy), modern science, and all the other fields of knowledge that would lead to his integral enterprise, from the start he took the novel approach of including as many truths as possible from every system he came across. All of these "correct but partial" truths were integrated into one encompassing integral theory, a "Metatheory" or "Theory of Everything." By taking such a comprehensive approach, Wilber realized he'd become a "methodological outlaw," since he was availing himself and so many different fields of study to so many possible methods of inquiry, from bodywork to group therapy, from yoga to intellectual study, from psychotherapy to meditation, from science to religion, as well as the many other forms of knowledge acquisition. After catapulting to world renown with his first book *The Spectrum of Consciousness* (1977), Wilber consciously shunned academia or any orthodox training that would curtail his voracious thirst for knowledge. Instead, the young philosopher labored as a dishwasher to meet his expenses, which gave him the requisite freedom to explore his studies in whichever way his wisdom quest would take him. As he explains in the new foreword to the paperback edition of *A Sociable God* (1983, 2006): "I was a methodological outlaw in the very inclusiveness of the methodology itself. My approach was outlawed in both cultural and countercultural academies, not because it was partial, but because it was radically holistic. I included those things that shouldn't be included, I embraced those methodologies that were pox-ridden for the orthodox, I loved those injunctions despised by those in power, I reached out to those experiences on the margin and beyond. In including all sides of the argument, I was disowned by all sides."[2] This was all done in an attempt to be as *inclusionary* as possible, not to just deny authority or be eclectic.

At the time, Wilber was only aware that he was using a radically inclusionary principle by actively engaging all of these various disciplines or methods of inquiry and methodologies. Years later, he calls this type of all-embracing approach "Integral Methodological Pluralism" (or IMP), which is best summarized, according to Wilber, with the phrase "Everybody is right"—although only partially ("true but partial"). The integral philosopher had already noted years before (1982): "We are faced not with several errors and one truth, but with several partial truths, and how to fit them together is the supreme puzzle."[3] For the integral approach, therefore, there can *only* be a pluralism of methodologies, as Wilber recently defined in a current writing (2005):

> **Integral Methodological Pluralism**… means that we allow (and rely on) every major mode of acquiring experience—every major methodology, paradigm, injunction, exemplar technique, and so on, because each of them, without exception, is delivering some important piece of the overall puzzle…. Integral methodological pluralism… includes the most amount of truth from the most number of sources based on the most amount of evidence in the most holistic fashion possible… and for [that] simple reason it honors and includes more truth than any of the alternatives.[4]

This brings up another one of the unique clarifications brought forward by Wilber's precise work, and that is the fact that the word "paradigm" has often been misinterpreted and misused by many contemporary theorists, especially by many of the so-called New Age or "New Paradigm" theorists. Originating in popularity with Thomas Kuhn's 1962 landmark book *The Structure of Scientific Revolutions*, the word "paradigm" was chosen by Kuhn to suggest a "constellation of facts, theories, and methods" to indicate that a paradigm is an "actual scientific practice [that will] provide models from which spring particular coherent traditions of scientific research."[5] In this case, the various and numerous "scientific revolutions" are seen as "paradigm shifts," thus indicating the transformation of one paradigm to another, where both *practices* and *theories* (or models) are being used to define the paradigm. Other theorists, however, took this interesting and explanatory idea and applied it to areas of interest other than the advancements of science. Although Kuhn himself was quite meticulous about the use of the word "paradigm" (in the second edition, he even complained it had created "misunderstandings"), its use in the popular lexicon had caused Wilber to claim that it's "one of the great misunderstood concepts of our era,"[6] therefore, with Phase-4 he's been on a mission to correct this grievous error of contemporary thought by more appropriately realigning it with its original meaning.

As a result of Kuhn's popularity (among the intelligentsia), many theorists began to see a paradigm as being something more like a worldview overall-encompassing theory, so that even today's dictionaries define "paradigm" as "a model, a pattern," thus placing an emphasis on the accompanying intellectual theory, and not the exemplar or methodology disclosing certain worldviews and variables of consciousness. While a model is an important part of a paradigm, its most critical aspect seems to be the "actual practices" that reveal or disclose certain information or data in the acquisition of knowledge. However, with the revolutionary changes of the 1960s, many theorists, perhaps understandably, exploited Kuhn's powerful observations by co-opting it to mean a general worldview, such as Marilyn Ferguson did in her immensely popular book *The Aquarian Conspiracy* (1980): "A paradigm is a framework of thought (from the Greek *paradeigma*, 'pattern'). A paradigm is a scheme for understanding and explaining certain aspects of reality…. A paradigm shift is a distinctly new way of thinking about old problems."[7] Yet, as we've just seen, theories are only half of the story—the other half is *practice.*

Injunctive Strand: The Real Paradigm

Since Ken Wilber has been emphatically critical of the distortion being made in contemporary thought about what a paradigm really is, he has therefore pointed out in *The Eye of Spirit* (1997): "Thomas Kuhn, in one of the greatly misunderstood ideas of our time, pointed out that normal science proceeded most fundamentally by way of what he called *paradigms* or *exemplars*. A paradigm is not merely a concept, it is an *actual practice*, an injunction, a technique taken as an exemplar for generating data."[8] According to Wilber, therefore, a paradigm "refers to the *methodologies of enacting new phenomena*, not merely to the theories that attempt to explain them."[9] As a consequence, the integral paradigm is *not* suggesting a shift from one theory to another "theory of everything," just creating another worldview to be memorized, another concept to accept, but rather, Wilber is suggesting we need to include and integrate *all paradigms* with an *inclusionary pluralism* (which is in contradistinction to postmodernity's *exclusive pluralism*). This is where an *Integral Methodological Pluralism* becomes extremely useful and practical.

In clarifying the role of paradigms, what's being highlighted is the *injunctive strand* in the "three strands of knowledge accumulation," i.e., injunctions, disclosures/data, and confirmation/rejection (see chapter 4). The injunctive paradigm, simply put, means if you want to know something, then "do this!"; for example, you must look through a telescope to see Jupiter's moons, or look through a microscope to see a cell; or learn mathematics to understand quantum physics; or practice meditation or contemplation to know Spirit. Therefore, Wilber's currently found it necessary to emphasize that a *paradigm* or *injunction* is a "type of social practice, mode of production, concrete behavioral injunction, or experimental exemplars… [that] generate, enact, bring forth, and illumine new types of experiences, occasions, data, phenomena."[10] *Engaging the injunction*, following the exemplar, exercising the practice—*doing the yoga*—is the actual method or methodology for disclosing new truths—but, the important point is: *You have to do them!*

Of course, Wilber has cooked up some tasty analogies, such as this one from *Eye to Eye* (1983): "[A paradigm or injunction] is precisely like a cookbook: You give recipes and invite the reader to go out and perform the recipe, actually do it, and then taste the results. You are not supposed merely to learn the recipes, memorize the recipes, and then claim you're a cook. But that's what many—not all—of the proponents of the new paradigm have in mind…. The new paradigm is just a new menu, but nobody's talking about the meal anymore, and that bothers me…. And the only way you actually know the transmental is to actually transform. You cook the meal and eat it, you don't emboss the menu."[11]

Integral Methodological Pluralism: A Meta-Paradigm

This Integral Approach, in summary, suggests that in our knowledge or wisdom quest, we must eat a variety of meals (i.e., enact paradigms), and then integrate what's been gained by embracing everything, from dust to deity, from dirt to Divinity. Only *then* can we make better value judgments and construct our models because now we're being inclusionary of *all maps* and methodologies (yet, of course, never mistaking any of them for the actual territory). As we've mentioned, with Wilber/Phase-5, the integral theorist has been calling this approach Integral Methodological Pluralism—or IMP—which is a "meta-paradigm" designed to be an all-embracing *inclusionary* paradigm that integrates all other paradigms. By taking the integral approach, which claims "Everybody is right" (since "no one can be 100 percent wrong"), then *all partial truths are included* (yet transcended) in an attempt to honor and include the partial validity of all values in the spectrum of consciousness (i.e., all-levels), and in all the domains of the Kosmos (i.e., all-quadrants). In other words, each methodology or paradigm contributes "*inherent ingredients* in today's spiral of growth and development."[12]

In a pivotal Wilber/Phase-5 essay that captures the essence of these intentions, called "The Many Ways We Touch" (now a chapter in volume 2 of *The Kosmos Trilogy*), Wilber has specifically outlined some basic definitions involved with such an *inclusionary pluralism* or Integral Methodological Pluralism (IMP):

- **Integral**—means this *meta-paradigm* is not eclectic (or selecting what seems best from varied sources) but invites all views and practices (or paradigms) into the mix in order to create an "integral tapestry of unity-in-diversity that slights neither the unity nor the diversity";

- **Methodological**—means by operating with and using real paradigms, exemplars, or a *set of actual practices* and behavioral injunctions, this will bring forth the various levels of reality and consciousness being investigated or inquired;

- **Pluralism**—means there are "no privileged paradigms" (no absolutisms) for "there is no overriding or privileged injunction (other than to be radically inclusive)" for an integral approach is an *inclusive pluralism* (unlike postmodernity's *exclusionary pluralism*).

Such inclusiveness is informed by all forms of human *inquiry* (or a knowledge search), which Wilber defines as "inquiry, or ways that we look for truth, or meaning, or information, or feelings, or insights, or collaborative sharing, and so on. In all forms of *inquiry*, in any quadrant, we are looking for something."[13] The particular methodology that's being used and enacted will disclose, generate, light up certain forms of data, including first-, second-, and third-person perspectives. Since this involves an AQAL Approach, Wilber tours the quadrants by pointing out some of the major forms of inquiry already found in each, such as the following:

- **Upper-Right Inquiry** ("It")—sensory empiricism; facts; sensorimotor dimensions of holons;

- **Upper-Left Inquiry** ("I")—first-person modes of inquiry (and being-in-the-world); "my own mind" (subjective); introspection;

- **Lower-Right Inquiry** ("Its")—third-person inquiries on the collective (systems-theory inquiry); organism-environment systems or the ecological web-of-life (which is itself embedded in larger webs); systems behavior;

- **Lower-Left Inquiry** ("We")—intersubjective inquiry (such as hermeneutics) covering mutual understandings between subjects or the cultural dimension ("the great postmodern discovery: every holon has an intersubjective dimension"); shared semantics ("exchanges of signifiers"); cultural backgrounds; collaborative inquiry; participatory pluralism.

With such a broad range and comprehensive sweep, or "theory of everything," including all the methodologies that disclose all forms of knowledge (on any level, in any quadrant), Wilber continues to list some of IMP's various parts and advantages:

- **Paradigmatic**—means that IMP makes room for all the major modes of inquiry, creating a careful compilation of all the primary paradigms or methodologies of inquiry;

- **Meta-paradigmatic**—is the "essence of Integral Metatheory" ("Everybody is right") which tries to conscientiously relate all the various paradigmatic strands to each other, which include:

  o **AQAL indexing** or "**simultracking**"—is when all the various phenomena in all the various domains (all levels, all quadrants, etc.) are simultaneously tracked according to the accepted methodologies of those particular domains;
  o **no absolutisms**—of any domain over the others, where no wave (level), stream (line), quadrant, or state, etc., is privileged or considered absolute (other than, of course, the Absolute itself that includes-yet-transcends *all forms* in the Formlessness of nondual Spirit);
  o **ILP** or **Integral Life Practice**—when "a full range of human potentials are simultaneously engaged and exercised in order to *enact* and bring forth any higher states and stages of human potential in all quadrants and on all levels";

   o   **Integrative Tool-Kit**—can be applied to *social ills* as well as *individual pathologies* thus providing "second-tier solutions" to social and individual problems, which will involve, as Wilber explains, "sustained inquiries into ways that will allow *each wave* (e.g., purple, red, blue, orange, green) to freely explore its own potentials but in ways that those waves would not construct if left to their own exclusionary practices."[14]

IMP or Integral Methodological Pluralism, therefore, is the type of inclusionary metatheory or pluralistic methodology that embraces all views, yet also transcends them all in the One Taste of nondual Spirit (or God). By doing so, the Integral Vision involves both theories *and* practices, for it's the *practices* that disclose the data that then informs the *theories*, and then in a "feedback loop" the *theories* support (or modify and correct) the *practices*. This type of integral approach brings *depth* (or all-levels) to the domains of self, culture, and nature (or all-quadrants), therefore, it corrects Flatland reductionism (the "disaster" of modernity), as well as the materialistic nihilism and narcissism (the Bad News of postmodernism) so prevalent in today's world. This type of AQAL integralism also provides the *operating system* that can be practically applied to all types of endeavors in all the domains of existence, thus providing a viable platform for genuine integral *theories* and transformative *practices* leading to the unfolding of our higher potentials.

IOS Basic: Integral Operating System

One of the more creative aspects of Ken Wilber's work is that he's always refining and simplifying his presentations in various ways. Although his Integral Model seems to always be capable of increasing its complexities, especially with its multivariable nature (such as with levels, lines, states, etc.), or with the variety of "cross-referencing" and "simultracking" schemes (such as holonic indexing, the Wilber/Combs Matrix, etc.), it still remains a fairly simple system composed of some basic elements. According to Wilber, since AQAL Metatheory is able to include all partial truths (eliminating absolutisms), or "orienting generalizations" gathered from "all known systems and models of human growth—from ancient shamans and sages to today's breakthroughs in cognitive science," then its pluralistic inclusiveness becomes a guiding framework for better organizing any activity or understanding any phenomena in the Kosmos.

Motivated in part from his recent public outreach, such as with Integral Institute and Integral University, Wilber has adequately distilled his more complex AQAL Map into what's now called an Integral Operating System—or IOS—in order to highlight its underlying simplicity. Wilber has recently summarized these ideas in the multimedia package titled *The Integral Operating System, Version 1.0* (2005, Sounds True, Inc.). In a recent essay titled "Introduction to Integral Theory and Practice: IOS Basic and the AQAL Map," Wilber has simplified this even further into what he calls "IOS Basic" *(Integral Operating System Basic),* where he explains: "More advanced forms of IOS are available, but IOS Basic has all the essential elements to get anybody started toward a more comprehensive, inclusive, and effective approach."[15] This is, in other words, the basics of where Wilber's at.

IOS Basic simplifies the multiple variables into "five simple factors" that summarize the basic elements in the AQAL Matrix as including: (1) quadrants, (2) levels, (3) lines, (4) states, and (5) types (as we've seen extensively in the previous chapters). Importantly, the integral philosopher defends this positions by reminding us, "These five elements are not merely theoretical concepts; they are aspects of your own experience, contours of your own consciousness."[16] As we've learned, they represent all-levels in the Great Nest of Spirit as they appear in self, culture, and nature (or all-quadrants) which are even evidenced by their embedment in all major human languages the world over (as the first-, second-, and third-person perspectives of "I, We, and It").

In its essence then, IOS is a way of analyzing any situation or existent phenomena from the point of view of an AQAL "all-quadrants, all-levels, all-states, et al." or integral perspective. Wilber therefore affirms the reasons for using an Integral Operating System: "IOS automatically *scans* all phenomena—interiors as well as exteriors—for any quadrants, waves, streams, or states that are not being included in awareness. IOS then acts to redress this imbalance and help move the system toward a more integral and inclusive stance.... IOS, although a third-person operating system, simply acts as a reminder, a *self-scanning alert,* that there might be more feelings than are presently being allowed to surface, and points one in the direction of a more integral embrace."[17] In other words, the Integral Operating System is the way to begin applying AQAL Metatheory.

Wilber lists several aspects that immediately become available by using

IOS Basic or an effective *Integral Operating System*, which is based upon exercising an integral methodological pluralism inherent in an overall AQAL Metatheory, including these advantages listed below:

- **IOS "touches all the bases"**—whatever field a person is working in, be it business, medicine, psychotherapy, art, law, ecology, or simple everyday living, IOS helps make sure you're "touching all the bases" by utilizing and accessing the full range of resources for any situation, thus assuring a greater likelihood for success;

- **IOS more easily accelerates growth/development**—when integrally touching all the bases by running IOS, this approach helps to orient yourself (or your field or business, etc.) to more easily appreciate, more fully exercise, and more adequately use all of the variables and evolutionary potentials of Kosmos-consciousness, thus allowing a deeper participation in the glorious journey of self-discovery and awakening;

- **IOS is only a map**—IOS is consciously aware that it is "only a map, not the territory," that it's "merely a third-person system of signifiers," therefore, it's not just a matter of learning or memorizing a new theory but actively engaging and enacting *injunctive practices* (as with Integral Methodological Pluralism);

- **IOS is a neutral framework**—this means IOS does not tell you what to think, force any particular ideology, nor coerce your awareness in any fashion since it's only suggesting what's necessary to be more comprehensive and integral, and that is, by including, at a minimum, all these variables and basic elements (AQAL);

- **IOS can be used by any discipline**—perhaps most important, since the AQAL Matrix embraces all possibilities, from human to otherwise, then all disciplines and methods of inquiry can be positively effected by applying an integral approach, from medicine to art to business to spirituality to politics to ecology (see IOS Apps below). In this case, as Wilber claims: "We can, for the first time in history, begin an extensive and fruitful dialogue between all of these disciplines,"[18] because now there's access to a common language and a common operating system that's universal in its embrace.

As a useful analogy to explain how to apply and access IOS, Wilber has resorted to using computerese by suggesting a person can install the "self-scanning software" of the AQAL Model to make sure all of the basic elements of existence are being included in any integral analysis. First, one "downloads" the basic elements of AQAL Metatheory by learning and understanding the basic contours of the integral approach (where "Everybody is right"). Once the program's been "installed," so to speak, then one runs his own projects by scanning them with a "holonic indexing" (or "holonic conferencing") system based on an AQAL database in order to see which *quadrants* (interiors and exteriors), *levels* (in the spectrum of consciousness), *lines* of development, *states* of consciousness, various horizontal *typologies*, etc., are being activated or overlooked with any occasion or with any phenomena. Then it becomes clearer what needs to be more adequately addressed or rebalanced; in other words, with IOS, it's possible to be *more integral*, more embracing, by involving deeper understandings and wider perspectives.

IOS, therefore, becomes a "multipurpose Integral Toolkit," in which case, as Wilber tells us, "cross-paradigmatic judgments can believably be made."[19] Allan Combs, in explaining his own integral vision in his brilliant book *The Radiance of Being: Understanding the Grand Integral Vision; Living the Integral Life* (2002), cleverly calls the use of Wilber's integral theories as applying an "AQAL litmus test," because, as he explains, "The AQAL approach can be a powerful way to re-examine just about any kind of activity. If nothing else, it keeps us from overlooking major omissions that become obvious when we turn the topic over in the light of the AQAL approach."[20] Combs accurately recognized his colleague's overall intentions: "Wilber himself is not an advocate of any particular discipline or practice. Rather, he claims that the AQAL approach gives us both a map and a litmus test with which we can assay any practice or life style."[21] In other words, these are some more of the advantages gained by understanding where Wilber's at.

IOS and Integral Methodological Pluralism, which is activated by understanding at least the broad outlines of the AQAL Matrix and its underlying metatheory, then becomes an invaluable aid for a fractured world that's often engaged in the violent war of worldviews. Yet, since IOS is not telling or forcing anyone what to think or what to do—it's a "neutral framework"—

then it's only *suggesting* that in order "to include all the important possibilities, be sure to include first- [I/you/she/he] and second- [we/us] and third-
person [it/its] perspectives." Only this type of integral approach will bring
about a genuine global healing and positive development, thus our integral
visionary presents his case again by saying, "Precisely because IOS is a neutral
framework, it can be used to bring more clarity, care, and comprehensiveness to virtually any situation, making success much more likely, whether
that success be measured in terms of personal transformation, social change,
excellence in business, care for others, or simple happiness in life."[22]

In this case, at the very least, people and institutions across the entire
matrix of existence can become more "integrally developed" and thus be more
open to, as Wilber explains, more *"integrally informed practices...* whether
one is a doctor, a lawyer, a janitor, or a waitress."[23] As human beings, if we
want to grow and develop as we reach for the promises of our evolutionary
potentials, then we need to be sustained and nurtured by a healthy sociocultural environment based in a thriving natural biosphere (all lower holons),
in other words, *we all need to be more integral.* We do this by "touching all
bases" with all the domains of the Kosmos (matter to body to mind to soul
to spirit) in order to broaden our search for more comprehensive solutions
and practical applications for our fractured and myopic problems promul-
gated by first-tier thinking and a Flatland materialism bereft of depth and
meaning. An Integral Vision, especially the one proposed by Ken Wilber,
intends to counter this dreadful situation by more consciously embracing
reality and then by *applying* and *practicing* this wisdom in the "real world."

AQAL Pragmatic Applications: IOS Apps

Now that we've reviewed the *Integral Operating System* (IOS), based in an
AQAL Metatheory using an *Integral Methodological Pluralism* (IMP) as its
method of inquiry (disclosing all domains of knowledge), then we can better
see the many ways these integral theories can be practically applied to "real
world" endeavors. This has become especially relevant since Ken Wilber has
been interacting with a larger (and growing) number of people in the new
millennium. He's also been meeting with a wide variety of leaders and professionals in numerous fields who have been reading his written works, then
implementing their own version of his integral theories, often making their
own invaluable contributions. This approach alone has encouraged Wilber,

and his colleagues and investors, to establish Integral Institute (I-I), a leading-edge integral think tank, as well as Integral University, the educational arm of I-I that's being run and taught by the many associates who've already been attracted to a more integral approach (see chapter 3).

Indeed, since the Wilber/Phase-4 presentation of the *four quadrants* or AQAL Model, Wilber's integral philosophy has become more accessible to a greater number of people in more practical ways, yet of course no one has to accept all of his assertions, such as with the theories about the transpersonal (spiritual) levels. The integral pandit pointed this out in *One Taste* (1999):

> With Wilber/Phase-4 (the four quadrants, each with a dozen or so levels), there is an almost *instant applicability* to most endeavors, because the four quadrants cover a multitude of ordinary events. You do not have to include, or even believe in, the higher and transpersonal levels [Phases 1-3] of each quadrant in order to find the quadrants themselves useful. And the four quadrants *are* useful precisely because they give a simple, easily understood way to fight the flatland reductionism so prevalent in the modern and postmodern world. Since unmitigated reductionism is imply *false*, this reductionism will adversely affect or even cripple your efforts in any and all fields, from business to politics to education—and thus the four quadrants give you an immediate way to avoid this crippling. And *that* will pay off in everything from more responsible politics to more efficient education to increased profits.[24]

This is mostly because, as we've amply seen, the AQAL Model covers the interiors and exteriors of both individual and collective systems, including the worldwide sociocultural milieu. The examples of how the AQAL Metatheory is being applied in the real world are becoming endless (I can't keep track of them)—as they should be: For any real "Theory of Everything" should offer something to, well, nearly *everybody*. In fact, the integral philosopher was heard to humorously note: "My work used to reach those interested in satori; now it reaches those interested in soap."[25] From dishwasher to soap promoter; sometimes it's simply amazing to find out all the places where Wilber's at. Let's briefly review a few examples demonstrating some of the various applications or "apps" of an *Integral Operating System* (IOS)—called "IOS Apps"—which are being used by a wide variety of modern fields.

Integral Medicine

The Integral AQAL Model is immediately applicable to medicine, thus it's an excellent example of how the four quadrants provide an effective tool for analysis and management; consequently, it's already being adopted by some innovative health care facilities around the world. First, it's possible to *scan* for the *"all-quadrants"* aspects that are all involved in the cause and management of illness and medical treatment. Since orthodox or conventional medicine is a classic Upper-Right quadrant approach, which emphasizes the *exterior* physical organism, then it suggests the various physical interventions (such as with surgery, drugs, medication, and behavioral modification). The Integral Approach, however, brings all four quadrants into the picture, therefore it places an added emphasis in the *interior* states and conditions of the patient (such as emotions, psychological attitudes, imagery, and intentions as well). The Left-Hand quadrants, or the interior conditions of the individual self, should also play important roles in any comprehensive medical care, as well as the standard Upper-Right treatments based on the exterior conditions of the individual body. Yet as important as these subjective and bodily factors of the individual are, they also have embedded relationships with both the Lower-Left (or *cultural*) and the Lower-Right (or *social*) quadrants. The dominant society's attitudes and cultural worldview toward any particular illness or disease, from care and compassion to derision and scorn, will have a profound impact on how individuals deal with their illnesses. The Lower-Right quadrant, of course, concerns the material, economic, and social factors involved in medical health and treatment, including everything from the food being consumed to the type of hospital, medicine, or medical care that's even made available (such as how close is access, or how affordable, etc.).

Next, one needs to run an appropriate analysis of the *"all-levels"* factors involved in health, which refers to the fact that individuals have, at a minimum, the levels of *physical, emotional, mental,* and *spiritual* operative in each of the quadrants. Obviously, physical causes play a large part in overall health, as do physical cures (especially with physical accidents and traumas), yet so do the emotional and mental and spiritual components have an immense influence. Researchers the world over have added immeasurably to a better understanding of this type of "multilevel" nature of disease and its attending cure (including invaluable contributions from the great wisdom traditions, shamanic to Tibetan). Wilber briefly summarizes his views on why this holonic approach is so important for medicine: "In short, a truly effective and comprehensive medical plan would be *all-quadrant, all-level:* the idea is simply that each quadrant or dimension—I, we, and it—has physical, emotional, mental, and spiritual levels or waves, and a truly integral treatment would take all of these realities into account. Not only is this type of integral treatment more *effective*, it is for that reason more *cost-efficient*—which is why even organizational medicine is looking at it more closely."[26]

Integral Business

The applications of the Integral Model and AQAL Approach have recently mushroomed in business, leadership, and management, perhaps, again, because the applications of the four quadrants are more immediate and obvious. In business, Wilber explains the immediate applicability in *A Theory of Everything* (2000): "The *quadrants* give the four 'environments' or dimensions in which a product must survive, and the *levels* give the types of values that will be both producing and buying the product."[27] For example, "value hierarchies," or "VALS" are already having an enormous influence on business, and when they're combined with the four quadrants (which show how these levels of values appear in the four different environments) this gives management and business "a truly comprehensive map of the marketplace (which covers both traditional markets and cyber markets)."[28]

Management training and leadership programs based on an integral model have consequently begun to flourish in the past few years, with more to come. For example, associates of Integral Institute have already been spearheading a drive to offer Integral Leadership Seminars, which have been a huge success so far, attracting people from various fields and businesses. Of course, they are emphasizing a full-rounded, complete AQAL Approach, while considering the marketplace, products, economics, and the customer, while also placing an added emphasis on the *interior* dimensions, such as personal values, conflict resolution, business responsibility, integral ethics, and even the larger picture of "integral spirituality." Reforming business and leadership in the context of an Integral Theory and Integral Practice (with the integral meta-paradigm) is providing new meaning to individual and collective action, evolution, learning, and development.

Integral Art

Many times people have the misconception that since Wilber's integral theories are mostly about philosophy and psychology that they don't have much relevance to such humanistic pursuits as the Arts, whereas this is far from the truth. Personally, Wilber is quite the connoisseur of Art (with a capital "A") in all its forms and styles (including Music), knowing the history of art quite well and having a high appreciation for the great masters of art, including everything from painting to literature to music (classical and modern) to architecture to even high fashion.[29] Wilber has applied his spectrum approach to art by the early 1980s, culminating in an essay titled "In the Eye of the Artist: Art and the Perennial Philosophy" (first appearing in the second edition of *Eye to Eye*, 1986). It was later readapted as an introduction to the beautiful book of visionary paintings published by his good friend, the extraordinary artist Alex Grey, in *Sacred Mirrors: The Visionary Art of Alex Grey* (1990), and in my humble opinion, one of the most mind-blowing and beautiful books ever published (check it out!).

Wilber summarized an aspect of his interest in Art (and music) by saying, "A truly comprehensive paradigm (or inclusive world view) ought to have something to tell us not only about science, but also about art. For art is not just a way of doing, it is fundamentally a way of knowing."[30] More important, he recognized the spectrum of consciousness and the modes of knowing (the "three eyes" of the flesh, mind, and spirit), quickly offers a well-defined "critical theory of art," such as making sure to cover *all-levels* (or degree of depth) and *all-quadrants* (or interior and exterior factors). Wilber clarified in *Eye to Eye* (1986): "Here is the crucial point: When it comes to a critical theory of art, what eye, or eyes, is the particular artist using? …The critical question is this: Using the medium of sensibilia, is the artist trying to depict represent, or evoke the realm of sensibilia itself, or the realm of intelligibilia, or the realm of transcendelia?"[31] The integral approach is then able to critically gauge and critique the degrees of conscious *depth* (or the depth of consciousness) that the artist brings to his or her artwork, as the integral critic points out, "In the artist's own spiritual growth and development, subtler and subtler experiences, emotions, and perceptions would come into view, and it is the artist's duty to portray these subtler experiences (transcendelia), and thus to evoke them and encourage them in those who witness with care the finished work."[32] With the right eye, any number of levels of consciousness can be seen (and enjoyed) in Art.

Wilber continued these considerations further when he was invited to write an essay that he titled "How Shall We See Art?" published in the artbook *Andrew Wyeth: America's Painter* (1996) by Martha R. Severens (later adapted as the chapters just reviewed in *The Eye of Spirit*). Here Wilber summarized his main concerns: "An integral theory of art and literary interpretation is thus the multidimensional analysis of the various contexts in which—and by which—art exists and speaks to us: in the artist, the artwork, the viewer, and the world at large."[33] Understanding art integrally, particularly art criticism (involving the critique of artworks and artists), puts us in a better position to appreciate the possibilities involved with great works of art, works which will move our heart, mind, soul, and spirit in endless ways.

In *The Eye of Spirit* (1997), Wilber further explored the AQAL analysis of art with two chapters titled "Integral Art and Literary Theory: Part 1 and Part 2," two of his favorite chapters in the book. By using an "integral hermeneutics" (or the *means of interpretation*) to first acknowledge that "all meaning is context-bound" (or that "meaning is context-dependent"), then Wilber examines some of the preferred theories of today's critical theories, such as the "hidden intent: symptomatic theories," or "art is in the artwork," or "art is in the viewer," or "unconscious intentions," etc. For the integral approach to use all of these approaches in a "correct but partial" fashion, allows us to critically understand, as Wilber tells us, "I am saying, the nature and meaning of art is thoroughly *holonic*.... Further—and this is the crucial point—*each context will confer different meaning on the artwork*."[34] He therefore summarized: "The holonic nature of reality—contexts within contexts forever—means that each of these theories is part of a nested series of truths.... And an integral art and literary theory—covering the nature, meaning, and interpretation of art—will of necessity be a holonic theory: concentric circles of nested truths and interpretations.... A comprehensive art and literary theory will of necessity be concentric circles of enveloping truths and interpretations."[35] Art, as a creative reflection of the Kosmic Mandala or the Great Nest of Spirit, will continue to reveal all of its levels and novel possibilities as well as its infinite depth.

Integral Feminism

Another area of interest of Ken Wilber's theories that has been cited by critics as being deficient is in regard to the feminine force of life and to feminists' theories; yet again, this is far from the truth. Overall, Wilber's integral psychology and theories have always been concerned with humans in general, men and women alike, although he certainly recognizes the need to differentiate from each other their valuable qualities and gifts (see chapter 14). Therefore, the integral psychologist summarizes his principal concerns in *A Theory of Everything* (2000): "With this more integral approach, we can trace development through the great waves and streams of existence, but also recognize that males and females might navigate that great River of Life using a different style, type, or voice. This means that we can still recognize the major waves of existence—which, in fact, are *gender-neutral*—but we must fully honor the validity of *both* styles of navigating those waves."[36] In other words, since women and men navigate the same basic waves of the Kosmic Mandala (or AQAL Matrix), then together they'll be cocreating the possibilities for all humans and their communities, supporting and loving each other, healing and correcting one another, in our mutual quest to gain ultimate liberation and freedom in enlightened consciousness.

Consequently, Wilber believes that an integral feminism "can actually command the respect of male and female theoreticians," where it's implemented so "neither gender orientation is in any fashion privileged or made paradigmatic."[37] In the process, he presents an impressive command of feminist literature and research by identifying "at least a dozen major schools of feminism (liberal, socialist, spiritual, eco, womanist, radical, anarchist, lesbian, Marxist, cultural, constructivist, power), and the only thing they all agree on is that females exist."[38] Naturally, his recommendation is for "a much more integral approach," one that would "bring an 'all-quadrant, all-level' approach to sex and gender issues—an integral feminism."[39] This is mostly because from the AQAL perspective "all of those factors—behavioral, cultural, and social (at each of their developmental levels)—will have a strong hand in determining how *individual* men and women experience their own embodiment, engenderment, and gender status."[40] An integral analysis, therefore, will have a better chance of correctly identifying deficient elements and providing the overall framework to encourage further development that honors both halves of humanity.

Integral Education

Ken Wilber has pointed out that although he's an "integral" and "holistic" philosopher, that doesn't mean he necessarily supports "holistic educational approaches," because, in his opinion, they tend to arise from the "green meme" of pluralistic relativism (where all approaches are flatly equal). By this criticism, Wilber tells us that "many 'holistic' approaches are either sadly flatland (based on systems theory, or merely the Lower-Right quadrant), or they stem ponderously and rather exclusively from the 'green meme' [of Spiral Dynamics], which means a type of pluralistic approach that nobly attempts not to marginalize other approaches, but in fact, marginalizes hierarchical development, and thus often ends up sabotaging actual growth and evolution."[41] Whereas, for the integral approach, the pandit explains in *A Theory of Everything* (2000): "A truly integral education does not simply impose the green meme on everybody from day one, but rather understands that development unfolds in phase-specific waves of increasing inclusiveness."[42] A full-spectrum approach to education, therefore, would honor and develop all of those levels (or basic waves) of human evolutionary growth, from preconventional to conventional to postconventional, including all the lines (or streams) of development, and all the other variables of consciousness (multiple intelligences, talents, etc.), into an all-inclusive integral embrace.

An AQAL or "all-quadrant, all-level" education naturally places a premium emphasis on encouraging healthy developmental growth through all the stages or fulcrums in the spectrum of consciousness evolution. This means, of course, from infancy to Enlightenment, from birth to beyond death, and everything in-between; or, as Wilber reminds us, "To use Jean Gebser's version, consciousness fluidly flows from archaic to magic to mythic to rational to integral waves, and a genuinely integral education would emphasize, not just the last wave, but *all* of them as they appropriately unfold."[43] Integral pioneer and American Buddhist scholar Robert Thurman (also associated with Integral Institute) summarized these ideals (inspired by the Buddhist's educational vision) in his book *Infinite Life: Seven Virtues for Living Well* (2004): "Buddhists believe that the primary purpose of any society is to educate its individuals. And the goal of education is not to prepare people for some other task or life purpose, but rather to enlighten. As the fundamental tool for ridding ourselves of delusion and finding the truth, education is the highest purpose of human life. Our society should offer every citizen ample opportunity for individual growth. Only through education can people achieve personal development. Only through personal development will society evolve."[44] Once more, understanding the tetra-meshing (or interdependence) of the spectrum of consciousness (all-levels) with the individual and the sociocultural domains (all-quadrants) is indispensable in providing a true human education.

An AQAL education, because it's "all-quadrant" as well as "all-level" (and "all-line, all-types," etc.), consequently places a justified importance on the institutional social and cultural dimensions (the collective quadrants). This includes, as Wilber points out, "the *organizational structures* of the schools (administration and faculty) and the *core curriculum* offered to students."[45] Numerous educators and institutions have already been implementing their own approaches to an "all-quadrant, all-level" education (inspired and based upon Wilber's AQAL theories), both in conventional schools and in schools for the developmentally challenged. This is an exciting and vitally important territory for the integral approach to explore and implement practical and pragmatic applications for an AQAL education, especially since it's so critical to the health of our children and the future of our world. Naturally, then, this overall topic of integral education is a prime focus at the Integral Institute of Integral Education (a branch of Integral Institute), and is of great interest to all the dedicated teachers and pupils everywhere.

Integral Ecology

The embracing or inclusive (holonic-holarchical) quality of the AQAL Model is a crucial understanding for integral ecology as well, especially since as Wilber has accurately pointed out in *Sex, Ecology, Spirituality* (1995): "The bios [biosphere] is a part of the Kosmos [Great Nest of Spirit], but not part of the cosmos [physiosphere], and in that move we have forever disavowed reductionism."[46] In other words, because the biosphere (nature) transcends-and includes the physiosphere (matter) by adding "something more" (new emergents), and since the noosphere (mind) transcends-and includes the biosphere, then the biosphere is a *part* of the noosphere, but not vice versa. By emphasizing that holonic evolution generates emergent qualities, Wilber recognizes that the noosphere contains the biosphere, for it's compounded of its basic features, but it's also added unique features that are not present in the biosphere alone. This is because, as Wilber points out again, "Each senior wave transcends and includes its junior, as shown by the enveloping nests. *In that sense*, it is quite correct to say that the mind transcends and includes the body, or that the noosphere transcends and includes the biosphere."⁴⁷ This radical notion of seeing the natural world as being a compound component of the noospheric mind has been confusing for many ecologists and deep ecologist theorists, yet it actually allows for a sacred reverence for both spheres without succumbing to reductionism.

For Wilber and the integral approach, these are crucial distinctions which must be made for it's the only way "we can emphasize the crucial importance of the biosphere with having to *reduce* everything to the biosphere."⁴⁸ Consequently, Wilber has been a stern critic of many ecological theories, especially since they tend towards "retro-romantic" views that elevate and worship nature (or the biosphere) at the expense of the mind and reason (see chapter 14). In contrast, the integral philosopher points out that by differentiating between the material nature (with a small "n") of the biosphere (the lower levels in the Great Nest) and the spiritual Nature (with a capital "N") of nondual Spirit (which transcends all), then this view is actually in deep agreement with nature mystics (such as Emerson). Nature (or the biosphere) is a manifestation of Spirit, but it's not Spirit itself. In this sense, Wilber has always maintained, as he stated in *Up from Eden* (1981): "Nature is not something set apart from mountains, eagles, rivers, and people, but something that, as it were, runs through the fibers of each and all. In the same way, the Absolute—as the Nature of all natures—is not something set apart from all things and events. The Absolute is not Other, but, so to speak, is sewn through the fabric of all that is."⁴⁹

These subtle but important distinctions of an "integral ecology" are being explored at the Integral Institute of Integral Ecology (a branch of Integral Institute), led by such respected ecologists as Sean Hargens and ecological philosopher Michael Zimmerman. Professor Zimmerman has astutely championed these ideas that have been made clear with Wilber's nested model of a *holarchy* (matter to body to mind to soul to spirit) within the philosophical circles of deep ecology, a community that often takes offense at hierarchical schemes (including the traditional "Great Chain") because they appear to demote nature at the expense of "man." Zimmerman therefore summarizes Wilber's significance:

> Wilber's central point, with which I am in basic agreement, is this: whichever species happen to possess the powers of awareness with which humans have been gifted, possessing such awareness means that a species "includes" the biosphere, in the sense of containing

and going beyond the levels of complexity involved in constituting the biosphere. Far from justifying derelict treatment either of the biosphere or of the life forms belonging to it, this capacity for transcending the biospheric imposes the responsibility of respecting and appropriately caring for all life, human or otherwise. That so many people, modern and otherwise, fail to live up to this responsibility indicates to what extent humankind lacks genuinely integrated awareness, but is instead dis-integrated and thus governed by greed, aversion, and delusion.[50]

The AQAL Approach, therefore, is a vigorous opponent of the naïve yearning for retro-romantic premodern revivals (such as with ecomasculinists and ecofeminists), while yet simultaneously being a strong critic of the abusive technological exploitation of the natural world by the "industrial ontology" of modernity (see Chapter 14). As we've already seen, this allows Wilber's integral approach to include the crucial contributions of modernity while also embracing the dignity and wisdom of premodern indigenous peoples, yet without privileging or elevating either to superior status (see chapter 4). As a result, although his views have been sharply contested, Wilber is widely admired for bringing forward this unique approach (AQAL) and its ambitious attempt to integrate nature, humankind, and Spirit in a way that "allows us to honor the physiosphere, the biosphere, the noosphere and theosphere, but by trying to reduce one to the others, but by acknowledging and respecting the vitally crucial role they all play in this extraordinary Kosmos."[51] In other words, an integral ecology situates the physical world, the natural environment, the mental realms, and the spiritual domains all in their appropriate relationship with the Kosmos at large, while simultaneously seeing them as manifestations of nondual Spirit.

By now, everyone should know that the survival of all humans and "more significant" collective societies are interrelated and interdependent on the lesser "more fundamental" holons of nature (the biosphere), our eco-family of minerals, air, water, plants, animals, and all living creatures. As integral ecologist Sean Hargens summarizes, "Integral Ecology recognizes that for an *eco*centric approach to manifest in ourselves, and our communities, we have to work together to stabilize *world*centric patterns of being in relationship.... Integral Ecology offers a comprehensive approach to environmental issues which takes into account all of the known dimensions of human beings in their complex interactions with wild, rural, and urban nature. Integral Ecology attempts to integrate the levels of body, mind, and spirit as they appear in the areas of self, culture, and nature."[52] Since the Integral Vision recognizes that all the "lower" levels are forms of Spirit-in-action, then we have responsibilities to care for and protect our more fundamental foundations, suggesting not only a truly integral ecology but an effective "environmental ethics," which we'll turn to next.

Environmental Ethics: A Holarchy of Values

With the emergence of AQAL Metatheory, Wilber has also developed an integral system of "environmental ethics" based on a holarchical (or nested hierarchical) model of reality and consciousness (the Great Nest of Spirit). As we just saw with a genuine *integral ecology*, each sphere of the Kosmos (*physio, bios, nous*) are all a valuable and fundamental components in our compound existence, therefore, an integral approach maintains they all must be rightly honored and not exploited. As he accurately summarized in *Sex, Ecology, Spirituality* (1995): "The biosphere is indeed *more fundamental* than the noosphere, not because it is higher but precisely because it is lower and shallower, and the lower in any evolutionary sequence must always come first and always be honored *first and foremost.*"[53] In other words, all lower levels are always part of our compound makeup as human, and from the position of Spirit, *everything* in the Kosmos is *part* of our sacred and spiritual makeup.

As it turns out, an integral approach ends up synthesizing the major schools of environmental ethics (including biodiversity, animal rights, holarchical ranking, and stewardship), which are generally based on an *axiology*, or the *theory of values* (an environmental axiology). By taking a holonic approach, Wilber places an emphasis on holons, or all *relative* whole/parts, where each has "its own relative *wholeness*, and its own relative *partness*,"[54] as we've seen, all holons are nested in a great holarchy (of transfinite whole/parts). In *A Brief History of Everything* (1996), Wilber's integral approach recognizes, at a minimum, the following *"values"* for a genuine "Environmental Ethics"[55] of compound holons (including humans):

- **Ground Value**—most fundamentally, all holons (whole/parts) are a manifestation of the Divine (nondual Spirit);

- **Intrinsic Value** (intrinsic = essential nature)—the value of a holon, as a *whole*, with *agency* (or autonomy); "The more of the Kosmos that is enfolded into its own being—that is, the *greater its depth*— then the greater its *intrinsic value*."

- **Extrinsic Value** (extrinsic = external nature)—the value of a holon, as a *part*, situated in *communion* (or interdependent relationship with other holons); "The more it is a part [such as with an atom], the more *extrinsic value* it has."[56]

- **Rights**—a holon, as a *whole* (with *intrinsic value*), has *rights* to express its relative autonomy;

- **Responsibilities**—a holon, as a *part* (with *extrinsic* value), has *responsibilities* to the maintenance of that whole.

These definitions present some clear implications for *ethics* and *value judgments*, such as, for example, "the ape is more *intrinsically valuable* than the atom because it is more conscious," or "the atom has enormous *extrinsic value*, instrumental value, for other holons, because it is an instrumental part of so many other wholes."[57] Yet, perhaps most important, Wilber goes on to explain some of the ethical implications for all of us, since as human beings we have *rights*, therefore, "human beings are the most advanced and thus possess the most rights, but these rights do not include the right to instrumentally plunder other living [or nonliving] entities, since they, too, possess certain basic but significant rights." Concurrently, this means as human beings we also have *responsibilities* "because human beings have relatively more depth than, say, an amoeba, we have more *rights*—there are more conditions necessary to sustain the wholeness of a human—but we also have many more *responsibilities*, not only to our own human societies of which we are parts, but to all the communities of which our own subholons are parts." Being *whole* humans that are a living *part* of a larger nested Kosmos, then we must equally exercise, with wisdom and compassionate care, both our *rights* and *responsibilities* to the entire environment (inside and outside), therefore, we're in the position to make very practical and real applications based on these theoretical environmental ethics. In *A Brief History of Everything* (1996), Wilber reviews these environmental ethics in greater detail:

> I think we want an environmental ethics that honors all three types of value for each and every holon—*Ground value, intrinsic value,* and *extrinsic value.* We want our environmental ethics to honor all holons without exception as manifestations of Spirit—and also, at the same time, be able to make pragmatic distinctions about the differences in intrinsic worth.... In other words, our first pragmatic rule of thumb for environmental ethics is: in pursuit of our vital needs, consume or destroy as little depth as possible. Do the least amount of harm to consciousness as you possibly can. Destroy as little intrinsic worth as possible. Put in its positive form: protect and promote as much depth as possible [the Basic Moral Intuition].[58]

This view of ethics based on a "holarchy of value" (i.e., *more depth = greater value*) indicates that as human holons, or the holons of planet Earth with the greatest depth (thus *"more significant"*), it is our *responsibility* (in communion with *"less fundamental"* holons) to protect "the health of the entire spiral where no one level is privileged," an idea known as the "prime directive" (see next chapter). All the lower holons comprising our compound makeup are *"more fundamental"* (less depth, greater span), although *"less significant,"* thus as Wilber explained with Tenet #9 (of the 20-Tenets): "Destroy any holon, and you will destroy all of the holons above it and none of the holons below it."[59] Overall, the integral pandit concludes: "Our first pragmatic rule of thumb for environmental ethics is: in pursuit of our vital needs, consume or destroy as little depth as possible.... Put in its positive form: protect and promote as much depth as possible."[60]

This is also called the Basic Moral Intuition (or BMI), which basically means: "Do the least amount of harm to consciousness as you possibly can. Destroy as little intrinsic worth as possible."[61] Only a truly integral approach, or one that includes *all-levels* (or depth), as well as all interiors and exteriors (or *all-quadrants*), will be able to assist humanity in making these type of clear *value judgments* and *qualitative distinctions* (ultimately, based on authentic spiritual realizations). These are obviously ethical issues that are of vital importance to human civilization and life on this planet, a planet that's embroiled in a destructive Flatland modernity and intolerant premodernity.

Yet, even more so, this is a philosophy that understands by developing the full spectrum of *structural potentials* inherent or enfolded in the compound human being (and all human beings) via an integral enlightened education and psychology, then when we awaken into our *always already* Enlightened Condition, we realize we embrace *all holons*, or the whole Kosmos (the entire AQAL Matrix), as our inherent nature, i.e., as the Ground value where "all holons are a manifestation of the Divine." This divine embrace of reality, transcending all and including all (in nondual Spirit), being totally free yet fully in love, then this is when our wisdom mind (of transcendence) is moved by our compassionate heart (of immanence) to love all things, to embrace and care for all holons (of any level), and to shine a beacon of integral strength and enlightened Happiness to all and All. Perhaps, with more people awakening to the "second-tier" consciousness exhibited by integral human beings (or the "centaur in vision-logic"), and by living and applying these type of integral ethical values, then they will indeed serve the emergence of an Integral Age, an age of humankind built with a world philosophy that promotes *Unitas Multiplex* or "unity-in-diversity." Perhaps, this "New Age" of human possibilities is available to all of us (and our descendents)—to the whole human family—that is, if further evolutionary growth and educational development is actually practiced, whole-bodily exercised, and pragmatically applied. These are just some of the subjects we'll explore in greater detail next (in part III), the place of not only where Wilber's at, but where Wilber's going.

PART III

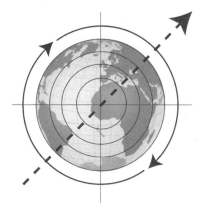

WHERE'S WILBER GOING?

In true and unobstructed evolution, we take all the lower levels with us, out of love and compassion, so that *all levels* eventually are reconnected to Source. To negate everything is to preserve everything; to transcend all is to include all. We must go whole-bodily to God; failing that, we fall into dissociation, repression, inner fragmentation. Ultimate transcendence is thus *not* ultimate annihilation of the levels of creation, but rather their ultimate inclusion in Spirit. The final transcendence is the final embrace. Thus, at ultimate Enlightenment or return to Spirit, the created world can still exist; it just no longer obscures Spirit, but serves it. All the levels remain as *expressions* of Atman, not substitutes for Atman.

—Ken Wilber, *Up from Eden* (1981)

CHAPTER TWELVE

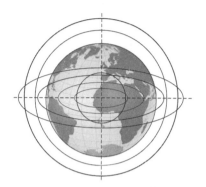

The Integral Age (at the Leading Edge)

I believe that the *real revolutions* facing today's world involve, not a glorious collective move into transpersonal domains, but the simple, fundamental changes that can be brought to the magic, mythic, and rational waves of existence.... For every person that moves into integral or higher, dozens are *born into the archaic.* The spiral of existence is a great unending flow, stretching from *body* to *mind* to *soul* to *spirit,* with millions upon millions constantly flowing through that Great River from source to ocean.... [Thus] the *major problem* remains: not, how can we get everybody to the integral wave or higher, but how can we arrange *the health of the overall spiral,* as billions of humans continue to pass through it, from one end to the other, year in and year out? In other words, most of the work that needs to be done is work to make the lower (and foundational) waves more healthy in their own terms.

—Ken Wilber, *A Theory of Everything* (2000)

IN THE PREVIOUS SECTION, WE HAVE REVIEWED IN DETAIL THE BASIC waves and multiple variables (including streams, types, states, etc.) that make up the AQAL Matrix—a multileveled Kosmos of consciousness (Knowing) and existence (Being), including interiors and exteriors manifesting in self, culture, and nature (the four quadrants). We've seen that these dynamics are not static but are situated in a vast "morphogenetic developmental space" that tetra-meshes and tetra-evolves as the "Great Nest" of Spirit-in-action, which is progressively driven by Eros or "the gentle persuasion of love." We saw how this Universe Story has unfolded the various spheres of existence, a Kosmic Mandala manifesting and correlating the material *physiosphere*, the pranic *biosphere*, the mental *noosphere*, and the inner subtle *theosphere*, the various domains which are all "shading into Spirit" (or radiant Divine Emptiness). We saw how this same developmental process appears in human beings, men and women alike, together paralleling or recapitulating the evolution of the entire universe, yet while still being open to new creative emergents and future potentials. This involves the growth and development of all human beings, present and future, including all races, all cultures, and the entire expanse of humanity set within the environment of the planet Earth, while all being eternally grounded in nondual Spirit.

In this section, we will look more closely at how this extraordinary evolutionary process of Spirit-in-action is active in the realm of human history and in each individual, especially as documented by the AQAL Metatheory of Ken Wilber. It may be useful, therefore, to see how an "integral consciousness" has been recognized by several theorists of consciousness evolution, including Wilber, as being a crucial link in humanity's incredible journey "*up from Eden*" (to echo Wilber's provocative title to his fourth book), or the development from the prepersonal to personal structures consciousness. Let's begin with one of the major influences on Wilber's integral theories regarding the historical unfolding of the structures of consciousness, before then examining the contours and possibilities of an "Integral Age" emerging in the new millennium, thus bringing attention to the dire necessity in our troubled times to acquire "an Integral Vision for a world gone slightly mad."[1]

Jean Gebser: Historical Emergence of Consciousness Structures

Another significant purveyor of the word "integral" has been the Swiss-German sociocultural philosopher Jean Gebser (1905–1973), an underappreciated theorist and scholar who was one of first to recognize that history can be measured by observing the unfolding emergence of what he called the "structures of consciousness."[2] Gebser was one of the first and most gifted scholars of the twentieth century to cross-reference enough research material collected by a global-dominated world to detect the various *psychohistorical structures* of consciousness that have emerged in the course of human history. He designated them as the archaic, the magic, the mythic, the mental, and the integral (which we'll review in more detail below). The depth of Gebser's pioneering work is outstanding and deserves much attention and study, as well as to be sublimely appreciated for its literary beauty. In regard to our interests for this book, Gebser also had a rich influence on Ken Wilber's theories, especially in relation to the historical emergence of the structures of consciousness.

One of Gebser's more significant conclusions, in the words of Georg Feuerstein's authoritative study *Structures of Consciousness* (1987), was that he also saw these structures of consciousness as being "not merely historical relics but active co-constituents of the modern psyche."[3] This is because the previous structures of consciousness are actually *transcended-yet-included* in humanity's holonic development; therefore, these past waves of awareness are still *psychically active* in us today. This is another example of how an integral approach can pluralistically include *all of the previous worldviews* that are available to humankind in the spiral of development. An AQAL scan or cross-analysis can first detect and differentiate these various basic waves or levels (and lines) of development on the way to *embracing them all* as being an important part in our compound makeup and human inheritance, thus this becomes a way to gain a deeper understanding of ourselves and our collective history.

Gebser's career culminated in the 1950s with the publication in Europe of his magnum opus titled in German as *Ursprung und Gegenwart*, which was later published in English with the translated title of *The Ever-Present Origin* (1949, 1953).[4] *The Ever-Present Origin* is a detailed 600-page summary about the evolution of the different identifiable structures of consciousness that Gebser had been researching during the previous decades. But since this detailed book wasn't published in English until 1985 (by Ohio University Press), the delay in translation has caused to Gebser to be a somewhat obscure, although highly admired, scholar in English-speaking academia.

Fortuitously, when Ken Wilber was working on his own book about the historical evolution of consciousness in the late 1970s, he came across one of

Gebser's only English-translated essays which had been published in 1972 by the respected theosophist journal *Main Currents in Modern Thought*[5] (this was the very same journal that had published Wilber's first essay in 1974). Gebser's "Foundations of the Aperspectival World"[6] is a provocative essay that shows the power of his pioneering observations, which had delineated the unfolding stages of consciousness in human history. These ideas were a significant contribution for Wilber since they reaffirmed his own observations about cultural and historical evolution, which he would soon formulate into his own groundbreaking *Up from Eden: A Transpersonal View of Human Evolution* (1981), one of the primary Wilber/Phase-2 source books.

Although both of these scholars approached the subject of human consciousness evolution from quite different angles (with Gebser's approach being more historical/literary and Wilber's being more psychological/philosophical), their conclusions were still essentially the same in that they recognized the same basic characteristics for each of these emergent structures. Nevertheless, because Wilber was working decades after Gebser's pioneering work, he had even more research material at his command. This importantly included a profound access to the deep resources of Eastern mysticism (a topic that Gebser had only begun to explore), thus Wilber's fully developed model includes the entire spectrum of consciousness, which evolves from the archaic-magical to the mental-ego to, ultimately, nondual Enlightenment (see chapter 10). By including the so-called *transpersonal* structures of consciousness, which Gebser had overlooked, Wilber's AQAL Model ends up transcending-yet-including Gebser's outline, especially since Gebser only posited one level (the *integral-aperspectival*) beyond reason (the *mental*). Wilber, on the other hand, includes at least four major recognizable structures beyond the rational (the *psychic, subtle, causal,* and *nondual*). In this case, Wilber's approach easily embraces the strides made by Gebser, and therefore puts him in a position to accurately critique some of Gebser's conclusions (although he shows a high level of admiration).[7] Technically, for example, AQAL Metatheory currently identifies Gebser's "structures" of consciousness as mostly resembling the cultural "worldviews" of psycho-historical development (evident as the collective interiors of the Lower-Left quadrant).

Although Gebser was also a well-known poet laureate who presented his arguments in a gifted and articulate manner, his conclusions and meticulous scholarship was thoroughly grounded in well-presented archaeological, anthropological, and historical evidence. Consequently, he presented a *reconstructive* theory of "emergent evolution" that chronicles the historical "mutations" that can be quantified or summarized as the various "structures" or "modalities" of consciousness evolution. According to Gebser, as we've mentioned, since each senior structure envelops the previous junior stages, from *archaic* to *magic* to *mythic* to *mental* to *integral,* then they're still active and observable in us today (another reason they must be thoroughly understood).

Gebser's work and data, especially as presented in *The Ever-Present Origin* (1949, 1985), carefully defines each structure's major epoch of human history, including their principal features, which are labeled with the following useful terms:[8]

- **Archaic consciousness**—is the most primitive structure going back to the early beginnings of humankind from over 3,000,000 years ago with the protohumans or hominids (such as *Australopithecus afarensis, Homo habilis,* perhaps some of *Homo erectus*); it's dominated by *instincts* and lacks self-consciousness or a symbolizing ego, therefore, there exists a relative strong fusion of self and world, or subject and object (thus Gebser related it to *deep sleep*); representative image: *uroboros* or the circled snake biting its own tail, because it's suggestive of unconscious narcissism and union.

- **Magical consciousness**—is when humanity's rudimentary self-sense begins to emerge with the rise of images and symbols (and the probable rise of protolanguage), yet it's still based in a visceral and *emotional fusion* of self and nature (thus Gebser related it with *sleep*), therefore, there's a desired manipulation of the environment by magic or magical action (including rudimentary rituals); representative image: "Sorcerer of Trois Frères" cave painting showing the art of magical consciousness and the close fusion of self and nature, although this is only the initial stage of differentiation.

- **Mythic consciousness**—involves a fully lateralized brain (two hemispheres), the use of language, and imaginative ability, therefore it has a more crystallized self-consciousness and *symbolizing ego* that shows a greater differentiation *(polarization)* between self and world, yet it's still somewhat dreamlike compared to later mental consciousness (thus Gebser related it to *dreaming*); beginning of

seasonal rituals and cyclic time (including calendars) which supports Neolithic villages, and which in turn leads to the rise of civilization and codified mythologies (as traditionally defined); therefore, it puts prominence on the group "we" (rather than the "I" of
the crystallized ego), thus forming the first urban cities and then
early empires; it is mostly circular, cyclic, mythic, ahistorical.

- **Mental consciousness**—is when the dualistic separation of self
  and world are complete (egoic consciousness), therefore, it has a
  strong individualistic sense of identity with the "ego" (thus Gebser related it to *wakefulness*); time is *historical* (or an arrow) instead
  of cyclic, while space has *perspective* (or is three-dimensional and
  perspectival); this inner split of self and world nevertheless leads to
  logic and self-reflexive thought ("thinking about thinking"), forming larger groupings of people (empires and nations), and has made
  possible the great adventures of science and technology (although
  Gebser claimed that *rational consciousness* was a "deficient mode" of
  this awareness); as examples, Gebser focused on the "Greek miracle"
  (the Axial Age), while the Renaissance was seen as a recapitulation
  of this achievement; the mental modality of consciousness was con-
  solidated with the invention of writing and other basic civilizational
  arts, therefore, it probably arose in other places before Greece (as
  Gebser conceded); it is mostly rational, self-reflexive, perspective,
  linear (progressive), historical.

These outlines of humankind's major eras and epochs, from the ancient
and recent past, from prehistory to history, indicate that the modern world
has generally evolved to the mental structure of consciousness, which is its
current average-mode or "center of gravity" (epitomized with formal rationality and science). However, as Gebser also detected, there are deep schisms
and psychopathologies evident in modern consciousness; thus, for example,
he claimed "rational consciousness" is actually a "deficient form" of mental
consciousness. This is a common observation among numerous theorists,
including Wilber, who points to the various forms of *dissociation* and *repression* rampant in the modern world, claiming it's the result of a pathological mental-egoic structure (and therefore must submit to appropriate treatments).

Integral Aperspectival Awareness

Fortunately, based on the evidence that Jean Gebser was gathering since the advent of the twentieth century, he came to truly believe, and then effectively demonstrated that there was a new structure of consciousness beginning to emerge—the "integral structure." The rise of this new awareness or structure of consciousness is able to bring together or *integrate* all the multiple perspectives of the preceding structures (archaic, magic, mythic, mental), which is what propelled Gebser to christen this new structure:

- **Integral-Aperspectival consciousness**—*aperspectival awareness* is the capacity to add together all the perspectives or worldviews generated by all the lower stages or structures of consciousness (including perspectival rationality), since this is when the lower structures of consciousness become more fully conscious or "transparent" to the individual; in this case, the self begins to master deficient elements to attain and sustain maturity and equilibrium; there's an increased sense of self-transparency, freedom from anxiety, openness, emotional availability and fluency, participatory freedom, personal responsibility, bodily presence (rather than abstraction from life), the ability for genuine intimacy, equanimity, reverence for all life, the capacity for service and love;[9] importantly, as Wilber points out (following Gebser), "*vision-logic*, or the *integral-aperspectival mind*, adds up all the perspectives *tout ensemble*, and therefore *privileges no perspective as final*; it is aperspectival."[10]

Aperspectival-integral awareness is at the heart of Gebser's concerns, especially since he began to document its rise and appearance (in the 1930s). As examples, he pointed to the then-living representatives, such as Einstein and his revolution of physics and cosmology, or Picasso and his fracturing of perspectival realism, or to Stravinsky, to Frank Lloyd Wright, and a host of other leading-edge pioneers of the early twentieth century.[11] Feuerstein later commented that "Gebser presented a richly documented model, which culminated in the insight that we are witnessing today the possible beginnings of a new structure of consciousness, what he called the 'aperspectival-integral' consciousness."[12] In Gebser's estimation, the emergence of integral awareness is critical for world stability, therefore, he prophetically proclaimed in an article from *Main Currents in Modern Thought* (1974): "The growth of a new, integral consciousness is important, even decisive for our times, for it is a theme of universal scope, embracing the whole of humanity. As such, it deserves to be treated as a coherent whole, for the common destiny of Asia and the Occident [the West] depends largely upon the extent to which this new consciousness is realized."[13]

Although they both have prophesied its emergence, Gebser and Wilber are fully aware that this integral awareness is *not* a guaranteed event, but rather, it involves everyone's responsibility and active participation in order to stabilize this higher stage of development. As Feuerstein explains, "The mutation of the integral consciousness demands our conscious collaboration in order to become fully effective....Without this personal actualization of integral values, it will not be possible to replace the desecrated mental-rational consciousness that has led to today's global crisis. Consequently, humanity's future would be more than uncertain."[14] Wilber has reported the same basic conclusion in *Sex, Ecology, Spirituality* (1995):

> Neither Gebser nor I (nor Murphy nor Habermas, nor any of the evolutionary-oriented theorists) see the emergence of the "aperspectival worldcentric" structure as being a sure thing, as being somehow guaranteed. Not only does evolution, as Michael Murphy put it, meander more than progress; not only, when it does progress, is there always the "dialectic of progress" [the "Good News" and "Bad News" of each structure/stage]; there is also the ever-lurking possibility that the whole thing might simply blow up, that evolution will take a wrong turn (in the short run), but a wrong turn that includes us.... Nor does the fact that the integral structure is integral guarantee that the necessary integration will in fact occur. The claim is simply, to put it in the terms we have been using, that the integral structure *can* integrate the physiosphere, the biosphere, and the noosphere—it has the *potential* for that integration. Whether that potential becomes actual is up to you and me; it depends on the concrete actions that each of us takes. As always, we have to make the future that is given to us.[15]

This is pretty close to where Wilber's at, right there along with the rest of us, and, like many of us, he's working hard to help the world embrace a *more integral*, or integral-aperspectival, view of reality. Like all higher-order emergents, this integral consciousness offers its own healing solutions for the dissociations and limitations of the lower levels, in this case, especially with the preceding mental-rational consciousness of the modern industrialized world.

Ken Wilber: Historical Evolution of Collective Worldviews (Lower-Left quadrant)

As mentioned, Ken Wilber was so impressed with the groundbreaking work of Jean Gebser and his monumental conclusions on the evolution of consciousness, that he openly acknowledged his debt by hyphenating Gebser's clearly recognizable designations with his own more obscure terms. Wilber had already chosen representative images from ancient mythology, such as the *uroboros* (encircled snake eating its own tail) representing *pleromatic* embeddedness, the *typhon* (half-reptile, half-human) representing the *bodyego* or the self identified with instinctual, biological impulses, and the *centaur* (half-horse, half-human) representing the *integrated bodymind* at the edge of the transpersonal. Gebser's terms, therefore, seemed to ideally round off Wilber's more exotic names, which is what gave birth to the Wilber/Phase-2 designations, as he explains in *Sex, Ecology, Spirituality* (1995): "I will often hybridize Gebser's terminology to match Piaget's substages, so that we have a continuum of archaic, archaic-magic, magic, magic-mythic, mythic, mythic-rational, rational, rational-existential (and into vision-logic, psychic, etc.). These particular names are, of course, arbitrary; but the actual stages they refer to are based on extensive empirical/phenomenological research. I also believe these names (such as magic, mythic-rational, etc.) help to capture the essential 'flavor' of each stage and substage."[16] This close similarity with Wilber's psychological structures (as presented in *The Atman Project*) were seamlessly correlated with Gebser's historical structures (as presented in *Up from Eden*) in order to clarify this long and torturous climb "up from Eden" and from the prepersonal realms to realize the highest possible potentials of the human race.

Wilber, of course, has been influenced by the research and ideas of many of the world's greatest evolutionary thinkers, scientists, and philosophers, from Adi Da to Aurobindo to Bergson to Hegel to Teilhard de Chardin to Berdyaev to Schilling to Cassirer, Frobenius, Gebser, Jantsch, Jaynes, Neumann, Smuts, Whitehead, Whyte, and numerous others. But perhaps it's the German philosopher Jürgen Habermas and his excellent hermeneutic interpretation of reconstructive historical evidence, such as presented in *Communication and the Evolution of Society* (1976, 1979), which resonates best with Wilber's own work and conclusions (though Habermas does not include the higher transpersonal levels of development). In fact, Wilber believes that Habermas's "unending genius," including his "brilliant outline of... the universal stages of consciousness development," is enough to warrant him being praised as "the world's greatest living philosopher."[17] Although their ideas were independently derived, Wilber still agrees with many of Habermas's insights and philosophical positions, thus he repeatedly turns to him for support and inspiration, especially in the more recent Wilber/Phase-4/5 writings.

When adopting the AQAL Approach years after his first contact with Gebser's work, Wilber now defines the sociocultural structures as being the "worldviews" or "worldspaces" of consciousness (collective interiors of the Lower-Left quadrant). They're also identified as being *"transitional structures"* of consciousness, since they act more like *"developmental lines,"* than the more permanent and *enduring structures*, clarifications that were made very explicit during Wilber/Phase-3, such as with *Transformation of Consciousness* (1986). These cultural worldviews, therefore, are *"phase-specific"* because the lower structures are subsumed and included (yet transcended) by the emerging higher-order structures of consciousness. In other words, the older worldviews are significantly left behind or phased out while yet remaining somewhat accessible or partially available, and thus *psychically active* in us today (to varying degrees). For example, a rational mind can access mythic thinking, but it doesn't generally translate its experiences from that lower, junior worldview (as its "center of gravity").

The major historical epochs of human consciousness are brilliantly covered in Wilber's masterpiece on the subject, the Phase-2 masterpiece *Up from Eden: A Transpersonal View of Human Evolution* (1981). The transpersonal theorist deftly showed how the unfolding stages of *phylogeny*, or collective human evolution, follow the same evolutionary patterns and emerging stages as that of *ontogeny*, or the stages of individual human development documented so well in *The Atman Project: A Transpersonal View of Human Development* (1980), which was written in conjunction with *Up from Eden* (its sister volume). The presentations of this detailed study have generally been buttressed by subsequent research, but now, of course, they're modified to fit the AQAL Matrix of "all quadrants, all levels, all lines," especially evident in the Wilber/Phase-4/5 writings.[18] By recognizing the basic evolutionary arc that develops from the *prepersonal* (archaic, magic, mythic) to the *personal* (mythic-rational, egoic, integral) to the *transpersonal* (psychic, subtle, causal, nondual), Wilber gave an amazing review of the evolution of human consciousness, presented in an immaculate writing style and mastery of the information. See Figure 12-1.

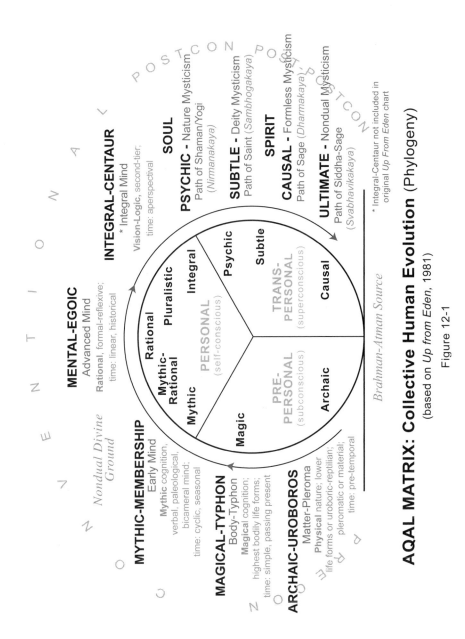

AQAL MATRIX: Collective Human Evolution (Phylogeny)
(based on *Up from Eden*, 1981)

Figure 12-1

Another one of the more important and novel achievements of Wilber's transpersonal studies of human evolution (beyond Gebser's or anyone else's) was the clear recognition of what he calls the "Average-mode" and "Advanced-Tip modes" of human consciousness development. By using the spectrum model of consciousness development, Wilber effectively demonstrated it's possible to "trace *two* parallel strands of evolution as they actually occurred *historically*."[19] By incorporating the research of transpersonal psychology (and the wisdom traditions), the integral historian explains how the *average-mode* awareness of the popular masses were evolving from *archaic* to *magic* to *mythic* to *mental* consciousness, while "a *correlative* evolution of advanced, growing-tip" individuals, yet far less in number (the "rare few"), were evolving from the *psychic* to *subtle* to *causal* to *nondual* stages of transpersonal awareness. These are, respectively, the *shaman/yogis* (masters of psychic/nature mysticism), the *saints* (masters of subtle/deity mysticism), the *sages* (masters of causal/formless mysticism), and the *siddhas* (masters of nondual mysticism) of world history, all of whom are the actual progenitors of humankind's sacred inheritance.[20]

When reviewing Wilber's basic worldviews as they emerge historically, there needs to be an understanding about their estimated *dates* of emergence. Although Gebser's emergent model and Wilber's transpersonal views on the evolution of historical consciousness often intersect, there's still a contested debate on the "exact dates" of emergence created by the complexity of the problem and the lack of extant historical evidence. With the continuing discovery of more archaeological, paleoanthropological, and historical artifacts being unearthed all the time, it's always been a challenge for these types of complex projects that attempt to reconstruct the vast sweep of written and unwritten history. In Wilber's work, all dates are general approximations and were never supposed to be fixed or rigid determinations; thus he tends to dismiss critics who suggest his overall views are incorrect simply because some of the dates aren't exact enough. Nevertheless, the historical evidence for the unfolding development of consciousness is staggering, thus it provides plenty of details needed to outline the principal characteristics of each level and historical era in human development.

The basic characteristics of the unfolding *average-mode* "structures" of consciousness now identified as the historical cultural "worldviews" (Lower-Left quadrant of collective interiors), with their approximate date of origin, are listed below:

- **Archaic-Uroboros**—(approx. date of origin: 5.0–3.0 million years B.P.)—emerged with the "Dawn Human" of prepersonal Eden; the early protohumans or hominids (such as *Australopithecus afarensis*, etc.); representative image: *uroboros* (or the encircled snake); also the "pleromatic-uroboric" (the Greek word *pleroma* stands for "undifferentiated fullness");

- **Magical-Typhon**—(approx. date of origin: 750,000–50,000 B.P.)— emerging with the Neandertals and Cro-Magnons (and probably earlier with late *Homo erectus*); a sense of self is emerging with "more complex paleosymbols, modifiers, commands, and some nouns,"[21] but still fused closely with nature; therefore Wilber concludes with an insightful understanding, that is, "The first men and women… were not just simple hunters and gatherers—they were magicians,"[22] which also means that their advanced-tip *shaman* "was the first great voyager into realms of the superconscious,"[23] especially the *psychic* and *low subtle* realms *(nature mysticism);* representative image: *typhon* or the mythic Greek titan who was half human and half serpent thus showing the still semi-mergence in the reptilian-naturic realms of the previous archaic stage;

- **Mythic-Membership**—(approx. date of origin:
  - **Low Period**: begins with the "creative explosion": 50,000-35,000 BP to the Neolithic revolution: 10,000 BCE;
  - **High Period**: the rise of classical civilizations: 3500 BCE— 1500 CE)—with greater self-consciousness there emerged an increased fear of "the other" that leads to greater use of "substitute gratifications," including organized war, murder, and wealth (money), as well as increased "leisure time" (accumulated from collective surplus) that allowed further explorations of the higher structural potentials of human beings, which led to the first advanced-tip saints and sages (or the explorers of the higher transpersonal realms, especially the *subtle, high-subtle,* and *causal* domains); the average-mode masses, however, were mostly living in the worldview of mythic-membership and *concrete myths* (based cognitive concrete operations), which are taken as literal facts;

moral values are *ethnocentric* (or membership) oriented and *conventional (rule/role mind),* thus they're very much alive in us today;

- **Mental-Rational** or **Mental-Egoic**—the rise of *rational-perspectival* thinking *(formal-rational),* including objective modes of thinking and reflection (including the transition stage of *mythic-rational*); representative image: Hero (solar ego); subdivided into three main periods with approx. dates of origin:

  ○ **Low Period** (2500–500 B.C.E.)—the pinnacle of classical mythic civilizations, including increased "death seizure," the emergence of "the Hero," kingship, money, mass-scale war, yet also the tools of civilization, such as mathematics, writing, the calendar (linear time);

  ○ **Middle Period** (500 B.C.E.–1500 C.E.)—begins with the Axial Age (500–300 B.C.E.), including increased rational, not mythic, interpretations of transpersonal realities; continual rise of the patriarchy and social hierarchies;

  ○ **Late Period** (1500–present)—culminates with the rise of modernity, modern science, and the "Industrial Age" (technological innovation), including an increased autonomous self that uses rational or self-reflexive thought to more efficiently *operate on* the world of nature and ideas (by transcending yet including them); includes the rise of democracies, various liberation movements (such as for slaves and women), declaration of human rights, equality under the law, etc., which are the *dignities* or "good news" of modernity, yet they're counterbalanced by the *disasters* or "bad news" of modernity, including the reductionistic "collapse of the Kosmos" into materialism;

- **Integral-Centaur** (approx. date of origin: emerging since twentieth-century)—embodied in the technological-economic base of global communications, the "Information Age" that's capable of supporting *"worldcentric"* awareness or *"universal integralism"* (*unitas multiplex* or "unity-in-diversity"); self awareness is *aperspectival* (multiple perspectives), cognition based in *vision-logic* (or *network-logic*) which ties together or integrates the multiple perspectives with integral analyses and met-paradigms; representative image: *centaur* or half-horse (representing the body) integrated with half-man (representing the mind).

In another insightful study on the evolution of consciousness, including humanity's possible future development, Duane Elgin in *Awakening Earth: Exploring the Evolution of Human Culture and Consciousness* (1993), uses an instructive graphic to depict the overlapping and emergent quality of historical consciousness evolution. I have modified this idea to depict the emerging epochs of human history, as basically presented by Wilber's depictions of the unfolding structures of consciousness in the long and arduous journey *"up from Eden"* (not fit to scale). See Figure 12-2 (next page).

In reviewing these "grand stories" of human history, it's important to point out that both Wilber and Gebser, unlike many European historical scholars, philosophers, and scientists, are *not* exhibiting the typical *Eurocentric prejudice* when elucidating the evolutionary journey of "Man." As concerned critics have often complained, evolutionary views will often suggest and justify the continuing dominance of Western civilization and/or of modern science, yet these two integral theorists are very careful *not* to commit these types of self-centered offenses against the family of humanity. Wilber therefore explains his defense in using evolutionary theories: "The constant downside of developmental theories is that the highest stage is usually, by strange coincidence, evidenced by the proponent of the theory. I hasten to point out that I have never made such a claim myself, though I am often accused of it."[24] For one, with Wilber's full-spectrum approach, there are even transpersonal levels of development following that of the integral-centaur (or mature ego), which have been exhibited by advanced-tip individuals from all the world's cultures.

In addition, as we've mentioned, the integral historian insists this approach is actually a *reconstructive* history based upon verifiable evidence and the fallibility principle (both objective and intersubjective strands), not just personal (or subjective) preferences and eclecticism. Yet, Wilber doesn't deny their interpretative value, either, as he clearly explained in a footnote to *Up from Eden* (1981), where he claims the conclusions to this reconstruction of humankind's evolution "up from Eden" are based on "a hermeneutical or interpretive reading of the text of history (evolution), set in a developmental-

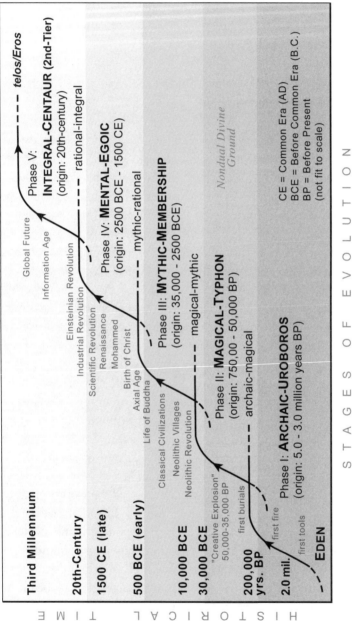

Historical Emergence of Collective Worldviews (Lower-Left quadrant)

(based on Ken Wilber, *Up From Eden*, 1981; *Sex, Ecology, Spirituality*, 1995; modified from Duane Elgin, *Awakening Earth*, 1993)

Figure 12-2

logic derived from a phenomenological inquiry into the deep structures of consciousness development [as first set forth in *The Atman Project*]."[25] In other words, the entire historical drama is still open to appropriate modification based on further interpretive readings, which is then verifiable by a community of adequately-trained interpreters (or integral scholars).

Again, Wilber does not claim that his or any other presentation or historical worldview has the whole picture, but rather he's only suggesting, "They are all simply snapshots of the great River of Life, and they are useful when looking at the River from that particular angle."[26] In this case, an all-embracing Integral Vision provides a meaningful context that honors the entire spectrum of historical worldviews. Wilber points out in *A Theory of Everything* (2000): "The more of these worldviews [that] can be seamlessly included in a larger vision, the more accurate the view of the Kosmos that emerges. This more encompassing view then acts not only as an aid in individual transformation but as a *holistic indexing system* for the numerous worldviews themselves, showing their relation to each other and the irreplaceable importance of each."[27] Such Integral Operating Systems (or IOSs) set within an AQAL meta-paradigm becomes an extremely useful analytical tool by including, yet transcending, all the previous worldviews. Thus, Wilber succinctly reviews his use of Gebser's insights in further expanding his own integral evolutionary theories in *Sex, Ecology, Spirituality* (1995):

> In *Up from Eden* (and *Eye to Eye*) I followed the groundbreaking work of Jean Gebser in recognizing four major epochs of human evolution, each anchored by a particular structure (or level) of *individual* consciousness that correspondingly produced (and was produced by) a particular *social worldview*. These general stages Gebser called the archaic, the magic, the mythic, and the mental. I (and to a lesser extent Gebser) further suggested that each of *these structures of consciousness generated a different sense of:* space-time, law and morality, cognitive style, self identity, mode of technology (or productive forces), drives or motivation, types of personal pathology (and defenses), types of social oppression/repression, degrees of death-seizure and death-denial, and types of religious experience. The archaic, the magic, the mythic, and the mental worldviews in the *social holon* are each correlated with a particular *individual* structure of consciousness (the co-evolution of macro and micro).[28]

For Gebser, the unfolding structures of consciousness emerge through a positive mutation or transformation to another worldview, which then generates a different perspective for the emerging self set within its particular historical and sociocultural context. For Wilber, this occurs because the evolution of consciousness is always an AQAL or "all-quadrants, all-levels, all-lines" affair, therefore it avails itself to *cross-indexing* and the integration of multiple perspectives (until the transcendence of all worldviews in Divine Realization or Enlightenment). Such an inclusionary meta-worldview or integral perspective finds it's possible to include all peoples and all cultures and all historical times, yet without privileging any one view as being better than the other. Thus it provides a global and universal vision of tolerance and increased depth, while simultaneously being perceptive enough to encourage further development beyond the conflicts of the earlier stages and less-evolved worldviews.

Techno-Economic Eras (Lower-Right quadrant)

Since the debut of Wilber/Phase-4 and the AQAL Approach in the 1990s, Ken Wilber has more clearly correlated the historical evolution of collective consciousness (interior Lower-Left quadrant of cultural values and worldviews) with the technological-economic or "techno-economic" systems as they're associated with their historical eras or periods of dominance (mostly evident in the social systems of the exterior Lower-Right quadrant). By understanding and observing their interaction and tetra-meshing, Wilber has made some important and novel observations (which can't be reviewed in depth here). In the important 1997 essay, "An Integral Theory of Consciousness," the author summarized the AQAL approach by recognizing "the modes of *material production* (e.g., foraging, horticultural, agrarian, industrial, informational) have a profound and constitutive influence on the actual contents of *individual* consciousness, and thus an understanding of these *social determinants* is absolutely crucial for an integral theory of consciousness."[29] Once more, this shows the importance of the AQAL or all-quadrants, all-levels feedback loop in constructing an integral analysis and critical theory of historical evolution, which is being clearly emphasized in Wilber/Phase-5, especially with the activities and presentations of Integral Institute and Integral University.[30]

A quick outline taken from *A Brief History of Everything* (1996) reviews some of Wilber's characterizations of the various Techno-Economic Eras that act as a social-systems platform (exterior Lower-Right quadrant) for the unfolding worldviews of consciousness (collective interior Lower-Left quadrant), which are fundamentally involved in sustaining individual consciousness (individual interior Upper-Left quadrant):

- **Foraging (archaic-magic)**—the hunter-gatherers of the original primal tribes and tribal societies; they had sharply delineated social roles (men did hunting, women gathering), yet they placed no particular emphasis on either the male or female value sphere; Wilber acknowledges: "The primal tribes are literally *our roots,* our foundations, the basis of all that was to follow, the structure upon which all subsequent human evolution would be built, the crucial ground floor upon which so much history would have to rest";[31]

- **Horticulture (magical-mythic)**—beginning of agriculture based upon the simple hoe where research shows that 80 percent of the foodstuffs in these societies were produced by *women* (while the men still hunted), therefore the social systems were mostly *matrifocal* (or feminine-centered); involving the "Great Mother" archetype; often had human sacrifice and magical fertility rituals; short life expectancy; cyclic time following the seasonal currents of nature;

- **Agrarian (mythic)**—the shift from hoe to plow placed an emphasis on *men* and male labor, therefore the social systems became *patriarchical* (or masculine-oriented), which led to increasing polarization of the sexes; Wilber explains: "Where females work the field with a hoe, God is a Woman; where males work the fields with a plow, God is a Man";[32] involves increased use of mythic images and codified mythologies; specialized classes; extended cultural endeavors (e.g., mathematics, writing, metallurgy, warfare); membership empire building;

- **Industrial (mental-rational)**—rise of the industrial modern world with science and technology that substitutes human and animal muscle with machine power, consequently, gender-neutral engines help foster liberation movements, such as for women, slaves, and the worker; Wilber summarizes: "Biology was no longer destiny... Men and women both need to be liberated from the horrendous constraints of agrarian polarization. Industrialization began this *liberation...* but we need to continue developing this freedom and transcendence.";[33] the downside (or Bad News) of attending social ills, pollution, overpopulation, atomic/nuclear weapons, etc.;

- **Informational (integral)**—the widely acknowledged shift into the "Information Age" (or the "Age of the Noosphere"), which includes the microchip/digital revolution, therefore, Wilber explains: "Global communications have made global and integral consciousness a widespread possibility. This global network of technology, this new nervous system for collective consciousness, does not, however, in any way guarantee that individuals will in fact develop to an integral level in their own case. It *facilitates*, but does *not* guarantee. Moreover, global or planetary does not necessarily mean integral";[34] downside (or Bad News) is global instability, threat of resource collapse, and loss of value and meaning (or depth).

These techno-economic conditions are mostly involved with the lower levels of "material exchange," epitomized with archetypal analysts such as Karl Marx and Adam Smith, for they generate and support the foundational base upon which the higher structures of human activities can emerge and be made effective, therefore the appropriate use and management of these techno-economic levels of exchange cannot be overemphasized.

Compound Levels of Exchange (AQAL)

In the concluding chapter of *Up from Eden* (1981), Wilber reasoned that his full-spectrum account of human evolution, with its structural levels of nested human development, could provide "the eventual core of a truly unified, critical sociological theory,"[35] a rich intellectual idea he explored further in *A Sociable God* (1983) and subsequent writings. An "integral sociological theory," Wilber argued, "might best be constructed around a detailed, multi-disciplinary analysis of the developmental-logic and hierarchic *levels of exchange* that constitute the human compound individual."[36] He therefore outlined the "Levels of Exchange" by following the unfolding spectrum of consciousness, which includes each level's basic paradigm of exchange, plus an example of their corresponding *archetypal analyst*, briefly listed below:

1) **Material Exchange**—involving the *physical-uroboric* level "whose paradigm is food consumption and food extraction from the natural environment; whose sphere is that of manual labor (or technological labor); and whose archetypal analysts is Marx."

2) **Pranic Exchange**—involving the *emotional-typhonic* level "whose paradigm is breath and sex; whose sphere is that of emotional intercourse, from feeling to sex to power; and whose archetypal analyst is Freud."

3) **Symbolic Exchange**—involving the *verbal-membership* level "whose paradigm is discourse (language); whose sphere is that of communication (and the beginning of praxis); and whose archetypal analyst is Socrates."

4) **Mutual Exchange**—involving self-recognition of the *mental-egoic* level "whose paradigm is self-consciousness or self-reflection; whose sphere is that of mutual personal recognition and esteem (the culmination of praxis); and whose archetypal analyst is Hegel (in his writings on master/slave relationship)."

5) **Intuitive Exchange**—involving the *psychic* level "whose paradigm is siddhi (or psychic intuition in its broadest sense); whose sphere is shamanistic kundalini; and whose archetypal analyst is Patanjali."

6) **Archetypal-Deity Exchange**—involving the *subtle* level "whose paradigm is saintly transcendence and revelation (nada); whose sphere is subtle Heaven (Brahma-Loka); and whose archetypal analyst is Kirpal Singh [Sufi master]."

7) **Formless Exchange**—involving the *causal* level "whose paradigm is radical absorption in and as the Uncreate (samadhi); whose sphere is the Void-Godhead; and whose archetypal analyst is Buddha/Krishna/Christ."[37]

These *compound levels of exchange* or *relational exchanges* constitute the interaction or tetra-meshing of the compound individual with the sociocultural environment across the entire AQAL Matrix (in all quadrants, on all levels, etc.). Consequently, since these levels are *not manifest* at birth, they must be grown and developed by adjusting to the physical world, then to the emotional world, then to the verbal, and so on, following the entire spiral of development. Therefore, as in all developmental processes, there can and will be *exchange distortions, emergent contaminations, dissociations, repressions*, and a host of other maladies that can go wrong anywhere along the way. Integral psychology addresses these pathological conditions by suggesting effective treatments for re-balancing and stable adaptation, which then leads to further growth and development.

The figure below lists some of the corresponding characteristics, exchange modes, principal paradigms, spheres of awareness, and examples of archetypal analysts for each of the basic "levels of exchange" (mostly situated in the Lower-Right quadrant). See Figure 12-3.

By acknowledging the entire AQAL Matrix of development, the full spectrum of consciousness in self, culture, and nature, this type of *Integral Operating System* (IOS) provides numerous advantages and therapeutic remedies by permitting and guiding development to proceed as naturally and holistically as possible. These models of Integral Theory and Integral Practice, therefore, have extremely important social and political implications, a topic beyond this brief review. These are the important areas of investigation still wide open for other integral pioneers to explore and make their valuable interpretive conclusions leading to increased integral solutions and practical applications, with deeper understandings of history and society.

Spiral Dynamics Integral

Another important model of cultural development that's emerged in significance during Wilber's recent AQAL phase is the pioneering work of "Spiral Dynamics," a developmental organization based on the original work and research done by Clare Graves in the 1970s. This has become especially effective with its more integral form called Spiral Dynamics integral or SDi, which is now being run by integral visionary Don Beck and his associates. By the late 1990s, Wilber came into contact with the work done by Spiral Dynamics, which was being taught and implemented with worldwide effectiveness by

STRUCTURE/ WORLDVIEW	EXCHANGE MODE	PRINCIPLE PARADIGM	SPHERE OF AWARENESS	CHARACTERISTICS	ARCHETYPAL ANALYST
NONDUAL SELF	*ULTIMATE EXCHANGE*	Paradox	Formless Form	free love-bliss; Divine Enlightenment	Buddha/Krishna/ Christ
CAUSAL SELF	*FORMLESS EXCHANGE*	Radical Absorption; Nondual Emptiness	Void-Godhead	meditative surrender	Buddha/Krishna/ Christ
SUBTLE SELF	*ARCHETYPAL-DEITY EXCHANGE*	transcendence; revelation	subtle heavens; One God/Goddess	meditative insight; archetypal dimensions	Kirpal Singh
PSYCHIC SELF	*INTUITIVE EXCHANGE*	psychic intuition (siddhi)	shamanistic kundalini (yoga)	spiritual awakening; transpersonal awareness	Patanjali
UNIVERSAL-INTEGRAL SELF	*GLOBAL-NETWORK EXCHANGE*	universal-global; eco-consciousness	integral-aperspectivism	ecological-planetary awareness; heart opening. spiritual awareness	Gebser
MENTAL-RATIONAL SELF	*MUTUAL EXCHANGE*	self-reflection; self-consciousness; "worldcentric"	mutual personal recognition/esteem	independence; democracy; social justice; educated mind	Hegel/Jefferson
MYTHIC-MEMBERSHIP SELF	*SYMBOLIC EXCHANGE*	language; communication; "ethnocentric"	discourse; community	politics, community awareness, brotherhood; mythic awarenesses	Socrates
MAGICAL-TYPHONIC SELF	*LIFE-ENERGY EXCHANGE*	breath, sex, power "egocentric"	emotional intercourse	magic; family, health,	Freud
ARCHAIC-UROBOROS SELF	*MATERIAL EXCHANGE*	bio-material production; food consumption; food production;	manual labor; technology	economics; material distribution; nature; web of life	Marx

AQAL MATRIX: Compound Levels of Exchange

Figure 12-3

Beck and Christopher Cowan (one of their projects was helping end apartheid in South Africa). Dr. Beck has become a founding member and active participant in Integral Institute while reintroducing the "spiral of development" with an all-quadrant awareness and multileveled presentation.

Both models distinguish between the different levels or stages of consciousness development, but Spiral Dynamics' system uses a color scheme to symbolize the various developmental "memes" or "value memes," now defined by Wilber as "*a basic stage of development that can be expressed in any activity.*"[38] The memes of Spiral Dynamics are similar to the evolutionary "worldviews" of the AQAL Matrix, thus Wilber emphasizes the fact that "Beck and Cowan affirm that memes (or stages) are not rigid levels but *flowing waves*, with much overlap and interweaving, resulting in a *meshwork* or *dynamic spiral* of consciousness unfolding."[39] Importantly, these memes are systems of values that not only apply to the worldviews of entire societies, but they also apply to the *mind-sets* of individuals (being part of their compound makeup). These descriptions fits in ideally with Wilber's pluridimensional, tetra-evolving AQAL Matrix composed of the waves and streams in the dynamic Great Nest of Spirit. Consequently, Ken Wilber has agreeably reviewed Spiral Dynamics in some of his recent Phase-4 books, while Don Beck continues his worldwide promotion of Spiral Dynamics, a portal that's easily found on the World Wide Web (www.spiraldynamicsgroup.org and www.spiraldynamics.net).

Understandably, Wilber used the color memes of Spiral Dynamics as another effective tool, with minor limitations, in presenting the developmental evolution of collective worldviews (Lower-Left quadrant). One of the unique gifts of this approach is it helps defuse people's reactions to being categorized by surface types, such as with skin color or economic class, for instead it puts the emphasis on the "color of the meme" or the developmental stage of growth (which can always be modified). Moreover, since all of these worldview memes are *structural potentials available in each and every individual,* then research continues to confirm that further development is the best and most effective method for solving the world's current problems and deadly social ills. For example, by becoming familiar with the various memes (and remembering their representative colors), then it's possible for anyone to run an AQAL Integral Operating System, or IOS scan, as a way to recognize the various waves being activated in any occasion, and then identify those most in need of rebalancing to heal deficiencies and pathologies.

Called the "Spiral of Development," the basic developmental scheme of Spiral Dynamics recognizes *two tiers* or basic groupings of memes (worldviews). The first six levels are marked by "First-Tier Thinking," consisting of the primary "subsistence levels," whose identifiable characteristic is that each first-tier meme or worldview cannot *fully appreciate the existence of the other memes.*[40] Therefore, there's usually divisiveness between these various levels and mind-sets of development. Listed below are brief outlines of these First-Tier Memes in the spiral of development, including their "color" and principal mode of consciousness, plus their population percentage and effective political power (including their correlation with Wilber's worldview):

First-Tier Memes—the "subsistence levels," usually fragmented and divisive;

- **Beige—Instinctual** (survival sense); automatic existence; (Wilber: Archaic-Uroboros)
  Archaic consciousness; (0.1 percent of the adult population, 0 percent power); a natural environment where humans rely on instincts to stay alive; food, warmth, sex, safety;
- **Purple—Magical-Animistic**; tribalistic existence; (Wilber: **Magical-Typhon**)
  Tribal consciousness; kin spirits, tribes; (10 percent of the population, 1 percent of the power); a magical place alive with spirit beings and signs; family rituals, shamans, blood oaths;
- **Red—Power Gods**; egocentric existence; (Wilber: Mythic-Membership)
  Warrior consciousness; early civilizations; (20 percent of the population, 5 percent of the power); a jungle where the strongest and most cunning survive; feudal kingdoms, rebellious youth, epic heroes;
- **Blue—Mythic Order**; mythic existence; (Wilber: Mythic-Rational)
  Traditional consciousness; conformist rule; (40 percent of the population, 30 percent of the power); an ordered existence under control of an ultimate truth; ancient nations; religious, mythic;
- **Orange—Scientific-Achievement**; materialistic existence; (Wilber: Mental-Rational)

Modern consciousness; power drives: nations; (30 percent of the population, 50 percent of the power); a marketplace full of possibilities and opportunities; individualistic, achievement-oriented;

- **Green—Sensitive Self;** personalistic existence; (Wilber: early Vision-Logic)
  Postmodern consciousness; network self; (10 percent of the population, 15 percent of the power); a human habitat sharing life's experiences; human rights, multiculturalism, relativism.

The accompanying figure represents a graphic of enveloping circles of memes to represent the "spiral of development" (and their corresponding colors) as closely correlated with Wilber's basic worldviews and structures of consciousness (Lower-Left quadrant). See Figure 12-4.

In this easily recognizable and understandable developmental scheme, the culmination of the first-tier memes is reached with the "*green meme,*" or the "sensitive self," the general self-sense of postmodern consciousness (making up 10 percent—25 percent of the population in developed countries). The "many gifts of green" (or its positive attributes), and the "mean green meme" (its negative ones), have become topics of critical focus in much of Wilber's later Phase-4 work, especially in relation to the dis-ease he calls "*boomeritis*" (or Baby Boomer narcissism). This is an infliction of green pluralism that's become one of the primary obstacles in the further emergence of integral consciousness and second-tier thinking, the next level of collective development (see next chapter).

Jump to Second-Tier Consciousness (Integral-Centaur)

After the development of the first-tier memes (beige to green), the evidence points to a "quantum leap" or "momentous jump" in consciousness, which is when, in Graves' words, "a chasm of unbelievable depth of meaning is crossed."[41] This revolutionary shift from the first-tier memes, including the highly developed green meme (relative pluralism), is now referred to as Second-Tier Thinking, which includes the *yellow* (or integrative) and *turquoise* (or holistic) memes. With second-tier awareness it's possible to, as Wilber emphasizes, "for the first time, *vividly grasp the entire spectrum of interior*

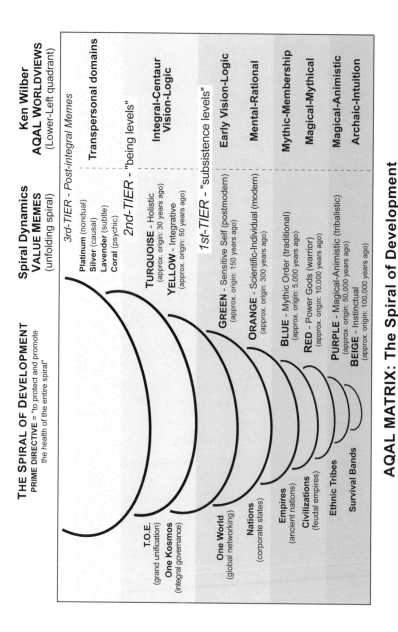

AQAL MATRIX: The Spiral of Development
Memes & Worldviews (Lower-Left quadrant)
(adopted from Spiral Dynamics)
Figure 12-4

development, and thus see that each level, each meme, each wave is crucially important for the health of the overall Spiral."[42] Since the first-tier memes are incapable of appreciating the other memes of development, then second-tier thinking is finally able to care for the entire spiral of development, a monumental breakthrough or quantum jump in consciousness development, as Graves puts it.

This is roughly the same fulcrum transformation (F-6) that Wilber calls the "integral-centaur," which operates with the cognitive capacity of "vision-logic" or "network logic" (see next chapter). In simple terms, *vision-logic* is defined as "a logic of inclusion, networking, and wide-net casting... a logic of nests within nests within nests, each attempting to legitimately include all that can be included. It is a *vision-logic*, a logic not merely of trees but also of forests. Not that the trees can be ignored. *Network-logic* is a dialectic of whole and part."[43] This is the stage of awareness that's now emerging with the "leading-edge" population of integral consciousness.

Wilber generally defines the *green* meme, with its pluralistic worldview (relative pluralism), as constituting the emergence of *early* vision-logic, while *middle* and *late* vision-logic constitute the *yellow* and *turquoise* memes of Second-Tier Awareness, briefly reviewed below:

Second-Tier Memes—the "being levels," flex flow; (Wilber: Centaur Vision-Logic)
- **Yellow**—**Integrative**; cognitive existence (Graves); (Wilber: Middle Vision-Logic)
  Integrative consciousness; (1 percent of the population, 5 percent of the power); a chaotic organism forged by differences and change; systems thinking, integrative structures;
- **Turquoise**—**Holistic**; experientialistic existence; (Wilber: Late Vision-Logic)
  Integral-centauric consciousness; (0.1 percent of the population, 1 percent of the power); an elegantly balanced system of interlocking forces; holonic, global networks and meshworks.

Consequently, Wilber's work with Beck, including their participation in Integral Institute, has encouraged Spiral Dynamics to more fully integrate AQAL Metatheory by acknowledging the all-quadrants aspect, as well as including the all-levels of development. Also, with agreement from Beck, Wilber has gone on to more fully flesh out the higher-order transpersonal stages (which were missing from the original meme color scheme of Spiral Dynamics), which are now called Third-Tier Awareness listed briefly below:

Third-Tier Memes—(Wilber: **Transpersonal domains**)

- **Coral—Psychic** *(nature mysticism)* or the "way of the shaman-yogi,"
- **Lavender—Subtle** *(deity mysticism)* or the "way of the saint,"
- **Silver—Causal** *(formless mysticism)* or the "way of the sage,"
- **Platinum—Nondual** awareness *(nondual mysticism)* or the "way of the siddha-sage."

Indeed, with Spiral Dynamics, and particularly with Don Beck's integral work, Wilber has found another friend and colleague committed to delineating, and then applying the knowledge gained from better understanding the dynamics involved with the unfolding structures of consciousness. According to Wilber, Spiral Dynamics and its supporting evidence, including the all-important "jump to second-tier consciousness," verifies the *integrative power of centauric vision-logic,* which indeed suggests there's an evolutionary (and revolutionary) shift in consciousness under way in the new millennium. This integral awareness of Second-Tier Thinking is setting the stage for a genuine Integral Age to emerge, that is, if the divisive nature of the battling first-tier memes can be outgrown through promoting the healthy development of the entire spiral, both collectively and individually.

Prime Directive: Health of the Entire Spiral

One of the important benefits gained from these developmental and integral perspectives, including with Spiral Dynamics and Wilber's AQAL Metatheory, is they're capable of affirming the necessity to *care for all* of the worldview memes of consciousness evolution. This will always be of prime importance, because, as Wilber logically points out, "Every person, in every culture, no matter how 'high' or 'advanced,' is *born at square one* and begins the great unfolding from there."[44] He calls this being "born at beige" since beige is the lowest meme in the spiral of development. For every infant, child, and adult, every stage and developmental level in the entire spiral of evolution must be cared for, rightly attended, and dutifully served in order to bring forth the positive qualities of each stage (and each person), for obviously without appropriate care, pathological symptoms will appear. This seriously means that no level or stage (beige to platinum, archaic to nondual) can be overlooked, undervalued, or privileged over the others, for all are necessary for healthy development (although the degree of depth will determine their *significance* or *fundamental* value).

Both Spiral Dynamics and AQAL Metatheory, therefore, have quantified these evolutionary dynamics (and truths) into some important *moral imperatives,* which they have articulated into the following formulations:

- **Prime Directive**—is Spiral Dynamics' dictum which concludes, in Wilber's words, "The health of the entire spiral is the *prime directive,* not preferential treatment for any one level,"[45] therefore, "the *prime directive* is thus to act in ways that, to the best of our judgment, will protect and promote the health of the entire spiral of development, and not to unduly privilege a favorite wave."[46] The point is to embrace and care for all the memes and developmental stages, from high to low, as all being vitally necessary to the overall health of the entire evolutionary process (which in humans range from the archaic to enlightenment, from beige to platinum).

- **Basic Moral Intuition (BMI)**—is defined as being that which "*protects and promotes the greatest depth for the greatest span*" (based on evolutionary tenet #8: "Each successive level of evolution produces greater depth and less span"), therefore, the BMI indicates the intention or imperative to increase as much evolutionary depth as possible for as many holons as possible. This is particularly applicable to human holons, who exhibit the greatest capacity for potential depth (reaching from the archaic to enlightenment), yet their developmental growth must be protected and cared for from the very beginning (being "born at beige"). Importantly, Wilber summarizes: "We want to protect and promote *the greatest depth for the greatest span.* Not just preserve the greatest depth—that's fascist and anthropocentric [human-oriented]—and not just preserve the greatest span—that's totalitarian and ecofascist [nature-oriented]—but rather preserve the greatest depth for the greatest span."[47] This becomes a *moral imperative* for appropriate action, both socially (collectively) and individually (personally).

While these are noble ideals, it's easy to recognize the major difficulty in that every human being is *always* "born at beige," i.e., at the very beginning of the spiral of evolutionary development. This becomes *the challenge of our times*, for as Wilber emphatically emphasizes: "The major problem remains: not, how can we get everybody to the integral waves or higher, but how can we arrange *the health of the entire spiral*, as billions of humans continue to pas through it, from one end to the other, year in and year out? In other words, most of the work that needs to be done is work to make the lower (and foundational) waves more healthy in their own terms."[48] Obviously, this will take the coordinated efforts of society-at-large and of every individual, from government to educational systems, from local communities to nation-states to the international order, as well as with the cooperative efforts of the global commons.

This is the Integral Vision's compassionate call for tolerance and the embrace of all of reality, from matter to mind to God, as embodied in the interiors and exteriors of self, culture, and nature (or all levels appearing in all four quadrants). This inclusive understanding or attitude is similar to the "Bodhisattva Vow," which Wilber once mystically marveled at in understanding its profound significance in his fourth book, *Up from Eden* (1981):

> Ultimately, in the compound individuality of the sage, all the lower levels are allowed to participate in absolute Enlightenment and bathe in the glory of Spirit. The mineral, as mineral, the plant, as plant, and the animal, as animal, could never be enlightened—but the Bodhisattva takes all manifestation with him to Paradise, and the Bodhisattva vow is never to accept Enlightenment until all things participate in Spirit. There is, to my mind, no nobler conception than that. Thus, at ultimate Enlightenment or Return to Spirit, the created world can still exist; it just no longer obscures Spirit, but serves it. All the levels remain as expressions of Atman, not substitutes for Atman.[49]

This principle of embracing reality, as we mentioned, also recognizes that *all of the memes* or worldviews of consciousness are still active in us today (due to their transcend-and-include quality); therefore, they can be *reactivated at any time* since we inherit the past with the compound nature of our human individuality. Wilber further clarifies: "One of the main conclusions of an all-level, all-quadrant [AQAL] approach is that each meme— each level of consciousness and wave of existence—is, in its healthy form, *an absolutely necessary and desirable element* of the overall spiral, of the overall spectrum of consciousness."[50] Consequently, this compassionate embrace of all "correct but partial" half truths confers a moral direction and responsibility in the healing of our divisive global situation, including proactively serving the future education and health of all who are living here now, and all who are yet to come.

A Gentle Pacer of Transformation

By understanding the unfolding stages involved in the evolution of consciousness (which became explicitly clear in Phase-2), Wilber recognized that every culture generally encourages growth only up to its particular level of development, therefore, "beyond that level," he noted, "you're on your own."[51] This is a society's "center of gravity," where he explained further in *The Eye of Spirit* (1997): "The center of gravity of a given culture tends to act as a 'magnet of development': if you are below that average, the magnet pulls you up; if you try to go beyond it, it pulls you down."[52] As a result, Wilber had observed back in *Eye to Eye* (1983): "Every society has to act as a *pacer of transformation* up to its average expectable level of structural adaptation, and thus it must provide authentic modes of transformation up to and including that level (generally, this task falls to family, educational, and occasionally religious systems)."[53] Since the people of any given culture or society are always "born at beige," then it becomes absolutely necessary for society and culture to *enact pacers of transformation* that provide for the highest level of development possible (ultimately Enlightenment), as well as following the *prime directive* to care for the entire spiral of consciousness evolution.

In addition, Wilber has also commented that no one can be *coerced* to evolve, that integral thinking or practice can never *be forced* on anyone, especially into the higher levels. As he states in a recent publication (2000): "What is required is *not* to force liberal pluralism, conservative values, or holistic ideas on anybody, but to foster the conditions—both interior and exterior—that will allow individuals and cultures to develop through the spiral at their own rate, in their own way."⁵⁴ This type of attitude and integral approach, therefore, requires the need for appropriate yet compassionate incentives for further development and education. In his recent Phase-4/5 writings, Wilber's been using the phrase "a gentle pacer of transformation" to compassionately indicate this need to educate yet also encourage the continual development of consciousness (and thus the progressive improvement of the culture-at-large). He therefore recommends we will always need to use "a gentle *pacer of transformation* for the full spectrum of human resources [is] inviting people to grow and develop their full potentials—interior and exterior—to the best of their abilities."⁵⁵ By running cross-level and cross-quadrant analyses (an IOS scan), an AQAL Approach becomes an effective tool for making sure all the bases are covered, therefore better serving the healthy development and integration of both self and society.

An Integral Age at the Leading Edge: The Integrative Power of Vision-Logic

As we've seen, these developmental models of consciousness show the initial glimmerings of an "integral consciousness" or Second-Tier Awareness that's beginning to emerge during this new millennium of human history. Since they show that integral awareness is anchored in an actual stage of human development, then it's easier to understand why the idea of a possible "new age" will actually be an "Integral Age" of consciousness development. As we also learned, both Jean Gebser and Ken Wilber agree in their analysis that the general or "average-mode" of development reached by "Western (Occidental) Man" is basically the *mental-rational* structure, which is expressed with the prevailing worldviews of modernity. They also acknowledge that next struggling structure that's emerging is the "integral" structure, which integral psychology labels as the cognitive capacity of the "integral-centaur anchored in vision-logic," yet they also conclude this is far from a sure thing (we'll explore the centaur in more detail in the next chapter).

In today's age, both scholars, and most social critics, are quick to agree that the positive advancements of the modern world are being dramatically offset by the horrible disasters generated by its pathological dissociations. Not only is there a pervasive materialistic reductionism (a flatland with no depth), but there's the obvious examples of two monumentally destructive world wars, the dangerous depletion of the natural environment, ethnocentric genocides, fundamentalist reactionism, and plenty of other Bad News scenarios. Yet, these evolutionary views also maintain that these modern disasters are mostly being driven by serious pathologies and dissociations, and are not to be attributed to the actual mental structure itself. As a result, they conclude this desperate condition will continue to haunt humankind until a more comprehensive awareness is able to effectively integrate these fractured structures of consciousness in a more positive fashion.

Only by healing, embracing, and honoring (by transcending-and-including) the lower levels (archaic, magic, mythic, mental) do these models even suggest there's a possibility to manifest the higher potentials of integral and transpersonal consciousness (psychic, subtle, causal, nondual). Only by encouraging evolutionary development, they suggest, will there emerge more encompassing, and therefore, more tolerant structures of awareness. Only the evolution of consciousness, in other words, can correct these warring, destructive, and dysfunctional problems created by a sprawling world culture drowning in its own diversity (lost without unity). The integral approach, therefore, provides a meta-paradigm that includes the ancient, traditional roots, yet it does so in a manner that's capable of growing beyond them as well. With the prime directive, the AQAL Approach acknowledges that in order to be *more integral*, then we must accept the previous worldviews of humankind in a universal embrace. Only if this happens will we ever come close to realizing a true integral millennium.

Speaking as an integral visionary, in Wilber's first book published on the cusp of the new millennium, on the opening page he first recognized the rich potentials of this possible "new age" of humankind, yet he also realizes it's coupled with extreme difficulties, as he explained in *A Theory of Everything* (2000):

> We live in an extraordinary time: all of the world's cultures, past, and present, are to some degree available to us, either in historical records or as living entities. In the history of the planet Earth, this has never happened before…. From isolated tribes and bands, to small farming villages, to ancient nations, to conquering feudal empires, to international corporate states, to global village: the extraordinary growth toward an integral village that seems human-

ity's destiny.... So it is that the leading edge of consciousness evolution stands today on the brink of an integral millennium—or at
least the possibility of an Integral Millennium—where the sum total of extant human knowledge, wisdom, and technology is available to all.[56]

While these observations may appear idealistic to some, it seems inevi-
table to others, yet because of the complexity of the developmental process, the integral philosopher is quick to warn: "There are several *obstacles*
to the integral understanding even in the most developed populations."[57]
One of the most obvious is that the *average-mode* consciousness, even in the
modern world, is far "from integral anything and in desperate need of its
own tending,"[58] especially since most people are primarily trying to evolve
up to the stage of a well-adapted mental-rational or self-autonomous existence (orange meme). Although this is the basic "center of gravity," or the
typical level of development reached in most developed societies, there are
still large portions of the world's population operating from the previous
mythic and mythic-rational structures (blue meme), while many others still
live from magical-mythical consciousness (purple/red memes). However, it's
the next stage of "vision-logic" or Second-Tier Thinking that provides the
higher-order emergent that transcends-yet-includes the mental-rational, as
well as the magical and mythic levels, therefore, Wilber confidently assures
us: "What rationality has put asunder, vision-logic will unite."[59] This development of consciousness is the key to the doorway into an Integral Millennium "where the sum total of extant knowledge, wisdom, and technology is
available to all."

Consequently, by following the available evidence these evolutionary
theorists are justified in claiming there are in fact signs of a worldcentric
integral consciousness emerging, for more and more people are moving toward
a more inclusive *universal integralism* (by whatever name). With this possibility in mind, Wilber optimistically concludes in *Sex, Ecology, Spirituality*
(1995): "Any way we slice the evolutionary pie, [this] is where we stand
today: on the verge of a planetary transformation, struggling to be secured
by rationality and completed by vision-logic, and embedded in global-
planetary social institutions."[60] Indeed, these are inspiring words coming
from a man who has, in general, been fairly pessimistic (actually, realistic)
about the dawning of any "New Age," but that's mostly because a great deal

of New Age thinking is a "regressive slide" into magical and mythical or prerational (prepersonal) consciousness, therefore it often lacks authentic transformative practices into the transpersonal domains. The actual integral-centaurs themselves, or those people developing integral consciousness, will comprise some type of "cultural elite at the leading edge," since they're moving beyond the conventional stage of the mental-rational (or modernism). However, it's important to understand that such positive developments are not an exclusive club reserved for only a few, for *everyone is invited* to join this "cultural elite" by developing the inherent and inalienable structural potentials found within us all. This type of elitism is not a superior group, but a highly-developed one in which everyone has a certain responsibility to develop and evolve ("the vow to grow"), both individually and collectively.

"An Integral Age at the Leading Age,"[61] therefore, has become a descriptive phrase used in Wilber/Phase-5 to draw attention to this higher-order emergent that can overcome some of the dissociations present in today's current world situation. If we actively participate with the natural developmental drive of evolution, then this creative "leap" to integral thinking will be one of the most significant shifts in the entire evolutionary journey. Consequently, Wilber continues to champion the idea that "In short, we appear to be entering *an integral edge at the leading edge* (with significant portions of the culture at large to follow).... An integral age at the leading edge, a big picture of many forests, an age of synthesis arising from the ruins of pluralism washed ashore."[62] Most of his confidence comes from the evolutionary evidence that outlines the successive unfolding stages of consciousness development while simultaneously acknowledging the progressive nature of evolution driven by a divine telos (Eros) of Spirit-in-action.

By accessing recent sociological evidence collected by numerous reputable researchers, Wilber points out that these studies and surveys show that at the turn of the twentieth/twenty-first century, the USA population is basically subdivided into four main groupings, which themselves follow the unfolding worldview memes (Lower-Left quadrant), which are briefly reviewed below:

- **Traditional** (Blue meme)—25 percent of the U.S. population, including *mythic-rational* and *mythic-religious* thinking, thus with *conventional* moral values (such as "family values"), therefore, they're usually *conservative* in political understanding;

- **Modern** (Orange meme)—40 percent of the U.S. population, including the *mental-rational* and *formal-rational* thinking, thus still has *conventional* moral values, such as with science and modern educational systems, thus, they're usually *liberal* in political understanding;

- **Postmodern** (Green meme)—20 percent of the U.S. population, includes the intelligentsia or academia promoting *pluralistic relativism* ("political correctness"), with *postconventional* moral values; greens (or *early vision-logic*) are usually *worldcentric*, although they're unable to make value judgments since they're extremely antihierarchical (i.e., no depth) and antiauthoritarian, therefore, they present an "obstacle" to further integral thinking;

- **Integral** (Second-Tier)—2 percent or less of the U.S. population, with 1.5 percent at the *yellow* meme (or *early vision-logic*), and only 0.5 percent at the *turquoise* meme (or *middle-to-late vision-logic*), therefore, they exhibit *postconventional* moral values; including "autonomous" and "integrated" morality or the "quantum jump" to "second-tier thinking" (Spiral Dynamics).

These statistics point out that the majority of the U.S. population (60 percent) is basically traditional (blue) and modern (orange), while close to 25 percent of the population has developed to the basic wave of green relative pluralism (postmodernism), the wave just preceding integral second-tier awareness. This includes many of the so-called "Baby Boomers" and the mind-set of academia, which is one reason why Wilber has been particularly critical of their narcissistic tendencies and translative spirituality, or what he calls *"boomeritis"* (see chapter 14). On the other hand, if the smaller "integral part" of the population (2 percent) can conceivably swell to 5 percent, or 10 percent or more in the next couple of decades, then this would have a significant impact on the world at large. Because academia has generally been under the sway of postmodern pluralism for the past few decades, it has actually contributed to "today's climate of cultural wars"[63] (as does the "irony of liberalism"), however, there are signs that this is giving way to *more integral* approaches, which must be encouraged to continue.

Wilber believes the evidence indicates this increasing emergence of integral consciousness, as with any evolutionary emergent, will continue unfolding "at the growing tip, the leading edge, or the avant-garde (by whatever appellation)—in academia, the arts, social movements, spirituality, thought leaders."[64] Integral *theories*, he contends, will necessarily assist in establishing more *integral practices*, including *Integral Transformative Practices* (ITP) and *integral applications* (AQAL apps), which in turn affect both individuals and the larger population in an AQAL feedback loop. In a recent published conversation with Allan Combs, Wilber points out that these emerging integral thinkers or centaurs "will have a voice, and they will demand integral approaches to everything—business, politics, education, medicine—because they will have an integral consciousness that will demand integral food or they will get hungry."[65] This change or emergence has already begun, and continues to grow, especially with the recent founding of social integral institutions, such as with Integral Institute, Integral University, and many other "real world" movements, from business to politics to education to spirituality (see chapter 11). These will be the real integral adventures and second-tier solutions that will create and support any type of integral consciousness leading to an Integral Millennium or Integral Age, if there's to be one.

As we'll continue to see, integral psychology maintains it's only with "the integrative power of centauric vision-logic," or the development into second-tier thinking (the yellow and turquoise memes), that the possibilities for a genuine "Planetary Culture" or a true "World Federation," will open up and emerge for the global commons (see last chapter). This is when "second-tier solutions" will become available as viable alternatives to today's fractured dilemmas, therefore, Wilber outlines some of the benefits expected to be seen with a rising culture of integral awareness, as he points out in *Sex, Ecology, Spirituality* (1995):

> It is the *integrative power of vision-logic*, I believe, and not the indissociation of tribal magic or the imperialism of mythic involvement that is desperately needed on a global scale. For it is *vision-logic* with its centauric/planetary worldview that, in my opinion, holds the only hope for:
> * the integration of the biosphere [nature/body] and noosphere [mind],
> * the supra-national organization of planetary consciousness,

- the genuine recognition of ecological balance,
- the unrestrained and unforced forms of global discourse,
- the nondominating and noncoercive forms of federated states,
- the unrestrained flow of worldwide communicative exchange,
- the production of genuine world citizens, and the enculturation of female agency (i.e., the integration of male and female in both the noosphere and the biosphere) –all of which, in my opinion, is nevertheless simply the platform for the truly interesting forms of higher and transpersonal states of consciousness lying yet in our collective future— if there is one.[66]

This type of planetary or worldcentric awareness is built upon the integrated bodymind utilizing vision-logic and integral consciousness, which itself is built upon authentic *transformative* practices. Only by applying theories into actual practice will the world be truly transformed into the next appropriate level of development, thus, once more, Wilber simply confirms this developmental truth: "The revolution, as always, will come from the *within* and be embedded in the *without*."[67] Yet, with a "prime directive" that states one of the most important tasks facing humanity is it must ensure the health and safety of the entire "spiral of development," then this alone should raise the "center of gravity" for the general population as a whole. But, as always, the future is what *we* make it, and, as Wilber constantly reminds us, there's still a lot of work to be done. First, by learning the value of more integral models of reality, and then by exercising compassion and wisdom cultivated with authentic transformative spirituality, then we can more effectively allow the evolutionary thrust of Spirit-in-action to push us forward with the gentle persuasion of love, once again leading humanity on toward a brighter future. Only together will we initiate this "Integral Revolution," not because it's a fad or the popular thing to do, but because it's the next emerging stage of human consciousness development: the stage of the "integral-centaur anchored in vision-logic," which we'll turn to next.

CHAPTER THIRTEEN

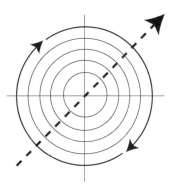

Evolution of the Integral-Centaur

This more generous stance calls for an "integral approach" to overall transformation, an approach that honors and incorporates many lesser transformative and translative practices—covering the physical, emotional, mental, cultural, and communal aspects of the human being—in preparation for, and as an expression of, the ultimate transformation into the always-already present state.

—Ken Wilber, *One Taste* (1999)

Ken Wilber's Integral-Centaur

AS WE SAW IN THE PREVIOUS CHAPTER, JEAN GEBSER'S *INTEGRAL-APERSPECTIVAL worldview* is very similar to what Ken Wilber has called the "integral-centaur" structure or basic wave of consciousness development. For Wilber, the worldview (of the Lower-Left quadrant) is called *"centauric"* and *"existential"* (which we'll examine in a moment), whereas the cognitive stages of development (of the Upper-Left quadrant) is called *"vision-logic"* and *"network-logic,"* which follows (by transcending-and-including) the mental-egoic and mental-rational developmental structures of consciousness.

Wilber's designator of the ancient Greek *Centaur*, which is a mythic creature that is half horse, half human, to signify the conscious integration of body and mind is an image for it's often used by modern psychology, such as by Hubert Benoit, E. H. Erikson, Loevinger, Broughton, Graves, and others, to indicate a "self-actualized" person, the epitome of personal evolution. Thus Wilber clarified in *Eye to Eye* (1983): "This integrated self, wherein mind and body are harmoniously one, we call the 'centaur.' The centaur: the great mythological being with animal body and human mind existing in a state of at-one-ment."[1] In Wilber's first book, *The Spectrum of Consciousness* (1977), he defined the centaur following Benoit (in *The Supreme Doctrine*): "We will also be calling *existential awareness* by the name '*centaur awareness*': the awareness not of a horse-man ruling over his horse, but rather of a *centaur*, a total, self-governing organism."[2] A few years later, in *The Atman Project* (1980), he dedicates an entire chapter to this important level of conscious development, before continuing further in-depth examinations in *Sex, Ecology, Spirituality* (1995) and other Phase-4 books.

Some astute observers have noted that possibly the Centaur, which is often portrayed as a violent and beastly man-horse in mythology, is not such a good symbol for the more peaceful, integrated, and self-actualized human being. The centaurs, who were pictured in Greek mythology as being compounded of a horse's body and legs topped with a man's torso, arms, and head, were often said to lead a wild and violent life, including raging battles, brawls, rapes, and riotous revelries.[3] As a result, they were often representing the dark, unruly forces of nature, not necessarily the most attractive image for a highly developed integral structure of consciousness. However, the myths also showed this higher-order integration by picturing the human as being united with one Earth's finest creatures, the noble horse, since in actuality ancient people were extremely fond of the horse. According to some scholars, the centaur is the only compounded monster of antiquity (i.e., animal + human) to which *any* good traits are assigned, therefore, they ultimately transcend (yet include) their degraded, brutish forms or reputations.[4]

In particular, there was the wise centaur named Chiron who was unlike his beastly brothers, for he was noted for his wisdom and gentleness. Chiron, a friend to Apollo, was learned in the art of prophecy, music, hunting, warfare, and importantly, in medicine, for it was Chiron, for example, who taught the master-physician Asclepius the fine arts of healing. Even the image of the *caduceus*, whose staff of intertwining snakes (which in yoga symbolizes the awakening of kundalini as rises up the spinal column to open the seven chakras) is clearly associated with Chiron, the healer centaur. Therefore, I suggest, it is this type of centaur that becomes an apt symbol for the consciously integrated body and mind, the first real steps into the transpersonal stages of human development. Not only does Chiron represent the transcendence of the beastly animal-body (typhon), usually represented by his unruly brothers, but this centaur also shows the deeper transcendence of the mind (via the awakening of kundalini and higher psycho-physical development). Therefore, the image of the centaur can rightly be seen as an appropriate symbol representing the next major phase of consciousness evolution (the integral), which emerges after the mental-egoic structure by completing the integration/transcendence of the body and mind.

Wilber's second book, *No Boundary* (1979), emphasizes this centauric awareness is such a way that makes it a valuable guidebook to this advanced stage of development (see, for example, Seymour Boorstein's recommendations in *Clinical Studies in Transpersonal Psychotherapy*).[5] Wilber clearly explains how readers, by following some basic psychological principles, may come to understand their own existential stage of development and how to better integrate the body and mind as a whole (such as integrating the "shadow" and "personae") on the way to the transpersonal domains (and "no-boundary awareness"). However, as Wilber points out, this is best accomplished with the assistance and guidance of trained professionals (including psychotherapists and adept-gurus). Listed below are some of the characteristic descriptions used by Wilber to define the "Integral-Centaur" and "centauric awareness":

- The more we are capable of resting in the centaur, the more we are capable of founding our lives on, and giving our lives over to, this wider store of natural wisdom and freedom.[6]

- All in all, the centaur level is the home of (1) self-actualization, (2) meaning, and (3) existential or life-death concerns. And the resolution of all of these requires a whole-bodied full-minded awareness, a current of feeling-attention which floods the bodymind and utilizes the entire psychological being.[7]

- On the centaur level, you still have access to the ego, the body, the persona, and the shadow; but because you are no longer exclusively identified with one as against the others, all of these elements work in harmony. You have befriended them all and touched each with acceptance. There are no intractable boundaries between them and so no major battles.[8]

- To find centauric meaning in life—fundamental meaning—is to find that the very processes of life itself generate joy. Meaning is found, not in outward actions or possessions, but in the inner radiant currents of your own being, and in the *release* and *relationship* of these currents to the world, to friends, to humanity at large, and to infinity itself.[9]

- In general, all of the characteristics of the centaur (intentionality, vision-image, bodymind integration) represent or reflect *higher-order unities*, new and higher forms of Atman-telos. This is why most centauric therapists (humanistic and existential), are always talking about either a "higher-level unity" or an "underlying unity"—a unity of ego, body, mind, and emotion.[10]

- [The integral-centaur] represents the stage where mind and body, after being clearly differentiated, are then brought into a higher-order integration. This is the level of humanistic-existential psychology/therapy, of self-actualization, of existential meaning.[11]

- This "union of feeling [body] and knowledge [mind]" is one of the general definitions of the mature centaur.[12]

In the fulcrums of self development (see chapter 10), this is Fulcrum-6 in Wilber's spectrum psychology, for it reflects the mature stage of adulthood that confronts the "existential" crisis of being alive and finding purpose or true meaning to life. Wilber has always been in strong agreement with those psychologies that maintain this is a crucial turning point in maturity, as he explained in *A Brief History of Everything* (1996): "One of the characteristics of the *actual self* of this stage (the centaur) is precisely that it no longer buys all the conventional and numbing consolations—as Kierkegaard put it, the self can no longer tranquilize itself with the trivial. The emergence of this more authentic or existential self is the primary task of Fulcrum-6. The finite self is going to die—magic will not save it, mythic gods will not save it, rational science will not save it—and facing that cutting fact is part of becoming authentic. This was one of Heidegger's constant points. Coming to terms with one's mortality and one's finitude—this is part of finding one's own authentic being-in-the-world (authentic agency-in-communion)."[13]

This mature stage of adulthood (Fulcrum-6) brings about a self-assured, autonomous, emotionally secure, well-functioning, self-healing, and integrated self-system, probably best documented by Humanistic Psychology or the "Third Force" of psychology. This level of integration, emerging after the differentiations of the rational-ego (and self-autonomy), corresponds to recent research from academic psychology, such as with Loevinger's *autonomous* and *integrated* stages, or Jenny Wade's *authentic*, or Spiral Dynamic's yellow and turquoise memes (second-tier), or Arlin's *postformal*, among many others. It also roughly corresponds to the observations of other social theorists monitoring social evolution, such as with Duane Elgin's *integral awareness*, or Peter Russell's *global brain*, or Willis Harman's *new paradigm*, or Charles Reich's *Consciousness III*, or Paul Ray's *cultural creatives*, or even Marilyn Ferguson's "Aquarian Conspiracy,"[14] although large segments of these populations are still operating in the immediately preceding level or "green meme" (see next chapter). Nonetheless, as we saw in the last chapter, the integral worldview of the centaur isn't really the promised "New Age," although it is another mutational or transformational shift in humankind's consciousness evolution, and in that sense only, is it a possible New Age in overall development, but it's certainly not any promised "Golden Age" of humanity.

In AQAL Phase-4, Wilber clarified his concerns (and those of his critics) when claiming it's the integral-centaur with a cognitive capacity of vision-logic that can better integrate the body and mind into a higher-order integration, as he did in *The Eye of Spirit* (1997):

> [The integration of mind and body] is, of course, a relative affair and a matter of degrees. One might even make the argument that the mind and body are not truly integrated until radical Enlightenment, and I would not argue with that. But generally speaking, I describe the centaur as the integration of mind and body because:

1)   this directly follows the evidence of Loevinger, Brough-
     ton, Graves, and others; and

2)   the centaur, as the great transition from the gross body-
     mind to the subtle bodymind, represents the "final" inte-
     gration of that gross bodymind.

3)   More technically: because vision-logic is on the edge of
     the transmental, the self of vision-logic is increasingly
     disidentifying with the mind itself. Because vision-logic
     transcends formal rationality, it can more easily integrate
     formal reason and body.[15]

By indicating a new level of emergence in consciousness (on the way to Enlightenment), as Wilber continues to explain, "This new centauric aware-ness transcends (but includes) so much of the verbal-mental-egoic dimen-sion, that the entire dimension itself becomes *increasing objective*, increas-ingly transparent, to centauric awareness."[16] In other words, he continues, "*centauric-integral awareness* integrates the body and mind in a new trans-parency, the biosphere [body] and the noosphere [mind], once finally dif-ferentiated, can now be integrated in a new embrace."[17] As a consequence, the body is much more relaxed and open, not as contracted and blocked, while the mind functions better through a further transcendence of mental and egoic patterning, dilemmas, and false selves (or personae).

The figure was presented in 1977 by Wilber in *The Spectrum of Con-sciousness* (adopted from Alexander Lowen's *Depression and the Body*, 1972)[18] to help graphically portray some of the benefits gained with centauric inte-gration. See Figure 13-1.

The psychological evidence shows that the newly emerging structure of integral consciousness or the centaur is a whole-body condition (defined as *psychosomatic* by Feuerstein) since the body and mind are integrated in a wider embrace and a deeper transcendence. The body is "resurrected," so to speak, from the alienation of the mental-egoic mind which is now tran-scended like never before. Thus Gebser scholar Georg Feuerstein points out in *The Structures of Consciousness* (1987): "It is a whole-bodily event of feel-ing through the *lived* body. It does not take flight from bodily experience in any form. Rather it is grounded in one's unmitigated acceptance of, or pri-mal trust in, corporeality. *It is the transparent body-mind.*"[19] This integrated

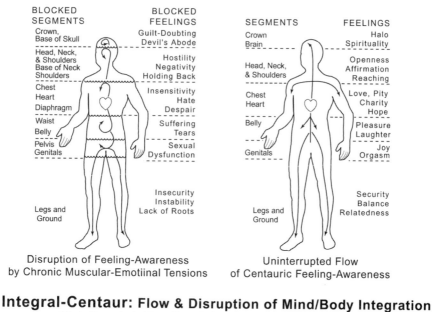

BLOCKED SEGMENTS	BLOCKED FEELINGS	SEGMENTS	FEELINGS
Crown, Base of Skull	Guilt-Doubting Devil's Abode	Crown Brain	Halo Spirituality
Head, Neck, & Shoulders Base of Neck Shoulders	Hostility Negativity Holding Back	Head, Neck, & Shoulders	Openness Affirmation Reaching
Chest Heart Diaphragm	Insensitivity Hate Despair	Chest Heart	Love, Pity Charity Hope
Waist Belly	Suffering Tears	Belly	Pleasure Laughter
Pelvis Genitals	Sexual Dysfunction	Genitals	Joy Orgasm
Legs and Ground	Insecurity Instability Lack of Roots	Legs and Ground	Security Balance Relatedness

Disruption of Feeling-Awareness by Chronic Muscular-Emotiinal Tensions

Uninterrupted Flow of Centauric Feeling-Awareness

Integral-Centaur: Flow & Disruption of Mind/Body Integration
(Illustrations adapted from Alexander Lowen, *Depression and the Body*, 1972, and used by Ken Wilber in *The Spectrum of Consciousness*, 1977)

Figure 13-1

bodymind of the centaur, then, introduces the platform for a new emergent cognitive capacity known as "vision-logic," which we'll examine next.

Integral-Centaur in Vision-Logic

Technically, this stage of integral consciousness is the "centaur in vision-logic,"[20] which Wilber (by following Loevinger's summary of Broughton's highest stage) most simply defines as: "*Mind* and *body* are both experiences of an *integrated self*."[21] As mentioned, the worldview or worldspace of the integral-centaur (situated as the Lower-Left quadrant) correlates with the individual self (Upper-Left quadrant) exhibiting the cognitive capacity called "vision-logic" or "network-logic," which is, as we noted, similar to Gebser's *integral-aperspectival* structure of consciousness. Wilber again reviews the characteristics of centauric vision-logic in *A Brief History of Everything* (1996): "Vision-logic or network-logic is a type of synthesizing and integrating awareness.... Vision-logic adds up the parts and sees networks of interactions.... So the highly integrative capacity of vision-logic supports an equally integrated self. Which is why I call the self of this stage the *centaur*, representing an integration of the mind and the body, the noosphere and the biosphere, in a relatively autonomous self—which doesn't mean isolated self or atomistic self or egocentric self, but rather a self integrated in its networks of responsibility and service."[22]

The stage before vision-logic, remember, is the mental-ego with its highly developed cognitive capacity of *rationality* (the orange meme), which Gebser referred to as the *"rational-perspectival,"* and which Wilber identifies the *"mental-rational"* or *"formal-rational"* (formop). Its higher-order characteristics are that rationality can take on *multiple perspectives*, including increased tolerance for different cultures and ideas, hence its moral values become more *"worldcentric"* in orientation (beyond egocentric and socio-ethnocentric worldviews of the magical and mythical mind). Yet, with the emergence of centauric vision-logic, then the self can not only "reasonably decide the individual issues," but this level of cognition is better able to bring all these multiple perspectives together in a larger, more integral "truth vision." Thus, Wilber succinctly proclaims, "Rationality gives all possible perspectives, vision-logic adds them up into a totality."[23] The integral psychologist further defines the traits of vision-logic in *Integral Psychology* (2000): "Where perspectival reason privileges the exclusive perspective of the particular subject, vision-logic *adds up all the perspectives*, privileging none, and thus attempts to grasp the integral, the whole, the multiple contexts within contexts that endlessly disclose the Kosmos, not in a rigid or absolutist fashion, but in a fluidly holonic and multidimensional tapestry."[24]

The self at this stage has become more *aware of* both body and mind as *experiences*, and thus the body and mind begin to become "transparent" (Gebser's term) to the *observing self* (or the Witness), therefore, the centauric self "can be aware of [both body and mind] as objects in awareness."[25] Consequently, Wilber summarizes this stage of development: "Centauric-integral awareness integrates body and mind in a new transparency; the biosphere and the noosphere, once finally differentiated, can now be integrated in a new embrace."[26] Specifically, he further defines: "More technically: because vision-logic is on the edge of the transmental, the self of vision-logic is increasingly disidentifying with the mind itself. Because vision-logic transcends formal rationality, it can more easily integrate formal reason and body."[27] Yet, the integral psychologist also constantly reminds us that he and other relevant theorists do not "see the emergence of the 'aperspectival worldcentric' structure as being a sure thing, as being somehow guaranteed," thus he continues to comment in *Sex, Ecology, Spirituality* (1995): "Nor does the fact that the integral structure is integral guarantee that the necessary integration will in fact occur. The claim is simply, to put it in the terms we have been using, that the integral structure *can* integrate the physiosphere, the biosphere, and the noosphere—it has the *potential* for that integration. Whether that potential becomes actual is up to you and me; it depends on the concrete actions that each of us takes. As always, we have to make the future that is given to us."[28]

The figure below represents the integral centaur in the four quadrants (of self, culture, and nature), thus graphically reviewing this stage of development by using some of Wilber's defining characteristics. See Figure 13-2.

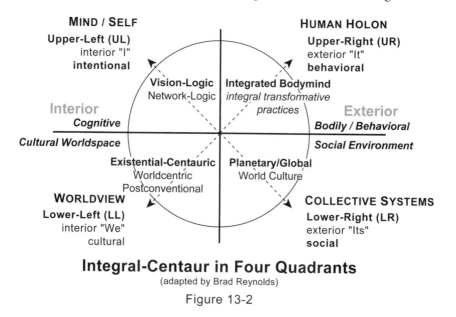

Integral-Centaur in Four Quadrants
(adapted by Brad Reynolds)
Figure 13-2

Now, as the third millennium dawns, Wilber is still one of the loudest champions of integral consciousness and the positive advantages gained by taking an integrative approach to life and the world's problems. By offering an AQAL Metatheory that brings forward an *Integral Operating System* (IOS), based on valid knowledge claims gathered from an *Integral Methodological Pluralism* (IMP), and one that's also grounded in *Integral*

Transformative Practices (ITP), then we can see why the integral bodhisattva is waving his "sword" of enlightening wisdom by boldly proclaiming: "The great quest for postmodernity, I will argue, is for the bodymind integration of the Centaur anchored in worldcentric vision-logic, and there are signs everywhere that this is in fact occurring."[29] Yet, as always, it's up to each one of us to encourage and enact our own developmental growth, compassionately and with wisdom, while actively and lovingly promoting the development and happiness of all others. This importantly includes those struggling with the lower levels of adaptation, since every living being may be better served in their need for a deeper embrace of love and care (the "prime directive"). This will have profound healing effects on the pathological expressions of any level in the spiral of development, for it encourages us all to reach for our higher potentials and possibilities while sincerely celebrating our precious and dynamic play within this sacred divine dance of Spirit-in-action.

Postmodern Aperspectival Madness

As with every stage of development, even integral consciousness has its downsides and pathologies (or Bad News and disasters), which in this case is when all the multitude of perspectives (aperspectival) of vision-logic become overwhelming. Then the self can slip into a common malady of postmodernism, or what Wilber calls "aperspectival madness, a dizzifying paralysis of will and judgment."[30] Sometimes translated as "everything is relative," it's when "all perspectives start to become relative and interdependent; there is nothing absolutely foundational; no final place to rest your head and say, I've got it!"[31] This often leads, as we saw, to an *existential crisis* or when the self questions its existence and the universe it's living in (even asking "Should I die?"), which, in a positive response, should propel a person into a search for deeper meaning and higher development.

This can be especially true for postmodernists, as Wilber insightfully explains: "The postmodern poststructuralists, for example, have gone from saying that no context, no perspective, is final, to saying no perspective has any advantage over any other, at which point they careen uncontrollably in their own labyrinth of ever-receding holons, lost in aperspectival space."[32] From the integral point of view, however, as Wilber also points out, "The fact that all perspectives are *relative* does *not* mean that no perspective has any advantage at all. That all perspectives are relative does not prevent some from still being relatively better than others all the time! Worldcentric is better than ethnocentric is better than egocentric, because each has more depth than its shallower predecessors."[33] Thus, the vision-logic of the integral-centaur emerges and a more authentic self begins to *transcend* the agonizing separate-self sense with a higher-order awareness of consciousness (and an even wider embrace), which will include the soul (psychic, subtle) and spirit (causal, nondual) or the transpersonal domains of consciousness.

Yet, even with this advanced integration, it's still important to realize that the integral-centaur is not a mystically enlightened self, for it's only developed to the stage of self-actualized maturity involving the holistic bodymind, but not the complete development to whole-body Enlightenment (the ultimate stage). Nonetheless, by following the evolutionary "form of development," the integration of one advanced level (in this case, the mental-rational) has become unsatisfactory, therefore, only a higher-order integration will truly satisfy (and heal), thus the next level beckons the self to higher development. Consequently, with "the bodymind integration of the centaur" the self finally finds itself, as Wilber emphasizes, *"on the brink of the transpersonal."*[34]

More than Integral: Transpersonal

As we also noted in the previous chapter, since there are many similarities between his evolutionary model and that of Jean Gebser, Ken Wilber has respectfully paid his debt and installed Gebser's theories to buttress his own views on the evolution of historical consciousness (especially as he specifically described them in *Up from Eden*). Yet, at the same time, Wilber would go on to immediately add the "transpersonal" domains to complete the spectrum of consciousness approach, which is fully accounted for in the AQAL Matrix, but not in Gebser's model. Nevertheless, as Wilber biographer Frank Visser noticed, "In Gebser's (and Wilber's) opinion four simple words—archaic, magical, mythical, and mental—enable us to describe the whole of the complex history of the consciousness of humankind."[35] For Wilber, of course, these were more accurately tagged the archaic-uroboros, magical-typhon, mythic-membership, and mental-ego.

These agreements aside, however, Wilber's discovery and presentation of the *pre/trans fallacy* during Phase-2 (the late 1970s) that accounted for both the prepersonal *and* transpersonal stages of development quickly led him to conclude that Gebser had made some important errors, including his interpretation of the "Origin" (or *Ursprung*). Since the pre/trans or pre/post fallacy is the "confusing of *pre*-rational structures with *trans*-rational structures simply because both are *non*-rational,"[36] then Wilber noted that some of Gebser's attributes for the integral structure could actually be attributed to the prepersonal, not the transpersonal, realms (these arguments, however, are too detailed to chronicle here). Yet, Feuerstein, a personal student during Gebser's last years, understood this oversight made by his teacher, especially after thoroughly studying Wilber's more recent model, therefore he claimed the "careful distinction between *pre-rational, rational,* and *trans-rational* phenomena is not only an important ordering device, it is also a critical framework that allows us to assess the authenticity of religious expressions."[37] This, of course, refers to Wilber's inclusion of the *transpersonal* structures into his developmental model, an area of interest that Feuerstein, a world-known scholar of yoga, clearly recognized and appreciated.

The Turn Within (to the Depths of the Divine)

In turning to the transpersonal structures of consciousness (psychic, subtle, causal, nondual), Wilber proceeds on the premise of recognizing the importance of *turning within* to access these deeper (or higher) reaches of consciousness. The reason for this is simple, as he formulates in *Sex, Ecology, Spirituality* (1995): "increasing development = *increasing* interiorization = *decreasing* narcissism (or decreasing egocentricism)."[38] This is because, Wilber continues to explain, "each stage of evolution, in whatever domain, involves a new emergence and therefore a new depth, or a new interiority, whether that applies to molecules or to birds or to dolphins; and that each new within is also a going beyond, a transcendence, a higher and wider identity with a greater total embrace. The formula is: going within = going beyond = greater embrace."[39] Therefore, the integral psychologist confirms the precise process involved in the evolution of consciousness: "The more one *goes within, the more one goes beyond,* and the more one can thus embrace a *deeper identity* with a *wider perspective*."[40] In other words, by turning within we embrace more without, since "every *within* turns us *out* into more of the Kosmos."[41] This is, as we've seen, a major premise of integral psychology and transpersonal psychology (the "fourth force" of modern psychology), and it sets the stage for further developmental growth beyond even the self-actualized individual (or integral-centaur).

In order for the deeper domains of the transpersonal to open themselves to an individual's awareness, that individual must engage the appropriate *injunctions* (exemplars, paradigms), or disciplined *practices*, in order to *turn within* and awaken these structural potentials of humankind as we evolve through "the depths of the divine."[42] For humans, this necessarily involves meditation (or contemplation), thus Wilber again notes, "Meditation is one of the single strongest antidotes to egocentrism and narcissism (and geocentrism and anthropocentrism and sociocentrism)."[43] This intentional engagement of the interior will therefore be included in any application of authentic transformative practices, as Wilber again notes, "This general movement of *within-and-beyond* is nothing new with humans: it is a simple continuation of the Kosmic evolutionary process, which is 'self-development through self-transcendence,' the same process at work in atoms and molecules and cells, a process that, in the human domains, continues naturally into the superconscious, with precisely nothing occult or mysterious about it."[44] In this case, it becomes a natural responsibility for us all in further the evolution of consciousness.

Although Gebser had been deeply concerned with the "spiritual" in many respects, his primary theoretical weakness stemmed from his lack of knowledge about Eastern mysticism, an area of wisdom that Wilber is most conversant (as is Feuerstein). Therefore Wilber's spectrum of consciousness model went on to propose several basic waves beyond "the integral" (or that of the integrated centaur), which were first called the "transpersonal" stages during the 1970s. In order to remind us that *trans*-personal doesn't mean "impersonal," or that it somehow completely negates the personal, then Wilber has clarified, "I think it's very important for us to remember that *transpersonal* mean 'personal *plus*,' not 'personal minus'."[45] Consequently, this means we are entering the realms of the soul, for as the integral psychologist summarizes, "The first rule of the soul is: it is transpersonal."[46]

In this case, these domains of *subtle soul* and *causal spirit* are the "higher" possibilities (or *structural potentials*) of our species as the spiral of development continues to unfold for anyone who engages the appropriate training and practices. As we've mentioned, they have generally been researched by the field of transpersonal psychology, as well as by the great wisdom traditions, and they're expertly reviewed in every one of Wilber's books. Indeed, this larger embrace and holistic integration of all the structures of consciousness lays a sturdier foundation for the psychological (and practical) *turn within* as awareness becomes freer to open up and experience the transpersonal realms and further evolution, thus, once more, it's important to emphasize the need for authentic *integral transformative practices* covering all levels in all quadrants.

Integral AQAL Therapy & Therapists

As we've seen, Wilber's first book, *The Spectrum of Consciousness* (1977), began by recognizing the only real way to gain enlightened wisdom is by actively *engaging* the "nondual mode of knowing," which itself requires *doing* the *injunctive practices* of higher development (such as meditation or contemplative prayer). Yet, as we've also seen, the foundations to these higher transpersonal stages (psychic, subtle, causal, and nondual) are built upon the healthy functioning of the lower stages in an adequate fashion (culminating with the integral-centaur or the integrated human being). Thus integral psychology always encourages healthy development at every stage of growth, including psychotherapeutic treatments and healing of any pathology on any level (matter, body, mind, soul, spirit). Therefore, Wilber highly recommends: "So even as you advance in your own spiritual unfolding, consider combining it with a good psychotherapeutic practice, because spiritual practice, as a rule, will not adequately expose the psychodynamic unconscious."[47] Since this aspect of integral practice is "a union of East and West," or the "marriage of Freud and the Buddha," then he heartily suggests: "Render unto Freud what is Freud's, and render unto Buddha what is Buddha's. And best of all, render unto the Divine all of yourself, be engaging all that you are."[48] And that, of course, includes not only the mind and soul (psyche), but also the body, the realm of *soma* (literally, Greek, for "the entire body"), the corporal and living base for the unfolding spirit of the individual human holon.

In regard to the physical-somatic (or bodily) therapy, contrary to some critic's opinion about a high-minded intellect being lost in the world of mental ideas, Wilber has always maintained, as he did in *Eye to Eye* (1983): "I am a staunch supporter of body-oriented therapies and recommend them, along with diet and exercise, as the first step of any overall therapy. We all seem generally out of touch with the body and must begin by rebuilding the base."[49] Personally, the integral psychologist has always been a huge advocate of physical exercise and somatic health, including natural diets and other vital body therapies. Indeed, as he reported in his private journal *One Taste: Daily Reflections on Integral Spirituality* (1999), he personally has been doing hatha yoga for decades, and since the early 1990s, he's become a "weight-lifting fanatic."[50] As a result, he confirms a simple fact: "My experience is that when the bodymind is strong and healthy—not ascetically starved and despised—it is all the easier to drop it, transcend it, let it go. Precisely because the bodymind is running smoothly, with no distracting glitches, it doesn't hold awareness obsessively circling around it."[51] Naturally, the integral approach involves *all the levels* in the spectrum of consciousness, from matter/body (gross) to mind/soul (subtle) to spirit (causal).

In addition, of course, a full-spectrum psychology also honors the mind (and reason), or the intellect, as well as the bodily base. By more effectively understanding the importance of eliminating the *pre/trans fallacy* in relation to today's world, Wilber began establishing this inclusive premise during Phase-2 (1981): "The single greatest service that trans-personalists, as well as humanists, could now perform is to champion, not just trans-reason, but an honest embrace of simple reason itself. Trans-personalism does indeed *negate* ego and reason, but it must also *preserve* them."[52] By recognizing the full-spectrum in the Great Nest of Spirit (and the AQAL Matrix) we now know that "Soul and Spirit *include* body, emotions, and mind, they do not erase them."[53] Full-spectrum health, therefore, requires they're all appropriately handled (and maintained) in combination and conjunction with each other and overall development.

This has recently led Wilber to propose the establishment of a "General Practitioner or GP of the spirit," that is, a "spiritual GP," or a "full-spectrum therapist," a qualified therapist who has "at least theoretical familiarity with all levels of the spectrum of consciousness—*matter, body, mind* (magic, mythic, rational, and integral-aperspectival), *soul* (psychic and subtle), and *spirit* (causal and nondual). They should also be familiar with the types of pathologies that can occur at each of those levels."[54] He further details this proposal in *Integral Psychology* (2000): "A full-spectrum therapist works with the body, the shadow, the persona, the ego, the existential self, the soul and spirit, attempting to bring awareness to all of them, so that all of them may join consciousness in the extraordinary return voyage to the Self and Spirit that grounds and moves the entire display. In short, *a full-spectrum therapist is an archeologist of the Self.* But, this is an archeology that unearths the future, not the past…. To move from egocentric to ethnocentric to worldcentric to theocentric is to ascend into greater and wider and higher spheres of release and embrace, transcendence and inclusion, freedom and compassion."[55] These are qualified therapists, men and women, who serve full-spectrum development and the further evolution of consciousness.

For one, this is a good place to access the "integral psychograph," which plots the various developmental *lines* (or streams) as they evolve through the different basic *levels* (or waves) in the Great Nest, thus helping determine what type of practices will be most effective for each individual and their different degrees of development (see chapter 10). For integral psychology, Wilber explains, "All of these developmental lines can be entered on an *individual's psychograph*, which is actually a graph of one's 'at-home-ness' with the world."[56]

Then it's a matter of circling around the quadrants (of self, culture, nature) to get an AQAL "snapshot" of what's required for further health and growth. An AQAL or "all-quadrant, all-level" psychology, of course, fully maintains that "All four quadrants mutually interact (they are embedded in each other), and thus *all* of them are required in order to understand pathologies in *any* of them.... A malformation—a pathology, a 'sickness'—in any quadrant will reverberate through all four quadrants, because every holon has these four facets to its being.... And so on around the four-quadrant circle. Crippling one quadrant [whether individual interiors or exteriors or social and cultural systems] and all four tend to hemorrhage.... That is why a truly integral therapy is not only individual but cultural, social, spiritual, and political."[57] Practically speaking, then, the purpose of these integral practices is to appropriately exercise and transform the body, the emotions (or heart), the mind, the soul, and our spirituality all in relation to self and others, culture and society, the body and natural environment, in order to harmoniously to live life to its fullest, realizing our greatest (and highest) potentials. Or as Wilber puts it best, "Practice them diligently, and coordinate your integral efforts to unfold the various potentials of the body-mind—until the bodymind itself unfolds in Emptiness, and the entire journey is a misty memory from a trip that never even occurred."[58]

Integral Life Practices (ILP): Change the Mapmaker!

"Walk the walk," as they say, or really moving integral *theory* into real life *practice* has always been where Wilber's mostly at, and yet still, he's finding ways to expand its reach (see chapter 14). The whole point of optimum health and well-functioning, for Wilber, "is to be fully at home in the body and its desires, the mind and its ideas, the spirit and its light. To embrace them fully, evenly, simultaneously, since all are equally gestures of the One and Only Taste [the Divine]." Indeed, these are the characteristics of the enlightened nondual sage—or *jiva-mukta* (in Sanskrit, "living liberated" or "one liberated while still alive")—our ultimate potential and happiness. This would naturally involve the self-system *exercising* and *surfing* the entire AQAL Matrix, i.e., all-levels in all-quadrants by actually *practicing* or "engaging the injunctions," in other words, most directly, "*doing the yoga!*" For instance, "Integral Yoga" is a practice developed by Aurobindo (and his student Haridas Chaudhuri), which was specially designed to be, Wilber explains, "a practice that unites both the *ascending* and *descending currents* in the human being—not just a transformation of consciousness, but of the body as well."[59] In a similar manner, the integral psychologist clearly maintains in *The Eye of Spirit* (1997): "This yogic injunction, exemplar, or practice is the real *transpersonal paradigm*, and without it (or something similar to it), you have no authentic transpersonal anything. At the very least, you must incorporate the necessity for this injunction into your system."[60] In other words, without authentic *practice* and subjective *transformation*, you will never really *walk the walk*.

In *A Theory of Everything* (2000), Wilber continues to emphasize using "a more integral map" to provide "a way to change the mapmaker," thus pointing to the limited effectiveness of even his own theoretical books and writings:

> What is required, in my opinion, is not simply a new integral theory or a new T.O.E., important as that is, but also a new *integral practice*. Even if we possessed the perfect integral map of the Kosmos, a map that was completely all-inclusive and unerringly holistic, that map itself would not transform people. We don't just need a map; we need ways to change the mapmaker! Thus, although most of my books attempt to offer a genuinely integral vision, they almost always end with a call for some sort of integral practice—*a practice that exercises body, mind, soul, and spirit in self, culture, and nature* (all-level, all-quadrant [or AQAL]).[61]

With the new millennium approach of the four quadrants (of Wilber/Phase-4/5), the integral theorist integrates *all-quadrants* and *all-levels* (including all states, lines, types, et al.), with each having their own methodologies, paradigms, and practices. The instructions are simple and direct: "Anybody can put together their own integral practice. The idea is to simultaneously exercise all the major *levels* and *dimensions* of the human bodymind—physical, mental, social, cultural, spiritual."⁶² This approach has evolved into what Wilber currently calls "Integral Lifee Practices" (or "ILP"), which is being heavily promoted by Integral Institute and other integral pioneers.

Orininally inspired by "Integral Transformative Practice" (or "ITP"), this idea was developed by two of the principal pioneers in the "human potential movement," i.e., Michael Murphy (founder of the famous Esalen Institute in Big Sur, California), and George Leonard (aikido master and well-known writer for *Look* magazine during the 1960s). Based upon years of leading-edge research conducted by some of the brightest minds in the human potential movement, their idea is to promote an *all-level* (body, heart, mind, soul, spirit) approach to human health by exercising the full range of human capacities and structural potentials. In their summary book on the subject, *The Life We Are Given: A Long-term Program for Realizing the Potential of Body, Mind, Heart, and Soul* (1995), they stress the necessity for each person to engage in a "*long-term program* for personal growth, joining physical, psychological, intellectual, and spiritual disciplines."⁶³ They also maintain that this project should be guided by scientific research as well as by the traditional injunctive practices, thus Murphy summarizes: "ITP is the integration of evolutionary theory with contemplative lore, and modern discoveries related to personal and social transformation."⁶⁴ Murphy, also the author of the monumental book *The Future of the Body: Explorations into the Further Evolution of Human Nature* (1992), clearly outlines the basic principles behind a genuine *integral transformative practice*.

> By *integral* we mean an approach that deals with the body through an emphasis on a sound diet and exercise. Such an approach addresses the mind through reading, discussion, and the deepening of our cognitive abilities. It also deals with the heart through group processes and community activities while touching the soul through meditation and imagery processes. By *transformative*, we

mean a set of activities that produces positive change in a person or group. By *practice*, we mean long-term, regular, disciplined activities that, beyond any specific external rewards, are valued in and of themselves.[65]

Consequently, Wilber has easily integrated this type of *all-level, full-spectrum* approach by adding the specific interests of the four quadrants into his conception of integral practice, thus placing it within a fully AQAL context in *A Theory of Everything* (2000): "*Integral Transformative Practice* attempts to exercise all of the basic waves of human beings—physical, emotional mental, and spiritual—in self, culture, and nature."[66] The point is to go around each quadrant, and then exercise the various *levels* of development which appear in those domains or *quadrants* of self/aesthetics/consciousness, culture/morals/ethics, and nature/science/environment. The directions, again, are easy: "The general idea of integral practice is clear enough: *Pick a basic practice from each category*, or from as many categories as pragmatically possible, and *practice them concurrently*—'all-level, all-quadrant' [or AQAL]."[67] Wilber, therefore, lists some representative examples of various practices from each quadrant:

Upper-Right quadrant (individual, objective, behavioral)—

- *Physical*
    - **Diet**—natural (organic) foods, vitamins, hormones, various food regimes, from Atkins to macrobiotics, etc.;
    - **Structural**—hatha yoga, weightlifting, aerobics, hiking, Rolfing, etc.

- *Neurological*
    - **Pharmacological**—various medications/drugs, where appropriate
    - **Brain/Mind machines**—to help induce theta and delta states of consciousness

Upper-Left quadrant (individual, subjective, intentional)

- *Emotional*
    - **Breath**—T'ai chi, yoga, bioenergetics, circulation of prana or feeling-energy, qi gong, etc.

o   **Sex**—appropriate sexuality; tantric sexual communion, self-transcending whole-bodies sexuality (based in heartfelt love)

- *Mental*
  - o   **Therapy**—psychotherapy, cognitive therapy, shadow work
  - o   **Vision**—adopting a conscious philosophy of life, visualization, affirmation

- *Spiritual*
  - o   **Psychic** (shamanic/yogi)—shamanic, nature mysticism, beginning tantric
  - o   **Subtle** (saint)—deity mysticism, yidam, contemplative prayer, advanced tantric
  - o   **Causal** (sage)—vipassana, self-inquiry, bare attention, centering prayer, Witnessing, formless mysticism
  - o   **Nondual** (siddha)—Dzogchen, Mahamudra, Shaivism, Zen, Eckhart, nondual mysticism

Lower-Right quadrant (social, interobjective)

- *Systems*—exercising responsibilities to Gaia (Earth), nature, biosphere, and geopolitical infrastructures at all levels
- *Institutional*—exercising educational, political, and civic duties to family, community, state, nation, world

Upper-Left quadrant (individual, subjective, intentional)

- *Relationships*—with family, friends, sentient beings in general; making relationships (and loving) part of one's growth, decentering the self
- *Community Service*—volunteer work, homeless shelters, hospice, etc.
- *Morals*—engaging the intersubjective world of the Good (morality), practicing compassion in relation to all sentient beings.[68]

The accompanying figure summarizes some of these representative practices involving the exercise, practice, and adequate *performance* of the various injunctions and methodologies enacting the four *quadrants* and *levels* or basic waves of existence in the AQAL Matrix. See Figure 13-3.

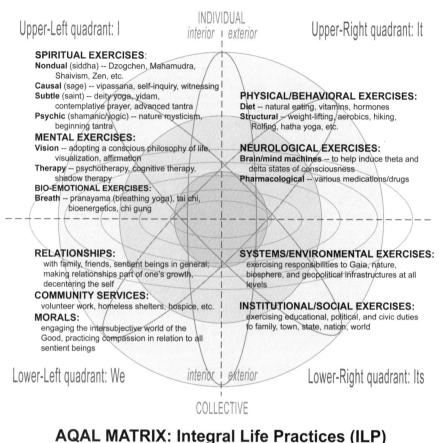

AQAL MATRIX: Integral Life Practices (ILP)
(some examples from *One Taste*, 1999)
Figure 13-3

These integral pioneers are proclaiming that only a genuine integral approach—in whatever guise or possible system (for there can be many, including traditional ones)—will be able to naturally and effectively encourage everyone to reach for the "farther reaches of human nature," as Maslow once termed it. As we've seen (in chapter 10), it takes an integral psychology based in a theoretical developmental understanding combined with a practical and pragmatic evolutionary approach to recommend the proper *transformative* practices, not just *translative* developments or improvements and stabilization on a certain level of consciousness (although these are important too). This includes transforming "temporary *states* into permanent *traits*," for as we are reminded again in *One Taste* (1999): "Whereas peak experiences can, and usually do, come spontaneously, in order to sustain them and turn them from a peak into a plateau—from a brief *altered state* into a more *enduring trait*—*prolonged practice* is required."[69] Once more, this is the difference between *translation* (the horizontal adaptation to a particular level) and *transformation* (the vertical growth to another level), thus generating "a spirituality that transforms."[70] For Wilber, this means, bottom line, "The point is simple: If you are interested in genuine transformative spirituality, find an authentic spiritual teacher and *begin practice*. Without practice, you will never move beyond the phases of belief, faith, and random peak experiences. You will never evolve into plateau experiences, nor from there into permanent realization. You will remain, at best, a brief visitor in the territory of your own higher estate, a tourist in your own true Self."[71] To practice takes motivation and understanding, a supportive environment, and most importantly, the "vow to grow" and *evolve*.

Once more, as always, this puts the ball back into our court, for the inspiration must ultimately come from within in order to be, well, to "be all that you can be." The best society and the environment can do (and this *is* their *responsibility*) is to provide adequate support for self-development, for people can't be forced to grow, to evolve. The integral psychologist plainly points this out: "Since you cannot *force* plants or people to grow, all you can really do is *set the conditions* that best allow the growth to occur (like water the plant). The State cannot demand the growth, but it can demand the conditions, and this it has traditionally done in the widely accepted demand for compulsory education."[72] The best the State can do (since "the state shall neither favor nor sponsor a particular version of the good life") is to provide, as Wilber says, "an atmosphere of encouragement."[73] What we can do, in response, is maintain our "vow to grow," which is exactly what Wilber advises: "In addition to self-esteem and accepting yourself the way you are now, you *also* need to meet yourself with real challenges and real demands—with real wisdom and real compassion—and therefore *vow to grow*, develop, and evolve into your own highest Estate."[74] The AQAL advice, therefore, will always be: "Take one or more practice from each of the levels of your own being—matter to body to mind to soul to spirit—and exercise *all of them* to the best of your ability, individually and collectively."[75] What better advice could anyone offer? Beside, all that is really required is just "adequate competence," not complete mastery.

This sensible approach to the spectrum of human potentials integrally involves family, community, society, global, universal, and spiritual relationships. However, since the requirement for further growth or evolution is only an adequate adaptation, or "adequate competence," to the lower foundational levels, then this will act as a true base for the higher unfolding of Spirit and Divine awareness. Wilber is very clear about this in *Sex, Ecology Spirituality* (1995): "It is merely necessary to develop an *adequate competence* at that stage, in order for it to serve just fine as a platform for the transcendence to the next stage,"[76] to which he later reaffirmed in *One Taste* (1999): "You absolutely do *not* have to develop perfect mastery of a lower stage before you can move to a higher stage—all that is required is a certain vague competency."[77] In other words, one doesn't have to fully master a stage of development, just show an adequate competency (for instance, a person doesn't have to be like Einstein to adequately master mathematics.) Then when the higher transpersonal and spiritual levels are exercised, engaged, and genuinely practiced, as we turn deeper within to embrace the Kosmos without, we will naturally enter into the time-honored and sacred practices of meditation and mystical contemplation.

The effectiveness of this type of integral approach for overall well-being is being demonstrated by the thousands of people who report they have been genuinely inspired by Wilber's Integral Vision for it becomes an encouragement to increase their own unfolding practices of self-development and self-transcendence. They do this by addressing the different levels or quadrants that need the greatest attention in order to improve or develop further to a greater degree of competence. For as the master psychologist summarizes in *Integral Psychology* (2000): "Each individual *discovers* the depths that are collectively given to all of us (we all have bodies and minds and souls and spirits, and none of us created those); but each individual discovers these depths by *creating* the surface features of each wave that will be *uniquely* his or hers (what you do with the body, mind, soul, and spirit: that is truly up to you). As always, we have to make the future that is given to us; and the full-spectrum therapist is an assistant in this extraordinary voyage that is both discovery and creation."[78] This is the real call of the leading-edge Centaurs: a call to authentic whole-body (mind-soul-spiritual) disciplined practice, thus, this is certainly a very important place where Wilber's at, for as we'll see next, this is how he takes his stand in bringing a *more integral* message into the "Flatland" reductionism of a modern "world gone slightly mad."

CHAPTER FOURTEEN

Flatland & Boomeritis (in a World Gone Slightly Mad)

All subjective truths (from introspection to art to consciousness to beauty) and all intersubjective truths (from morals to justice to substantive values) were collapsed into exterior, empirical, sensorimotor occasions. Collapsed, that is, into dirt. Literally. The great nightmare of scientific materialism was upon us....—a nightmare I have also called Flatland.... So in our quest for an integral holism, we want to *honor all four quadrants*, and not merely privilege one of them in a reductionism blatant [atomistic] or subtle [holistic].

—Ken Wilber, *Integral Psychology* (2000)

An Integral Vision (for a World Gone Slightly Mad)

WITHOUT LOOKING TOO HARD IT'S OBVIOUS TO MOST PEOPLE THAT the world at large is in dire circumstances—thus there's certainly the need for "an integral vision in a world gone slightly mad," as Ken Wilber aptly subtitled his Phase-4 book *The Eye of Spirit* (1997). Overpopulation, lack of resources, worldwide poverty, tribal genocide, species extinction, climate alteration, and the continuing war of worldviews and armed insurrections

317

(or violent revolutions) are only some examples of the difficult decisions facing global humanity. Although the "miracles" of science and technology abound, their arrogant hubris and conceit coupled with an unquestioned belief in the "promise of progress" to fix everything, from biogenetics to toxic pollution to cultural homogeneity, actually creates a frightening future if these powerful energies are not restrained with real wisdom and authentic ethical values. Postmodernity, although a blessing with its liberation movements of cultural tolerance, has still fostered a devastating dilemma of diversity where no one view can be held sacred or any better than any of the others, thus the universal currents of humankind are covered over with superficial surface values, while what the world really needs is a deeper global embrace, now more than ever.

To accomplish this without resorting to traditional approaches, which is impossible in a modern/postmodern world, will require a truly integral approach that can effectively untie Left (liberals) and Right (conservatives), Eastern and Western philosophies, science and spirituality. It will require the resurrection of interiors back into a collapsed Kosmos that has created a crippling war of worldviews overrun by a misguided scientific reductionism while traditional religious values seems to only encourage intolerant ethnocentric rivalries, thus leaving the contemporary person without an authentic moral compass in today's emerging global culture. This disastrous reductionism of modernity has left the world drowning in disposable surface values commercialized for mass consumption which only perpetuates a demoralizing "flatland" of despair and dissemblance. Consequently, people too often escape into a vast array of distractions and "substitute gratifications," from TV to movies to sports to cars to drugs to sex to the daily grind of work and family. However, all of these fall far short of true fulfillment and freedom, which the mystics claim is found only in Enlightenment or the complete transcendence of the desirous separate-self sense and its fear of death (and others). But since substitutes will never satisfy, then there's still the aching need for a genuine spirituality, not mythic absolutisms, for verifiable evidence, not media hype, for compassionate politics, not corporate wrangling, and it is to this deeper understanding that the Integral Vision lends a light.

Wilber summarized these dire circumstances on numerous occasions, such as on the last page of *Up from Eden* (1981), where he complained, "Through substitute seeking (Eros) and substitute sacrifices (Thanatos), a person propels himself or herself through the ocean of other equally driven souls, and the violent friction of these overlapping Atman projects sparks that nightmare called history."[1] Fifteen years later he summed up the same situation on the last page of his monumental book *Sex, Ecology, Spirituality* (1995), by saying, "Today's world of modernity gone slightly mad: Myth for the peasants, flatland naturalism for the intelligentsia."[2] A situation to which he later reported, "Many people looked at me and said, 'Only slightly?'"[3]

All of these issues and more are being addressed by numerous "post-postmodern" integrative philosophies, but perhaps none more so than the AQAL Approach. Importantly, this is not just a static theory of ideas but a call to real *integral transformative practices*, a sacred demand for *action*—to *do the yoga!* Unlike most paradigms, the Integral Vision isn't just proposing another philosophy to be learned or memorized; just another worldview among many, for it offers a wide enough embrace to include *all worldviews*, from the premodern to the modern to the postmodern. It accomplishes this by serving the process of true development that naturally recognizes a *value hierarchy* that can justly and compassionately distinguish the better and more evolved from the less evolved, showing how all can be rightly engaged in the further growth of love (and morality) to the heights and depths of the human potential. This vision engenders this revolution by uniting the Enlightenment of the West and East, which calls for the inalienable rights to both political *and* spiritual freedoms, a clarion call to humanity's true liberation and the real pursuit of happiness in the coming millennium. But first, the obstacles created by the previous millennia and their crippling worldviews must be overcome and released through their integration and transcendence, beginning with the disastrous flatland reductionism of modernity.

Flatland: The Disaster of Modernity

"Book Two" of *Sex, Ecology, Spirituality* (1995) was originally titled "Flatland" for it began Wilber's strong critique against the reductionism of modernity (or the various philosophies used by science and the modern world), including the general trends of postmodernity following in its wake. Wilber's criticism is especially harsh on the materialistic reductionism, whether atomistic or holistic, for it has led to an exaggerated *"scientific materialism"* (also known as *scientism*). He calls this reductionism the "collapse of the Kosmos" into a meaningless "Flatland," because it claims everything in the universe (including all interiors) is nothing more than "dead" physical matter (only exteriors). This means all the levels (of matter, mind, soul, spirit) of the Kosmic Mandala are collapsed or reduced to the lowest levels (of matter-only), therefore, for modernity there's nothing alive with spirit or consciousness (or depth and meaning). As Alfred North Whitehead (1861–1947) famously bemoaned, modern science thinks the universe is "a dull affair, soundless, scentless, colorless; merely the hurrying of material, endlessly, meaninglessly" (to which he pointedly added, "Thereby, modern philosophy has been ruined").[4]

For AQAL Metatheory, this materialism technically means that "Flat-land is simply the belief the *only the Right-Hand [exterior] world is real*—the world of matter-energy, empirically investigated by the human sense and their extension (telescopes, microscopes, photographic plates, etc.). All of the interior worlds are reduced to, or explained by, objective/exterior terms."[5] Wilber's integral critiques are designed to counter this and bring depth back into the scientific and modern reductionism rising from the "smoking ruins of Kant," first by recognizing, and then overcoming, the two primary forms of *reductionism* found in modern flatland:

- **Gross reductionism (atomistic)**—the positivist Ego camp committing the error of materialistic science; in AQAL terms: *gross reductionism* reduces all Left-Hand interiors to the Right-Hand exterior quadrants (matter)

- **Subtle reductionism (holistic)**—the "web-of-life" Eco camp committing the error of the Romantics; in AQAL terms: *subtle reductionism* reduces all Left-Hand interiors to the Lower Right quadrant (exterior holistic systems).[6]

Importantly, Wilber identifies this reductionistic collapse of the multi-leveled Kosmos as being the "disaster of modernity" (or the "bad news" of the modern world epitomized with the phrase "No more Ascent!"), which is a *dissociated* pathological condition that must be overcome or outgrown. However, unlike many of modernity's critics, Wilber also asserts a strong defense of the "dignity of modernity" (or the Good News of the modern world epitomized with Voltaire's rallying cry of "No more myths!"),[7] which includes the "immensely positive aspects of modernity, for it gave us the liberal democracies; the ideals of equality, freedom, and justice, regardless of race, class, creed, or gender; modern medicine, physics, biology, and chemistry; the end of slavery; the rise of feminism; and the universal rights of humankind."[8] Based on the dialectic of progress, Wilber emphasizes that the dignity of modernity is based on the *differentiation* of "the cultural value spheres" (i.e., the "Big Three" of *self* or "I," *culture* or "We," and *nature* or "It/Its"), whereas the disaster involves the *dissociation* (instead of differentiation) of the Big Three where the values of science, scientific materialism, and technological innovation, have come to dominate the domains of culture/ morality and the self/aesthetics.

In extending his developmental analysis of Western philosophical history, Wilber maintains that on the positive side, the "Age of Reason" involved the emergent shift from the mythic and mythic-rational to the rational worldviews as larger numbers of people had an increased access to *formal operational thought* (or *formal-rationality*) This includes reason's increased "space of possibilities," which has helped to ignite a series of social liberation movements that continue to this day. Wilber's Integral Vision once more defends the appropriate development of a strong mental-ego structure of consciousness based on mature self-autonomy (fulfilled with the integral-centaur), therefore, this philosophy embraces and includes the increased cognitive capability of reason and rationality (leading to vision-logic).

To counter these forms of modern reductionism, AQAL Metatheory is an integral call to resurrect not only *all-levels* of existence (epitomized by the premodern Great Chain of Being), but also *all-quadrants* (or the differentiations of modernity), which lays the foundation for the integration of real science and authentic religion (see chapter 4). Consequently, the necessary "task of postmodernity" is to realize, as Wilber explains, a "constructive postmodernity: the integration of art, morals, and science, at every level of the extraordinary spectrum of consciousness, body to mind to soul to spirit."[9] By doing so, the interiors of consciousness are rescued from reductionistic materialism, even given scientific validity, thus propelling humanity to grow beyond the Flatland wreck of a disastrous modernity, while yet still retaining its very important and positive dignities.

Retro-Romantics: Regress Express

With Wilber's Phase-4 books (1995–2000), not only was the integral philosopher instigating a strong integral critique against Flatland scientific materialism (both atomistic and holistic), but he also increased his attack on the postmodern versions of the Romantic ideology and their "recaptured-good-ness" models. In their favor, the original Romantics of the eighteenth and nineteenth centuries were a concerned form of intellectual reaction to the modern program of heightened rationality, especially the dissociative "disas-ters of modernity," yet, fortunately, their desire for wholeness also produced some of the most moving works of art ever created by the human spirit. Unfortunately, however, they also thought the "march of civilization" was a *devolution* from some past glorious "Golden Age" or "Paradisical Eden," therefore, since they generally recommend a "return to the past" as the solu-tion to modern ills, Wilber often labels them the "retro-Romantics."

As a way to metaphorically (yet sarcastically) critique these Romantic trends still active in the modern world, often expressed as popular "New Age" or "New Paradigm" theories, or what Wilber calls "Eco-Romantic" holistic theories, some of the Phase-4 writings strongly denounce their regressive slide to prerational thinking (and elevationism). He even polemically labels them "retro-Romantics," since they want to board their "Regress Express," or take the "Way Back Machine," and go back to some sort of utopian ideal (such as the earlier Romantics did by thinking ancient Greece was the pris-tine society). Yet, Wilber complains, this is nothing more than calling for the revival of premodern societies, including these two popular versions of Eco-Romanticism found in today's modern/postmodern culture:

- **Eco-feminists**—those postmoderns who believe we should resur-rect Goddess worship, such as that found in Neolithic villages, since, as Wilber explains, "for the ecofeminists, the especially hallowed period is that immediately preceding agrarian Greece, namely, the horticultural societies that flourished from roughly 10,000 B.C.E. to 4000 B.C.E., before the rise of the early empires and the agrarian 'patriarchy' in general."

- **Eco-masculinitists**—those postmoderns who believe we need to resurrect tribal lifestyles for, as Wilber explains, "the ecomasculinists (deep ecologists) [want] to push back even further into prehistory, to the previous stage of *foraging*, beyond which one cannot go (prior to foraging were apes). This *must* be the pure and pristine and 'non-dissociated' state, because there is no further destination left on the Regress Express."[10]

By taking this approach, the Romantics often *elevate* prerational or pre-personal (including magical and mythic) worldviews to higher levels than they actually are, such as with the "Noble Savage," thus mistaking them for rational and transrational (or transpersonal) developments. The integral view, of course, maintains this is the classic *pre/trans fallacy* (i.e., confusing *prepersonal* and *transpersonal* realities), an error that actually cripples future evolutionary possibilities. This critical analysis, of course, began nearly two decades earlier with the transition from the "recaptured-goodness" model of Wilber/Phase-1 to the evolutionary "growth-to-goodness" model of Wilber/Phase-2.[11] As a result, the AQAL Phase-4 books were even sometimes polemical in tone, for as Wilber explained later (1997): "You are never so vicious toward a theory as toward one that you yourself recently embraced."[12] Nonetheless, Wilber clarifies the overall intentions of the integral approach by acknowledging "even in the evolutionary arc itself, we want to balance the growth-to-goodness model and the recaptured-goodness model, both of which have much to offer."[13] This is a fine line of understanding, but one that only the pre/trans fallacy can clarify.

In answer to theses type of postmodern reactions to the *dissociations* (or pathological differentiations) of modernity and its regressive tendencies, the Integral Vision counters by strongly supporting an *evolutionary* model as being the best way to integrate this raging war and theoretical stand-off between the Ego (or materialists) and the Eco (or Romantics). Only with an integral evolutionary awakening, claims Wilber, will we be able to put an end to this "two-thousand-year-old battle at the heart of the West's attempt to awaken."[14] For as the integral pandit precisely and poetically notes in *The Marriage of Sense and Soul* (1998): "It is tomorrow, not yesterday, that our vision must be turned. And Idealism began in part with exactly that realization, and exactly that attack on Romanticism. The God of tomorrow, not the God of yesterday, comes to announce our liberation."[15] This is a situation AQAL Metatheory addresses directly by effectively including, as a foundational principle, the necessity to *practice*—to *engage the injunction* or *do the yoga*—by offering a radically inclusive methodological pluralism set within the context of integral transformative practices. In other words, evolution always has a chance to produce a better tomorrow and an improved present, but, as always, the future is what we make it.

Boomeritis & the Mean Green Meme (MGM)

In reviewing the integral social critique of his own "boomer" generation (arising out of the 1960s), it's still important to remember that Ken Wilber actually has much admiration and sympathy with the first generation in human history to enter en masse the stage of development known by Spiral Dynamics as the "green meme," the highest stage of development in first-tier thinking. Indeed, Wilber rightly commends the "many gifts of green" by recognizing that "green discloses, not a rational uniformitarianism that tends to ignore and marginalize anything not of its ilk, but a beautiful tapestry of multiple contexts, richly different cultural textures, pluralistic perceptions, and individual differences, and it becomes sensitive (the sensitive self!) to all of those often unheard voices. We have seen that every meme makes an invaluable contribution to the health of the overall spiral, and this pluralistic sensitivity is one of the great gifts of green."[16] Remember, the green meme emerges after scientific-rationality (orange), which emerged after conventional mythic-empires (blue), which emerged after magical-mythic tribalism (purple), etc., in the spiral of development (see chapter 12).

Nonetheless, the pluralistic relativism of green, and especially its anti-hierarchical stance, has caused it, according to Wilber, "to turn its guns on all post-green [or second-tier] stages as well, with the most unfortunate results. This has made it very difficult, and often impossible, for green to move forward into more holistic, integral constructions."[17] This "downside of green" and its insistence on *pluralistic relativism* and *deconstructionism* has diminished its ability to make value judgments and qualitative distinctions, especially when shunning any type of natural hierarchy (or holarchy). This problem is compounded by the fact that today's academia, and culture studies in particular, have been under the heavy sway of the postmodern green for over three decades. Since, according to Spiral Dynamics, first-tier memes tend to resist the emergence of second-tier memes, and since green is the highest stage of first-tier development, then the population of green consciousness can actually become one of the biggest obstacles to second-tier (or integral) development.

In this case, Wilber's postmodern critique has been particularly harsh on the pluralistic green meme mostly because "it is only *from* the stage of pluralism (green) that integralism can emerge (holistic second tier)."[18] This is where the "leading-edge" of greens (comprising approximately 25 percent of the U.S. population) could possibly shift into second-tier awareness (the yellow and turquoise memes), and in doing so swell the current 2 percent population of second-tier into higher percentages (see chapter 12). In turn, this could considerably effect the integral direction of the entire population of the planet. This is a large part of what's motivating Wilber to become such a strong social critic, even alienating some of his peers in the process (especially the Eco-Romantics and neopagans, etc.). However, the heat is worth it, for as the new century dawns the integral philosopher believes that "by highlighting our fixation to the green meme, we can begin more readily to transcend and include its wonderful accomplishments in an even more generous embrace."[19] This is exactly what has led Wilber, in this case, to his insightful yet somewhat controversial diagnosis of "boomeritis."

For quite some time, Wilber had been eyeing the situation of his own generation—the "Boomers" or "Baby Boomers" (or those people, particularly in America, born during the post-WWII boom of 1946–1964)—especially in regard to their increased interest in spirituality outside of conventional religion and the traditional church. During his early books (especially Phase-2), Wilber had already strongly criticized the "Dharma Bum" approach to spirituality. By the time the 1990s were coming to a close, he had identified that most Boomers (from hippies to yuppies) were engaging in mostly *translative* (not *transformative*) spirituality. Therefore, many of the green New Age Boomers were promoting, according to Wilber, "not a new authenticity—or way to find actual transcendence of the self—but a new legitimacy—or way to give meaning to the self."[20] In other words, Wilber agreed with researchers like Parson, Bellah, et al., that most Boomers were involved with a "person-centered civil religion" (PCCR) which, unfortunately, can be summarily characterized as being "antihierarchical, anti-institutional, anti-authority, antiscience, antirationality, and deeply subjectivistic."[21]

With an integral spectrum psychology, and epitomized in his Phase-2 book *A Sociable God* (1983), Wilber critically points out the important differences between "translation," which is a *horizontal* means of verifying legitimacy at a certain level (or stage of consciousness), and "transformation," which is the *vertical* transcendence to another higher-order level of consciousness (see chapter 10). The failure of *translative spirituality* is that all occasions of adaptation or assimilation to lower levels are basically in service to the self at that level (which is why it's justly described as being *legitimate*), therefore they're not *transformative* at all. In other words, as Wilber noticed, the "Me

Generation" is laced with a heavy dose of narcissism (or *subjectivism*) in their spirituality, which isn't too surprising as the title suggests.

By the end of the twentieth-century, this observation ignited Wilber's strong critique of the narcissistic or self-centered tendencies of the Boomers by labeling their dis-ease with the odd-sounding name of "boomeritis," which he defines as: "*Boomeritis* is that strange mixture of very high cognitive capacity (the green meme and noble pluralism) infected with rather low emotional narcissism—exactly the mixture that has been noted by so many social critics."[22] In this case, bolstered by narcissistic attitudes, such as "Fight the system!" and "Don't tell me what to do!" Wilber sees the laudable pluralism of green sink into "an often belligerent and reactionary defense—what might be called in this case 'the mean green meme' (which is especially the home of boomeritis)."[23] Therefore, the "mean green meme" (or "MGM") and *boomeritis* have become important critical tools in Wilber's push for a more integral revolution, especially since, as he points out in *A Theory of Everything* (2000): "It is now boomeritis and the MGM that are some of the primary roadblocks to a truly integral, more inclusive approach."[24] To counter these obstacles, he's been relentless in his critical attacks in order to encourage the green meme to more actively engage in *authentic transformative practices* and make the "quantum jump" to second-tier thinking (and to the higher transpersonal structures of consciousness).

Boomeritis: *A Postmodern Novel That Will Not Set You Free*

After publishing several Phase-4 books, as we mentioned, Wilber began his analysis and diagnosis of "boomeritis," or the narcissistic person-centered tendencies of the Baby-Boomer generation. Since this critical analysis was based on mounds of empirical evidence he had been collecting for years, as well as upon the views of other social critics, Wilber first decided to write a scholarly treatise on the subject. Yet, he (and others) were finding that its harsh critical tone, plus the possible negative impact from those being critiqued, prompted him to rewrite it several times, until he finally ended up couching it in a more readable novel format. The year of 2002 finally saw the publication of *Boomeritis: A Novel That Will Set You Free* (by Shambhala Publications), Wilber's first attempt at writing a fictitious novel, or what he calls "a postmodern novel," since he's trying to embody many of the characteristics he was criticizing (such as narcissism and irony).

Boomeritis, the novel, is actually another literary device created by Wilber to continue his strong critique of the "mean green meme," or the narcissistic tendencies of many modern and *postmodern relative pluralists* or the "green meme." Mostly the didactic passages are aimed at those postmodern theorists who have hijacked academia and popular culture the past three decades, which is one of the reasons why the narrative is set at a university (at the fictitious Integral Center). Seen through the mind and voice of a Gen-Xer college student (narcissistically named Ken Wilber), the author takes everyone on a wild ride through a series of classroom lectures peppered with fantasy sequences, ecstatic drug experiences, political scenarios, youthful sex, mis-guided parents, narcissistic victims, and just about everything else within the electrified interconnected world of postmodernity and modernity, even giving hints of tantric God-Realization (or orgasmic Goddess-communion). These various experiences, therefore, become a means to review and critique the plethora of today's worldviews and attitudes. Even the subtitle itself is an ironic put-down of the many best-selling self-help books that are so popular among Boomers.

Some of these critical ideas had been snowballing partly because Wilber had come under some intense critical attack by many of the academic green proponents of pluralistic relativism since the emergence of the Phase-4/5 AQAL Model in 1995. Thus, he's had a lot to say about the matter, especially since the characteristics of boomeritis are some of the main obstacles in the emergence of a worldwide Integral Culture. Since these developmental comments on boomeritis are an important integral critique of contemporary culture, then the prolific philosopher wrote hundreds of pages detailing his arguments that first appeared as "sidebars" and "endnotes" (endnotes to a novel!, he sighed). These were posted on Shambhala's website during the early years of the new millennium, but they'll now be published together with the novel *Boomeritis* in upcoming *The Collected Works of Ken Wilber, Volume Ten* (2006).

Whatever else it may be, *Boomeritis* is an amazing postmodern novel that clearly intends to point the way out of today's pluralistic madness by suggesting the way of authentic transformative methodologies based on a wildly embracing meta-perspective. Once again, Wilber ends up championing *real practice*, not just theories to be memorized or another "new-paradigm" to read about. Using the green meme (the sensitive, ecologically-based self) as an excellent encapsulation of Boomer concerns, from the noble to the regressive, Wilber has swung his sharp sword of critical wisdom into action and has punctured many of the favorite theories and philosophies of boomer narcissism, including the majority of university academia and their preference for deconstructionism and relative pluralism. Nonetheless, in caring for the entire spiral of development (from beige to platinum), the integral approach is instigating the transformative evolution to the higher-order levels of individual and collective consciousness. And, as we've seen, this directly entails the "leading-edge cultural elite," from whatever generation, with their further embodiment of integral consciousness (and aperspectival vision-logic), not the narcissistic madness of the current modern world.

From Postmodernity to Universal Integralism

In addition to his penetrating analyses of modernity, Ken Wilber's Phase-4/5 writings have also demonstrated a masterful understanding of, and respect for, postmodernity, the general trend of philosophy following in the wake of modernity. Wilber sums up their most important (but partial) truth: *"Interpretation is an intrinsic feature of the fabric of the universe:* there is the crucial insight at the heart of the great postmodern movements,"[25] or in short, "interpretation: the heart of the postmodern."[26] Yet, of course, he also levels a strong integral critique at postmodernity as well, especially at their "extreme" trends, or "strong versions," such as with *deconstructionism, poststructuralism,* and an exaggerated *relative pluralism* and *nihilistic narcissism* (sometimes called *"boomeritis"* by Wilber). In *The Marriage of Sense and Soul* (1998), the integral philosopher concisely and brilliantly summarized his views on postmodernity's attempt "to deconstruct the world" as being in an attempt to counter the dissociations and disasters of flatland modernity by undermining science in its own foundations (e.g., dismissing the representative paradigm or science's "myth of the given").[27]

In reviewing postmodernism, Wilber first reviews the all-important *"the linguistic turn* in philosophy" that was begun by pioneering linguist Ferdinand de Saussure (1857–1913), since this set the stage for twentieth-century postmodernity with "the general realization that language is not simply a representation of a pregiven world, but also has a hand in the creation and construction of that world."[28] This linguistic insight has led to most forms of postmodern poststructuralism, which Wilber reviews in depth by emphasizing that the "three postmodern core assumptions are quite accurate, and need to be honored and incorporated in any integral view," including the following versions of Postmodernism:

- **Constructivism/deconstructionism**—maintains that "reality is not in all ways simply pregiven, but in some significant ways is a construction, an interpretation";

- **Contextualism**—maintains that "meaning is context-dependent, and contexts are boundless";

- **Integralism**—maintains that "cognition must therefore unduly privilege no single perspective [*integral-aperspectivalism*]."[29] Therefore, for Wilber, this provides the possibility for a *"constructive postmodernism"* (not just a deconstructive one) that genuinely integrates the best of premodernity (the *levels* of the Great Nest of Spirit) and modernity's differentiations (the *quadrants* or Big Three of self, culture, and nature), all tied together with the discovery of evolution, yet, as Wilber reassures us, this will be presented "not in a rigid or absolutists fashion, but in a fluidly holonic and multidimensional tapestry."[30]

The positive versions are the Good News of postmodernity, whereas the Bad News, as Wilber skillfully explains, is that because "depth takes a vacation," and "language collapses," then "postmodernism came to embrace surfaces, champion surfaces, glorify surfaces, and surfaces alone."[31] This leads to postmodern irony and cynicism, based on a worldview that claims there is "no value, no meaning, and no qualitative distinctions of any sort," thus humanity's left with a "disenchanted world" (Weber), a "disqualified universe" (Mumford), the nightmare of "one-dimensional man" (Marcuse). This is part of the reason why postmodern "aperspectival madness" (or extreme relativism), which claims every view is equally correct ends up erecting a postmodern "Tower of Babel," a condition where Wilber only hears "each voice claming to be its own validity, yet few of them actually honoring the values of the others."[32] Yet still, he reminds us, "postmodern pluralism" or "relative pluralism" is built upon the multiple perspectives of *early vision-logic*, a necessary and important stage in the spiral of consciousness development. Pluralistic relativism has yet to discover the value of *evolutionary depth* as the way to unite all the multiple perspectives or all the "true but partial" voices singing in the universal choir of unrelenting diversity. AQAL Metatheory, on the other hand, makes this inclusive evolutionary approach the basis of its postmodern mission.

A truly integral model, or what Wilber calls "the path of constructive postmodernism" (such as AQAL Metatheory) represents the "quantum jump" to second-tier thinking with a developmental holism that can even unite science and spirituality (see chapter 4). Thus Wilber foresees a "brighter promise" for the future: "And *that* marriage would allow us to move forward to the bright promise of a *constructive postmodernity*: the integration of art, morals, and science, at every level of the extraordinary spectrum of consciousness, body to mind to soul to spirit."[33] This "universal integralism" will naturally promote a tolerant and compassionate "unity-in-diversity"—or a *Unitas Multiplex*—built upon recognizing the many levels and dimensions in the Great Holarchy of Spirit. As the integral visionary explains, "*integral-aperspectivism*—this unity-in-diversity, this *universal integralism*—discloses global interconnections, nests within nests within nests, and vast holarchies of mutually enriching embrace, thus converting pluralistic heapism into integral holism."[34] This alternative of a fully integral approach gives birth to more optimistic solutions to many of modern Flatland problems by reintroducing "the within, the deep, the interior of the Kosmos, the contours of the Divine."[35] Such an embrace of reality, as we've learned, could possibly herald the true "New Age" as the Integral Age, thus Wilber optimistically concludes in *A Theory of Everything* (2000): "The advantage of second-tier integral awareness is that it more creatively helps with the solutions to [the world's] pressing problems…. In all these ways and more, we could indeed use an Integral Vision for a world gone slightly mad."[36] One of the more effective remedies, therefore, will be to stop turning a blind eye to the role of the feminine in human development and evolution itself.

Integrating the Feminine

Another common misunderstanding made by some critics of Wilber's work is that his integral theories undervalues, or misses entirely, the importance of women and feminine values, yet this is an unjustified criticism. What Wilber does do is *not* elevate their importance nor privilege the feminine or feminist position, not because he's a man, but rather because their concerns have always been an integral part of his overall philosophy and politics.

From his earliest books, Wilber has addressed the feminine, including the dynamics involved between masculine and feminine values, between male and female interactions, between the historical effects of the patriarchy and matriarchy. With the AQAL Approach, Wilber has attached great impor- tance to developing an "integral feminism," with an accompanying inte- gral "gender studies," including the valuable contributions being made by contemporary women scholars who are beginning to use a fully-developed integral model (see chapter 11).

According to Wilber, the evidence clearly shows that "men and women both develop through the same *gender-neutral basic structures* or expanding spheres of consciousness," although each does have their own emphasis or tendencies, which are expressed "in a different voice" (after Carol Gilligan). In a chapter dedicated to the subject titled "Integral Feminism: Sex and Gender on the Moral and Spiritual Path," he summarized in *The Eye of Spirit* (1997): "Men tend to develop through these expanding spheres with an emphasis on *agency*, rights, justice, and autonomy, whereas Women tend to develop through the same holarchical spheres based more on *communion*, responsibil- ity, relationship, care, and connection."[37] Because the integral approach main- tains that all holons exist in relationship as *agency-in-communion* (whether male or female), then it also insists that "neither the male nor female disposi- tion is itself higher or lower, or deeper or wider, on the nested holarchy of basic structures."[38] Integral theory, in other words, brings together women and men while appreciating their differences and unique gifts.

By embracing both halves of humanity as being valuable participants, Wilber affirms that AQAL Metatheory needs to constantly "keep our eye on both the profound similarities as well as the intricate differences between men and women, and resist the urge to sink our discussion in an ideologi- cal fervor to promote one at the expense of the other."[39] A genuine integral approach honors and includes the uniqueness of women and men while recognizing their *androgynous* nature or their *universal deep features* of being human. Ultimately, and all of this is accounted for in Wilber's sophisti- cated integral approach, because of men and women's *trans*-personal nature, then in the higher developments of consciousness both the Male (Shiva) and Female (Shakti) are "married" (or united and transcended) in the Unifying Heart of Tantra or nondual Oneness.

In addition, an integral reading of history shows that both men and women have always worked together in pushing humankind forward in its

progressive development, including during the historical rise and dominance of the patriarchy (a condition which, according to Wilber, too many
feminists claim to be only the victims). In this case, as a counter to current
feminist thought, the integral pandit concludes in *Sex, Ecology, Spirituality*
(1995): "Women do not have to take back their power because they never
gave it away; they co-selected, with men, the best possible societal arrange-
ments under the extremely difficult environmental and social conditions
of the time."[40] Wilber therefore emphasizes that in actuality "Female Liberation" has only been possible because of the positive gains made during
the modern age of rational self-autonomy. Equal rights have only become
possible with an industrial age that clearly differentiates the *noosphere* (or
the powers of the mind) from the *biosphere* (or the powers of the body), a
fact many feminists overlook. Wilber maintains that "when the noosphere
and the biosphere were finally differentiated, *biology was no longer destiny*,"[41]
then this development has allowed women to more equally participate in
both worlds, since in the mental world physical strength becomes *irrelevant*
(although preserved yet negated).

Built upon the growing platform of an *industrial technological-economic
base* (created by the mental-rational Machine Age and Industrial Age), Wilber argues that it was this historical process of development that's set the
stage for the planetary liberation of *both* men and women. However, due
to the dreadful dissociations of the traditional patriarchy, which supports a
male-dominated political sphere, then the necessary elevation of the feminine role to equal status will only serve the emerging Integral Age. In fact,
Wilber proclaims in *Sex, Ecology, Spirituality* (1995): "At this time in history—in *today's* world—it is especially the role of the *female as historical
agent* that can *bridge the two values spheres* [of masculine and feminine]."[42] In
the early phases of his work, Wilber was already aware of the vital evolutionary role that women, and the feminine archetypal energies, would play in
bringing about the holistic emergence of centauric awareness in our current
times. In *Up from Eden* (1981), for instance, he announced: "The new Hero
will be centauric (which means mind and body united and not dissociated),
whole-bodied, mentally androgynous, psychic, intuitive *and* rational, male
and female—and the lead in this new development most easily can come
from the female, since our society is *already* masculine-adapted."[43] In other
words, the feminine is indispensable in lifting humanity and future generations into the higher developmental potentials of consciousness evolution.

As we've already seen, it's the emerging of the "centaur" (or integrated bodymind) with its "vision-logic" (or second-tier awareness) and its *universal integralism* that develops beyond (yet includes) the modern egoic-rational consciousness (and all the other first-tier memes). Therefore, it will be both female and male centaurs working together who will initiate the integral revolution for a new planetary culture. They will act from both *within* and then from *without,* thus integrating the concerns of modern liberals with traditional conservatives, and finally marrying science and spirituality with wisdom and compassion. Only with women and men side-by-side does humanity have a chance of developing and applying an increased awareness that cares for all people, child and adult, as well as all other sentient beings on this sacred planet Earth. Another effective remedy, therefore, will be to stop turning a blind eye to necessary process of unfolding human development and evolution itself.

Irony of Liberalism: Developmental Blindness

Unlike the various visions of extreme postmodernity, whose theories Wilber has consistently criticized (based on a thorough understanding of their literature), the vision of integral multiculturalism (or a genuine *unitas multiplex*) doesn't fail to incorporate the evolutionary fact that "cultural tolerance is secured only by rationality as universal pluralism."[44] By taking a *developmental view* based on the evidence of evolution, including that found in human psychology, Wilber was able to see that *"pluralistic relativism is actually a very high developmental achievement,"*[45] a fact the pluralistic relativists themselves have been overlooking. As we've seen, the postmodern developments of individual freedom, the tolerant inclusion of multiple perspectives *(aperspectival),* and the liberation from unfair conventions, are evidence of *postconventional* and *worldcentric* development, or what integral psychology calls *post-formal cognition* or *vision-logic* and *network-logic* (of the integral-centaur).

In this case, since the emergence of Wilber/Phase-4/5, the integral theorist has been on a serious mission to counter this "great irony of liberalism," which unintentionally denies its own stage of development. As he points out in *A Theory of Everything* (2000), because liberalism itself is the product of a whole series of interior stages of consciousness development, evolving from egocentric to ethnocentric to worldcentric, then ironically, *"The liberal stance itself is the product of stages that it then denies*—and there is the inherent contradiction of liberalism."[46] By denying the unfolding structures of consciousness, the modern liberal makes a *performative contradiction*, so like the conservatives, the moderns, and the postmoderns (including greens) they find themselves caught in a materialistic Flatland collapse of the Kosmos. Consequently, Wilber strongly believes this is "the most pressing political issue of the day, both in America and abroad, [to find] a way to integrate the tradition of liberalism with a genuine spirituality."[47] According to AQAL Metatheory, of course, this is accomplished by integrating the interiors and exteriors (or the four quadrants) with all the developmental levels and stages in the spectrum of consciousness.

In a note to the reader titled "On God and Politics," the integral philosopher opens *The Eye of Spirit* (1997) by strongly suggesting it's absolutely crucial to find a new conception of God (and Spirit) that finds resonance with the noblest aims of liberalism. As a solution, liberalism must become *progressive* and *evolutionary*, instead of resorting to Romantic fantasies of returning to the past or regaining a lost primal goodness. The best way to *protect* true diversity and multiculturalism, according to Wilber, is to engage the difficult demand for growth and postconventional goodness, the worldcentric stance of the integral-centaur anchored in vision-logic. Without encouraging developmental growth beyond the magic, mythic, and mental-egoic worldviews, then the sad irony will remain that worldcentric liberalism will always be sabotaging its own higher-order agenda (of political freedom).

Integral Politics: Uniting Liberals & Conservatives

The moral imperatives of evolutionary understanding, such as voiced by Spiral Dynamics (with its "prime directive") and Ken Wilber's Integral Vision (with its "basic moral intuition"), is definitely applicable in the real world of politics and economics (also known as *realpolitik*). One of the approaches currently being explored by integral thinkers is to suggest a possible "Third Way" politics that moves beyond the traditional dualism of Left liberals versus Right conservatives. Thus the goal of a genuine "Integral Politics" is to unite the best of the liberals and conservatives philosophies by conceding that each has a "true but partial" stance to offer. The optimal approach, in this case, would be to construct a more integral model of politics integrating the best of the *premodern conservatives* (blue), *modern liberals* (orange), and *postmodern pluralists* (greens) with the emerging postliberal stance of the integral-centaur, or the postconventional moral development of *universal integralism.*

Based on a developmental understanding, Wilber's political views were first clearly articulated in the engaging last chapter to *Up from Eden* (1981) appropriately titled "Republicans, Democrats, and Mystics." In these closing pages, the integral philosopher began by first outlining "the eventual core of a truly unified, critical sociological theory" (based around the "hierarchic *levels of exchange*"), which he then collapsed into the three basic worldviews explaining why human beings suffer (and how to alleviate that). In response to the problem of human suffering, Wilber insightfully observed that the modus operandi of the "Republicans" (or conservatives), the "Democrats" (or liberals), as well as the world's Mystics (or sages), could be summarized as:

- **Liberals**—the *objective* Democrats or *progressive* Humanist-Marxist approaches—or those who "tend to believe in *objective causation...* that is, if an individual is suffering, the typical liberal tends to blame objective social institutions (if you are poor it is because you are oppressed by society)."

- **Conservatives**—the *subjective* Republicans or *traditional* Freudian-Conservative approaches—or those who "tend to believe in *subjective causation...* [that is] the typical conservative tends to blame subjective factors (if you are poor it is because you are lazy)."[49]

- **Nondual Mystics**—the sages who universally claim that "men and women are unfree because there exists a belief in the existence of a 'true' self in the first place," therefore, these highly evolved soul claim that "we are not to repress or unrepress the self, but rather undermine it; transcend it; see through it."[50]

Simply put, liberal/humanists tend to emphasize the "exterior" *social* causes, while conservative/traditionals tend to emphasize the "interior" *subjective* causes. An "Integral Politics," of course, includes both, for as Wilber simply states: "A true Third Way would emphasize both interior development and exterior development."[51] A genuine "all-level, all-quadrant" or AQAL approach to politics involves all the *stages* of development (or all-level) in combination with all the *interiors and exteriors* as they appear in self, culture, and nature (or all-quadrant). But still, most importantly, this "theory of everything" also includes the mystic's point-of-view as well. Wilber expertly explains their solution to human suffering: "The aim of the mystics is to deliver men and women from their battles by delivering them from their boundaries. Not manipulate the subject, and not manipulate the object, but transcend both in nondual consciousness.... The ultimate solution to unfreedom, then, is neither Humanistic Marxist, nor Freudian-Conservative, but Buddhist: *satori, moksha, wu,* release, awakening, *metanoia.*"[52]

Since the new millennium, Ken Wilber has been working with various political theorists and several well-known politicians, first by offering his own general orientations towards the Left and Right (such as those stated above), and then adopting some of their important insights as well, including communications with "advisors to Bill Clinton, Al Gore, Tony Blair, and George W. Bush, among others."[53] As another example, the political theorists Lawrence Chickering (*Beyond Left and Right,* 1993) and Drexel Sprecher have differentiated the "order" and "free" wings of the Left liberalism and the Right conservatism. Wilber summarizes their insights in *A Theory of Everything* (2000): "The *order wings* of both Left and Right wish to impose their beliefs on all, usually via government, whereas the *free wings* of both ideologies place the rights of individuals first," therefore, "the interior quadrants are right/conservative [subjective causation], and the exterior quadrants are left/liberal [objective causation]."[54] In significant ways, these "political quadrants" align themselves to the *upper quadrants* (of individuals), which are the individual's "free" aspects, while the *lower quadrants* are the collective or "order" aspects. Once more, an AQAL analysis expands upon the traditional approaches to political theory by emphasizing the need to include both.

Based upon these original observations about "Democrats, Republicans, and Mystics," integral political theory recognizes each of their advantages (or Good News) and their disadvantages (or Bad News). An alternative "Integral Politics," therefore, solves the conventional dilemma of Left/Right politics by honoring both sides of the debate, while also providing a positive third alternative:

- **Liberalism** (liberal Left)—its Good News is its "emphasis on individual freedom," "rejection of [conventional] herd mentality," "economic and political freedoms," etc., yet its Bad News could be summarized by saying "religious tyranny was simply replaced by economic tyranny."[55]

- **Conservatives** (conservative Right)—its Good News is its "deep contexts of family, community, and spirit," the "fabric of community," yet their Bad News which generates an ethnocentric "cultural tyranny."[56]

- **Integral Politics** (Third Way)—its Good News is its "integration of real science and authentic spirituality" by integrating the world-views of *premodernity* (*all-levels* of the Great Chain), *modernity* (*all-quadrants* of the Big Three), and *postmodernity* (their integration), the Bad News is it's a higher-order development, therefore the lower levels must be cared for first to create a developmental base and foundation for further consciousness evolution.

By making sure that both interior *and* exterior causes are taken into account, then these detailed and complex AQAL cross-analyses are extremely fruitful in finding viable solutions to many current political concerns. Since an AQAL Metatheory offers one of the sturdiest foundations yet for achieving these integrative goals, then Wilber concludes "an 'all-level, all-quadrant' [AQAL] approach once again can serve as a theoretical basis for a truly integrated political orientation."[57] As a widely respected modeling scheme, the integrative capacity of the AQAL Approach provides "second-tier solutions" beyond the traditional and modern approaches, which too often reflects their own deficiencies and prejudices. The integral approach, on the other hand, offers a way to reunite what's been fragmented by moving beyond the previous limitations of earlier worldviews and their ethnocentric eras. In this case, it seems nothing could be more pertinent for our global times, especially with the polarized politics in the United States. The actual details for this type of integration, of course, are yet to be seen, but this important dialogue to one of humankind's most critical concerns: the effective management of local, national, international, and global politics, is finally becoming *more integral* in its approach, thus finding room to include the full spectrum of reality and all the world's people.

Spiritual Humanism: Eastern & Western Enlightenment

The answer for many of these political issues that are beginning to be offered by centauric vision-logic and *universal integralism*, according to Wilber, is evidence of an emerging "spiritual liberalism," or "spiritual humanism," a concept that ties together and underlies all of his Phase-4/5 books.[58] In *The Eye of Spirit* (1997), he specifically outlined this integral agenda for establishing an authentic spirituality that also includes the scientific and political foundations made by the Enlightenment of the West: "The gains of the liberal Enlightenment need to be firmly retained, but set in the context of a spirituality that profoundly defuses and answers the very real and very accurate objections raised by the Enlightenment. It will be a spirituality that rests on, not denies, the Enlightenment [of the West]. It will be, in other words, a liberal Spirit."[60] In other words, it's not just a modern liberalism lost in flatland madness (reductionism), but one that's also based on the gain of authentic mysticism, epitomized by the Enlightenment (or God-Realization) highly-valued in the East.

In *The Marriage of Sense and Soul* (1998), the integral philosopher brilliantly integrates the ideals expressed by both the "Western Enlightenment," which he defines as "the assertion that *the state does not have the right to legislate or promote any particular version of the good life*," with those of the "Eastern Enlightenment," which he simply defines as "*any genuine spiritual experience.*"[61] Since Western Enlightenment offers the people *political freedom*, and Eastern Enlightenment offers the people *spiritual freedom*, then both forms together (which includes the entire spectrum of consciousness) become the necessary ingredients for true human happiness and genuine world peace.

This great quest for a "spiritual humanism," or a "transcendental naturalism" (by whatever name you wish), is inherently *political* since it's keenly aware of, and actively participating, in the "real world" (see chapter 4). From an integral perspective, therefore, *authentic spirituality* will always be a *political act*, for it's deeply aware of its rights and responsibilities to others and the environment (as a human holon with agency-and-communion). This healthy integration of premodern religion (authentic spirituality) with modern science (deep sciences) not only "marries science and religion," but it gracefully unites the truly liberal Enlightenment of the West (exercising political freedoms) with the truly sacred Enlightenment of the East (exercising spiritual freedoms). A more integral vision for a world gone totally mad could not be had.

Scientia Visionis: *Evolutionary Politics*

By placing a strong emphasis on the evolutionary development of Spirit-in-action, Wilber is moved to present an eloquent postmodern defense of Idealism, the nineteenth-century evolutionary philosophy that arose in response to science's discovery of evolution (extending beyond the reductionistic implications of Charles Darwin). Idealism was epitomized with the brilliant minds and philosophies of such towering geniuses as Friedrich von Schelling (1775–1854), one of Wilber's all-time favorites, and another favorite, G. W. F. Hegel (1770–1831). Although they both produced a "truly stunning vision" proposing an evolutionary process of "God-in-the-making," Wilber insightfully criticizes the fact they "possessed *no yoga*—that is, no tried and tested practice for reliably reproducing the transpersonal and superconscious insights that formed the very core of the great Idealist vision," therefore, the glory of their evolutionary vision was relegated to "mere metaphysics."[60] AQAL Metatheory, on the other hand, directly addresses this problem by effectively including, as a foundational principle, the necessity to *practice*, to *engage the injunction*, to *do the yoga*, yet occurring within the context of *Integral Transformative Practices* and a thoroughly developed *Integral Post-Metaphysics* (see chapter 5).

Unlike the Idealists, however, who had "no yoga" or a way to developmentally reproduce their transpersonal insights, the Integral Vision offers a pluralism of methodologies disclosing the entire spectrum of consciousness, from matter to nature to mind to soul to God, evolving the self in the spiral of development from ignorance to ego to Enlightenment. According to Wilber, this healthy union of real religion with broad deep sciences is probably the best way to realize the *summum bonum* of the Good Life, for it honors all people wherever they live in the spiral of evolutionary development as well as honoring the divinity within us all. Thus the Integral Vision finds it absolutely necessary to promote these integral theories and transformative practices, not by violence, force, and coercion, but "through the powers of advocacy and example" enacted as a "gentle pacer of transformation" (see chapter 12).

This is where the possibility of any real "New Age" or "Integral Millennium" exists: with the authentic practices and evolutionary transformation of individuals who will then influence institutional and global transformation, if there's to be one. Thus, we find the integral prophet proclaiming with his last words on the last page of his mighty magnum opus, *Sex, Ecology,*

Spirituality: The Spirit of Evolution, or volume 1 of *The Kosmos Trilogy*, where exactly the world is at: "And so there we stand now, at rationality, poised on the edge of transrational perception, a *scientia visionis* that is bringing here and there, but ever more clearly, to all sorts of people in all sorts of places, powerful glimmers of a true Descent of the all-pervading World Soul."[61] The Integral Vision—a *scientia visionis* (or deep science) combined with authentic spiritually (or real religion)—is a world philosophy and theory of everything which wants to attain our political freedoms—epitomized by the Enlightenment of the West—along with our spiritual freedoms—epitomized by the Enlightenment of the East—and in doing so, possibly initiate a genuine global evolution revolution.

CHAPTER FIFTEEN

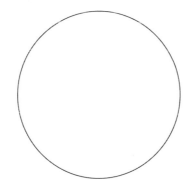

Where Wilber's Going: The Integral Revolution

Each transformation is a process of death and rebirth: death to the old level, and transformation to and rebirth on the newly emergent level. And, according to the sage, when all layers of self have been transcended—when all deaths have been died—the result is only God in final Truth, and a new Destiny beyond destiny is resurrected from the stream of consciousness.

—Ken Wilber, *A Sociable God* (1983)

Dharma Combat: A Shout from the Heart

AFTER REVIEWING THROUGHOUT THIS BOOK WHERE WILBER'S AT, OR AT least *partially*, hopefully we now have a better understanding why this type of Integral Vision is so significant—it will act as a gentle pacer of transformation through the spiral of evolutionary development, both individually and collectively. Although, as I've mentioned, it's impossible to say *exactly* where Wilber's at, it's always possible to say what Wilber's doing—emancipatory writing!—or the literary and intellectual expressions that are attempting to serve the liberation of human beings. Another way to see this is as "dharma combat," or the intellectual and philosophical arguments in support of non-dual Enlightenment (or God-Realization). Importantly, this liberation is not to be achieved with just temporary "peak experiences," or all-encompassing "theories of everything," but it must become an enduring way of life based upon an authentic spirituality transforming "states into traits," thus more fully realizing the spectrum of our inherited human potentials.

Throughout this book I have suggested that by elucidating his "integral vision," Wilber's something like a modern-day version of the Bodhisattva Manjushri, known for his piercingly sharp intellect, since Wilber, too, in his own times, is a smart defender of the true path of Enlightenment (both gradual and sudden). Yet as we've also seen, in Wilber's case it's done with a cognitive model called the "AQAL Matrix" and "AQAL Metatheory" based on centauric vision-logic grounded in nondual Spirit. By waving his "pen" of penetrating insight (actually, fingers dancing across the feather-light keyboard of an IBM ThinkPad), the integral pandit has been for years engaging in an intense intellectual battle to clarify and support the nondual position of enlightened realization (and ego transcendence), yet done with an *Integral Post-Metaphysics* that includes the positive achievements gained by the modern scientific and postmodern mind. Consequently, like a true bodhisattva, this integral pandit wants to enlighten the whole entire Kosmos, to shower everyone with the Good, the True, and the Beautiful. But, as always, it's still up to all of us. Nonetheless, since Wilber's books are published and sold in a popular spiritual marketplace that generally promotes paths geared to "empowering" the self, then his powerful indictments on the pathologies of the mental-ego, especially the self's regressive slides into prepersonal realms, has made his work less than desirable for a large number of contemporary theorists and writers.

"Dharma combat" is a useful term, therefore, in describing the intellectual defense of the "Dharma" (with a capital "D"), a Sanskrit word meaning the "lawful order of the universe." In more general terms (i.e., non-Buddhist), it indicates the universal "Teaching of Truth" given by the world's enlightened spiritual masters, from Buddha to Jesus to Mohammed to the Dalai Lama to Adi Da (thus sometimes called "the Perennial Philosophy," also known in India as *"sanatana dharma"* or the "eternal truth/teaching"). The Dharma, as a teaching, explains the divine nature of things (the Kosmos), including the reasons for the sufferings of the self, since the real Truth (i.e., God or *sunyata*) is within consciousness and thus within all human beings, regardless of race, culture, type, or surface value. Defenders of the Dharma, therefore, in order to make their case for the finer points of these esoteric and complex teachings, will often have to argue for authentic *vertical transformation* with the continued transcendence of the ego-I (or the self). Transformation of consciousness, in other words, instead of *horizontal translation* or adjusting to a particular level of development, is what opens the way towards divine realization. In most cases, the mind needs a strong presentation that's able to critically break through the confusions and illusions of the ego-I or the various levels of self-identity, including those inherited from our collective worldviews. Since Enlightenment involves ego-transcendence, not egoic fulfillment, then the separate-self often feels uncomfortable and threatened in the face of such powerful spiritual demands. This is when clever defenses of nondual knowing might sometimes come across as an "angry wisdom," or being overly harsh and too critical of the other less-than-enlightening theories propagated all around. But, in this case, it's a message that clearly "shouts from the heart," for it's sincerely based in a compassionate love that only wants to serve everyone's happiness in finding out that they, too, are God or Spirit.

Once again, by identifying the important differences between surface structure *translation* (or adaptation *to* a level) and deep structure *transformation* (or the change *between* levels), which Wilber summarizes in his important essay, "A Spirituality That Transforms: Translation versus Transformation" (now found in *One Taste*): "There is the angry wisdom that shouts from the heart: we must, all of us, keep our eye on the radical and ultimate transformative goal. And so any sort of integral or authentic spirituality will also, always, involve a critical, intense, and occasional polemical shout from the transformative camp to the merely translative camp."[1] In this case, the true *call for transformation* comes from an integrated head and heart, from intelligent wisdom coupled with loving compassion. Ultimately, as we've seen, the final transformation is divine Enlightenment (nondual mysticism), a condition of humanity that's been demonstrated most fully with the enlightened teachers (saints and sages) of humankind (especially with the advanced *gurus*). These enlightened teachers and spiritual adepts from across the centuries and around the world, male and female alike, are the ones whom the *pandits* defend and support with their intellectual debates and rational talents. Importantly, as the traditions claim (such as those in India), these intellectuals pandits must also be spiritual practitioners involved with meditation and other transformative disciplines, for they must know for themselves the actual transpersonal insights they're intellectually learning about and defending (see chapter 6).

As we have clearly seen, one of Wilber's main missions with AQAL Metatheory, and that of Integral Institute and Integral University, is the attempt to bring *depth* and *meaning* (and hence *qualitative distinctions* and *value judgments*) back into today's complicated yet flattened world of scientific/capitalistic materialism. As a result, some of his strong critical analysis of today's current theories have sometimes resulted in polemic critiques that have shown little mercy for the errors of Flatland materialists (whether atomistic or holistic), or for the prerational tendencies of retro-romantics and their erroneous elevation of magical and mythic thinking to a superior status.

Yet strong arguments from the head and heart are exactly how it should be in the world of real philosophy, for it's anchored in the true "love of wisdom." Nonetheless, by taking this type of sharp critical approach, Wilber's actually exercising what's called "Real Compassion," a combination of head and heart that brings together, as the integral pandit explains, "wisdom and compassion, so it makes *judgments* of care and concern: it says some things are good and some things are bad, and I will choose to act only on those that are informed by wisdom and care."[2] This is qualitatively different from what's been despairingly referred to as "Idiot Compassion" (the terms come from Trungpa Rinpoche), which is a just another form of being agreeable though a person may think they're actually being kind (or compassionate) by allowing anything to happen. In this case, a person's really not making judgments at all, thus Wilber criticizes this attitude as only offering a "tepid egalitarianism," or an extreme "political correctness," two versions of exaggerated modern-day pluralistic relativism.[3]

According to Wilber, *idiot compassion* errors by massaging or consoling the ego by supporting its desires and wants, therefore, although providing some forms of legitimate *translation* (or horizontal integration), it usually remains stuck in that level's liabilities and limitations. *Real compassion*, on the other hand, is a call to authentic *transformation* (or vertical development and ego-transcendence), thus it has to make "qualitative distinctions" based on a "ranking of values" and "hierarchical judgments,"[4] all of which originate in natural holarchies (such as the Great Nest of Spirit). Therefore, the integral pandit insists in *One Taste* (1999): "We need to learn to *consciously* make qualitative distinctions. We need to make judgments on degrees of depth."[5] This is the stand of *dharma combat*, the philosophical technique that Wilber sometimes uses in his intense social critiques of modern Flatland or the various Eco-Romantic movements. He thereby becomes involved in a noble "battle" encouraging genuine *transformation of consciousness* into "the depths of the divine" leading to God knows where. Hence, Wilber's shout for transformative change, whether sweet, rational, or angry, is *really* being compassionate, although, at times, he doesn't suffer fools or the egoic-contraction.

The purpose of this type of intellectual challenge is to shake the ego out of its slumbering sleep of ignorance, to awaken it from of its dualistic dilemmas in order to transcend itself in the nondual consciousness of reality which is *always already* its real essence and true identity (one's Original Face). In other words, Wilber's philosophy is no "grandmother Zen," another form of idiot compassion that wants to be "kind" to the ego, like your caring grandmother (which has its appropriate place). Instead, with piercingly sharp critiques and demanding intellectual dissertations, this integral bodhisattva is issuing, as he says, "a thundering shout from the heart that translation is not enough."[6] As a social critic of today's Flatland world, including a harsh diagnosis of *"boomeritis"* that critiques the narcissistic tendencies of his own generation, or when he's coming down hard on psychology's fascination with mythic archetypes (including astrology and neopagan worship), Wilber has the right to complain that too many "boomers want to be told that their ego is God, their self-contraction is Spirit."[7] Yet from the point of view of authentic spirituality, this laissez-faire attitude is unacceptable, therefore, it must be argued against with a deeper understanding that reaches for a higher calling based on more integral wisdom.

However, Wilber still tries not to be sanctimonious, for he too recognizes the danger of being overly critical or just being obnoxious, as he concedes, "It is one thing if you are being offensive because you are engaged in angry wisdom or dharma combat, quite another if you are simply being a neurotic creep."[8] Consequently, our judgments need to be exercised with "skillful means" (*upaya* in Sanskrit), which are the methods of compassion combined with wisdom that are adeptly applied by caring individuals to help guide their fellow beings to liberation (or Enlightenment). Once this is done, however, the important point remains: Wise and compassionate judgments are definitely necessary and extremely vital to overall health and developmental growth.

Although some missteps have undoubtedly been made (for nobody's perfect), overall Ken Wilber's work can be seen as an effective form of dharma combat, or when a philosopher defends his or her positions with intense critical resolve. Not only has this philosopher helped point a modern light towards the transrational glory of Divine Enlightenment, but he's done so explicitly to bring *depth* and *meaning* back into today's ironic and complicated world of Flatland materialism and ethnocentric intolerance. By integrating the confusing cornucopia of premodern, modern, and postmodern knowledge systems, Wilber's delivering his message with a penetrating criticism and passionate "shout from the heart," and yet, fortunately, he does so with some of the most eloquent and diamond-clear prose you'll ever read in the annals of world philosophy.

Intellectual Samurai: Emancipatory Writing

In a revealing essay titled "Mind and the Heart of Emptiness: Reflections on Intellect and the Spiritual Path," soon published after the debut of and reaction to *Sex, Ecology, Spirituality* (1995), Ken Wilber cleverly pointed out that in general the "new age movement" has a major problem with the verbal rational mind (or rationality), the powerful formal-reflexive intellect that's been harnessed by the modern mind (and especially by science). Naturally, he indicates this is probably because we correctly do intuit that we must "go beyond the mind" in order to be authentically *trans*-rational, the goal of meditation. However, in some people's zest to go transrational, he insightfully notices that they "too often end up uncritically embracing anything that is *non*-rational, including many things that are, frankly, *pre*-rational, regressive, infantile, and narcissist."[9] In other words, people often make the *pre/trans fallacy* by confusing the prepersonal domains with the transpersonal ones (like the retro-Romantics do). This developmental error is clarified and avoided with an evolutionary AQAL Metatheory, thus anyone benefits immensely from its correction. Therefore, Wilber's gone on to criticize many of the New Age circles for having an "ambivalent relationship to our own intellectual and rational capacities," for, in actually, as he explains, "Rationality is *better* than pre-rational, but worse than trans-rational." By embracing the entire spectrum of consciousness (or all-levels), then Wilber's integral psychology has become a staunch defender of the rational mind and mental-reason by insisting that it's an appropriate (and necessary) stage of developmental growth, not just an antagonist to be defeated (although, granted, it too must be transcended in further consciousness evolution).

By using a psychological model that's brought into alignment with the sacred teachings of nondual Enlightenment, or the true Dharma (or "Teaching of Truth"), then Wilber's also able to justifiably criticize the fallacious stances taken by an domineering intellect or a reductionistic rational mind, which often likes to reject not only the lower, prerational realms, but also the higher transrational truths as well. This is obviously the condition of our overly rational modern and postmodern worldviews, especially since the advent of scientific materialism, which has created its own set of dangerous liabilities. This then forces the transpersonalist Wilber to highly recommend that all rational intellectuals, or most modern people of any persuasion, would do well "to pursue, first and foremost, a spiritual discipline... [as] a way to set the mind aside and open to a grand and greater [transrational] glory." In this case, he thankfully observes "when the intellect is polished until it becomes radiant and shining, it is a staunch defender of a Truth and Beauty that reaches quite far beyond its own capacities, and in that reach it serves its master [Spirit] more than faithfully." In other words, this entails the integration of a shining bright intellect with a radiant love-filled heart, which are, as we saw earlier (see chapter 6), the very qualities of a bodhisattva intellectual pandit (perhaps like Manjushri).

Consequently, Wilber's likened this approach to becoming an "intellectual samurai," for if the mind is truly trained and properly disciplined (and always transcended), then the mind can be "genuinely made into a servant, [for] the intellect is a fast and furious path to enlightenment." This enlightened intellectual approach is also the way of Jnana Yoga, or a branch of India's royal yoga that focuses on using the intellect and mind, based on wisdom and insight, to ultimately transcend the mind altogether and rediscover its innate oneness with Atman/Brahman (or God). The other complimentary path to jnana is the devotional path of Bhakti Yoga, which exercises an open heartfelt-surrender of the ego-I to the divine yet without using thoughts, but rather more via *feeling* (in other words, it simply relies on the *heart* more than the mind). The way of the intellect, however, needs to constantly exercise "skillful means" *(upaya)* in combination with "real compassion," for as we just saw, it's really based on an intellectual wisdom that's been tempered with heartfelt understanding. Yet still, according to Wilber, this skillful compassion comes when the mind is blazing "so brightly that they [jnani yogis] sizzle the ego in the process." Nonetheless, with the true practices of an authentic spirituality, a person will naturally develop an integrated head and heart connected with a vibrant, healthy body and supportive environment, although today, as Wilber embarrassingly notes, "Many people simply cannot believe that intense intellectual accomplishment could possibly be coupled with emotional sensitivity." Contrary to some critics' assertions, however, the exercising of a strong compassionate intellect has certainly been the case with Ken Wilber (and his multidimensional integral "theories").

For the Integral Vision, as we've seen throughout this book, the only real and true solution is to actually "Do the yoga!"—to keep *evolving* with a committed "vow to grow." Once again Wilber simply asserts the plain undeniable fact: "At some point, you and I must stop this intellectual headtripping, and begin actual spiritual practice." This is why, of course, he freely admits his approach is designed basically to "use the mind to beat the mind, and point to the trans-mental, the over-mental, the radiant and luminous shining in the Emptiness of all that arises." This can give the appearance that this integral critical philosophy often plays the "good cop, bad cop," first, since it offers, as Wilber explains, "a strong criticism of the merely prerational, in an attempt to get people up to rationality, and then an equally intense attack on rationality, in an attempt to open people to the transrational." When this intellectual method is embraced and understood in the context of authentic transpersonal practice, then the rational mind becomes a wise and compassionate servant to the higher unfolding potentials of consciousness, including the transpersonal stations of soul and spirit.

Since Wilber intentionally writes in the integral language arising from centauric vision-logic, as we've already seen, then AQAL Metatheory is not intended to be transmental (an impossibility for all mental "maps"), yet it's still geared toward a transpersonal enlightened understanding (or the transcendence of all stages and states). Thus the integral pandit explains some of the motivation behind his writings in *One Taste* (1999): "Each of us still has to find a genuine contemplative practice—maybe yoga, maybe Zen, maybe Shambhala Training, maybe contemplative prayer, or any number of authentic transformative practices. That is what advances consciousness, not my linguistic chitchat and book junk."[10] This is exactly the same to what he was professing two decades earlier when he curtly commented in *Eye to Eye* (1983): "The only major purpose of a book on mysticism should be to persuade the reader to engage in mystical practice."[11] Nearly twenty years later, the best advice Wilber has to give still beats at the heart of his writings, for he explains, "The point is simple: if you are interested in genuine transformative spirituality, find an authentic spiritual teacher and *begin to practice*. Without practice, you will never move beyond the phases of belief, faith, and random peak experiences. You will never evolve into plateau experiences, nor from there into permanent realization. You will remain, at best, a brief visitor in the territory of your own higher estate, a tourist in your own true Self."[12] From an integral or developmental perspective, that indeed would be a tragedy.

By engaging dharma combat with an integral attitude that's able to include yet transcend the mental intellect, then this American bodhisattva paints a titillating picture of possible liberation for all human beings. In *One Taste* (1999), Wilber explains in some detail how he actually sees his own work as being expressed within a lineage that's called "emancipatory writing," which is a noble attempt, in his words, to bring "intellectual light in the service of liberation—helping to undo repression, thwart power, and shun shallowness."[13] Other writers in this genre have included the past few centuries worth of intellectuals and philosophers, especially those people writing within the tradition of humanism, or even a "humanistic rational pluralism," like with notables such as Voltaire, Ralph Waldo Emerson, Henry David Thoreau, Walt Whitman, Nietzsche, Schelling, Schopenhauer, Kierkegaard, Oscar Wilde, Ezra Pound, Madam Blavatsky, Thomas Mann, Christopher the common denominator of these intellectuals was "an intense desire to acquire, to advance, and to disseminate knowledge—a wish to improve the lot as well as the administration of humankind, as assumption of responsibility—*l'intelligence oblige*—and with a passion, no tamer word will do, for truth."[14] Another way to look at this, of course, is to see these passionate intellectual pleas as being part of the task that must be taken up by the emerging leading-edge integral-centaurs (and the other modern-day "bodhisattvas"), or all those integrated souls who are genuinely concerned for the liberation of everyone in this modern/postmodern world and its interconnected global environment and planetary community.

In the new millennium, however, this enlightening emancipatory philosophy is not coming down from the heights of the Himalayas, since this particular version is arising from a tall funny smart bald contemporary Manjushri who's sitting right smack in the middle of the USA, high in rooftops of the Rocky Mountains where he networks with thousands of people via the worldwide digital Internet and the published written word. This time, as we've seen, the integral words of liberation are being hammered out on a high-performance notebook computer, and are then being downloaded into the electronic mind streams of global consciousness. This Western Vedanta American Buddhist intellectual samurai pandit, this modern mad mystic, who's probably without peer in today's fractured world of reactive philosophies, has fortunately been aiming his critical wisdom and heart-awakened intellect of incredible computing-power in order to encourage the true liberation of all sentient beings, wherever they may reside. In any case, Ken Wilber, whether he's seen as a genius or as an annoyance, does speak in a voice that's sometimes strong and fierce, yet it's also one that's been tendered and educated with a wise and compassionate heart, let alone being so breathtakingly articulate it can send shivers up your spine. In any case, this beckoning Integral Vision is standing up strong on this threshold of a new millennium urging us all on to a greater revolution in the evolution of consciousness.

The Integral Revolution: The Founding Mothers & Fathers

Since the Integral Vision of Ken Wilber deals fully with the "real world," and isn't just wandering around in idealistic streams of abstract ideas, then we should've learned by now that with the AQAL Matrix, both the interiors and exteriors of individuals and collective systems are inexorably linked and intermeshed. Not only does the transformation of consciousness that comes from within have a profound effect on the outer world and its relations, but the outer world also has a profound effect on the transformation of consciousness. Thus, there is an "AQAL feedback loop" involving all the "quadrants" of self, culture, and nature as they tetra-evolve through the basic waves of the Kosmic Mandala. The Integral Vision, as we've seen, maintains that genuine *integral transformative practices* (ITP) will help initiate this further evolution of consciousness. Wilber reviews this AQAL transformative process that involves the interaction of the sociocultural individual or all-quadrant transformation: "The overall movement of cultural transformation is from the:

- **Upper-Left** (U-L) of individual cognitive potential to the
- **Lower-Left** (L-L) of collective worldviews, at first marginalized, but finally embedded in the

- **Lower-Right** (L-R) social institutions, at which point these basic institutions automatically help reproduce the

- **Lower-Left** worldview (L-L) and socialize the individual Upper-Left (U-L) in succeeding generations, acting as *pacers of transformation*—a transformation first started or begun in a moment of individual creative emergence and transcendence."[15]

As we've seen, the emerging higher-order structure of consciousness appearing in our time is that of the integral centaur or the holistically integrated bodymind, embodied in those individuals cognitively operating from vision-logic, whether male or female. These are today's (and tomorrow's) men and women who will cocreate a "cognitive potential" for future evolution, as Wilber expertly outlines in *Sex, Ecology, Spirituality* (1995): "As for the coming transformation itself, it is being built, as have all past transformations, in the hearts and minds of those *individuals* who themselves evolve to centauric planetary vision. For these individuals create a "cognitive potential" in the form of *new worldviews* (in this case, centauric-planetary) that in turn feed back into the ongoing mainstream of *social institutions*, until the previously "marginalized" worldview becomes anchored in institutional forms which then catapult a collective consciousness to a new and higher release. *The revolution, as always, will come from the within and be embedded in the without.*"[16]

Consequently, in his recent Phase-5 writings, Wilber has been pointing out that "knowledge revolutions," or the emergence of a new way of thinking and living, are best supported by a combination of *"new paradigm-practices"* and *"new theories-maps,"* since they better explain the multitude of data into a new meta-paradigm. This is how the "scientific revolutions" that Kuhn was referring to came about, and it's often how with new models and paradigms that the political and social "revolutions," or other radical changes, in the larger society occur. As one example, Wilber refers to the estimation that the European Renaissance was initiated and carried forward by a group numbering around one thousand people. In the initial phases, these knowledge revolutions are embraced by only a handful of individuals emerging at the leading-edge of consciousness evolution, only to later be followed by the larger culture or community. As another example, the small intellectual and social gatherings of seventeenth-century France, or the philosophical *salons* of the French Enlightenment, helped bring about the modern age and establish democratic social institutions (including the shift from the mythic blue meme to the scientific orange). These leading-edge elites, in other words, become the *pacers of transformation* for the society as a whole, and they call for others to step forward and realize the depths of their own innate potentials.

Consequently, Wilber is encouraging the networking of "nascent integral salons [that are] spontaneously forming around the world," as being an effective way to become involved with the emerging integral consciousness revolution. Indeed, as we've seen, this is one of the primary functions of Integral Institute and Integral University (see chapter 3). As another result, the integral centaurs (or integrated men and women) will also seek out new "leaders" and "visionaries" to light the way in promoting further change and evolutionary growth in whatever way possible. Wilber has recently examined some of these issues in depth in the Phase-5 essay titled "The Many Ways We Touch," where he says these integral salons are exercising "the *social practice* of *dialoguing*… a social practice, paradigm, or injunction of dialogical discourse within an elite subculture."[17] This naturally includes the production of new books and written treatises, audiovisual presentations and community activities, all of which will help, as he explains, to "implement the new paradigm or practices on a wider scale, by revolution if necessary."[18] Thus, the *micro-practices* of individuals and communities will effect and transform the *macro-practices* of the technological-economic base, which, in turn, will effect the progressive development of individuals, meshing with the cycles and circles of change in an all-quadrant process (or tetra-mesh).

Since the "Age of Information" is simply, as Wilber explains, the "Age of Noosphere," then this will include the *cyber-technology* of personal computers, and of course the Internet (or information superhighway), which may (or may not) be the techno-economic platform for the merging integral consciousness. He further clarifies in *Sex, Ecology, Spirituality* (1995): "The *platform* for an emerging world culture is being built by international markets of material-economic exchange, and by the increasingly free exchange of rationality structures, particularly empiric-analytic science and computer-transmitted information, all of which are supra-national in essential character."[19] Indeed, this leads him to indicate in the fine print to *SES:* "From within the informational neural network of a global commons will come the voices indicating liberation."[20] Nevertheless, this doesn't mean the Internet and advanced computer technology will automatically become "enabling technologies," nor will they guarantee that any higher-level transformation actually takes place. This is because, for one, any form of a higher-stage (rational) technology can be "high-jacked" by the lower worldviews, and then used for egocentric and ethnocentric purposes (this partially explains, for example, the horrors of Auschwitz and other modern atrocities).

Once again, we must clearly understand that the future is *ours* to create by more fully acknowledging the entire AQAL Matrix of reality, the full-spectrum of consciousness, from the development of interiors to the application of exterior realities. With interior consciousness development, based on some type of methodological pluralism that's exercising transformative practices (thus encouraging development from precon to con to postcon), then from this development there will emerge the cutting-edge individuals living at the leading-edge of global consciousness evolution. These new "integral leaders" will emerge from all walks of life as they further initiate the transition to an integral Planetary Culture. They are the new group of women and men—call them the "integral-centaurs"—who will be working together from a new level of conscious adaptation (vision-logic). They are already pushing for more responsibility from national governments and international corporations to halt their ideologically brutal war games and the exploitation of the natural environment and human population, in doing so they're already exercising a genuine care for the entire spiral of evolutionary development.

Wilber predicts that these integral-centaurs will be "the Founding Mothers and Fathers of a second-tier or Integral Constitution," who will co-participants in service to the emerging "World Civilization" and "Planetary Culture." They will be the ones who will pragmatically apply the countless second-tier solutions that are arising from aperspectival vision-logic and networking-meshworks (while also accessing the higher transpersonal stages of consciousness adaptation). This will obviously have profound implications for the world-at-large, and for every individual. Therefore the political pandit considers some of the possibilities in a recent writing (2000): "This is the great and exhilarating call of *global politics at the millennium*. We are awaiting the new founding Fathers and Mothers who will call us to our more encompassing future, an Integral Constitution that will act as a gentle pacer of transformation for the entire spiral of development, honoring each and every wave as it unfolds, yet kindly inviting each and all to even greater depth."[21] Next, let's briefly review the contours of what such an integral revolution may look like as it provides developmental incentives for the genuine emergence of a truly integral Planetary Culture that celebrates its multivariate "unity-in-diversity."

Call of the Millennium: Integral Governance & World Federation (Transnationalism)

Living in the doorway to the third millennium of the Common Era, to reactively resist the forces of globalization is basically fruitless, for it is already upon us, as many writers have attested. The best option, therefore, is to better serve and promote its healthy emergence. Since Ken Wilber's AQAL Metatheory includes *all-levels, all-lines, all-quadrants*, etc. as they arise and appear in self, culture, and nature, then it's worth taking more seriously as being a viable alternative for a true world philosophy (as many people are already doing). Naturally, Wilber confidently confirms this possibility in *A Theory of Everything* (2000): "An 'all-quadrant, all-level, all-lines' approach is one of the best methods available for charting that extraordinary unfolding from egocentric to ethnocentric to worldcentric, in all its perilous ups and downs, thus making more friendly the waters leading to the promised land of worldcentric Civilization and *unitas multiplex*. And that is not a final end point, but simply a new beginning."[22] A new beginning for a genuine cosmopolitan "Global Village," a vision that's been a dream for countless people throughout human history, but now, for the first time, it's one that's attainable in our current millennium. Indeed, *everyone* is invited to this evolution revolution.

As we've seen, this integral revolution will probably be embodied in the developmental emergence of *integral consciousness* with its worldcentric global awareness, for it's that level of second-tier awareness that provides the best "foundation for a World Federation and council of all beings."[23] These will be the leading-edge centaurs (or the integrated bodyminds of self-actualized people cognitively operating in vision-logic) who will be the flesh-and-blood women and men who are, truly, the first *"true world citizens."* Research already shows, as Wilber points out, that *"true world citizenship* belongs not to national organizations but to *planetary organizations....*

The modern nation-state, founded upon initial rationality, has run into its own internal contradictions or limitations, and can only be released by a vision-logic/planetary transformation."[24] Integral politics, as we've seen, is suggesting that we need new forms of "integral governance" that will probably involve some type of a "pluralistic World Federation,"[25] which itself will be founded on worldcentric "transnational" principles and agreeable legal treaties. Wilber clarifies some of these political views in *A Theory of Everything* (2000): "What the world now needs is *the first genuinely second-tier form of political philosophy and governance.* I believe, of course, that it will be an all-quadrant, all-level [AQAL] political theory and practice, deeply integral in its structures and patterns. This will in no way replace the U.S. Constitution (or that of any other nation), but will simply situate it in global meshworks that facilitate mutual unfolding and enhancement—an integral and holonic politics."[26] It will be, in other words, a politics that's exercising its *rights* (as a part), while simultaneously (or integrally), exercising its *responsibilities* (as a whole).

The integral call for a genuine "World Federation" is based on a mutual tolerance and integration of all the basic waves and worldview memes, from the *premodern* (preconventional) to the *modern* (conventional) to the *postmodern* (postconventional), for its prime directive is to protect the healthy development of the entire spiral of consciousness, individually and collectively. This will not be a domineering "new world order" bent on mass-control and materialistic consumerism, but rather it will act in a proactive manner exercising a holistic and worldcentric embrace. This moral and conscious development expands self-identity, as we've seen, in a "spiral of compassion" that's unfolding morality from *"me"* to *"we"* to *"us"* to *"all of us,"* instead of just concentrating on the "we/us" (i.e., tribalistic or ethnocentric or nationalistic), or worse, only being concerned with "me" (i.e., egocentric). "All of us," the central message of "universal integralism," is exactly what encourages a tolerant "celebration of diversity,"[27] one that leads to a genuine *Unitas Multiplex* of "unity-in-diversity." The holonic embrace of each evolutionary stage of consciousness development, including all its types and surface variations seen throughout history (and prehistory), and currently alive in our times, is what will most fundamentally allow the full emergence of a true Planetary Culture and genuine World Federation.

The figure below represents the unfolding development of the major "emergent geopolitical systems" as found in collective human evolution (social holons in the Lower-Right quadrant) as they evolve from *tribal-kinship* (beige/purple) to *horticultural-villages* (red) to *agrarian-empires* (blue) to *industrial-nations* (orange/green) to a *planetary world federation* (second-tier or yellow/turquoise memes). See Figure 15-1.

Emergent Geopolitical Systems   **Techno-Economic System**

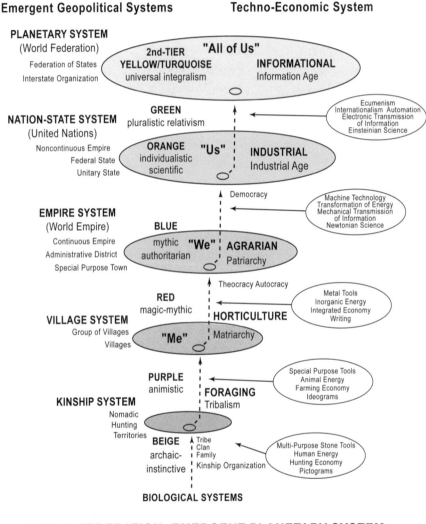

WORLD FEDERATION: EMERGENT PLANETARY SYSTEM
(Social Holons in Lower-Right quadrant)
(after Alastair Taylor, SDi, and *Sex, Ecology, Spirituality*, 1995)

Figure15-1

In this quest to promote a World Federation of *Unitas Multiplex* ("unity-in-diversity"), Wilber has outlined a few requirements that address the current global world order in today's twenty-first century, particularly with the current dominance of nationalism and international economics. Obviously, any Global Civilization or World Federation will have to involve the transformation of national institutions into some type of cooperative "Transnationalism," which will obviously involve very real world difficulties. The encouragement for this type of cooperation, Wilber explains, begins with "Nations voluntarily surrendering some of their sovereignty for the global betterment—therein precisely is the extremely difficult nature of this 'postnational' global transition."[28] In *Sex, Ecology, Spirituality* (1995), the author lists what the shift to *transnational worldcentric actions and integral leadership* would partially require:

> The global nature of this transformation is now being driven, particularly in its *technological-economic base*, by three interrelated factors:
>
> 1)   the necessity to protect the "global commons," the common biosphere that belongs to no nation, no tribe, no creed, no race;
>
> 2)   the necessity to regulate the world financial system, which no longer responds to national borders;
>
> 3)   the necessity to maintain a modicum of international peace and security, which is not so much a matter of major war between any two nations, but between a "new order" of loosely federated nations and renegade regimes threatening world peace [or "retribalization"].[29]

Once more, the AQAL Matrix "feedback loop" (or the tetra-meshing of all-quadrants, all-levels, all-lines, all-types, etc) involves the spectrum of *relational exchanges* across the span and depth of the global environment (including interiors and exteriors). Therefore, the integral pundit clarifies the priorities: "None of those physical and material and economic components *can be secured* in the long run without a *corresponding change in consciousness* among the citizens of the nations surrendering some of their sovereignty for the transnational good…. *They are literally transnational crisis demanding transnational, worldcentric responses.*[30] In wise response, integral politics recognizes the *educational opportunity* to develop "integral leadership" (via transformative practices) on local to national to corporate to international levels. They must start constituting and projecting geopolitical systems of "integral governance" in order to secure the global commons, the world financial system, and the international peace and security (the goals of transnationalism). Wilber captures this enormous challenge of a real "global politics" in *A Theory of Everything* (2000): "No *global systems* and *integral meshworks* are evolving out of corporate states and value communities. These *interdependent systems require governance* capable of integrating (not dominating) nations and communities over the entire spiral of interior and exterior development."[31] But *we* (all of us) are actually the governments, *we* are the leaders and the people, therefore, if *we* develop and evolve (inside), then so too will our world (outside). As always, the journey of a thousand miles begins with each step.

Indeed, Wilber prophetically proclaimed at the cusp of the new millennium (2000): "This is the great and exhilarating call of global politics at the millennium. We are awaiting the new global founding Fathers and Mothers who will frame an *integral system of governance* that will call us to our mutual encompassing future, that will act as a *gentle pacer of transformation* for the entire spiral of human development, honoring each and every wave as it unfolds, yet kindly inviting each and all to even greater depth."[32] This is what increases the probability for an "Integral Millennium," an idea Wilber first mentioned on the first page to *A Theory of Everything* (2000), where he suggests that for the first time in human history it's now possible to bring together all of the world's cultures, past and present, and thus finally create a real "Global Village" (a title originally coined by the futurist Marshall McLuhan), to enact a genuine "Integral Village" where the entire human family can gather in harmony and peace to celebrate their sacred unity-in-diversity. An idealistic vision and dream, perhaps, but it's one that seems to be humanity's evolutionary destiny, one way or another, for many people from countless generations have felt it beating deep in the depths of their hearts and minds, as well as expanding like light into the furthest reaches of our shared human nature. Our integral visionary, by following the available evidence, simply puts it this way:

> For the fact is, this is the dawning of the age of vision-logic, the rise of the network society, the postmodern, aperspectival, internetted

global village. Evolution in all forms has started to become conscious of itself. Evolution, as Spirit-in-action, is starting to awaken on a more collective scale. Kosmic evolution is now producing theories and performances of its own integral embrace.... And it is now the same Spirit-in-action, starting to become collectively conscious of itself, that has initiated an era of integral embrace—global village to communications internet to integral theories to network society—as it slowly binds together the fragments of a world that has forgotten to care.[33]

This integral "council of all beings," at the very least, will work toward securing and cultivating the health of the entire spiral of evolution, from protecting the minerals of matter to the biosphere's web-of-life to the valuable mythic prototypes and archetypes to reason's technological marvels and democratic mutual self-recognition to energetic psychic insight to subtle communion to enlightened relationship, et al. But first, as always, the entire process begins with each and every "I," and "me," growing outward in the evolutionary arc of consciousness to justly embrace the "we," and "all of us," scattered throughout the Kosmic Mandala of Spirit-in-action. For us, the Integral Vision showing where Wilber's at, finds that he's pushing us forward with another gentle persuasion of love to keep us evolving onward to an even truer tomorrow, whether in life or in death, whether as a part or as a whole. Thus, the integral visionary continues to shout loudly from the heart: "Without in any way denying the crucial importance of the ecological and economic and financial factors in the world-demanding transformation, let us not forget that they all rest ultimately on a correlative transformation in human consciousness: the global embrace, and its pluralistic World-Federation, can only be *seen*, and *understood*, and *implemented*, by individuals with a universal and global vision-logic... in a worldcentric embrace through which runs the blood of a common humanity and beats the single heart of a very small planet struggling for its own survival, and yearning for its own release into a deeper and a truer tomorrow."[34] As always, today and tomorrow, are what we all make it.

Where's Wilber Going? To the Grave or to the Bardos?

So where is Wilber ultimately going? In short, like us all, Ken Wilber will eventually die and pass on, for as he's been persistently reminding us, by quoting Shakespeare: "The skull grins in at the banquet." He once even claimed that he himself would want on his tombstone to be etched the plain words: "He was true, but partial..."[35] As we've seen, that's a damn good description of where Ken Wilber's at, but it may also be interesting to consider where he's going after death. Is it even possible to know? Who is the self or "I" that wants to know about securing its possible immortal existence? Who or what leaves the body on a journey to somewhere else (or not), whether it's a heaven or a hell (or whatever), sometime after death? From the view of materialism, it may be nothing more than "21 grams" missing, and when you're dead, you're dead.

Wilber's view of what happens after death, of course, is more Buddhistic, more transpersonal, more mystical in orientation. Thus, when he was drawing *Up from Eden* (1981) to a close, he concluded with a summary of the human being's predicament in life: "There is a way out: if men and women are truly miserable creatures because they have made death consciousness, they *can* go one step further and—transcending self—transcend death as well. To move from *subconsciousness* to *self-consciousness* is to make *death conscious;* to move from *self-consciousness* to *superconsciousness* is to make *death obsolete.*"[36] In other words, death is only transcended by releasing the separate sense of self that's been generated by the primary dualism between subject and object, between self and a vast universe, created as a boundary or a problem to be overcome. Consequently, before physical death the mystics claim that it is possible to make death obsolete by fully experiencing "the death of the ego," for they say this is the only way to know the Ultimate Truth, which they also say is the awareness that liberates a soul from the shackles of fear created by the separative divisions of the self, including the most primal fear of death or of its total annihilation. Wilber eloquently confirmed this view in his personal journal of *One Taste* (1999): "It dawns on me, yet again, that all spiritual practice is a rehearsal—and at its best, an enactment—of death. As the mystics put it, 'If you die before you die, then when you die, you won't die.'... Meditation is to practice that death right now, and right now, and right now, by resting in the timeless Witness and disidentifying with the finite, objective, mortal self that can be seen as an object. In the empty Witness, in the great Unborn, there is no death—not because you live forever in time—you will not—but because you discover the timelessness of this eternal moment, which never enters the stream of time in the first place."[37] For in the end, and during the process, it's really Only God.

Of course, Wilber has written about the "after death" process in several places, but perhaps none more vividly than with an insightful interpretation of *The Tibetan Book of the Dead,* found in the last chapter of *The Atman Project* (1980), titled "Involution." For the integral philosopher, the ascent and descent of the soul after death is similar to the process of "involution," or when causal Spirit (or pure Formlessness) descends into, and therefore creates, the gross dimensions of physical reality, including the Earth realm. He first clarified the title to this sacred source-text from ancient Tibet, by explaining, "The Tibetan title of the book is *Bardo Thotrol,* and Bardo means 'gap,' 'transition state,' 'intermediate state,' or as I prefer, 'in between','"[38] that is, the Bardos are the gap "in-between" a human being's death and a soul's possible rebirth into another lifetime (if one is so fortunate, claim the mystical Tibetans). According to the Tibetans, this forty-nine-day Bardo period can be basically subdivided into three major stages of Ascent (death) and Descent (rebirth), following the three major realms of the gross, subtle, and causal, which we'll be touring below.

Most mystics the world over have generally argued that immediately following physical death the soul (or the deeper-psychic self) first sees and experiences the bright Divine Light (of Atman/Brahman), which the Tibetans call the *Chikhai* or the "Clear Light of Reality." Wilber continues to beautifully explain what happens: "[This] is simply the state of the immaculate and luminous Dharmakaya, the ultimate Consciousness, the Brahman-Atman. This ultimate state is *given,* as a gift to all individuals: they are plunged straight into ultimate reality and exist *as* the ultimate Dharmakaya,"[39] which is, as we saw, in the West called God and Godhead. Perhaps, you've heard about this before, such as from the numerous people who have momentarily died, only to return and universally testify when they died, they saw "a Light at the end of the tunnel."

Although every person is gifted by divine grace with this Divine Vision after dying, unless a soul has prepared itself by doing appropriate spiritual and meditative practices during its lifetime, and is then consciously ready for this blissful Divine Communion, they will slip back down into the lower realms, and, if fortunate, possibly reincarnate. As we mentioned earlier, Wilber compares this process to *involution* or the "descent" of causal Spirit (as formlessness) into the gross material realm of matter and bodies. After death and seeing the light of God, perhaps surprisingly, the soul usually *contracts* away from the Divine intensity of Atman/Brahman (mostly "owing to unfamiliarity with such a state"), therefore, Wilber continues to explain this is when the soul "turns instead to forms of seeking, desire, karma, and grasping, trying to 'search out' a state of equilibrium."[40] What was at first freely "witnessed" by the True Self (Atman) has now become a series of attachments and burdens, for now the soul is caught in the "in-between" Bardo states as it continues to draw away even further from its own true condition (the Clear Divine Light).

As a result, after tasting this causal Emptiness, the soul is now involved with its own involution into the material realm, but first it slips down into the subtle realm, known as the *Chonyid* in Tibet, the realm of subtle lights and sounds and radiant archetypal deities (both peaceful and wrathful varieties). Our guide continues to clarify what's going on: "According to the Thotrol, most individuals simply *recoil* in the face of the divine illuminations—they *contract* into less intense and more manageable forms of experience."[41] Thus, these falling souls are uncontrollably "*attracted* to the lower realms, drawn to them, and find satisfaction in them."[42] However, once more, this is only the illusory existence of nonenlightenment, thus Wilber perfectly sums up the universal message of the mystics: "The only way the soul will not suffer this lack is when the soul *recovers* that Original Oneness as Brahman-Atman [Enlightenment]."[43] Indeed, this yearning to recover one's Original Face (as Zen would say) becomes the unfolding evolutionary drive of *Atman-telos*, or the "gentle persuasion toward love." This great drive is only fulfilled when Spirit-in-action becomes totally conscious of itself (through the depth and awakening of human holons) as being Consciousness Itself, the "Love-Bliss-Void" (or *sat-chit-ananda*) of the Divine.

In the meantime, while the soul continually seeks temporary *substitutes* to replace the lost Unity of Atman, this becomes the various levels in the *"spectrum of consciousness,"* or the Great Nest of Spirit, where, Wilber tells us, "Each level of the spectrum is thus constructed as a symbolic substitute for lost unity, so that ultimately each level of the spectrum is (prior to Enlightenment) a substitute for Atman-consciousness."[44] Now that separation has occurred, the subject-I continues to grasp and wander about seeking for substitute gratifications and other forms of release, including the desire for delightful subtle objects, until finally the wandering soul finds itself tossed down into the *Sidpa* or the gross-reflecting mind realm (such as with the Earth). However, since the soul's now in a domain of dualistic dualisms and gross energetic dimensions, it's possible, say the Tibetan mystics, to visually see visions of males and females intertwined in sexual union, in which case the deeper-psychic self or soul may be drawn down into a living rebirth as a human body. Falling into the lowest of all possible realms, the pleromatic and typhonic realm of body-union, the soul is found floating as fetus in a female womb, whereby the soul, as Wilber explains, "goes once again into a swoon, passes out, represses the whole Sidpa realm, and emerging from the mother's womb, wakes up in the gross realm, merged with the pleroma, forgetful of the whole affair."[45] Perhaps, this too seem vaguely familiar, since we've all probably been there, done that.

The wisdom traditions of humankind, therefore, maintain that mature human development acquired through the progressive evolution of consciousness is really a matter of the "Remembrance" or "The Remembering" of one's forgotten unity with Divinity or God Itself (which is, Wilber tells us, "the Buddhist *smriti* and *sati-patthana*, the Hindu *smara*, the Sufi *zikr*, Plato's recollection, Christ's *anamnesis*: all of those terms are precisely translated as *remembrance*"). Consequently, Wilber sums up by going straight to the point of being alive as a human holon (composed of matter, body, mind, soul, and spirit): "Evolution is a remembrance of involution—a rediscovery of the higher modes which were enwrapped in the lower ones during the soul's flight from God."[46] As the "perennial philosophy" of humankind also reminds us in culture after culture, century after century, Wilber too succinctly states the simple yet difficult goal of human life: "The soul's duty in this life is to remember." It's a rediscovery, in other words, of what's *always already* the truth and absolutely real.

In this case, as we've learned throughout this book, this American Buddhist philosopher isn't just another intellectual translator or trained scholar of Eastern philosophies. Rather, he's a living nondual mystic with a post-postmodern spin on the bodhisattva Manjushri, thus, just as we'd expect, he again reveals the nondual secret on the last page of *The Atman Project* (1981): "At that final remembrance, the impact of Only God in absolute Mystery and radical Unknowing dismantles once and for all the Atman-projects…. And because there is always only Atman, the Atman-project never occurred."[47] This notorious paradox compels the mystical pandit to muse at the incredible bliss of existence, as he did in *One Taste* (1999): "Ken Wilber is just a scab on my Original Face, and this morning I flick it off like a tiny insect, and disappear back into the Infinite Space that is my true abode."[48] It's the same for each one of us, that is, if we truly know our Original Face as the

Face of God. Yet, simultaneously, because he thoroughly understands this paradox, Wilber continues explaining, "But that infinite space is impulsive. It sings its songs of manifestation, it dances the dance of creation. Out of sheerest purest gossamer nothingness, now and now and forever now, this majestic world arises, a wink and a nod from the radiant Abyss. So I finish unpacking the books and go on about the morning's business."[49] As you continue exploring the depth of his writings and where Wilber's at, you will experience this divine paradox and understanding living at the very heart of his Integral AQAL Vision and global philosophy.

Could it be possible, now at the dawn of a new millennium, there's finally emerging a practical Theory of Everything that includes nondual Spirit by integrating science and religion so they can investigate and understand as one integral system the diverse unity of the AQAL Matrix, which includes human evolution and the journey of birth, life, and death, even extending beyond death? Yet, as always, the journey is ours to carry forward, for Ken Wilber's only another sentient being who arises for a while and then will pass away, just one more fragile life form floating in formless Clear Light. Yet in this case, no doubt, history will remember his name, at least for a time, because he has reminded us, in a much more integral way, how to transcend-yet-include "all-quadrants, all-levels." In the meantime, the man openly invites all sentient beings to actively participate in this emerging integral revolution that's already occurring *within* as it embodies a more enlightened reality *without*. Now that, as much as anything, is where Wilber's at.

ENDNOTES

Foreword

1. This is not to deny that Socrates and the pre-Socratic philosophers, as well as great thinkers in other cultures had not grappled with these questions as well, but in the West it was Plato who articulated and codified these questions into what would become systematic philosophical traditions.

2. Consistent with these reflections, Nietzsche's colorful comment on Plato and his teacher Socrates was that they stood the full-bodied (mythic-archaic) Greek attitude "on its head," meaning they transformed it into rational discourse.

3. For an exercise in obscurity just try reading Nietzsche's great book-length parable, *Thus Spoke Zarathustra!*

4. For a sophisticated argument consistent with this view see Fredric Jameson's work; especially his 1992 book, *Postmodernism, Or, the Cultural Logic of Late Capitalism*, Duke University Press.

5. A more complete definition of metaphysics is that branch of philosophy which deals with issues of ontology (what is being or reality?) and epistemology (how do we know it?).

6. To read Whitehead one has to acquire a new language!

7. Here Wilber enters the tradition of great American philosophers in another way. William James, who many regard as America's preeminent pioneer of psychology, consciousness research, and spirituality, characterized consciousness in terms of "pulses" – substantive events of experience. When, late in his life, he came to espouse the philosophy of "Radical Empiricism" – the nothing that *everything is experience* – he continued to theorize in terms of such pulses of experience. At this point, however, they were no longer merely "subjective," but like the occasions of Whitehead and Wilber, the very foundation of reality.

8. A phrase from Tibetan *rDzogs-chen* thought that refers to the holistic coming-into-being of the entire world in each moment of experience.

9. To complete the picture, each major perspective, say, the first person singular view, can actually be unfolded into two related but importantly different perspectives. One is the inner sense of experience itself, pure subjectivity, or in brain scientist Antonio Damasio's terms "the feel of…[whatever you are feeling]" The other is the "outer" appearance of this inner experience, or in Wilber's terms, "the look of a feel." Taking such an objective

attitude toward subjective experiences has led to "structural" theories of the mind, such as those of Sigmund Freud, Jean Piaget, Robert Kegan, and many others. Each of the other three major quadrants similarly unfolds into its own inner and outer perspectives.

Chapter One
Where Wilber's At: AQAL Reality

1. Ken Wilber, *A Theory of Everything* (2000), p. 2.

2. Ken Wilber, *The Marriage of Sense and Soul* (1998), p. 105.

3. Ken Wilber, *Integral Psychology* (2000), p. 56.

4. Ken Wilber, *One Taste* (1999), p. viii.

5. The preference of this author is to usually use the Phase-# designation since using Wilber's last name is too redundant and self-centered for mine or Wilber's tastes, although the Wilber/Phase-# is the most accurate representation.

6. Ken Wilber, foreword to *Ken Wilber: Thought as Passion* (2003, SUNY Press) by Frank Visser.

7. *Embracing Reality: The Integral Vision of Ken Wilber: A Historical Survey and Chapter-by-Chapter Guide to Wilber's Major Works* (2004) reviews each one of Wilber's previous books for their own sake, thus it's an excellent source guide to the breadth of Wilber's career. Consequently, it is a very useful compendium for easily ingesting Wilber's earlier phases, which are brilliant in and of themselves; thus if you want clarification of his principal ideas and his well-articulated definitions, then *Embracing Reality* becomes an indispensable resource that everyone, especially Wilber's students, should include in their library.

8. Ken Wilber, *Collected Works, Volume Eight (CW8)* (2000), introduction, p. 47.

9. Perhaps the best introductory Wilber/Phase-4 books to read are either his most concise books, such as *A Theory of Everything* (2000) or *A Brief History of Everything* (1996), yet the personal journals of *One Taste* (1999) affords perhaps the easiest overview of most of his important Phase-4/5 AQAL ideas (as well as chronicling many of Wilber's own spiritual practices and meditative experiences). As of 2005, for the best overview of the AQAL position, it's probably best to turn to *Integral Psychology* (2000), especially since it's his most complete and concise overview of the AQAL *integral vocabulary*, as is *The Marriage of Sense and Soul* (1998), another short yet detailed presentation reviewing "the task of premodernity" and the best means for integrating science and religion. But of course, *Sex, Ecology, Spirituality* (1995), vol. 1 in *The Kosmos Trilogy*, is the definitive AQAL text, as well as volume 2 (2006), the second 900-page volume, all of which are supplemented by the other more difficult, but engaging, Phase-4 texts, such as *The Eye*

of Spirit (1997), which has updated many of his earlier theories and concerns. Then there's *Boomeritis* (2002), a novel approach (his first "fiction" book) to presenting the AQAL Approach while focusing on the evolution and "spiral dynamics" of consciousness development (that is, taking a Phase-2 evolutionary approach, while a book's worth of detailed endnotes updates these concerns with the AQAL Phase-4 approach).

10. See: Frank Visser, *Ken Wilber: Thought As Passion* (2003), p. 15: "Thus in my opinion the teachings of Theosophy also serve to enrich any discussion about the validity of Wilber's vision"; also see: Visser's Chapter 7: "Ken Wilber In Perspective."

11. T. R. V. Murti, *The Central Philosophy of Buddhism* (1955), p. 104.

12. In almost all cases, his critics have shown a misreading of Wilber by presenting only a *partial* reading, where many, if not most, have concentrated on an earlier phase of writing and thinking—generally Phase-2 or the evolutionary, developmental period—in Wilber's overall career. The criticisms of Phase-4 and the AQAL approach has generally been more productive, where even many co-called "critics" (a number have even become friends) have been invited to participate in Wilber's Integral Institute and other projects.

13. See, for example, Michael Zimmerman, *Contesting Earth's Future: Radical Ecology and Postmodernity* (1994) or Zimmerman's excellent essay "A Transpersonal Diagnosis of the Ecological Crisis" in *Ken Wilber in Dialogue* (1998), ed. Donald Rothberg and Sean Kelly.

14. See Allan Combs, *The Radiance of Being: Understanding the Grand Integral Vision; Living the Integral Life* (2002).

15. See Georg Feuerstein, *Holy Madness* (1991), and Wes Nisker, *Crazy Wisdom* (1990).

16. Ken Wilber, foreword to *Finding God through Sex* (2002) by David Deida.

17. Georg Feuerstein, *Holy Madness* (1991), p. 5.

18. Ken Wilber, *Sex, Ecology, Spirituality* (1995), p. 271.

19. Ken Wilber, foreword to *Ken Wilber: Thought as Passion* (2003), p. xv.

Chapter Two
Unitas Multiplex: *An Integral Theory of Everything*

1. See *The Simple Feeling of Being: Embracing Your True Nature* (2004) by Ken Wilber; compiled and edited by Mark Palmer, Sean Hargens, Vipassana Esjorn, and Adam Leonard, p. 139.

2. See Ken Wilber, *A Theory of Everything* (2000).

3. Ken Wilber, *A Theory of Everything* (2000), p. 2 [italics added].

4. Ibid., p. xi.

5. Michael Murphy, back cover blurb on *Sex, Ecology, Spirituality* (1995) by Ken Wilber.

6. Stanislav Grof, *The Cosmic Game* (1998), p. xiii, p. 11.

7. Roger Walsh and Frances Vaughan, "The Worldview of Ken Wilber" in *Textbook of Transpersonal Psychiatry and Psychology* (1996), p. 71.

8. Ken Wilber, *One Taste* (1999), p. 345.

9. Ibid., p. 307.

10. Ibid., p. 334.

11. Ken Wilber, *Collected Works, Volume 4 (CW4)*, (1999), "Sociocultural Evolution," pp. 332-33.

12. Ken Wilber, *A Theory of Everything* (2000), p. 140; *Collected Works, Volume 8 (CW8)* (2000), introduction, p. 49.

13. Ken Wilber, *A Theory of Everything* (2000, Shambhala), p. 140: "True But Partial"; *Collected Works, Volume 8 (CW8)* (2000), introduction, p. 49.

14. Ken Wilber, *A Theory of Everything* (2000, Shambhala), p. 141.

15. See Ken Wilber, Excerpt B: "The Many Ways We Touch—Three Principles Helpful for Any Integrative Approach," November 2002.

16. Ken Wilber, "Odyssey: A Personal Inquiry into Humanistic and Transpersonal Psychology, *Journal of Humanistic Psychology*, vol. 22, no. 1 (Winter 1982): pp. 60-61.

17. Jack Crittenden, "What Is the Meaning of 'Integral'?" foreword to *The Eye of Spirit* (1997, Shambhala) by Ken Wilber, pp. viii-ix.

18. See Ken Wilber, *Sex, Ecology, Spirituality* (1995), pp. viii-ix.

19. Ken Wilber, *A Brief History of Everything* (1996), p. 18 [italics added].

20. Ken Wilber, *Integral Psychology* (2000), p. 187.

21. E. F. Schumacher, *A Guide for the Perplexed* (NY; Harper & Row, 1977); also see Anna Lemkow, *The Wholeness Principle* (Wheaton, IL: Quest Books, 1990), p. 16.

22. Ken Wilber, *The Spectrum of Consciousness* (1977), p. 42 [italics added].

23. Ken Wilber, *A Theory of Everything* (2000), p. 135 [italics added].

24. Ken Wilber, *Transformations of Consciousness* (1986), p. 6; while Aurobindo's integral philosophy, especially the teachings of evolution/involution, heavily influenced Wilber in the move from Phase-1 (spectrum of consciousness) to Phase-2 (evolution

of the spectrum), Wilber has said that Aurobindo became a hindrance in the move to Phase-4 (AQAL approach). (Personal communication to author.)

25. Haridas Chaudhuri, *The Evolution of Integral Consciousness* (1977), p. 17.

26. Dionne Marx and Dave Kendall, introduction, *The Evolution of Integral Consciousness* (1977) by Haridas Chaudhuri, p. 14 [italics added].

27. Roger Walsh and Frances Vaughan, "The Worldview of Ken Wilber" in *Journal of Humanistic Psychology*, vol. 34, no. 2 (Spring 1994): p. 19 [this paragraph, at the end of the essay, is not included in the version appearing in *Textbook of Transpersonal Psychiatry and Psychology*, Scotton et al., eds.].

28. Ken Wilber, *A Theory of Everything* (2000), p. 38 [emphasis added].

29. Ken Wilber, *The Marriage of Sense and Soul* (1998), p. 103.

30. Ken Wilber, *A Brief History of Everything* (1996), p. 42 [italics added].

Chapter Three

Wilber' Integral Internet of Jewels: Integral Institute & Integral University

1. See Tony Schwartz, *What Really Matters: Searching for Wisdom in America* (1995), Chapter 9: "Putting Consciousness on the Map: How Ken Wilber Married Freud and the Buddha"; and Frank Visser, *Ken Wilber: Thought as Passion* (2003).

2. Frank Visser, *Ken Wilber: Thought as Passion* (2003), p. 3.

3. Ken Wilber, *Up from Eden* (1981), p. 41n.

4. *The Oxford Dictionary of World Religions* (1997), p. 449.

5. *Kindred Visions* is an anthology (begun in 1998) by eighty of the finest philosophers, psychologists, and teachers from around the world who have alternative or complementary approaches to an Integral Vision, and who have used Wilber's version as a reflective foil to present summaries of their own work as well as offer insightful appreciations of Wilber's writings and integral philosophy, including contributions by Charles Taylor, John Searle, David Chalmers, Robert Kegan, Howard Gardner, Stan Grof, George Feuerstein, and many others.

6. Quote from opening page (not necessarily a mission statement), but it captures the essence of what I-I is attempting to accomplish.

7. All quotes about Integral Naked are from the website itself, January 2004.

8. Magazine advertisement, *What Is Enlightenment?* Issue 26, August-October 2004.

9. Beginning with Wilber/Phase-4, the phrase "I-I" has been used to refer to the highest state of consciousness, for it recalls Sri Ramana Maharshi who, as Wilber explains, "refers to the Self by the name 'I-I,' since the Self is the simple Witness of even the Ordinary 'I.' We are all, says Ramana, perfectly aware of the I-I, for we are all aware of our capacity to witness in the present moment" (*SES*, p. 306). Therefore Wilber often uses this phrase "I-I" in his mystical writings where he poetically, and beautifully, explains his realization of the Witness as the nondual ground of consciousness itself, therefore, also becoming an apt acronym for his institute and integral "think tank."

10. Ken Wilber, "Announcing the Formation of the Integral Institute" at www.wilber.shambhala.com [slight paraphrase].

11. Ken Wilber, Integral Institute website, "Join Us," Fall 2003.

12. Ken Wilber, Integral Institute website, "Integral University: A Multidimensional Matrix of Integral Learning," Fall 2003.

13. Ken Wilber, Integral Institute website, "Join Us," Fall 2003.

14. Ken Wilber, Excerpt B: "The Many Ways We Touch—Three Principles Helpful for Any Integrative Approach," November 2002.

15. "The Guru and the Pandit: Breaking the Rules: Andrew Cohen and Ken Wilber in Dialogue," *What Is Enlightenment?* (Fall/Winter 2002).

16. See *What Is Enlightenment?* August-October 2004, p. 29.

17. See integralnaked.org, "Luminous Arising: The Many Meanings of *The Matrix*," 9/10/2004.

Chapter Four
Wilber/Phase-4: The Marriage of Science & Religion: Correlating Exteriors & Interiors

1. See: Tony Schwartz, *What Really Matters* (1995), Chapter 9: "Putting Consciousness on the Map: How Ken Wilber Married Freud and the Buddha."

2. The title *The Marriage of Sense and Soul* was suggested by Random House, the New York publisher for this book (with blessings from Wilber's regular publisher, Shambhala Publications), since it came from the Oscar Wilde quote that opens the book: "There is nothing that will cure the senses but the soul, and nothing that will cure the soul but the senses." Also see Ken Wilber, *One Taste* (1999), the January entries for a description of Wilber's trip to New York City to sell his book to a larger publisher in order to encourage greater distribution and success; a goal that was accomplished in sales and recognition; for instance, it was even read by and publicly mentioned by then-President Bill Clinton and Vice President Al Gore.

3. Ken Wilber, *The Marriage of Sense and Soul* (1998), p. 14.

4. Wilber does not actually write out this formula as I have done, for I have taken the liberty for the sake of brief summary; see Ken Wilber, *The Marriage of Sense and Soul* (1998), p. 14: "To integrate religion and science is to integrate a premodern worldview with a modern worldview.... Thus, in order to integrate religion and science, we need to *integrate the Great Chain with the differentiations of modernity.*"

5. Ken Wilber, *The Marriage of Sense and Soul* (1999), p. 117: "*Interpretation is an intrinsic feature of the fabric of the universe,* and there, in a sentence, is the enduring truth at the heart of the great postmodern movements."

6. Ken Wilber, *Integral Psychology* (2000), p. 121.

7. Ken Wilber, *The Eye of Spirit* (1997), p. 58.

8. Ken Wilber, *A Brief History of Everything* (1996), p. 131.

9. Ken Wilber, *Integral Psychology* (2000), p. 149.

10. See Ken Wilber, *The Marriage of Sense and Soul* (1998), Chapter 1: "The Challenge of Our Times."

11. Ken Wilber, *The Marriage of Sense and Soul* (1999), pp. x-xi.

12. Ibid., p. 47.

13. Ken Wilber, *Integral Psychology* (2000), p. 158.

14. Ken Wilber, *The Marriage of Sense and Soul* (1999), p. 53.

15. Ibid., p. 47.

16. Ibid., p. 58.

17. Ibid., p. 80 [italics in original].

18. Ibid., p. 60.

19. Ibid., p. 25.

20. Ibid., p. 153.

21. Ibid., pp. 152-53.

22. Ibid., p. 155.

23. Ibid., pp. 155-56.

24. Ibid., pp. 158-59 [italics in original].

25. Ibid.

26. Ibid., pp. 162-63.

27. Ibid., p. 164.

28. Ibid., pp. 163, 166.

29. Ibid., p. 167.

30. Ibid., pp. 169-70.

31. Ibid., Chapter 11: "What Is Science?"

32. Ibid., Chapter 13: "The Stunning Display of Spirit."

33. Ken Wilber, *A Theory of Everything* (2000), p. 77.

34. Ken Wilber, *Eye to Eye* (1983), p. 183.

35. Ibid., p. 81.

36. Ken Wilber, *Integral Psychology* (2000), p. 75 [italics added].

37. See: KenWilber.com opening screen, Fall 2004.

38. Ken Wilber, *Integral Psychology* (2000), p. 75 [italics added].

39. Ken Wilber, *The Marriage of Sense and Soul* (1999), p. 182.

40. Ken Wilber, *A Theory of Everything* (2000), p. 66.

41. Ken Wilber, *Eye to Eye* (1983, 1986), p. 183.

42. See Ken Wilber, *Eye to Eye* (1983), Chapter 2: "The Problem of Proof"; Chapter 3: "A Mandalic Map of Consciousness."

43. Ken Wilber, *The Marriage of Sense and Soul* (1998), p. 196 [italics added].

44. Ibid., p. 197.

45. Ibid., p. 196.

46. Ibid., Chapter 14: "The Great Holarchy in the Postmodern World."

47. Ibid., p. 196 [italics added] and p. 76 [italics in original].

48. Ken Wilber, *Eye to Eye* (1983), p. 196.

49. Ken Wilber, *Integral Psychology* (2000), p. 288, 3n (last page of endnotes).

50. Ken Wilber, "An Integral Theory of Consciousness," in *Journal of Consciousness Studies*, vol. 4, no. 1, 1997 (now in *CW7*), p. 85 [italics added].

51. Ken Wilber, *Integral Psychology* (2000), p. 158 [italics added].

52. Ibid., p. 73.

53. Ibid., p. 172 [emphasis added].

54. Ken Wilber letter to Huston Smith, faxed to author July 25, 1995.

55. Ken Wilber, "An Integral Theory of Consciousness," in *Journal of Consciousness Studies*, vol. 4, no. 1, 1997 (now in *CW7*), p. 76.

Chapter Five
Wilber/Phase-5: Integral Post-Metaphysics: Transcending Spiritual Traditions

1. See "Welcome Message," at KenWilber.com, September 17, 2004.

2. See Ken Wilber, "An Integral Age at the Leading Edge" (Excerpt A), 2003, excerpted from vol. 2 of *The Kosmos Trilogy* (2005).

3. Ken Wilber, *Grace and Grit* (1991), p. 77.

4. See Ken Wilber, introduction to *Collected Works, Volume 8 (CW8)* (2000).

5. Ken Wilber, *The Eye of Spirit* (1997), pp. 63-64.

6. Ken Wilber, "The Neo-Perennial Philosophy," in *American Theosophist*, Special Fall Issue 1983, pp. 349-55 (reprinted in *The Quest*, Autumn 1992; now part of *The Eye of Spirit*, 1997, Chapter 2: "In a Modern Light: Integral Anthropology and the Evolution of Cultures"); also see Brad Reynolds, *Embracing Reality: The Integral Vision of Ken Wilber: A Historical Survey and Chapter-by-Chapter Guide To Wilber's Major Works* (2004, Tarcher/Putnam), introduction: "Ken Wilber's Personal Odyssey."

7. Ken Wilber, "The Neo-Perennial Philosophy," in *The Quest*, Autumn 1992, p. 20 [emphasis added].

8. Ibid.

9. See in particular Ken Wilber, *Up from Eden* (1981), Chapter 14: "I and the Father Are One"; and Ken Wilber, *Sex, Ecology, Spirituality* (1995), Chapter 8: "The Depths of the Divine."

10. See Ken Wilber, introduction to *Collected Works, Volume 8 (CW8)* (2000).

11. Ken Wilber, introduction to *Collected Works, Volume 8 (CW8)* (2000), pp. 53-55, 10n.

12. See Ken Wilber, introduction to *Collected Works, Volume 8 (CW8)* (2000).

13. Ken Wilber, *The Eye of Spirit* (1997), pp. 38-39; Ken Wilber, *One Taste* (1999), March 10.

14. Ken Wilber, *The Eye of Spirit* (1997), p. 39.

15. Ken Wilber, *Integral Psychology* (2000), pp. 8-9.

16. Ken Wilber, *One Taste* (1999), pp. 57-58 (March 10).

17. Ken Wilber, *Integral Psychology* (2000), p. 9.

18. Ibid., p. 10. [Italics added].

19. See Ken Wilber, "An Integral Age at the Leading Edge" (Excerpt A), posted 2003, excerpted from vol. 2 of *The Kosmos Trilogy* (2005).

20. Ken Wilber, *The Marriage of Sense and Soul* (1998), pp. 118-19 [italics in original; plus I substituted "interior" for "Left-Hand" and "exterior" for "Right-Hand" dimensions].

21. Ken Wilber, introduction to *Collected Works, Volume 8 (CW8)* (2000), p. 62, 30n.

22. See Ken Wilber, "An Integral Age at the Leading Edge" (Excerpt A), 2003, excerpted from vol. 2 of *The Kosmos Trilogy* (2005).

23. Ken Wilber, *Integral Psychology* (2000), p. 12.

24. See Ken Wilber, "An Integral Age at the Leading Edge" (Excerpt A), 2003, excerpted from vol. 2 of *The Kosmos Trilogy* (2005).

25. Sri Adi Da Samraj, *Water and Narcissus* (unpublished) by then Franklin Jones.

Chapter Six

Manjushri with a ThinkPad: "Spirit Exists."

1. Drawn from the opening quote to Frank Visser's *Ken Wilber: Thought as Passion* (2003), which quoted from an unpublished manuscript that Wilber wrote in 1987 called *The Great Chain of Being: A Modern Introduction To the Perennial Philosophy and the World's Great Mystical Traditions* (mentioned in *Grace and Grit*, p. 257).

2. Ken Wilber, *Grace and Grit* (1991), p. 246.

3. Alan Watts, *Myth and Ritual in Christianity* (1968), p. 15.

4. "The Great Tradition" is a term used by Wilber that originated with Sri Adi Da Samraj to describe "the total inheritance of authentic religious, spiritual, magical, and transcendental paths, philosophies, and testimonies from all the eras and cultures of humanity"; see: Adi Da (Da Free John), *Nirvanasara* (1982), and Adi Da, *The Basket of Tolerance* (unpublished).

5. See Ken Wilber, "An Integral Age at the Leading Edge" (Excerpt A), posted 2003.

6. Ken Wilber, *The Eye of Spirit* (1997), p. 43.

7. Ken Wilber, *A Brief History of Everything* (1996), p. 38.

8. Ken Wilber, *The Eye of Spirit* (1997), p. 43; Ken Wilber, "The Great Chain of Being," in *Paths Beyond Ego* (1993), p. 217.

9. Ken Wilber, *Eye to Eye* (1983, 1990), p. 307.

10. Ken Wilber, *Up from Eden* (1981), p. 4.

11. See Ken Wilber, *Sex, Ecology, Spirituality* (1995), p. 303.

12. Ken Wilber, *Up from Eden* (1981), p. 258.

13. Ken Wilber, *The Atman Project* (1980), p. 74.

14. Both definitions from Ken Wilber, *Up from Eden* (1981), p. 134.

15. Ken Wilber, *The Spectrum of Consciousness* (1977), p. 43 [italics added].

16. See Ken Wilber, *Eye to Eye* (1983), last chapter: "The Ultimate State of Consciousness," where the pandit gives an excellent presentation of the "Ultimate" by starting with the phrase from the *Chandogya Upanishad* that claims that the Absolute (Brahman) is "One without a second." Wilber concurs by explaining, "That inspired Upanishadic text does not describe the ultimate as the creator, controller, ruler, or lord of a second; neither does it speak of One opposed to a second, nor One outside a second, nor over, above, or beyond a second—but One without a second."

17. Ken Wilber, *The Eye of Spirit* (1997), pp. 281, 283.

18. Ken Wilber, foreword to *Talks with Ramana Maharshi* (2000, 2001), p. ix, xi; I have substituted the Western name "God" in place of "Brahman" (the Hindu name for God), which both Ramana and Wilber use in this example.

19. See *The Encyclopedia of Eastern Philosophy and Religion* (1989, 1994, Shambhala Publications), p. 128.

20. Ken Wilber, *One Taste* (1999), p. 126.

21. Ken Wilber, *The Atman Project* (1980), p. 74.

22. Ken Wilber, *Integral Psychology* (2000), p. 155.

23. Ken Wilber, *Up from Eden* (1981), p. 151.

24. See Ken Wilber, *Sex, Ecology, Spirituality* (1995), pp. 268-73: "Language and Mysticism"; also *The Marriage of Sense and Soul* (1998) as well as in Wilber's most recent Phase-5 writings.

25. Ken Wilber, *The Atman Project* (1980), p. 75.

26. Ken Wilber, *Up from Eden* (1981), p. 6 ["discovery of Wholeness" and "optical delusions" are from Einstein's' famous quote that Wilber had referred to earlier on the page].

27. Ken Wilber, *The Atman Project* (1980), pp. 73-74.

28. Ken Wilber, *The Eye of Spirit* (1997), p. 291.

29. Ken Wilber, *The Atman Project* (1980), p. 74.

30. Ken Wilber, *No Boundary* (1970), p. 142.

31. "Always Already," or pointing to our "ever-present awareness," often appears at the end of Wilber's books (after intense intellectual philosophical considerations), such as in *The Spectrum of Consciousness* (1977) with the last chapter titled "That Which Is Always Already," or in *Eye to Eye* (1983) with "The Ultimate State of Consciousness," or in *The Eye of Spirit* (1997) with "Always Already: The Brilliant Clarity of Ever-Present Awareness."

32. See Brad Reynolds, *Embracing Reality: The Integral Vision of Ken Wilber* (2004), introduction: "Ken Wilber's Personal Odyssey," pp. 1-69.

33. See Ken Wilber, "Odyssey: A Personal Inquiry into Humanistic and Transpersonal Psychology" in *Journal of Humanistic Psychology*, vol. 22, no. 1 (Winter 1982), especially about the Apollo and Vishnu complexes.

34. Ken Wilber, "Psychologia Perennis: The Spectrum of Consciousness," *Journal of Transpersonal Psychology*, vol. 7, no. 2, 1975, p. 83.

35. Ken Wilber, "Odyssey," p. 84.

36. Ibid.

37. Ken Wilber, *Sex, Ecology, Spirituality* (1995), p. 357.

38. See Ken Wilber, *Sex, Ecology, Spirituality* (1995), and its companion volume *A Brief History of Everything* (1996) for discussions on "Western Vedanta."

39. Ken Wilber, *One Taste* (1999), p. 136.

40. Ken Wilber, *The Eye of Spirit* (1997), p. 309, 1n; *Sex, Ecology, Spirituality* (1995), p. 358.

41. Ken Wilber, *Sex, Ecology, Spirituality* (1995), p. 358.

42. Ibid.

43. Mircea Eliade and Joan P. Couliano, *The Eliade Guide To World Religions* (1991, HarperSanFrancisco), p. 266.

44. In my previous book, *Embracing Reality: The Integral Vision of Ken Wilber* (2004), I do claim that Wilber is a person who has had (at least) a "taste" of, or been awakened to, the Enlightened Condition of consciousness and reality (which is ultimately inherent in every being). In the introduction, titled "Ken Wilber's Personal Odyssey," I review some of the conditions and spiritual masters that were available to Wilber on

his "personal odyssey" to his first *satoris* or *kenshos* in the late 1970s, and then with his continual development throughout the 1980s and 1990s. Yet I do not make the claim, nor has he ever made such a claim, that Wilber is a fully enlightened human being. Indeed, according to the wisdom traditions, there are advanced stages or subtle phases (or further transformations) that are available and can manifest within the condition of "whole-body Enlightenment." This human condition has been expressed or personally demonstrated in the human body-mind complex by some of the world's greatest saints and sages. Also, the wisdom traditions, as does Wilber, distinguish between the short, temporary or "sudden" "experience" of Enlightenment, and the fully-advanced, final, or "whole-body" disposition of permanent (or enduring and "gradual") Enlightenment, which is lived constantly in every moment (*sahaj samadhi* or the "open eyes" Enlightenment of nondual mysticism). Wilber's first major *satori,* on that graceful day in 1978, was more-or-less *temporary,* thus he does not claim to be a fully enlightened being, yet (as with all persons) the psycho-physical currents or enduring depths of Complete Enlightenment are still evolving (or unfolding) in his own case.

45. Ken Wilber, *One Taste* (1998, Shambhala), p. 351.

46. Robert Thurman, *Essential Tibetan Buddhism* (1995, 1997), p. 5.

47. Robert Thurman, *The Central Philosophy of Tibet* (1984, Princeton), p. 3.

48. Ken Wilber, *The Atman Project* (1981), p. 91.

49. Ken Wilber, *Collected Works, Vol. 3* (1999), introduction.

50. Ken Wilber clarifies further: "In India, as I have often pointed out, a distinction is made between a *pandit* and a *guru.* A pandit is a spiritual practitioner, who also has a flair for the academic or scholarly or intellectual, and so becomes a teacher of the Divine, an articulator and defender of the dharma, an intellectual samurai. A guru, on the other hand, is one who engages people directly and publicly, and who gets intimately involved with the ordeal of transforming their karma," in "Mind and the Heart of Emptiness: Reflections on Intellect and the Spiritual Path," in *The Quest,* Winter 1995, p. 21.

51. See Ken Wilber, *One Taste* (1999, Shambhala), pp. 222-26; *What Is Enlightenment?* "The Guru and the Pandit: Andrew Cohen and Ken Wilber," issues: Spring/Summer 2002; "Dialogue I: The Evolution of Enlightenment," Fall/Winter 2002; "Dialogue II: Breaking the Rules," Spring/Summer 2003; "Dialogue III: Exploring the Future of Religion."

52. Ken Wilber, *One Taste* (1999), September 15, p. 224 [italics added].

53. Ken Wilber, "Mind and the Heart of Emptiness: Reflections on Intellect and the Spiritual Path," in *The Quest,* Winter 1995, p. 22.

Chapter Seven
AQAL Metatheory: A Kosmos of Holons

1. Personal communication to author.

2. Ken Wilber, *Grace and Grit* (1991, Shambhala), p. 396; *One Taste* (1999, Shambhala), p. 54; *CW5* (2000, Shambhala), p. x.

3. See Ken Wilber, *One Taste* (1999, Shambhala), March 7 entry.

4. See Ken Wilber, "An Integral Theory of Consciousness," in *Journal of Consciousness Studies*, vol. 4, no. 1, 1997 (now in *CW7*).

5. See Ken Wilber, *Sex, Ecology, Spirituality: The Spirit of Evolution, Second Edition, Revised* (2000), first published in 2000 as *Collected Works, Volume Six (CW6)* and then in paperback, is a slightly modified version of the original for it includes a couple of extra graphics and some explanatory text (including "the mind/body problem" and offering "a diagrammatic overview").

6. Ken Wilber, *Sex, Ecology, Spirituality* (1995, Shambhala), p. 524 (last page).

7. Ibid., p. viii.

8. Ken Wilber, *Collected Works Vol. 6* (2000, Shambhala), p. xxiii.

9. Ken Wilber, *One Taste* (1999), p. viii.

10. Ken Wilber, *A Theory of Everything* (2000), p. 145, 1n.

11. Wilber's writings, I contend (as already suggested in Chapter 6), can be accurately seen as incorporating many of the major philosophical schools of Buddhism, from the "universal liberation" qualities of the T'ien T'ai school (and the *Lotus Sutra*), to the "mind-only" (or "consciousness-only") school of Yogachara, to the "gradual" and "sudden" Enlightenment teachings of Rinzai and Soto Zen, respectively, to the "Middle Way" of Madhyamika, to the "totality teachings" of the Hua-Yen. In my opinion, other than the *neti, neti* ("not this, not that") negation teachings of Nagarjuna (which maintain a purely nondual stance), which is Wilber's deepest affinity (as we've seen in Chapter 6), the resemblance seems to be especially true in comparison to the "full-rounded" models of reality taught by Hua-Yen Buddhism, which include the principal teachings on the Dharmadhatu. Hua-Yen Buddhism, founded in China by Fa-tsang (643-712) and further established by another professed incarnation of Manjushri, the sage Ch'eng-kuan (737-820), primarily teaches the "universal causality of the *dharmadhatu*" or the interdependence of all things on one another See: *The Encyclopedia of Eastern Philosophy and Religion* (1989, 1994, Shambhala Publications), p. 145.

12. Ken Wilber, *The Spectrum of Consciousness* (1977), p. 87.

13. Gavin Kilty, trans., *The Splendor of an Autumn Moon: The Devotional Verse of Tsong-khapa* (2001, Boston: Wisdom Publications), p. 289.

14. *The Perennial Dictionary of World Religions* (1981), p. 222.

15. Ken Wilber, *The Spectrum of Consciousness* (1977), p. 72.

16. Ken Wilber, "On the Nature of a Post-Metaphysical Spirituality" (2003), and in *What Is Enlightenment?* Spring/Summer 2003, p. 92.

17. Ken Wilber, *The Spectrum of Consciousness* (1977), Chapter 3: "Reality and Consciousness."

18. Ken Wilber, *Integral Psychology* (2000), p. 27.

19. Ibid., p. 90 [emphasis added].

20. Ken Wilber, *Collected Works, Volume 4* (1999), p. 231, from "Sheldrake's Theory of Morphogenesis" by Ken Wilber, originally in *Journal of Humanistic Psychology*, vol. 24, no. 2, 1984.

21. See Rupert Sheldrake, *A New Science of Life* (1981).

22. Ken Wilber, *Collected Works, Volume 4* (1999), p. 234 [italics added].

23. See Ken Wilber, "Toward a Comprehensive Theory of Subtle Energies," Excerpt C, posted January 2003 as an excerpt from vol. 2 of *The Kosmos Trilogy;* tentatively titled *Kosmic Karma and Creativity* (2006).

24. Ken Wilber, *Integral Psychology* (2000), p. 89.

25. Ibid., p. 12 [italics added].

26. Ken Wilber, *The Eye of Spirit* (1997), p. 49.

27. See Ken Wilber, "Introduction To Integral Theory & Practice: IOS Basic & the AQAL Map," Integral Institute essay, 2003, p. 30.

28. Jan Smuts, *Holism and Evolution* (1926), p. 99.

29. Ken Wilber, *The Atman Project* (1980), p. 1 [italics in original].

30. Ken Wilber, *The Atman Project* (1980), p. 1; also see Jan Smuts, *Holism and Evolution* (1926, NY: Macmillan).

31. See Ken Wilber, "Preface to the Second Edition, Revised," *Sex, Ecology, Spirituality* (1995, 2000).

32. F. E. Peters, *Greek Philosophical Terms* (1967), p. 84.

33. E. F. Schumacher, *A Guide for the Perplexed* (1977), p. 14 [italics in original]; Schumacher is also the author to the popular *Small Is Beautiful* (1973), which introduced the idea of "appropriate technology."

34. See Arthur Koestler, *The Ghost in the Machine* (1967), p. 49; *Janus: A Summing Up* (1978), p. 27.

35. Ken Wilber, *Sex, Ecology, Spirituality* (1995), p. 33 (page before the listing of the first tenet).

36. Ken Wilber, *Sex, Ecology, Spirituality* (1995), pp. 22-23.

37. Arthur Koestler, *Janus: A Summing Up* (1978), p. 34.

38. Ken Wilber, *The Eye of Spirit* (1997), p. 40.

39. Arthur Koestler, *The Ghost in the Machine* (1967), p. 103; Ken Wilber, *Sex, Ecology, Spirituality* (1995), p. 21: "All hierarchies are composed of holons, or increasing orders of wholeness... [therefore] the correct word for 'hierarchy' is actually *holarchy*."

40. Ken Wilber, *Sex, Ecology, Spirituality* (1995), p. 31 [italics in original].

41. Ibid., p. 23, plus, 18, 24.

42. Ibid., p. 24.

43. Ken Wilber, *A Theory of Everything* (2000), p. 143, 1n.

44. Ken Wilber, *Sex, Ecology, Spirituality* (1995), p. 31.

45. Ken Wilber, *Integral Psychology* (2000), p. 279, 15n.

46. Ibid.

47. Stephen Hawking, *A Brief History of Time: From the Big Bang To Black Holes* (1988), p. 1.

48. See Ken Wilber, *Sex, Ecology, Spirituality* (1995), p. 35: "There is an old joke about a King who goes to a Wiseperson and asks how is it that the Earth doesn't fall down? The Wiseperson replies, 'The Earth is resting on a lion.' 'On what, then, is the lion resting?' asks the King. 'The lion is resting on an elephant.' 'On what is the elephant resting?' 'The elephant is resting on a turtle.' 'On what is the...' 'You can stop right there, your Majesty. It's turtles all the way down'."

49. See Ken Wilber, *Sex, Ecology, Spirituality* (1995), Chapter 9: "The Way Up Is the Way Down."

50. Ibid., p. 40.

51. Ibid., p. 36.

52. Ibid., p. 46.

53. Ibid., p. 36.

54. Ken Wilber, *A Theory of Everything* (2000), p.143, 1n.

55. Ken Wilber, *Integral Psychology* (2000), p. 173.

56. Ken Wilber, *Sex, Ecology, Spirituality* (1995), p. 39 [italics added].

57. Ken Wilber, *The Marriage of Sense and Soul* (1998), p. 79.

58. Ibid., pp. 80, 9.

59. Ken Wilber, *Sex, Ecology, Spirituality* (1995), pp. 37-38.

60. Ken Wilber, *A Brief History of Everything* (1996, Shambhala), p. 19 [italics added].

Chapter Eight
AQAL Matrix: A Kosmic Mandala of Spitit-in-Action

1. Huston Smith, personal communication from Ken Wilber to author, July 25, 1995; also see: Huston Smith, back cover blurb on *The Spectrum of Consciousness* (1977, 1993, 2nd edition).

2. Arthur Lovejoy, *The Great Chain of Being* (1936, 1964), p. 26

3. Ken Wilber, *The Marriage of Sense and Soul* (1998), p. 7 [emphasis added].

4. Huston Smith, *Forgotten Truth* (1976, 1992), p. 62.

5. Ibid., pp. 3, 20-21.

6. Ken Wilber, *Integral Psychology* (2000), p. 236, 2n [italics added].

7. Ken Wilber, *Collected Works, Volume Eight (CW8)* (2000), p. 63, 31n [emphasis added].

8. Ken Wilber, *Integral Psychology* (2000), p. 236, 2n.

9. See Eric Jantsch, *The Self-Organizing Universe* (1980).

10. See Ervin Laszlo, *Evolution: The Grand Synthesis* (1987).

11. See Michael Murphy, *The Future of the Body* (1992)

12. Ken Wilber, *Sex, Ecology, Spirituality* (1995), p. 38; see *A Brief History of Everything* (1996), p. 19.

13. See Ken Wilber, *Eye to Eye* (1983), Chapter 3: "A Mandalic Map of Consciousness."

14. Ken Wilber, *The Atman Project* (1980), p. 80.

15. Ken Wilber, *Sex, Ecology, Spirituality* (1995), p. 88.

16. See Ken Wilber, *A Brief History of Everything* (1996), Chapter 2: "The Secret Impulse."

17. Ibid., p. 30.

18. Ken Wilber, *The Eye of Spirit* (1997), p. 157.

19. Huston Smith, *Forgotten Truth* (1975, 1992), p. 87.

20. See Ken Wilber, *Sex, Ecology, Spirituality* (1995), Chapter 2: "The Pattern That Connects." I have chosen to call what's usually listed as the "twenty tenets" by the designator "20-Tenets" in order to make it more obvious.

21. Ken Wilber, *Sex, Ecology, Spirituality* (1995), p. 34.

22. Ken Wilber, *Collected Works, Volume Seven (CW7)* (2000), p. 365.

23. Ken Wilber, *Sex, Ecology, Spirituality* (1995), p. 116 [both quotes].

24. Ibid., p. 34.

25. Ken Wilber, *Collected Works, Volume Seven (CW7)* (2000), p. 365.

26. See: Ken Wilber, *Sex, Ecology, Spirituality* (1995), pp. 35-78, 500, 502, 505 [20-Tenets]. A complete list of the 20-Tenets can also be found in *Collected Works, Volume Seven (CW7)* (2000), pp. 365-66.

27. Ken Wilber, *Sex, Ecology, Spirituality* (1995), p. 72; *Collected Works, Volume 2 (CW2)* (1999), introduction.

28. Ken Wilber, *A Theory of Everything* (2000), p. 168, 7n [italics added].

29. Definitions from Ken Wilber, *A Brief History of Everything* (1996), p. 332 [italics in original].

30. Ken Wilber, *A Theory of Everything* (2000), p. 168, 7n.

31. Ken Wilber, *The Atman Project* (1980), p. ix.

32. Ken Wilber, *The Marriage of Sense and Soul* (1998), p. 104.

33. Ken Wilber, *A Brief History of Everything* (1996), p. 10.

34. Ken Wilber, "Odyssey: A Personal Inquiry into Humanistic and Transpersonal Psychology, *Journal of Humanistic Psychology*, vol. 22, no. 1, Winter 1982, p. 59.

35. Ken Wilber, *A Brief History of Everything* (1996), p. 42.

36. Ibid., p. 38.

37. Ken Wilber, *The Eye of Spirit* (rev. ed., 2000), Chapter 12: "Waves, Streams, States, and Self—A Summary of My Psychological Model (Or, Outline of An Integral Psychology)."

38. Both *exocept* and *endocept* are terms used by Wilber from Silvano Arieti in *The Intrapsychic Self: Feeling, Cognition, and Creativity in Health and Mental Illness* (1967), a major influence on Wilber's early theories.

39. See Ken Wilber, *Sex, Ecology, Spirituality* (1995), pp. 18-19, from Goudge, *Encyclopedia of Philosophy, Vol. 2* (1967), ed. Paul Edwards, p. 474.

40. Ken Wilber, *The Eye of Spirit* (1997), p. 95.

41. Ken Wilber, *The Spectrum of Consciousness* (1977), p. 314 [all quotes this paragraph].

42. Ken Wilber, *Integral Psychology* (2000), p. 153.

Chapter Nine
AQAL Matrix: Four-Quadrant Holons

1. Ken Wilber, "An Integral Theory of Consciousness," in *Journal of Consciousness Studies*, vol. 4, no. 1, 1997 (now in *CW7*), p. 73.

2. Ken Wilber, *A Brief History of Everything* (1996), p. 119.

3. Ken Wilber, "An Integral Theory of Consciousness," p. 73.

4. See Ken Wilber, *A Brief History of Everything* (1996), pp. 72-73.

5. Ken Wilber, "An Integral Theory of Consciousness," p. 73.

6. Ken Wilber, *Sex, Ecology, Spirituality* (1995), p. 139.

7. Ken Wilber, "An Integral Theory of Consciousness," p. 77.

8. Ken Wilber, *A Brief History of Everything* (1996), p. 105.

9. Ken Wilber, *A Brief History of Everything* (1996), p. 106.

10. Ken Wilber, "An Integral Theory of Consciousness," p. 86.

11. Ken Wilber, *A Brief History of Everything* (1996), p. 109.

12. Ken Wilber, *A Brief History of Everything* (1996), p. 112 [italics in original].

13. Ken Wilber, "An Integral Theory of Consciousness," p. 79.

14. See Ken Wilber, *The Eye of Spirit* (1997), p. 20; also see Ken Wilber, "An Integral Theory of Consciousness," p. 77: Habermas's three validity claims (subjective truthfulness of I, cultural justness of we, and objective truth of its); Kant's three critiques: science or Its (*Critique of Pure Reason*), morals or We (*Critique of Practical Reason*), and Art and self-expression of the I *(Critique of Judgment);* Sir Karl Popper's "three worlds" (subjective, cultural, and objective); Three Jewels of Buddhism: Buddha (I), Sangha (We), and Dharma (It).

15. See Ken Wilber, foreword to the paperback edition of *A Sociable God* (1983, 2005), "Methodological Outlaw: My Life as a Dishwasher."

16. See Ken Wilber, *Kosmos Trilogy, Volume Two* (untitled, 2006); also see: "The Ways

We Are in This Together: Intersubjectivity and Interobjectivity in the Holonic Kosmos," by Ken Wilber, Excerpt C, posted January 2003.

17. Ken Wilber, *Sex, Ecology, Spirituality* (1995), p. 127.

18. Ken Wilber, *A Brief History of Everything* (1996), p. 121; *The Marriage of Sense and Soul* (1998), p. 50.

19. Ken Wilber, *The Marriage of Sense and Soul* (1998), p. 50; *A Brief History of Everything* (1996), p. 121.

20. Ken Wilber, *The Marriage of Sense and Soul* (1998), p. 50; *A Brief History of Everything* (1996), p. 120.

21. See Ken Wilber, *Kosmos Trilogy, Volume Two* (untitled, 2006); also see "The Ways We Are in This Together: Intersubjectivity and Interobjectivity in the Holonic Kosmos," by Ken Wilber, Excerpt C, posted January 2003.

22. Ken Wilber, *One Taste* (1999), p. 238; France's husband, Roger Walsh, responded by suggesting, as Ken tells us, with what "he calls 20/20: *Each quadrant* should have at least 20 percent representation in the [Integral Institute's] activities."

23. Ken Wilber, *Integral Psychology* (2000), p. 184 [italics added].

24. Ibid., p. 185 [italics added].

25. Ken Wilber, *A Theory of Everything* (2000), p. 154, 16n.

26. Ken Wilber, *Integral Psychology* (2000), pp. 192-93 [emphasis added].

27. Ibid., pp. 183, 184 [italics added].

28. Ibid., p. 234, 3n.

29. Ibid., p. 113.

Chapter Ten

AQAL Matrix: Integral Psychology: Evolution of the Self-System

1. Ken Wilber, *A Theory of Everything* (2000), p. 7.

2. Ken Wilber, *Transformations of Consciousness* (1986), p. 67.

3. See Ken Wilber, *Integral Psychology* (2000), Chapter 3: "The Self" [italics in original, bold added].

4. Ken Wilber, *The Atman Project* (1980), p. 34; also see: Ken Wilber, *Spectrum of Consciousness* (1977), *No Boundary* (1979); "persona + shadow = ego" is a simplistic

formulation Wilber presented in his earlier Phase-1/2 writings to quickly recapitulate traditional psychology.

5. Ken Wilber, *Integral Psychology* (2000), p. 28.

6. Ibid., p. 35.

7. Ibid., p. 36.

8. See ibid., Chapter 8: "The Archeology of Spirit"; an excellent AQAL (Phase-4) review packed with detail describing the various *fulcrums* in the development of the proximate self.

9. Ken Wilber, *The Atman Project* (1980), p. 79.

10. Ken Wilber, *A Brief History of Everything* (1996), p. 196; pp. 193-196: "On the Brink of the Transpersonal."

11. Ken Wilber, *The Eye of Spirit* (1997), p. 351, 17n; p. 384n: "These post-Enlightenment developments are the events that unfold in the space of *sahaj [samadhi]*, in the nondual space of simple, everpresent awareness, once the bodymind is self-liberated from the tortures of the self-contraction; that is, once it is recognized that the self-contraction does not exist, never did exist, and never will exist. Under that realization, the bodymind is transfigured into its own primordial condition, the naked luminosity that is its own remark, self-evidently, eternally."

12. Wilber has carefully reviewed the AQAL upgrade of integral psychology in his Phase-4 books, such as *Sex, Ecology, Spirituality* (1995), *A Brief History of Everything* (1996), and *The Eye of Spirit* (1997), but especially with *Integral Psychology* (2000).

13. Ken Wilber, *Sex, Ecology, Spirituality* (1995), p. 231.

14. Ibid., pp. 103, 233.

15. Ken Wilber, *Grace and Grit* (1991), p. 65.

16. Ken Wilber, "Intro to Integral Theory & Practice: IOS Basic and the AQAL Map," Integral Institute essay (2003), p. 12.

17. Ken Wilber, *Integral Psychology* (2000), p. 90.

18. Definitions and quotes from Ken Wilber, *Integral Psychology* (2000), Chapter 9: "Some Important Developmental Streams"; plus [in brackets], I've included the recent terms suggested by Andrew Cohen developed in cooperative dialogues with Wilber in the opening years of the new millennium; also see: "The Guru and the Pandit: Andrew Cohen and Ken Wilber in Dialogue: Following the Grain of the Kosmos: Dialogue V" in *What Is Enlightenment?* May-July 2004.

19. Wilber shows the streams as straight vertical lines, whereas I have slightly modified the graphic to depict their layered effect.

20. See Ken Wilber, *Integral Psychology* (2000), Chapter 9: "Some Developmental Streams."

21. Ken Wilber, *A Theory of Everything* (2000), p. 22 [italics added].

22. Ken Wilber, "Introduction to Integral Theory & Practice: IOS Basic & the AQAL Map" (2004, private essay), p. 8.

23. Ken Wilber, *The Eye of Spirit* (1997), p. 353, 22n.

24. Ken Wilber, *One Taste* (1999), p. 290.

25. Ken Wilber, *Integral Psychology* (2000), p. 29.

26. Ken Wilber, "Introduction to Integral Theory & Practice: IOS Basic & the AQAL Map" (2004, private essay), p. 28.

27. Ken Wilber, *Integral Psychology* (2000), p. 38.

28. Ibid.

29. Ibid., p. 30.

30. Ibid., p. 31 [Wilber only notes to see the figure which I've called a "holarchic mandala"].

31. Ken Wilber, *The Eye of Spirit* (1997), p. 352, 21n.

32. Ken Wilber, *One Taste* (1999), p. 288.

33. Ken Wilber, *Integral Psychology* (2000), Chapter 1: "The Basic Levels or Waves."

34. Ken Wilber, "Introduction to Integral Theory & Practice: IOS Basic and the AQAL Map" (2004), p. 12.

35. See Ken Wilber, *Integral Psychology* (2000), pp. 12-16: "Structures and States."

36. Ken Wilber, *Integral Psychology* (2000), Chapter 1: "The Basic Levels or Waves."

37. Ken Wilber, *One Taste* (1999), p. 125; also see: *The Eye of Spirit* (1997), pp. 46-47.

38. Ken Wilber, *Integral Psychology* (2000), p. 53, Chapter 4: "The Self-Related Streams."

39. Ken Wilber, *Integral Psychology* (2000), pp. 12-13.

40. See Ken Wilber, *Sex, Ecology, Spirituality* (1995), pp. 741-61, 17n; I had pointed out in a paper referenced in *SES*, where Wilber agreed "that we have a type of (limited but fluid) access to transpersonal states should not detract from the fact that temporary experiences are not the stuff of enduring wisdom-adaptation," yet he was also very clear that "*all* the domains of consciousness are simply *not* available (holographically or otherwise) to a particular subject of consciousness." For example, when a conventional mythic-believer has not developed "the formative structures of stable adaptation"

to maintain a vision-logic worldcentric stance then they must continue development through the enduring stages.

41. Ken Wilber, *Integral Psychology* (2000), p. 35, Chapter 3: "The Self."

42. Ken Wilber, *A Sociable God* (1983), p. 71.

43. Ibid., p. 69.

44. Ibid., p. 74.

45. Ken Wilber, *The Eye of Spirit* (1997), p. 319, 9n.

46. Ken Wilber, *A Sociable God* (1983), p. 68.

47. Ibid., p. 18.

48. See Ken Wilber, *Sex, Ecology, Spirituality* (1995), pp. 276-78: "Reconstruction of the Contemplative Path."

49. A review of Ken Wilber's own personal spiritual development can be found in *Embracing Reality: The Integral Vision of Ken Wilber: A Historical Survey and Chapter-by-Chapter Guide to Wilber's Major Works* (2004, Tarcher/Putnam) by Brad Reynolds; also see Ken Wilber's autobiographical accounts of his spiritual practices in "Odyssey: A Personal Inquiry into Humanistic and Transpersonal Psychology" (1982), now in *Collected Works Vol. 2 (CW2)*; *Grace and Grit* (1992); *One Taste* (1999) for examples of his personal practices.

50. Ken Wilber, *A Sociable God* (1983), p. 32.

51. The transpersonal levels and corresponding "path" that Wilber has used in outlining the various transpersonal stages of development in the late 1970s were inspired, in great part, by Sri Adi Da Samraj (then known as Bubba Free John and Da Free John), who had recently written such influential books as *The Method of the Siddhas* (1973, 1978), *The Paradox of Instruction* (1977), and *Enlightenment of the Whole Body* (1978), which Wilber had read and recommended with the highest praise (see *No Boundary* and *Up from Eden*, for example).

52. See Ken Wilber, *A Sociable God* (1983), Chapter 2: "The Hierarchy of Structural Organization."

53. See Ken Wilber, *Quantum Questions* (1984), p. 145-46n: "Because the natural realms are a *reduced* subset of, or are ontically *less than*, the mental-soul realms, then all fundamental natural processes can be essentially represented mathematically, but not all mathematical forms have a material application."

54. Ken Wilber, *The Atman Project* (1980), p. 72.

55. Ken Wilber, *The Atman Project* (1980), p. 74.

56. Wilber very effectively applied these developmental structures or levels of mysticism

to the historical development of humankind beginning with his classic Phase-2 study on human evolution, *Up from Eden* (1981), and then succinctly reviewed in *A Sociable God* (1983); he has carried these ideas forward via the AQAL Approach with the various Phase-4 books, such as *Sex, Ecology, Spirituality* (1995), *A Brief History of Everything* (1996), *The Eye of Spirit* (1997), *Integral Psychology* (2000), and in other writings.

57. Allan Combs, *The Radiance of Being* (2002), pp. 194-95.

58. Ken Wilber, introduction to *Collected Works, Volume 8 (CW8)* (2000), pp. 78-79n.

Chapter Eleven
AQAL Apps: Integral Theory into Integral Practice

1. Ken Wilber, from opening quote posted on www.KenWilber.com, January 2005.

2. See Ken Wilber, "Mythological Outlaw: My Life as a Dishwasher," in the new foreword to the paperback edition of *A Sociable God* (1983, 2006).

3. Ken Wilber, "Odyssey: A Personal Inquiry into Humanistic and Transpersonal Psychology, *Journal of Humanistic Psychology*, vol. 22, no. 1, Winter 1982, pp. 60-61.

4. See Ken Wilber, "Mythological Outlaw: My Life as a Dishwasher," in the new foreword to the paperback edition of *A Sociable God* (1983, 2005).

5. Thomas Kuhn, *The Structure of Scientific Revolutions* (1962, 1970), p. 1, 10.

6. Ken Wilber, *Sex, Ecology, Spirituality* (1995), p. 274.

7. Marilyn Ferguson, *The Aquarian Conspiracy* (1980), p. 26.

8. Ken Wilber, *The Eye of Spirit* (1997), p. 86.

9. Ken Wilber, "The Many Ways We Touch: Three Principles Helpful for Any Integrative Approach" (Excerpt B), p. 2.

10. Ibid.

11. Ken Wilber, *Eye to Eye* (1983, 1990), p. 199.

12. Ken Wilber, "The Many Ways We Touch," p. 9 [italics added].

13. Ken Wilber, "An Integral Age at the Leading Edge" (Excerpt A), p. 100.

14. All quotes from Ken Wilber, "The Many Ways We Touch."

15. Ken Wilber, "Introduction to Integral Theory & Practice: IOS Basic & the AQAL Map" (Integral Institute essay, 2003), p. 35.

16. Ibid., p. 2.

17. Ken Wilber, "An Integral Age at the Leading Edge" (Excerpt A), pp. 109-100 [italics added].

18. Ken Wilber, "Introduction to Integral Theory & Practice," p. 36.

19. Ken Wilber, "The Many Ways We Touch."

20. Allan Combs, *The Radiance of Being: Understanding the Grand Integral Vision; Living the Integral Life* (1995, 2002), p. 142; also see p. 283.

21. Ibid., p. 143; see in particular, Chapter 7: "All Quadrants, All Levels."

22. Ken Wilber, "Introduction to Integral Theory & Practice," p. 36.

23. Ken Wilber, "The Many Ways We Touch," p. 41 [italics added].

24. Ken Wilber, *One Taste* (1999), p. 251; also see Ken Wilber, *A Theory of Everything* (2000), pp. 251, 254.

25. Ken Wilber, *One Taste* (1999), p. 253.

26. Ken Wilber, *A Theory of Everything* (2000), p. 93.

27. Ibid., p. 94 [italics added].

28. Ibid.

29. See Ken Wilber, *One Taste* (1999) for many of Wilber's art interests and the wide range of styles he is interested in and adeptly able to comment on.

30. Ken Wilber, *Eye to Eye* (1983, 1986), p. 201.

31. Ibid., pp. 201-2.

32. Ibid., p. 208.

33. Ken Wilber, *The Eye of Spirit* (1997), p. 134.

34. Ibid., p. 112.

35. Ibid., p. 113 [emphasis added].

36. Ken Wilber, *A Theory of Everything* (2000), p. 48 [first italics added].

37. Ken Wilber, *The Eye of Spirit* (1997), p. 190.

38. Ibid.

39. Ibid., p. 191.

40. Ibid., p. 195.

41. Ken Wilber, *A Theory of Everything* (2000), pp. 95-96: "Integral Education."

42. Ibid., p. 96.

43. Ibid.

44. Robert Thurman, *Infinite Life* (2004), pp. 79-80.

45. Ken Wilber, *A Theory of Everything* (2000), p. 96.

46. Ken Wilber, *Sex, Ecology, Spirituality* (1995), p. 93.

47. Ken Wilber, *A Theory of Everything* (2000), pp. 97-98.

48. Ibid., p. 97.

49. Ken Wilber, *Up from Eden* (1981), p. 4.

50. Michael Zimmerman, "On Transpersonal Ecology" in *Ken Wilber In Dialogue* (1998), p. 388.

51. Ken Wilber, *A Theory of Everything* (2000), p. 99.

52. See Sean Hargens, "Integral Ecology: The *What, Who*, and *How* of Environmental Phenomena," paper for Integral Institute, version 4, March 14, 2004.

53. Ken Wilber, *Sex, Ecology, Spirituality* (1995), pp. 195-196.

54. Ken Wilber, *A Brief History of Everything* (1996), p. 331.

55. See ibid., pp. 328-35: "Environmental Ethics."

56. Definitions are from: Ken Wilber, *A Brief History of Everything* (1996), pp. 328-35: "Environmental Ethics."

57. Ibid., pp. 331-32 [all quotes in this paragraph].

58. Ibid., p. 334.

59. See Ken Wilber, *Sex, Ecology, Spirituality* (1995), pp. 61-63; also see Chapter 11 of this book for a more extensive discussion on the 20-Tenets of evolution, or "the patterns that connect" the Kosmos.

60. Ken Wilber, *A Brief History of Everything* (1996), p. 334.

61. Ibid.

Chapter Twelve
The Integral Age (at the Leading Edge)

1. The subtitle to Wilber's Phase-4 book *The Eye of Spirit: An Integral Vision for a World Gone Slightly Mad* (1997).

2. Although underappreciated in his time, Jean Gebser was highly admired and had many influential friends in Europe, consequently a new chair of "Comparative Civiliza-

tions" was created for him at the University of Salzburg; see Georg Feuerstein, *Structures of Consciousness* (1987).

3. Georg Feuerstein, *Structures of Consciousness* (1987), p. 9 (unfortunately, this study still remains out of print although the author has promised to remedy that situation).

4. In German, *The Ever-Present Origin* is called *Ursprung und Gegenwart,* where "*Ursprung* = "Primordial Origin" and *Gegenwart* = "Living Present," thus "The Ever-Present Origin."

5. Ken Wilber's first published essay was "The Spectrum of Consciousness," *Main Currents in Modern Thought,* November-December 1974, vol. 31, no. 2; Jean Gebser's article was "The Foundations of the Aperspectival World" published in *Main Currents of Modern Thought,* vol. 29, no. 2, 1972.

6. Jean Gebser "The Foundations of the Aperspectival World" in *Main Currents of Modern Thought,* vol. 29, no. 2, 1972, pp. 80-88.

7. Wilber and Gebser naturally disagree on other matters of detail but their general agreements far more support their similarities on the evolution of historical human consciousness. See Georg Feuerstein, *Structures of Consciousness: The Genius of Jean Gebser: An Introduction and Critique* (1987) for a comparison of Wilber's and Gebser's models, filtered through the intelligent insights of Dr. Feuerstein, an advanced practitioner and highly respected scholar of yoga and the spiritual traditions of India, as well as being a scholar of the psychohistory of humankind; also see G. Feuerstein, *Wholeness or Transcendence: Ancient Lessons for the Emerging Global Civilization* (1974, 1992).

8. In addition to Gebser's articles and books, these definitions of Gebser's terms owe much to Georg Feuerstein's essay "Jean Gebser's Structures of Consciousness and Ken Wilber's Spectrum Model" (unpublished); also see Georg Feuerstein, *Wholeness or Transcendence?* (1992), p. 18.

9. Georg Feuerstein, *Wholeness or Transcendence?* (1992), p.19.

10. Ken Wilber, *Sex, Ecology, Spirituality* (1995), p. 187.

11. See Ken Wilber's excellent review of Gebser's astute observations and examples of integral consciousness in *Sex, Ecology, Spirituality* (1995), p. 190.

12. Georg Feuerstein, *Holy Madness* (1991), p. 256.

13. Jean Gebser, "The Integral Consciousness," *Main Currents of Modern Thought,* vol. 30, no. 3, 1974, pp. 107-9.

14. Georg Feuerstein, *Wholeness or Transcendence?* (1992), p.19.

15. Ken Wilber, *Sex, Ecology, Spirituality* (1995), p. 191.

16. Ibid., p. 214 [italics added].

17. Ken Wilber, *The Eye of Spirit* (1997), pp. 20, 71.

18. See: Ken Wilber, *Sex, Ecology, Spirituality* (1995), *A Brief History of Everything* (1996), *The Eye of Spirit* (1997), *Integral Psychology* (2000), also "Sociocultural Evolution" in *Collected Works, Volume 4 CW4)* (1999).

19. Ken Wilber, *Up from Eden* (1981), p. 10.

20. See Ken Wilber, *Up from Eden* (1981); *Sex, Ecology, Spirituality* (1995); *A Brief History of Everything* (1996); *The Eye of Spirit* (1997).

21. Ken Wilber, *Up from Eden* (1981), p. 65.

22. Ibid., p. 39.

23. Ibid., p. 70.

24. Ken Wilber, *A Theory of Everything* (2000), p. 110.

25. Ken Wilber, *Up from Eden* (1981), p. 33n.

26. Ken Wilber, *A Theory of Everything* (2000), p. 6.

27. Ibid., p. 108.

28. Ken Wilber, *Sex, Ecology, Spirituality* (1995), p. 119.

29. Ken Wilber, "An Integral Theory of Consciousness," *Journal of Consciousness Studies*, vol. 4, no. 1, 1997, p. 90 (see *Collected Works, Volume 7*).

30. Wilber has introduced his AQAL views on the techno-economic eras in *Sex, Ecology, Spirituality* (1995), *The Eye of Spirit* (1997), *The Marriage of Sense and Soul* (1998), and in *A Brief History of Everything* (1996), especially in Chapter 3 titled "All Too Human." He has also promised an even more in-depth review in the upcoming volumes of *The Kosmos Trilogy*, especially with the one tentatively titled *Sex, God, Gender: The Ecology of Men and Women* (unpublished).

31. Ken Wilber, *A Brief History of Everything* (1996), p. 47 [italics added].

32. Ibid., p. 51.

33. Ibid., pp. 54-55.

34. Ken Wilber, *A Theory of Everything* (2000), p. 34.

35. Ken Wilber, *Up from Eden* (1981), p. 329.

36. Ibid., [italics added].

37. Ibid., pp. 329-30 [all quotes in list].

38. Quoted in Ken Wilber, *A Theory of Everything* (2000), p. 7.

39. Ibid., [italics added].

40. Ibid., p. 12.

41. Quoted in Ken Wilber, *A Theory of Everything* (2000), p. 11.

42. Ibid., [italics in original].

43. Ken Wilber, *Integral Psychology* (2000), p. 2.

44. Ken Wilber, *A Theory of Everything* (2000), p. 118 [italics added].

45. Ibid., p. 56.

46. Ibid., p. 118.

47. Ken Wilber, *A Brief History of Everything* (1996), p. 334.

48. Ken Wilber, *A Theory of Everything* (2000), p. 57; therefore, Wilber concludes: "The integral vision is one of the least pressing issues on the face of the planet."

49. Ken Wilber, *Up from Eden* (1981), p. 311n.

50. Ken Wilber, introduction to *Collected Works, Volume 7 (CW7)* (2000), p. 34.

51. Ken Wilber, *Eye to Eye* (1983, 1986), p. 284.

52. Ken Wilber, *The Eye of Spirit* (1997), p. 342, 17n.

53. Ken Wilber, *Eye to Eye* (1983, 1986), p. 267 [emphasis added].

54. Ken Wilber, introduction to *Collected Works, Volume 8 (CW8)* (2000), p. 39.

55. Ibid., p. 77n.

56. Ken Wilber, *A Theory of Everything* (2000), p. 1.

57. Ibid.

58. Ibid., p. 2.

59. Ken Wilber, *Sex, Ecology, Spirituality* (1995), p. 393 (sentence tense has been changed accordingly).

60. Ibid., p. 199.

61. See Ken Wilber, "An Integral Age at the Leading Age" (Excerpt A, 2002), which will appear as a chapter in *Sex, Karma, Creativity* (2005).

62. Ibid., pp. 6, 8 [italics added].

63. Ken Wilber, *A Theory of Everything* (2000), p. 2.

64. Ken Wilber, "An Integral Age at the Leading Age," p. 6.

65. See Allan Combs, *The Radiance of Being* (2002), Appendix II: "States, Structures, and Lines: A Conversation between Ken Wilber and Allan Combs," p. 312.

66. Ken Wilber, *Sex, Ecology, Spirituality* (1995), p. 187 [italics and bullets added].

67. Ibid., p. 197.

Chapter Thirteen
Evolution of the Integral-Centaur

1. Ken Wilber, *Eye to Eye* (1983, 1986), p. 90.

2. Ken Wilber, *The Spectrum of Consciousness* (1977), p. 130 [italics added].

3. Arthur Cotterell, *The Encyclopedia of Mythology* (NY: Smithmark, 1996), p. 49.

4. See *The Age of Fable: The Illustrated Bullfinch's Mythology* (NY: Macmillan, 1997), p. 98.

5. See, for example, Seymour Boorstein, *Clinical Studies in Transpersonal Psychotherapy* (1997), p. 134: "In the course of my seeing John, I suggested that he read *No Boundary*, by Ken Wilber. He was particularly interested in Wilber's developmental schema, which posits that existential concerns are a normal and even desirable developmental phase."

6. Ken Wilber, *No Boundary* (1979), p. 117.

7. Ibid., p. 120.

8. Ibid., p. 133.

9. Ibid., pp. 119-20.

10. Ken Wilber, *The Atman Project* (1980), p. 142.

11. Ken Wilber, *Up from Eden* (1981), p. 319.

12. Ken Wilber, *A Theory of Everything* (2000), p. 150, 13n.

13. Ken Wilber, *A Brief History of Everything* (1996), p.193.

✓ 14. Noted in Georg Feuerstein, *Wholeness or Transcendence?* (1992), p. 19; see Duane Elgin, *Awakening Earth: Exploring the Evolution of Human Culture and Consciousness* (1993, NY: William Morrow); Peter Russell, *The Global Brain: Speculations on the Evolutionary Leap to Planetary Consciousness* (1983, LA: Jeremy P. Tarcher); Willis Harman, *Global Mind Change: The Promise of the 21st Century* (1988, 1998, SF: Berrett-Koehler Publishers); Charles Reich, *The Greening of America* (1983, LA: Jeremy P. Tarcher); Paul Ray and Sherry Ruth Anderson, *The Cultural Creatives: How 50 Million People Are Changing the World* (2000, NY: Three Rivers Press); Marilyn Ferguson, *The Aquarian Conspiracy: Personal and Social Transformation in the 1980s* (1980, LA: Jeremy P. Tarcher).

15. Ken Wilber, *The Eye of Spirit* (1997), p. 346, 23n; I have included the "more technically" point as a numbered bullet (although Wilber lists it as the next paragraph in his endnote).

16. Ken Wilber, *Sex, Ecology, Spirituality* (1995), p. 189.

17. Ibid., p. 188.

18. Wilber does criticize Lowen's overemphasis on the somatic dimension; see Ken Wilber, *One Taste* (1999), pp. 194-95: "But many body therapists completely confuse this integrated mind-and-mind union with *just* the body itself. You find this confusion in writers like Alexander Lowen and Ida Rolf and Stanley Keleman. They frequently elevate the body to the status of the centaur (or body-and-mind integrated unit), and you can tell they do this because there is virtually no discussion of the mind per se, the mind as mind—no discussion of rational ethics, of perspectivism, or postconventional morality, of mutual understanding, and so on."

19. Georg Feuerstein quoted in *Sex, Ecology, Spirituality* (1995) by Ken Wilber, p. 189.

20. See Ken Wilber, *Sex, Ecology, Spirituality* (1995), pp. 186-92: "The Centaur in Vision-Logic"; *A Brief History of Everything* (1996), pp. 190-92: "Fulcrum-6: The Bodymind Integration of the Centaur."

21. Ken Wilber, *Integral Psychology* (2000), Chapter 8: "Archeology of the Spirit."

22. Ken Wilber, *A Brief History of Everything* (1996), p. 191.

23. Ken Wilber, *Sex, Ecology, Spirituality* (1995), p. 185.

24. Ken Wilber, *Integral Psychology* (2000), p. 167.

25. Ken Wilber, *A Brief History of Everything* (1996), p. 191.

26. Ken Wilber, *Sex, Ecology, Spirituality* (1995), p. 189.

27. Ken Wilber, *The Eye of Spirit* (1996), p. 346, 23n.

28. Ken Wilber, *Sex, Ecology, Spirituality* (1995), p. 191.

29. Ibid., p. 521.

30. See Ken Wilber, *A Brief History of Everything* (1996), p. 192; pp. 192-93: "Aperspectival Madness."

31. See Ken Wilber, *A Brief History of Everything* (1996), p. 193; "everything is relative": p. 202.

32. Ken Wilber, *Sex, Ecology, Spirituality* (1995), p. 188.

33. Ken Wilber, *A Brief History of Everything* (1996), p. 193.

34. Ibid., pp. 190-92: "Fulcrum-6: The Bodymind Integration of the Centaur"; pp. 193-96: "On the Brink of the Transpersonal" [italics added].

35. Frank Visser, *Ken Wilber: Thought as Passion* (2003), p. 98.

36. Ken Wilber, *Transformations of Consciousness* (1986), p. 146.

37. Georg Feuerstein, *Structures of Consciousness* (1987), p. 143.

38. Ken Wilber, *Sex, Ecology, Spirituality* (1995), p. 255 [italics in original].

39. Ibid.

40. Ibid., p. 257 [italics in original].

41. Ibid.

42. Ibid., Chapter 8: "The Depths of the Divine."

43. Ibid., p. 257.

44. Ibid., p. 258.

45. Ibid., p. 280.

46. Ibid., p. 279.

47. Ken Wilber, *One Taste* (1999), p. 312.

48. Ibid., p. 213.

49. Ken Wilber, *Eye to Eye* (1983, 1990), pp. 235-36, and "especially Yoga, Rolfing, focusing, Alexander."

50. See Ken Wilber, *One Taste* (1999), pp. 128-29; the description "weightlifting fanatic" was communicated to the author.

51. Ibid., p. 129.

52. Ken Wilber, *Up from Eden* (1981), p. 328.

53. Ken Wilber, *One Taste* (1999), p. 300 [italics added].

54. Ibid., p. 127.

55. Ken Wilber, *Integral Psychology* (2000), pp. 109, 111.

56. Ibid., p. 115.

57. Ibid., pp. 112-13.

58. Ibid., p. 114.

59. Ken Wilber, *One Taste* (1999), p. 129 [italics added].

60. Ken Wilber, *The Eye of Spirit* (1997), p. 350, 11n.

61. Ken Wilber, *A Theory of Everything* (2000), p. 55.

62. Ken Wilber, *One Taste* (1999), pp. 129-130.

63. See Michael Murphy and George Leonard, *The Life We Are Given* (1995); from "Integral Transformative Practice (ITP)": Esalen Institute and Aikido of Tamalpais Announce a New Focused Network in Mill Valley, 1992/date unknown.

64. Michael Murphy, promo material for ITP.

65. Michael Murphy, "The Life We Are Given: An Interview with Michael Murphy" in *Science of Mind*, January 1997, p. 41.

66. Ken Wilber, *A Theory of Everything* (2000), p. 139 [italics added].

67. Ken Wilber, *One Taste* (1999), p. 131.

68. See Ken Wilber, *Integral Psychology* (2000), pp. 113-14; *One Taste* (1999), pp. 130-31.

69. Ken Wilber, *One Taste* (1999), pp. 315-16 [emphasis added].

70. Ibid., pp. 27-37: "A Spirituality that Transforms: Translation versus Transformation."

71. Ibid., p. 321.

72. Ibid., p. 258.

73. Ibid., p. 341.

74. Ibid., p. 259.

75. Ibid., p. 212.

76. Ken Wilber, *Sex, Ecology, Spirituality* (1995), p. 259.

77. Ken Wilber, *One Taste* (1999), p. 138.

78. Ken Wilber, *Integral Psychology* (2000), p. 100.

Chapter Fourteen

Flatland & Boomeritis (in a World Gone Slightly Mad)

1. Ken Wilber, *Up from Eden* (1981), p. 338 (last page).

2. Ken Wilber, *Sex, Ecology, Spirituality* (1995), pp. 523-24.

3. Ken Wilber, *Collected Works, Volume 7* (2000), p. 5.

4. Ken Wilber, *Integral Psychology* (2000), p. 61.

5. Ibid., p. 70.

6. Ibid., p. 71.

7. See Ken Wilber, *Sex, Ecology, Spirituality* (1995), Chapter 11: "Brave New World," and Chapter 12: "The Collapse of the Kosmos."

8. Ken Wilber, *Integral Psychology* (2000), p. 59.

9. Ibid., p. 73.

10. Ken Wilber, *The Marriage of Sense and Soul* (1998), p. 99.

11. Wilber/Phase-1 was epitomized with the books *The Spectrum of Consciousness* (1977) and *No Boundary* (1979), while Wilber/Phase-2 was epitomized with the books *The Atman Project* (1980), *Up from Eden* (1981), and *A Sociable God* (1983).

12. Ken Wilber, *The Eye of Spirit* (1997), p. 52.

13. Ken Wilber, *One Taste* (1999), p. 335.

14. See Ken Wilber, *A Brief History of Everything* (1996), Chapter 16: "The Ego and the Eco."

15. Ken Wilber, *The Marriage of Sense and Soul* (1998), p. 101.

16. Ken Wilber, *A Theory of Everything* (2000), pp. 28-29.

17. Ibid., p. 15.

18. Ibid., p. 29.

19. Ibid.

20. Ken Wilber, *One Taste* (1999), p. 232.

21. Ibid., pp. 230-36: "The New Person-Centered Civil Religion"; also see Ken Wilber, *A Sociable God* (1983), Chapter 7: "Present-Day Sociology of Religion."

22. Ken Wilber, *A Theory of Everything* (2000), p. 27; also see Chapter 2: "Boomeritis."

23. Ibid., p. 125.

24. Ibid.

25. Ken Wilber, *Integral Psychology* (2000), p. 160 [italics in original]; also see Ken Wilber, *The Marriage of Sense and Soul* (1998), Chapter 9: "Postmodernism: To Deconstruct the World."

26. Ken Wilber, *Integral Psychology* (2000), p. 160.

27. See Ken Wilber, *The Marriage of Sense and Soul* (1998), Chapter 9: "Postmodernism: To Deconstruct the World."

28. Ibid., pp. 124-25.

29. Ken Wilber, *Integral Psychology* (2000), p. 163.

30. Ibid., Chapter 13: "From Modernity to Postmodernity."

31. Ken Wilber, *The Marriage of Sense and Soul* (1998), p. 134.

32. Ken Wilber, *Integral Psychology* (2000), p. 171.

33. Ibid., p. 73.

34. Ibid., p. 172.

35. See Ken Wilber, *The Marriage of Sense and Soul* (1998), Chapter 9: "Postmodernism: To Deconstruct the World."

36. Ken Wilber, *A Theory of Everything* (1998), p. 58.

37. Ken Wilber, *The Eye of Spirit* (1997), p. 189 [emphasis added].

38. Ibid., p. 197.

39. Ibid., p. 200.

40. Ken Wilber, *Sex, Ecology, Spirituality* (1995), p. 570, 12n.

41. Ibid., p. 163 [italics added].

42. Ibid., p. 161.

43. Ken Wilber, *Up from Eden* (1981), p. 260 [caps added].

44. Ken Wilber, *Sex, Ecology, Spirituality* (1995), p. 202.

45. Ken Wilber, *Collected Works, Volume 6 (CW6)* (2000), p. viii.

46. Ken Wilber, *A Theory of Everything* (2000), p. 87 [italics in original].

47. Ken Wilber, *The Eye of Spirit* (1997), p. xiii.

48. Ken Wilber, introduction to *Collected Works, Volume 8 (CW8)* (2000), p. 21.

49. Ken Wilber, *Up from Eden* (1981), p. 333.

50. Ken Wilber, introduction to *Collected Works, Volume 8 (CW8)* (2000), p. 21.

51. Ken Wilber, *Up from Eden* (1981), p. 334.

52. Ken Wilber, introduction to *Collected Works, Volume 8 (CW8)* (2000), p. 20.

53. Ibid., p. 25.

54. Ken Wilber, *A Theory of Everything* (2000), p. xv, xvi.

55. Ibid.

56. Ken Wilber, introduction to *Collected Works, Volume 8 (CW8)* (2000), p. 25.

57. See Ken Wilber, *The Marriage of Sense and Soul* (1998), *A Theory of Everything* (2000), *Integral Psychology* (2000), *Boomeritis* (2002), and the new *The Many Faces of Terrorism* (2005).

58. Ken Wilber, *The Eye of Spirit* (1997), p. xvi.

59. Ken Wilber, *The Marriage of Sense and Soul* (1998), pp. 210, 209 [italics in original].

60. Ibid., Chapter 8: "Idealism: The God That Is to Come."

61. Ken Wilber, *Sex, Ecology, Spirituality* (1995), p. 524.

Chapter Fifteen
Where Wilber's Going: The Integral Revolution

1. Ken Wilber, *One Taste* (1995), p. 34; see: pp. 27-37: "A Spirituality That Transforms."

2. Ken Wilber, *One Taste* (1995), p. 100.

3. See Ken Wilber, *One Taste* (1998), pp. 99-102; "compassion" and "idiot compassion" are terms that originated with the Tibetan Buddhist tulku Chögyam Trungpa Rinpoche, who founded the Naropa Institute in Boulder, Colorado, in 1974, and who was a teacher and friend of Ken Wilber.

4. Ken Wilber, *One Taste* (1998), p. 100.

5. Ibid., p. 101.

6. Ibid., p. 35, 101.

7. Ibid., p. 102.

8. Ibid., p. 139.

9. Ken Wilber, "Mind and the Heart of Emptiness: Reflections on Intellect and the Spiritual Path," in *The Quest*, Winter 1995, p. 18; all quotes from this article.

10. Ken Wilber, *One Taste* (1999), p. 350.

11. Ken Wilber, *Eye to Eye* (1983, 1986), p. 199.

12. Ken Wilber, *One Taste* (1999), p. 321.

13. Ibid., p. 14.

14. Sybille Bedford quoted in Ken Wilber, *One Taste* (1999), p. 12.

15. Ken Wilber, *Sex, Ecology, Spirituality* (1995), p. 580, 43n.

16. Ibid., p. 197 [italics in original; last sentence italic added].

17. See Ken Wilber, "The Many Ways We Touch," pp. 4-5.

18. Ibid., p. 7.

19. Ken Wilber, *Sex, Ecology, Spirituality* (1995), p. 197.

20. Ibid., p. 581, 44n.

21. Ken Wilber, introduction to *Collected Works, Volume 8 (CW8)* (2000), p. 60, 17n [italics added].

22. Ken Wilber, *A Theory of Everything* (2000), p. 127.

23. Ken Wilber, *Sex, Ecology, Spirituality* (1995), p. 522.

24. Ibid., p. 186.

25. Ibid., p. 201.

26. Ken Wilber, *A Theory of Everything* (2000), p. 90 [italics added].

27. Ken Wilber, *Sex, Ecology, Spirituality* (1995), p 460.

28. Ibid., p. 200.

29. Ibid., pp. 199-200 [italics added]; see pp. 199-201: "Transnationalism."

30. Ken Wilber, *Sex, Ecology, Spirituality* (1995), pp. 199-200: "Transnationalism," [italics added].

31. Ken Wilber, *A Theory of Everything* (2000), p. 90 [italics added].

32. Ibid.

33. Ken Wilber, *Integral Psychology* (2000), pp. 193-94.

34. Ken Wilber, *Sex, Ecology, Spirituality* (1995), p. 201.

35. Ken Wilber, *Collected Works, Volume 8 (CW8)* (2000), p. 49.

36. Ken Wilber, *Up from Eden* (1981), p. 337 [italics added].

37. Ken Wilber, *One Taste* (1999), pp. 249-50.

38. Ken Wilber, *The Atman Project* (1980), p. 162.

39. Ibid., p. 163.

40. Ibid., p. 164.

41. Ibid., p. 165.

42. Ibid.

43. Ibid., p. 167.

44. Ibid., p. 168.

45. Ibid., pp. 172-73.

46. Ibid., p. 175.

47. Ibid., p. 176.

48. Ken Wilber, *One Taste* (1999), p. 152.

49. Ibid.

BIBLIOGRAPHY

Abbott, Edwin A. *Flatland: A Romance of Many Dimensions* (1884, 1984, Middlesex, England: Harmondsworth).

Adi Da, *The Knee of Listening* (1972, 2004, Middletown, CA: Dawn Horse Press).

Adi Da, *The Method of the Siddhas* (1973, 1978, Middletown, CA: Dawn Horse Press).

Adi Da, *The Paradox of Instruction* (1977, Middletown, CA: Dawn Horse Press).

Adi Da, *Enlightenment of the Whole Body* (1978, Middletown, CA: Dawn Horse Press).

Adi Da, *Eleutherios: The Only Truth That Sets the Heart Free* (1982, 1998, 2001, Middletown, CA: Dawn Horse Press).

Adi Da, *The Dawn Horse Testament* (1985, Middletown, CA: Dawn Horse Press).

Alexander, Jeffrey C., *The Meanings of Social Life: A Cultural Sociology (2003).*

Arieti, Silvano, *The Intrapsychic Self: Feeling, Cognition, and Creativity in Health and Mental Illness* (1967, New York, NY: Basic Books).

Aurobindo, Sri, *The Life Divine* (1939, 1990, Wilmot, WI: Lotus Light Publications).

Aurobindo, Sri, *The Essential Aurobindo,* Robert McDermott, ed., (1987, Great Barrington, MA: Lindisfarne Press).

Batchelor, Stephen, *Verses From the Center: A Buddhist Vision of the Sublime* (2000, New York, NY: Riverhead Books).

Beck, Don Edward, and Christopher C. Cowan, *Spiral Dynamics: Mastering Values, Leadership, and Change* (1996, Malden, MA: Blackwell Publishers).

Bellah, Robert N., *Beyond Belief: Essays on Religion in a Post-Traditionalist World* (1970, New York, NY: Harper & Row).

Benoit, Hubert, *[The Supreme Doctrine] Zen and the Psychology of Transformation* (1955, 1990, Rochester, VT: Inner Traditions).

Boorstein, Seymour, M.D., *Clinical Studies in Transpersonal Psychotherapy,* foreword by Ken Wilber (1997, Albany, NY: SUNY).

Brockelman, Paul, *Cosmology and Creation: The Spiritual Significance of Contemporary Cosmology* (1999, New York, NY: Oxford University Press).

Capra, Fritjof, *The Tao of Physics: An Exploration of the Parallels between Modern Physics and Eastern Mysticism* (1975, Boulder, CO: Shambhala Publications).

Capra, Fritjof, *The Turning Point: Science, Society, and the Rising Culture* (1982, New York, NY: Simon & Schuster).

Chang, Garma C. C., *The Buddhist Teaching of Totality: The Philosophy of Hwa Yen Buddhism* (1994, University Park, PA: Pennsylvania State University Press).

Chaudhuri, Haridas, *The Evolution of Integral Consciousness* (1977, Wheaton, IL: Quest Books).

Chickering, A. Lawrence, *Beyond Left and Right: Breaking the Political Stalemate* (1993, Oakland, CA: ICS Press).

Combs, Allan *The Radiance of Being: Complexity, Chaos, and the Evolution of Consciousness* (1995, St. Paul, MN: Paragon House).

Combs, Allan *The Radiance of Being: Understanding the Grand Integral Vision; Living the Integral Life,* foreword by Ken Wilber (2002, St. Paul, MN: Paragon House).

Cooper, Robin, *The Evolving Mind: Buddhism Biology, and Consciousness* (1996, Birmingham, AL: Windhorse Publications).

Cortright, Brant, *Psychotherapy and Spirit: Theory and Practice in Transpersonal Psychotherapy* (1997, Albany, NY: SUNY).

Cozort, Daniel, *Highest Tantra Yoga: An Introduction To the Esoteric Buddhism of Tibet* (1986, Ithaca, NY: Snow Lion Publications).

Crittenden, Jack, "What Is the Meaning of 'Integral'?" Foreword in Ken Wilber, *The Eye of Spirit* (1997, Boston, MA: Shambhala Publications).

Deida, David, *Finding God through Sex: A Spiritual Guide to Ecstatic Loving and Deep Passion for Men and Women,* foreword by Ken Wilber (2002, Austin, TX: Plexus).

Elgin, Duane, *Awakening Earth: Exploring the Evolution of Human Culture and Consciousness* (1993, New York, NY: William Morrow).

Encyclopedia of Eastern Philosophy and Religion, The (1989, 1994, Boston, MA: Shambhala Publications).

Ferguson, Marilyn, *The Aquarian Conspiracy: Personal and Social Transformation in the 1980s* (1980, Los Angeles, CA: Jeremy P. Tarcher).

Feuerstein, Georg, *Structure of Consciousness: The Genius of Jean Gebser: An Introduction and Critique* (1987, Lower Lake, CA: Integral Publishing).

Feuerstein, Georg, *Yoga: The Technology of Ecstasy,* foreword by Ken Wilber (1989, Los Angeles, CA: Jeremy P. Tarcher).

Feuerstein, Georg, *Holy Madness: The Shock Tactics and Radical Teachings of Crazy-Wise Adepts, Holy Fools, and Rascal Gurus* (1991, New York, NY: Paragon House).

Feuerstein, Georg, *Whole or Transcendence? Ancient Lessons for the Emerging Global Civilization* (1974, 1992, New York, NY: Larson Publications).

Feuerstein, Georg, *The Yoga Tradition: Its History, Literature, Philosophy and Practice,* foreword by Ken Wilber (1998, Prescott, AZ: Hohm Press).

Gardner, Howard, *Frames of Mind: The Theory of Multiple Intelligences* (1983, 1993, New York, NY: Basic Books).

Gebser, Jean, "The Foundations of the Aperspectival World," *Main Currents of Modern Thought,* Vol. 29, No. 2, 1972, pp. 80-88.

Gebser, Jean, "The Integral Consciousness," *Main Currents of Modern Thought,* Vol. 30, No. 3, 1974, pp. 107-9.

Gebser, Jean, *The Ever-Present Origin [Ursprung Und Gegenwart],* (1949, 1953, 1985, Athens, OH: Ohio University Press).

Gilligan, Carol, *In a Different Voice: Psychological Theory and Women's Development* (1982, 1993, Cambridge, MA: Harvard University Press).

Goleman, Daniel, *The Meditative Mind: The Varieties of Meditative Experience* (1988, New York, NY: Tarcher/Putnam).

Goswami, Amit, *The Visionary Window: A Quantum Physicist's Guide to Enlightenment,* foreword by Deepak Chopra (2000, Wheaton, IL: Quest Books).

Grey, Alex, *Sacred Mirrors: The Visionary Art of Alex Grey,* essay by Ken Wilber (1990, Rochester, VT; Inner Traditions International).

Grey, Alex, *The Mission of Art,* foreword by Ken Wilber (1998, Boston, MA: Shambhala Publications).

Grey, Alex, *Transfigurations,* with "Art and the Integral Vision: A Conversation with Ken Wilber and Alex Grey" (2001, Rochester, VT: Inner Traditions International).

Grof, Stanislav, *Beyond the Brain: Birth, Death, and Transcendence in Psychotherapy* (1985, Albany, NY: SUNY).

Grof, Stanislav, *The Cosmic Game: Explorations of the Frontiers of Human Consciousness* (1998, Albany, NY: SUNY).

Grof, Stanislav, *Psychology of the Future: Lessons from Modern Consciousness Research* ✓ (2000, Albany, NY: SUNY).

Habermas, Jürgen, *Communication and the Evolution of Society,* trans. Thomas McCarthy (1976, 1979, Boston, MA: Beacon Press).

Hargens, Sean, "Integral Ecology: The *What, Who,* and *How* of Environmental Phenomena," paper for Integral Institute, version 4, March 14, 2004.

Harman, Willis, *Global Mind Change: The Promise of the Twenty-First Century* (1988, 1998, San Francisco, CA: Berrett-Koehler Publishers).

Hawking, Stephen W., *A Brief History of Time: From the Big Bang To Black Holes* (1988, New York, NY: Bantam Books).

Hixon, Lex, *Coming Home: The Experience of Enlightenment in Sacred Traditions,* foreword by Ken Wilber, 1989 (1978, 1989, Los Angeles, CA: Jeremy P. Tarcher).

Hixon, Lex, *Mother of the Buddhas: Meditation on the Prajnaparamita Sutra,* foreword by Robert A. F. Thurman (1993, Wheaton, IL: Quest Books).

Huxley, Aldous, *The Perennial Philosophy* (1944, 1970, New York, NY: Harper & ✓ Row).

Jantsch, Eric, *Design for Evolution: Self-Organization and Planning in the Life of Human Systems* (1975, New York, NY: George Braziller).

Jantsch, Eric, *The Self-Organizing Universe* (1980, New York, NY: Pergamon).

Jantsch, Eric, and Conrad Waddington, eds., *Evolution and Consciousness: Human Systems in Transition* (1976, Reading, MA: Addison-Wesley).

Kegan, Robert, *The Evolving Self: Problem and Process in Human Development* (1982, Cambridge, MA: Harvard University Press).

Kilty, Gavin, trans., *The Splendor of an Autumn Moon: The Devotional Verse of Tsongkhapa* (2001, Boston, MA: Wisdom Publications).

King, Jr., Martin Luther, *A Testament of Hope: The Essential Writings of Martin Luther King, Jr.,* James Washington, ed., (1986, San Francisco, CA: Harper & Row).

✓ Koestler, Arthur, *The Ghost in the Machine* (1967, New York, NY: Viking Penguin).

Koestler, Arthur, *Janus: A Summing Up* (1978, NY: Vintage Books).

Kuhn, Thomas, *The Structure of Scientific Revolutions* (1962, 1970, 2nd ed., Chicago, IL: University of Chicago Press).

Laszlo, Ervin, *Evolution: The Grand Synthesis* (1987: Boston, MA: Shambhala, New Science Library).

Laszlo, Ervin, *The Creative Cosmos: A Unified Science of Matter, Life, and Mind* (1993, Edinburgh, United Kingdom: Floris Books).

Laszlo, Ervin, *The Whispering Pond: A Personal Guide To the Emerging Vision of Science* (1996, Rockport, MA: Element Books).

Lemkow, Anna, *The Wholeness Principle* (1990, Wheaton, IL: Quest Books).

Lowen, Alexander, *Depression and the Body* (1972, 1993, New York, NY: Penguin).

Maslow, Abraham, *The Farther Reaches of Human Nature* (1971, New York, NY: Viking Press).

Maslow, Abraham, *Religions, Values, and Peak-Experiences* (1964, 1970, New York, NY: Viking Press).

Mitchell, Stephen, ed., *The Enlightened Mind: An Anthology of Sacred Prose* (1991, New York, NY: HarperCollins).

Murphy, Michael, *The Future of the Body: Explorations Into the Further Evolution of Human Nature* (1992, Los Angeles, CA: Jeremy P. Tarcher).

Murti, T. R. V., *The Central Philosophy of Buddhism: A Study of the Madhyamika System* (1955, New Delhi, India: HarperCollins Publishers).

Nasr, Seyyed Hossein Nasr, *Knowledge of the Sacred* (1989, Albany, NY: SUNY).

Needleman, Jacob, *The Sword of Gnosis: Metaphysics, Cosmology, Tradition, Symbolism* (1974, 1986, Boston, MA: Arkana).

Nelson, John E, M.D., *Healing the Split: Integrating Spirit into Our Understanding of the Mentally Ill,* foreword by Ken Wilber, preface by Michael Washburn (1994, Albany, NY: SUNY).

Nisker, Wes, *Crazy Wisdon: A Provacative Romp Through the Philosophies of East and West* (1990, Berkeley, CA: Ten Speed Press).

Oxford Dictionary of World Religions, The, John Bowker, ed. (1997, Oxford, England: Oxford University Press).

Perennial Dictionary of World Religions, The, Keith Crim, ed. (1981, San Francisco, CA: Harper & Row).

Peters, F. E., *Greek Philosophical Terms: A Historical Lexicon* (1967, New York, NY: New

York University Press).

Pinker, Steven, *How the Mind Works* (1997, New York, NY: W. W. Norton).

Pinker, Steven, *The Blank Slate: The Modern Denial of Human Nature* (2002, New York, NY: Viking).

Ray, Paul, and Sherry Ruth Anderson, *he Cultural Creatives: How 50 Million People Are Changing the World* (2000, NY: Three Rivers Press).

Ramana Maharshi, *Talks with Ramana Maharshi: On Realizing Abiding Peace and Happiness,* foreword by Ken Wilber (2000, 2001, Carlsbad, CA: Inner Direction Publishing). ✓

Reich, Charles, *The Greening of America* (1983, Los Angeles, CA: Jeremy P. Tarcher).

Reynolds, Brad, *Embracing Reality: The Integral Vision of Ken Wilber,* foreword by Ken Wilber (2004, New York, NY: Penguin).

Rothberg, Donald and Sean Kelly, eds., *Ken Wilber in Dialogue: Conversations with Leading Transpersonal Thinkers* (1998, Wheaton, IL: Quest Books).

Russell, Peter, *The Global Brain: Speculations on the Evolutionary Leap To Planetary Consciousness* (1983, Los Angeles, CA: Jeremy P. Tarcher). ✓

Rowan, John, *The Transpersonal: Psychotherapy and Counseling* (1993, 1998, London, England: Routledge). ✓

Sagan Carl, *Cosmos* (1980, New York, NY: Ballantine Books).

Schumacher, E. F., *Small Is Beautiful: Economics as If People Mattered* (1973, London, England: Blond & Briggs; New York, NY: Harper & Row).

✓Schumacher, E. F., *A Guide for the Perplexed* (1977, New York, NY: Harper & Row).

Schuon, Fritjof, *The Transcendent Unity of Religions,* introduction by Huston Smith (1957, 1984, Wheaton, IL: Quest Books).

Schwartz, Tony, *What Really Matters: Searching for Wisdom in America* (1995, New York, NY: Bantam Books).

Scotton, Bruce, Allan B. Chinen, John R. Battista, eds., *Textbook of Transpersonal Psychiatry and Psychology,* foreword by Ken Wilber (1996, New York, NY: Basic-Books).

Severens, Martha R., *Andrew Wyeth: America's Painter,* with an essay by Ken Wilber (1996, New York, NY: Hudson Hills Press).

Sheldrake, Rupert, *A New Science of Life: The Hypothesis of Formative Causation* (1981, Los Angeles, CA: Jeremy P. Tarcher).

Sheldrake, Rupert, *The Presence of the Past: Morphic Resonance and the Habits of Nature* (1988, New York, NY: Times Books).

Smith, Huston, *The World's Religions: A Completely Revised and Updated Edition of* The Religions of Man (1958, 1991, San Francisco, CA: HarperSanFrancisco).

Smith, Huston, *Forgotten Truth: The Common Vision of the World's Religions* (1976, San Francisco, CA: HarperSanFrancisco).

Smith, Huston, *Why Religion Matters: The Fate of the Human Spirit in an Age of Disbelief* (2001, San Francisco, CA: HarperSanFrancisco).

Smuts, Jan *Holism and Evolution* (1926, London, England: Macmillan; 1973, Westport, CT: Greenwood Press).

Spencer-Brown, G., *Laws of Form* (1972, 1994, Portland, OR: Cognizer Company).

Surya Das, Lama, *Awakening the Buddha Within: Eight Steps To Enlightenment: Tibetan Wisdom for the Western World* (1997, New York, NY: Broadway Books).

Swimme, Brian and Thomas Berry, *The Universe Story: From the Primordial Flaring Forth to the Ecozoic Era: A Celebration of the Unfolding of the Cosmos* (1992, San Francisco, CA: HarperSanFrancisco).

Tarnas, Richard, *The Passion of the Western Mind: Understanding the Ideas That Have Shaped Our World View* (1991, New York, NY: Harmony Books).

Teilhard de Chardin, Pierre, *The Phenomenon of Man [Le Phenomene Humain]*, (1955, 1959, 1965, New York, NY: Harper & Row).

Thurman, Robert A. F., *The Holy Teaching of Vimalakirti: A Mahayana Scripture* (1976, 1992, University Park, PA: Pennsylvania State University Press).

Thurman, Robert A. F., *The Central Philosophy of Tibet: A Study and Translation of Jey Tsong Khapa's Essence of True Eloquence,* foreword by the Dalai Lama (1984, Princeton, NJ: Princeton University Press).

Thurman, Robert A. F., *The Tibetan Book of the Dead: Liberation through Understanding in the Between* (1994, New York, NY: Bantam Books).

Thurman, Robert A. F., *Essential Tibetan Buddhism* (1995, Edison, NJ: Castle Books).

Thurman, Robert A. F., *Inner Revolution: Life, Liberty, and the Pursuit of Real Happiness* (1998, New York, NY: Riverhead Books).

Thurman, Robert A. F., and Tad Wise, *Circling the Sacred Mountain: A Spiritual Journey through the Himalayas* (1999, New York, NY: Bantam Books).

Vaughan, Frances, *The Inward Arc: Healing In Psychotherapy and Spirituality* (1985, 1995, Nevada City, CA: Blue Dolphin Publishing)

Vaughan, Frances, *Shadows of the Sacred: Seeing through Spiritual Illusions,* foreword by Ken Wilber (1995, Wheaton, IL: Quest Books).

Visser, Frank, *Thought as Passion,* foreword by Ken Wilber (2003, Albany, NY: SUNY Press).

Walsh, Roger, *The Spirit of Shamanism* (1990, New York, NY: Tarcher/Putnam).

Walsh, Roger, and Frances Vaughan, "The Worldview of Ken Wilber" (Chapter 7) in *Textbook of Transpersonal Psychiatry and Psychology* (1996, New York, NY: BasicBooks).

Walsh, Roger, *Essential Spirituality: The Seven Central Practices to Awaken Heart and Mind: Exercises from the World's Religions to Cultivate Kindness, Love, Joy, Peace, Vision, Wisdom, and Generosity,* foreword by His Holiness the Dalai Lama (1999, New York, NY: John Wiley & Sons).

Washburn, Michael, *Transpersonal Psychology in Psychoanalytic Perspective* (1994, Albany, NY: SUNY Press).

Washburn, Michael, *The Ego and the Dynamic Ground* (1988, 1995, 2nd ed., Albany, NY: SUNY Press).

Watts, Alan, *Myth and Ritual in Christianity* (1968, Boston, MA: Beacon Press).

White, John, ed., *The Highest State of Consciousness* (1972, New York, NY: Doubleday).

White, John, *The Meeting of Science and Spirit: Guidelines for a New Age: The Next Dynamic Stage of Human Evolution, and How We Will Attain It* (1990, New York, NY: Paragon House)

White, John, foreword to 2nd ed. of Ken Wilber, *The Spectrum of Consciousness* (1977, 1993, Wheaton, IL: Quest Books).

Whitehead, Alfred North, *Process and Reality* (1929, 1978, New York, NY: Free Press).

Whitehead, Alfred North, *Adventures of Ideas* (1933, New York, NY: Free Press).

Whitmont, Edward C., *Return of the Goddess* (1992, New York, NY: Crossroad).

Whyte, Lancelot Law, *The Next Development in Man* (1948, 1950, New York, NY: Mentor Books).

Wilber, Ken, *The Spectrum of Consciousness* (1977, Wheaton, IL: Quest Books).

Wilber, Ken, *The Spectrum of Consciousness,* foreword by John White (1977, 1993, 20th Anniversary, Wheaton, IL: Quest Books).

Wilber, Ken, *No Boundary* (1979, Los Angeles: Center Publications; 1981, Boston: Shambhala Publications).

Wilber, Ken, *The Atman Project* (1980, Wheaton, IL: Quest Books)

Wilber, Ken *Up from Eden* (1981, New York, NY: Doubleday Books).

Wilber, Ken, *A Sociable God* (1983, NY: McGraw-Hill).

Wilber, Ken, *Eye to Eye: The Quest for the New Paradigm* (1983, NY: Anchor Press/ Doubleday; 1990, Boston: Shambhala Publications).

Wilber, Ken, *Quantum Questions* (1984, Boulder, CO: Shambhala New Sciences Library).

Wilber, Ken, *Transformations of Consciousness* (1986, Boston: Shambhala Publications).

Wilber, Ken, *Grace and Grit* (1991, Boston, MA: Shambhala Publications).

Wilber, Ken, *Sex, Ecology, Spirituality: The Spirit of Evolution* (1995, 2000 2nd Edition, Boston, MA: Shambhala Publications).

Wilber, Ken, *A Brief History of Everything* (1996, Boston, MA: Shambhala Publications).

Wilber, Ken, *The Eye of Spirit* (1997, 2001 revised paperback edition, Boston, MA: Shambhala Publications).

Wilber, Ken, *The Marriage of Sense and Soul: Integrating Science and Religion* (1998, New York, NY: Random House).

Wilber, Ken, *One Taste* (1999, Boston, MA: Shambhala Publications).

Wilber, Ken, *The Collected Works of Ken Wilber, Volumes 1-4* (1999, Boston: Shambhala Publications).

Wilber, Ken, *The Collected Works of Ken Wilber, Volumes 5-8* (2000, Boston: Shambhala Publications).

Wilber, Ken, *Integral Psychology* (2000, Boston, MA: Shambhala Publications).

Wilber, Ken, *A Theory of Everything* (2000, Boston, MA: Shambhala Publications).

Wilber, Ken, *Boomeritis: A Novel that will Set You Free* (2002, Boston: Shambhala Publications).

Wilber, Ken, *The Integral Operating System, Version 1.0* (2005, Sounds True, Inc.)

Wilber, Ken, foreword to Frank Visser, *Ken Wilber: Thought as Passion* (2003, Albany, NY: SUNY Press).

Wilber, Ken, *The Simple Feeling of Being: Embracing Your True Nature,* compiled and edited by Mark Palmer, Sean Hargens, Vipassana Esjörn, and Adam Leonard (2004, Boston, MA: Shambhala Publications).

Woodhouse, Mark B., *Paradigm Wars: Worldviews for a New Age* (1996, Berkeley, CA: Frog, Ltd.).

Zajonc, Arthur, *Catching the Light: The Entwined History of Light and Mind* (1993, NY: Oxford University Press).

Zimmerman, Michael, *Contesting Earth's Future: Radical Ecology and Postmodernity* (1994, Berkeley, CA: University of California Press).

INDEX

413